endorsed for
BTEC

BTEC Level 2 Technical Diploma

Digital Technology

D1394371

Learner Handbook

Rob Cadwell
Timothy Cook
Bernie Fishpool
Mark Fishpool
Ian Gibson
Colin Harber-Stuart
Karl Jones

Pearson

Published by Pearson Education Limited, 80 Strand, London, WC2R 0RL.

www.pearsonschoolsandfecolleges.co.uk

Copies of official specifications for all Pearson qualifications may be found on the website: qualifications.pearson.com

Text © Pearson Education Limited 2017
Typeset by Phoenix Photosetting, Kent
Original illustrations © Pearson Education Ltd 2017
Picture research by Aptara
Cover photo/illustration © koya979/Shutterstock.com

The rights of Rob Cadwell, Timothy Cook, Bernie Fishpool, Mark Fishpool, Ian Gibson, Colin Harber-Stuart and Karl Jones to be identified as authors of this work have been asserted by them in accordance with the Copyright, Designs and Patents Act 1988.

First published 2017

19 18 17 16
10 9 8 7 6 5 4 3 2 1

British Library Cataloguing in Publication Data
A catalogue record for this book is available from the British Library

ISBN 978 1 292 19663 3

Printed in Solvakia by Neografia

Acknowledgements
The publisher would like to thank the following for their kind permission to use their materials:

p. 171–172 © Warwick International Group Limited, used with the permission of Warwick Chemicals; **p. 242** © Tom's Planner N.V., used with the permission of Tom's Planner NV; **p. 306** a web server and R package for plotting arc diagrams of RNA secondary structures, R-chie © The University of British Columbia, www.e-rna.org/r-chie

The publisher would like to thank the following for their kind permission to reproduce their photographs:

(Key: b-bottom; c-centre; l-left; r-right; t-top)

123RF: Belchonock 008, Olga Serdyuk 038t, Andrii Starunskyi 040, Piotr Stryjewski 043, Prasit Rodphan 045, Kantver 051, Kjetil Kolbjornsrud 092, Goodluz 105, Scanrail 152, Samum 261bl, 261br, Duard Van Der Westhuizen 262tl, Shurik76 262tcr, Nopparat Wannasuk 262bl, Anton Samsonov 262bcl, Panitan Kanchanwong 262bcr, Rawpixel 284, Trinette Monkel 338, Mikkel Bigandt 350, Ammentorp 352; **Alamy Stock Photo:** Dpa Picture Alliance 032, SiliconValleyStock 039, Aleksey Boldin 170, British Retail Photography 325, Anatolii Babii 328, David J. Green 356; **Getty Images:** David Paul Morris/Bloomberg 038b, PC Plus Magazine 359; **Pearson Education Asia:** Coleman Yuen 262tr; **Shutterstock:** Panom Pensawang 002, Mile Atanasov 026t, MNI 026b, Seregalsv 042, Zapp2Photo 046, Bikeriderlondon 066, Mimagephotography 076, Ford Prefect 082l, Tlorna 082r, Metrue 083, Auremar 102, Dragon Images 104, Dotshock 148, Zlikovec 154, KieferPix 182, Sergey Nivens 216, Oleksiy Mark 256, Denis and Yulia Pogostins 260, 262br, Makaule 261tl, Galushko Sergey 262tcl, O.Bellini 275, LDprod 322, Icons vector 343, Jakub Zak 351

All other images © Pearson Education

The publisher would like to thank the following:

Michael Bowkunowicz for his invaluable help and advice in developing this learner handbook
Susannah Fountain for her professionalism, diligence and dedication towards the production of this learner handbook.

Websites
Pearson Education Limited is not responsible for the content of any external internet sites. It is essential for tutors to preview each website before using it in class so as to ensure that the URL is still accurate, relevant and appropriate. We suggest that tutors bookmark useful websites and consider enabling students to access them through the school/college intranet.

Notes from the publisher
1.
In order to ensure that this resource offers high-quality support for the associated Pearson qualification, it has been through a review process by the awarding body. This process confirms that this resource fully covers the teaching and learning content of the specification or part of a specification at which it is aimed. It also confirms that it demonstrates an appropriate balance between the development of subject skills, knowledge and understanding, in addition to preparation for assessment.

Endorsement does not cover any guidance on assessment activities or processes (e.g. practice questions or advice on how to answer assessment questions), included in the resource nor does it prescribe any particular approach to the teaching or delivery of a related course.

While the publishers have made every attempt to ensure that advice on the qualification and its assessment is accurate, the official specification and associated assessment guidance materials are the only authoritative source of information and should always be referred to for definitive guidance.

Pearson examiners have not contributed to any sections in this resource relevant to examination papers for which they have responsibility.

Examiners will not use endorsed resources as a source of material for any assessment set by Pearson.

Endorsement of a resource does not mean that the resource is required to achieve this Pearson qualification, nor does it mean that it is the only suitable material available to support the qualification, and any resource lists produced by the awarding body shall include this and other appropriate resources.

2.
Pearson has robust editorial processes, including answer and fact checks, to ensure the accuracy of the content in this publication, and every effort is made to ensure this publication is free of errors. We are, however, only human, and occasionally errors do occur. Pearson is not liable for any misunderstandings that arise as a result of errors in this publication, but it is our priority to ensure that the content is accurate. If you spot an error, please do contact us at resourcescorrections@pearson.com so we can make sure it is corrected.

Contents

How to use this book

This handbook is designed to support you in developing the skills and knowledge to succeed in your BTEC Level 2 Technical course. It will help you to feel confident in taking the next step and to be ready for your dream job.

The skills you will develop during the course include practical skills that you'll need in your chosen occupation, as well as a range of 'transferable' skills and behaviours that will be useful for your own personal development, whatever you do in life.

Your learning can be seen as a journey which moves through four phases.

Phase 1	Phase 2	Phase 3	Phase 4
You are introduced to a topic or concept; you start to develop an awareness of what learning and skills are required.	You explore the topic or concept through different methods (e.g. watching or listening to a tutor or a professional at work, research, questioning, analysis, critical evaluation) and form your own understanding.	You apply your knowledge and skills to a practical task designed to demonstrate your understanding and skills.	You reflect on your learning, evaluate your efforts, identify gaps in your knowledge and look for ways to improve.

During each phase, you will use different learning strategies. As you go through your course, these strategies will be combined to help you secure the essential knowledge and skills.

This handbook has been written using similar learning principles, strategies and tools. It has been designed to support your learning journey, to give you control over your own learning and to equip you with the knowledge, understanding and tools to be successful in your future career or studies.

Getting to know the features

In this handbook you'll find lots of different features. They are there to help you learn about the topics in your course in different ways and to help you monitor and check your progress. Together these features help you:

- build your knowledge and technical skills
- understand how to succeed in your assessment
- link your learning to the workplace.

In addition, each individual feature has a specific purpose, designed to support important learning strategies. For example, some features will:

- help you to question assumptions around what you are learning
- make you think beyond what you are reading about
- help you make connections across your learning and across units
- draw comparisons between the theory you are learning about and real workplace environments

- help you develop some of the important skills you will need for the workplace, including planning and completing tasks, working with others, effective communication, adaptability and problem solving.

Features to build your knowledge and technical skills

Key terms

Terms highlighted **LIKE THIS** are 'Key terms'. It is important that you know what they mean because they relate directly to your chosen subject. The first time they appear in the book they will be explained. If you see a highlighted Key term again after that and can't quite remember its definition, look in the Glossary towards the end of the book – they are all listed there! Note that these key terms are used and explained in the context of your specialist subject or the topic in which they appear, and are not necessarily the same definitions you would find in a dictionary.

Practise

These work-related tasks or activities will allow you to practise some of the technical or professional skills relating to the main content covered in each unit.

> **Practise**
>
> If you own a mobile phone, write down:
> - the names of the ten apps that you use most often
> - how often you use them (for example daily, weekly, monthly).

Skills and knowledge check

Regular 'Skills and knowledge check' boxes will help you to keep on track with the knowledge and skills requirements for a unit. They will remind you to go back and refresh your knowledge if you haven't quite understood what you need to know or demonstrate. Tick off each one when you are confident you've nailed it.

> **Skills and knowledge check**
>
> ☐ Can you describe possible threats to data and systems?
> ☐ Can you explain the impact of not fully securing an IT system?
> ☐ Can you describe measures that can be used to protect IT systems and the data they hold?
> ☐ Can you explain the importance of appropriate backup procedures?
>
> ○ I can install, configure and/or update appropriate security features on a computer system.
> ○ I can use computer systems safely and ensure they are set up in a way that protects others.
> ○ I can select and configure appropriate backup procedures.

What if...?

Employers need to know that you are responsible and that you understand the importance of what you are learning. These 'What if...?' scenarios will help you to understand the real links between theory and what happens in the workplace.

What if...?

Your friend has recently started a new business making birthday cards. The business operates from home and has two laptop computers connected to the internet. Card designs are emailed to a local printing business by email. Neither laptop currently has any security software installed.

1 Why is it a security risk to have no security software installed?

2 Outline a series of actions that your friend should take to minimise the security risks of operating the computer system.

Pathway focus

This feature will help you to understand how the content of the unit relates to specific pathways. This will allow you to see how the content, especially of the mandatory units, can be related to the other units in your pathway. This will help you to build your understanding of how the different parts of digital technology can fit together. This feature appears in mandatory Units 1–3, which are shared between each pathway of the qualification.

Pathway focus

Digital Applications

In an IT support role, it is likely that you will be working with an existing network and you may be required to connect a device to the network or replace a component of that network such as a switch or network interface card.

Networking and Cybersecurity

In a networking and cybersecurity role, you may have to configure and set up the network itself, ensuring that it is robust and secure.

Link it up

Although your BTEC Level 2 Technical is made up of several units, common themes are explored from different perspectives across the whole of your course. Everything you learn and do during your course will help you in your final assessment. This kind of assessment is called 'synoptic'. It means that you have the opportunity to apply all the knowledge and skills from the course to a practical, realistic work situation or task.

The 'Link it up' features show where information overlaps between units or within the same unit, helping you to see where key points might support your final assessment or help you gain a deeper understanding of a topic.

This feature will also indicate where content in other units is relevant to particular pathways of the qualification. Where this is the case, the name of the pathway will appear in **bold** at the start of the 'Link it up' feature.

Step-by-step

This practical feature gives step-by-step descriptions of processes or tasks, might include a photo or artwork to illustrate each step. This will help understand the key stages in the process and help you to practise cess or technique yourself.

present information in a way that is helpful, practical and You can check off the items listed to ensure you think about individually, as well as how they relate to the topic as a collective

Features connected to your assessment

Your course is made up of several units. There are two different types of unit:

- externally assessed
- internally assessed.

The features that support you in preparing for assessment are below. But first, let's look at the difference between these two different types of unit.

Externally assessed units

These units give you the opportunity to present what you have learned in the unit in a different way. They can be challenging, but will really give you the opportunity to demonstrate your knowledge and understanding, or your skills, in a direct way. For these units you will complete a task, set by Pearson, in controlled conditions. This could take the form of an exam or onscreen test, or it could be another type of task. You may have the opportunity to research and prepare notes around a topic in advance to use when completing the assessment.

Internally assessed units

Internally assessed units involve you completing a series of assignments or tasks, set and marked by your tutor. The assignments you complete could allow you to demonstrate your learning in a number of different ways, such as a report, a presentation, a video recording or observation statements of you completing a practical task. Whatever the method, you will need to make sure you have clear evidence of what you have achieved and how you did it.

Ready for assessment

You will find these features in units that are internally assessed. They include suggestions about what you could practise or focus on to complete the assignment for the unit. They also explain how to gather evidence for assessment from the workplace or from other tasks you have completed.

Ready for assessment

- You will need to show that you can understand the protocols and applications used in networks.

- You should reflect on networking encountered during work placements, either as a user or when helping in technical support.

- You must be able to develop a secure network, review and troubleshoot it successfully.

- You need to develop a short report/presentation on the technologies used in networking and how they relate to topologies. It should include information on securing networks and how applications support efficient networking.

- You can gather evidence of your practical efforts in developing, securing and troubleshooting a network through the use of screen captures (for device and NOS configuration), photographs, video evidence and observation statements.

- Any review you produce for user groups on the network provided should include any observations made while troubleshooting the solution, including the issues diagnosed, the possible cause(s) and the solution found.

Assessment practice

These features include questions similar to the ones you'll find in your external assessment, so you can get some experience answering them. Each one relates to one or more Assessment Outcomes, as indicated in the top right-hand corner of this feature box. Suggested answers are given at the back of this book.

Assessment practice	AO2

Jamil Jackson runs a small business that prints documents received from clients sent by email using a file-sharing service. The business has anti-virus software installed but this is set to update manually only. Explain to Jamil:

- why it is important to keep anti-virus software up to date

- the benefits of updating software automatically.

Getting ready for assessment

This section will help you to prepare for external assessment. It gives information about what to expect in the final assessment, as well as revision tips and practical advice on preparing for and sitting exams or a set task. It provides a series of sample questions and answers that you might find, including helpful feedback, or 'verdicts', on the answers and how they could be improved.

Features which link your learning with the workplace

Work focus

Each internal unit ends with a 'Work focus' section which links the learning from the unit to particular skills and behaviours that are required in the workplace. There are two parts in each Work focus section:

1. **Hands on** – gives suggestions for tasks you could practise to develop the technical or professional skills you'll need on the job.
2. **Ready for work?** – supports you in developing the all-important transferable skills and behaviours that employers are looking for, such as adaptability, problem solving, communication or teamwork. It will give you pointers for showcasing your skills to a potential employer.

WORK FOCUS

HANDS ON

There are some important occupational skills and competencies that you will need to practise which relate to this unit. Developing these and practising them could help you to gain employment as an IT technician or helpdesk worker.

- Employers will expect you to understand a wide range of existing technologies and to be aware of some of the emerging technologies.

- Read sector publications, such as *Computer Weekly*, so that you can stay up to date.

- Use the internet and search for information about emerging technologies.

- Find sources of apps (for both Apple® and Android™).

- Find out more about devices that are used by organisations.

- Find out more about enabling technologies and where they can be used.

- Get used to using features such as Bluetooth.

Ready for work?

You will need to demonstrate that you have the skills and behaviours required to work on your own and with others to solve simple and complex problems. Being able to practise these skills and behaviours could help you gain employment as an entry-level database administrator.

1 Problem solving

- Are you able to design an effective database solution?

- Are you able to use the tools to validate data entry?

- Are you able to use queries effectively in order to search for data?

- Are you able to use reports to present information clearly?

- Are you able to use forms to facilitate easy data entry?

2 Communication

- Are you able to communicate with different people, including people with and without technical knowledge?

- Are you calm under pressure and able to communicate clearly to managers?

3 Managing information

- Are you able to accurately input records into a database with no errors?

- Are you able to decipher referential integrity errors and to develop a solution?

4 Working with others

- Are you able to support team members who may be trying to fix a fault that you have experienced before?

- Do you know your own strengths and weaknesses and are you able to escalate jobs to other people?

Pathway mapping

This table shows how the different units map into the different pathways of the qualification. This will help you to understand which units are relevant to your BTEC Technical Diploma, and also how the overall structure of your qualification works.

Unit 4: Working as an IT Support Technician does not appear in any of the Digital Technology pathways. It appears in the IT Support qualification and has been included in this handbook to provide coverage for all of the units in the suite of Technicals qualifications for IT.

	IT Support	Digital Technology		
		Data Management	Digital Applications	Networking and Cybersecurity
Set Up and Configure Technology Systems	███	███	███	███
Exploring Current and Emerging Technologies	███	███	███	███
Security Protection and Risk Management	███	███	███	███
Working as an IT Support Technician	███			
IT Service Solutions		███	███	███
Database Tools and Techniques		███		
Digital Applications Development			███	
Network Technologies and Applications				███
Organisational Data Systems		Synoptic		
Organisational Uses for Digital Media Systems			Synoptic	
Installing and Maintaining Networks				Synoptic

Contents

See Unit 8 for more information on network interface cards.

1 Set Up and Configure Technology Systems

Computers are a vital part of most activities within any organisation. How do members of staff in your organisation communicate with each other? How does a sales team communicate with customers? How does access to technology help employees to do their jobs effectively? Knowing which hardware and software to use and being able to set it up so it works efficiently are important parts of an IT professional's role and help ensure that an organisation remains productive.

In this unit, you will explore the basic components of computer systems, their uses and how hardware and software can be installed, configured (set up and modified), connected and used to make sure these systems effectively meet users' needs.

How will I be assessed?

This unit is internally assessed through assignments set by your tutor, based on the assessment criteria. The assignment will present you with a context for completing a number of practical tasks. Your assessment evidence may take the form of a portfolio of work that provides a range of evidence, which may include, but is not limited to, written evidence, screenshots, videos and witness statements. Your evidence should demonstrate that you can complete the required practical activities to the standard as outlined in the assessment criteria.

Assessment criteria

Pass	Merit	Distinction
Learning aim A: Install, configure and test hardware in a computer system to meet user requirements		
A.P1 Install hardware in a computer system safely to meet user requirements.	**A.M1** Install and configure hardware in a computer system safely, considering relevant factors to meet user requirements and testing for functionality.	**AB.D1** Set up, install and configure computer systems and mobile devices to meet user requirements confidently, considering all relevant factors and suggesting suitable alternative methods and components.
Learning aim B: Install, configure and test software on computer systems and mobile devices to meet user requirements		
B.P2 Install software to meet user requirements.	**B.M2** Install and configure software to meet user requirements, considering relevant factors and testing for functionality.	
Learning aim C: Apply appropriate security measures to computer systems and mobile devices		
C.P3 Apply security measures to a computer system and mobile device.	**C.M3** Apply security measures to computer systems and mobile devices, considering relevant factors and testing for functionality and ensuring back up of systems.	**C.D2** Apply security measures to computer systems and mobile devices thoroughly considering all relevant factors, testing for functionality and ensuring full back up of systems.

A Install, configure and test hardware in a computer system to meet user requirements

A1 Types of internal computer hardware components

Computers are made up of a number of different parts, or components, known as **HARDWARE**. These components each have a specific role in ensuring a computer functions properly and each can be changed or upgraded to meet a specific need. As an IT technician, you will need to understand how to identify computer components and how their features affect the working of a larger system.

Central processing unit

The **CENTRAL PROCESSING UNIT (CPU)** is the internal component responsible for controlling the computer, handling instructions and performing calculations. Through a process called the **FETCH-EXECUTE CYCLE** (the basic instruction cycle of a computer involving retrieving program instructions from memory, determining the action to be taken, then carrying out that action), the CPU ensures that instructions from the user or **SOFTWARE** are carried out. Software is the term used to describe the programs and other operating information used by a computer.

The performance of a CPU is affected by a number of factors, which you should consider when choosing a CPU for an information technology (IT) system. Table 1.1 shows some of the features you should consider and how they affect the performance of the CPU.

Table 1.1: Features of the CPU

CPU feature	Description of feature	Impact on performance
Clock speed	The number of 'pulses' a processor can perform per second.	The clock speed impacts on the number of calculations that can be performed per second. The more calculations a processor can perform, the faster it can execute (carry out) instructions.
Number of **CORES**	The core is the part of the CPU that processes the instructions.	The higher the number of cores, the more instructions a processor can perform at the same time.
Number of **THREADS**	A thread is the number of instructions each core can process at the same time.	The higher the number of threads, the more instructions each core can process at the same time. For example, a dual core processor with only one thread per core can execute two simultaneous instructions, whereas a dual core with two threads per core can execute four instructions at the same time.
CACHE size	The cache is a small, high-speed memory location.	Cache memory is designed to queue instructions and **DATA** (single or collected quantities, characters or values on which the computer performs operations) ready for use by the processor. The larger the cache size, the more instructions can be prepared before the processor needs them. This improves the execution speed of a computer.

While it may be tempting to choose the most powerful processor you can find, typically the more powerful a CPU, the more expensive it will be. Therefore, it is important to choose a processor that is right for the intended purpose. For example, an employee who will only be using word-processing software would need a much less powerful processor than one who will be processing large amounts of financial data as part of numerical **MODELLING** (processing data to identify trends and patterns to ask 'what if…?' questions).

Random-access memory

RANDOM-ACCESS MEMORY (RAM) is the computer's **VOLATILE** short-term memory (memory that only holds data when powered) and is used as a temporary store for program data and instructions. For example, when you are typing in a word-processing document, the instructions and data needed to keep the program running are stored in RAM so it can be accessed and used quickly by the CPU. When you save your work, a permanent copy is made on the hard drive, but a temporary copy will remain in RAM for you to work on until you close the program or turn off the power. The more RAM a computer has, the more temporary data can be stored at any one time. This means that the computer is less likely to slow down when performing demanding tasks or when multiple programs are open and running at once.

Power supply

A computer's power supply is responsible for providing power to the **MOTHERBOARD** (a printed circuit board that holds the CPU and its supporting components) and other computer components. Measured in **WATTS** (a standard unit for measuring electricity consumption), the power output for a power supply is dictated by the number and efficiency of the components in the computer. For example, a computer designed for simple office tasks that has only a single hard drive and integrated graphics would require less power than a computer designed to play high-specification computer games. This latter computer would contain high amounts of RAM, multiple hard drives and dedicated graphics cards.

Storage devices

The term **STORAGE DEVICE** can apply to any device or component that provides **NON-VOLATILE** (holds data even when the power is turned off), long-term storage for data, programs and files. These include the following types of drive.

- **OPTICAL DRIVE**: a drive that uses disk lasers to write to disk media, for example CD, DVD and Blu-ray.
- **HARD DISK DRIVE (HDD)**: a mechanical secondary storage device that uses spinning disks and magnetic **READ/WRITE HEADS** (a mechanical part of the hard drive that transfers data to and from the storage part of the hard drive).
- **SOLID-STATE DRIVE (SSD)**: a secondary storage device that uses **FLASH MEMORY** (electronically written memory) rather than mechanical parts.

Expansion cards

EXPANSION CARDS are components that plug in to the computer's motherboard to provide additional or enhanced functionality. The ability to add additional cards can be beneficial in the real-world environment as it allows companies to avoid spending vast amounts of money buying new computers. They can instead add additional cards to make a standard computer more suitable for a given task. As an IT professional, such as helpdesk support or an IT technician, you may have to give advice on what cards to select or even select and install them for the user. The following are examples of typical expansion cards.

Video cards

A VIDEO CARD usually contains additional processors dedicated to graphical processors (the GRAPHICS PROCESSING UNIT (GPU) is a processing chip optimised for computer graphical operations) and additional RAM. These are usually added to a system when additional power is required to render high-quality, detailed computer graphics or images, such as when playing computer games or editing photos and movies.

Audio cards

While many motherboards come with audio processors included, as with graphics cards, additional AUDIO/SOUND CARDS are added when more demanding or specific processing is required – for example, to provide high-quality surround-sound processing or to provide input and sound processing effects for musicians.

Network interface cards

A NETWORK INTERFACE CARD (NIC) allows a computer to connect to a COMPUTER NETWORK (a set of computers connected together to share resources). Wireless (Wi-Fi) and wired (Ethernet) network cards are available, the choice of which will depend on the user requirements and the available resources.

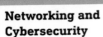

Link it up

Networking and Cybersecurity

See Unit 8 for more information on network interface cards.

Motherboard

The motherboard is also sometimes referred to as the mainboard. The motherboard provides connections and DATA-BUSES (internal computer connections that carry data and instructions between internal components) to allow the internal components to work together. Many modern motherboards contain integrated graphic and audio connections, as well as network connections, which reduces the need for separate audio, graphic and network interface cards.

System cooling

Computer processors can become extremely hot during operation and when they are run for extended periods of time, this heat can damage the processor. It is therefore important to keep the temperature of the processors as low as possible. Examples of typical system cooling components are listed here.

Fans

FANS are used in a computer to keep air flowing around the inside of the case in order to cool the CPU. Case fans help draw cooler air from outside the case and circulate it around the case. CPU fans are typically much smaller than case fans and blow air directly onto the CPU's heat-sink.

Heat-sink

A **HEAT-SINK** is attached to the CPU using a heat conductive gel. It is made of a heat conductive material and is designed to draw heat away from the chip. The component is designed to have a larger surface area than the chip and will typically have a number of 'fins' that the heat is drawn into, so that it can cool more quickly.

Liquid cooling

LIQUID COOLING is designed to reduce the overall temperature inside a computer system by pumping a cooled liquid through pipes that are distributed inside the computer. The liquid never touches the components but the cold temperature of the pipes helps keep the air temperature inside the computer low, allowing the fans and heat-sink to cool the CPU more efficiently.

A2 Types of computer peripherals

A **COMPUTER PERIPHERAL** is any external device or component that is not part of the core computer system. Peripherals will typically add functionality or a method of user control to a computer system. When working in the IT industry, you will need to understand the use and purpose of different input and output devices so you can effectively select the most appropriate peripherals for a specific task so that systems are used in the most efficient and productive way.

Pathway focus

Networking and Cybersecurity

In an IT support role, you will need to know what devices do and you may need to assist others in selecting appropriate peripherals to complete a given task. You will also need to be able to diagnose problems and replace peripherals as required.

Input devices

You use **INPUT DEVICES** to interact with, or control, a computer system. From entering data into a spreadsheet using a keyboard, to drawing a picture on a computer using a mouse or even a sensor that activates an automatic door, input devices are how users are able to interact with a computer system. You can use input devices for manual processes, such as keying in product names on an invoice, or automatic processes such as using a sensor to monitor the temperature in a room over a period of time.

Output devices

You can use **OUTPUT DEVICES** to provide a user with feedback from a computer system, and to send data to users or other systems. These outputs may be in the form of feedback to the user, such as an image onscreen or a sound, or to provide a physical output, such as a printed document.

Input and output devices

Some devices can provide both input and output from a system. While some of these are multiple devices combined into one unit, it is typical to consider them as a single device. For example, a game controller allows a user to input their instructions into a system but may provide output in the form of 'force feedback'. Force feedback is an example of the application of **HAPTICS** (the use of feedback through the sense of touch, such as vibration features when interacting with a smartphone's touch screen). In some cases, a storage device such as a hard drive may be considered to be both an input and output device as it can be used to receive output from one system and input it to another.

Practise

You work in the IT support department of a company. You have been asked by your manager to ensure that all computers in an office have the appropriate input, output and input/output devices to enable the staff to do their jobs effectively. Consider different tasks that a range of users may have to complete and list the devices you would suggest for them.

You could organise your thoughts in a table like this:

Job of user	Devices to be used	Reasons for choices
Graphic designer	Graphics tablet	Allows user to draw in a similar way to using pen and paper.
	Large screen HD monitor	Lots of detail required for producing accurate drawings.
	Large SSD	Graphic files typically use up a lot of storage space. SSD provides faster read/write operations.

Link it up

Digital Applications

For more information on the difference between wired and wireless connections (and how this affects a computer system), see Unit 5, B2.

A3 Connectors and ports

In order to function, computer components and systems need to be connected. Physical, or wired, connections are made up of two parts: the connector and the port. The **CONNECTOR** is the part of the wire that attaches to the device. The **PORT** is the part the connector attaches to, or plugs into. There is a vast array of connection types, each of which is suited to a job. Here we will consider physical/wired connections.

Connector

A wired connector – USB provides a multipurpose connection and is common across many different devices

Video

Depending on the graphics card, computers come equipped with a range of different video connections. Typically, these are used to connect the computer to a screen or similar output device. The following are examples of common video connections.

- **VIDEO GRAPHICS ARRAY (VGA)**: an analogue output that provides relatively low (by modern standards) resolution output. Subsequent higher-resolution versions include Super Video Graphics Array (SVGA) and Extended Graphics Array (XGA).
- **DIGITAL VISUAL INTERFACE (DVI)**: provides a digital output at a higher resolution than VGA that is gradually replacing VGA usage in modern computers. Variations include DVI, Micro-DVI and Mini-DVI.

USB

USB (UNIVERSAL SERIAL BUS) is a data connection port used to connect a range of peripherals such as printers and external storage media. USB also supports DC power output, removing the need for an external power source for some devices (such as external hard drives) and allows you to charge battery-powered devices such as smartphones.

eSATA

ESATA is a data port which uses the same connection type that is typically used to connect internal hard drives (SATA). It is typically used for connecting external storage devices. eSATA is slowly being replaced by USB 3.0 connections as the data transfer speeds of eSATA are faster than USB 2.0 but slower than USB 3.0.

Thunderbolt™

THUNDERBOLT™ is a combination port that provides data, video and DC power output. Thunderbolt supports high-speed data transfer and high-definition video. The Thunderbolt connection is also available in a number of mobile devices (such as smartphones and tablets) in the form of USB-C ports.

RJ-45

RJ-45 (REGISTERED JACK-45) is a data connector commonly used in computer networks. RJ-45 refers to the connector type at each end of an Ethernet cable and not the cable as a whole.

RJ-11

Although similar in appearance to an RJ-45, an **RJ-11** is a slightly smaller data connection that is used almost exclusively in telephone connections.

Audio

- *2.5 mm (mini) jacks*: these provide input and output of audio data and are used for microphones and headphones.
- *SPDIF*: this interface comes in a number of different connection formats, all of which provide high-quality, uncompressed sound data.

Link it up

Networking and Cybersecurity

See Unit 8 for more information about RJ-45 connectors.

Power

Many desktop power connections use standardised two- or three-pin power connections (see Figure 1.1) which connect the computer to the main AC power supply. Laptops tend to use a DC power input, so are connected to the mains power supply using a power adaptor. The power connections for laptops vary significantly between manufacturers and even individual models made by the same manufacturer.

Figure 1.1: Wired connections have many different connection ports. You should be able to identify the port in order to select an appropriate connection medium

HDMI

HDMI (HIGH-DEFINITION MULTIMEDIA INTERFACE) provides high-quality video and audio data transmission. This connection is typically used to connect monitors and other similar output devices.

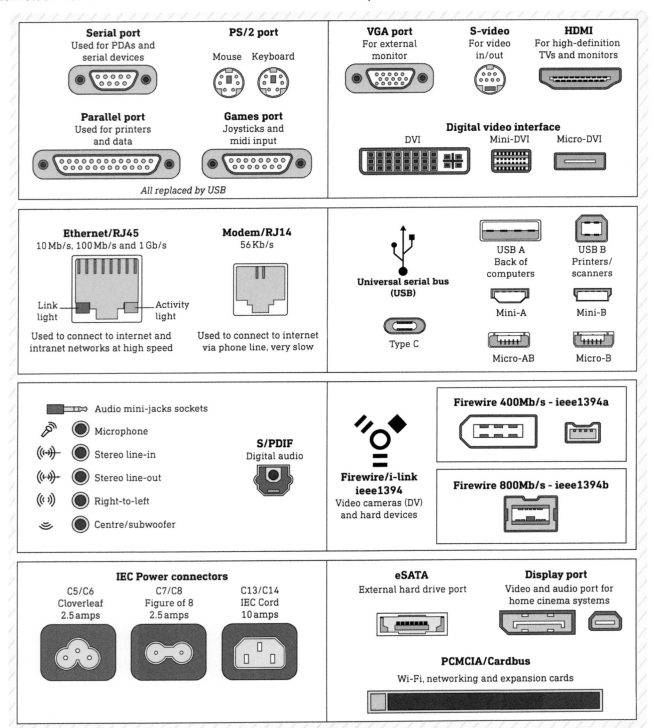

A4 Network devices and connection processes

A **NETWORK** can be defined as two or more devices connected for a common purpose. This may include provision of access to services such as internet connection or entertainment, or it may be to share common resources such as a shared printer in an office.

Networks are vital to the running of a modern organisation. They provide customers and employees with access to data and services so that the company can be effective. Loss of network connectivity can be devastating to a company.

Pathway focus

Digital Applications

In an IT support role, it is likely that you will be working with an existing network and you may be required to connect a device to the network or replace a component of that network such as a switch or network interface card.

Networking and Cybersecurity

In a networking and cybersecurity role, you may have to configure and set up the network itself, ensuring that it is robust and secure.

Network devices

Being able to identify what each component of a network does, and being able to provide connectivity and/or replace a faulty component, will make you an invaluable member of an IT support team.

Nodes and links

When visualising networks it is useful to think about them in terms of nodes and links. A **NODE** can be any connected computing device (such as a server or desktop) or it may be a network device (such as a router). **LINKS** are the parts of the network that join (or link) the nodes. This may include the Ethernet cabling that is part of a **LOCAL AREA NETWORK (LAN)** (a network based on geographical location such as an office or a school), or the **INTERNET BACKBONE** (the main data routes that connect internet service providers across the world) that connects a **WIDE AREA NETWORK (WAN)** (a network across a wider geographical area, for example connecting two buildings on opposite sides of a city).

Routers

A **ROUTER** is a device used to connect computer networks by sending data **PACKETS** (sets of data for sending over the internet or a network) from one router to the next. Modern home routers send data from the connected devices to the internet and back again. Most home routers are often multi-functional and perform tasks associated with other network components such as switches and wireless access points (see Figure 1.2).

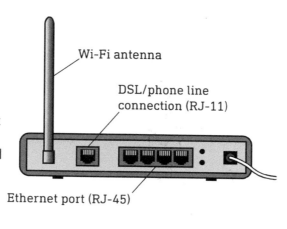

Wi-Fi antenna

DSL/phone line connection (RJ-11)

Ethernet port (RJ-45)

Figure 1.2: A typical home router often provides both internet and local area network connectivity

Link it up

Digital Applications

For more information on local and wide area networks, see Unit 5, B2 'Common networks used by organisations'.

Link it up

Networking and Cybersecurity

See Unit 8 for more information on nodes, routers, switches, wireless access points and hubs.

Switches

A **SWITCH** is a network component that directs internal network traffic. A switch uses packet switching to ensure data is sent only to the individual devices that require the data.

Hubs

A **HUB** is a simple networking component that allows computers to communicate. Unlike a switch, a hub will broadcast all data that is sent to all connected devices; devices other than the intended recipient will 'ignore' the sent data. Because the data is broadcast to all devices, hubs are extremely inefficient. They have been largely replaced with switches for networks within organisations but may still be used in small-scale (two or three computers) or home networks.

Network connection processes

In order to allow communication between devices that form part of a network, the device must be correctly configured. How this is done may vary depending on the device or **OPERATING SYSTEM (OS)** you are using (see B1), the type of connection you are using and whether you are connecting to a managed client-server network, a simple home network or even an **AD-HOC NETWORK** (temporary use of existing networks such as connecting to public Wi-Fi). However, there are some general concepts to consider.

Apply/verify connections for devices

When devices are connected to a network they are identified using an **IP (INTERNET PROTOCOL) ADDRESS** (a unique identifier/address for a device connected to a network). The IP address allows the server and other devices on the network to identify each connected device and communicate with it. The IP address is usually assigned by the server or home router, although it can be set manually if you want the device to regularly connect to it together with other devices (such as a shared printer). The IP address is a temporary address that applies only during the active connection.

As well as an IP address, a connected device can be identified by its **MEDIA ACCESS CONTROL (MAC)** address. This is a unique identifier that is assigned during the manufacturing process and cannot be changed. As the MAC address never changes, it can be used to filter connections to a router by individual devices.

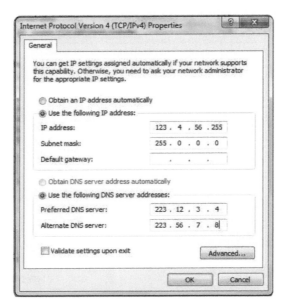

MAC Address	IP Address	Device Name	Time Connected
44:6D:57:BE:35:6B	192.168.0.2	Gib-Asus-Laptop	0days 02hrs 03mins 52s
F8:DB:7F:9C:54:DC	192.168.0.3	Android_356299042463503	0days 01hrs 22mins 51s
30:85:A9:54:A7:85	192.168.0.14		0days 02hrs 01mins 24s

You can manually set the IP address, and the MAC and IP addresses, of devices connected to a router

Manually specifying the IP address is most useful in a large network as it allows you to uniquely identify each piece of connected equipment, which helps with a range of maintenance and management tasks.

Install drivers

The computer's OS will usually install a driver for Network Interface Card (NIC) automatically. However, in some cases you may find you need to install new or updated drivers – for example, if you are using a newly manufactured NIC that was released after the version of the OS you are using, or if new drivers have been released to fix known problems.

For more on drivers, see B1 in this unit.

Set server identity and encryption type

When setting up a network or network connection point (especially when setting up a wireless network), if you want to allow ad-hoc connections, it is important to make the network access point both identifiable and secure.

The **SERVICE SET IDENTIFIER (SSID)** is the name assigned to the access point that allows the user, and the connected devices, to tell what network they are connecting to. To improve security, it is possible to prevent the router from broadcasting the SSID, ensuring only those who know it can connect.

2.4GHz Wireless Security	
Security Mode	WPA Auto
SSID	My_WiFi
	Up to 32 characters (case sensitive)
Passphrase or Security Key	ksisnwe12 ✕
	Between 8 and 63 characters (case sensitive)
Channel	Auto
Operating Channel	11

The SSID allows computers to identify the access point. Choosing the correct encryption and regularly changing the password improves security

When setting the SSID you can also choose the connection password and the type of **ENCRYPTION** that you wish to use. Encryption is when data is converted into a scrambled code and only someone with a translation key can unscramble it. The most common types are Wired Equivalent Privacy (WEP), Wi-Fi Protected Access (WPA) and WPA2. Each has its own benefits and drawbacks in terms of the levels of security it provides.

What if...?

Aleema runs a medium-sized business that specialises in financial advice for its clients. The staff all use laptops to connect to the office server using an open Wi-Fi connection that they also use to provide internet access for visitors.

Aleema would like to know the risks of using an open Wi-Fi connection for the work laptops and would also like to understand more about ways the connections could be protected.

Prepare a report for Aleema explaining the:

- potential risks to her business of using an open Wi-Fi connection

- benefits and drawbacks of different Wi-Fi encryption methods (WEP, WPA, WPA2), based on your own research.

Apply admin and user passwords

When setting up shared files or managing a multi-user network, it is important that you ensure data is protected and that users are only allowed access to parts of the network (or features of a device) that they require. Imagine the problems that might occur if everybody could view, modify and delete every file saved on a company's network.

Common, and good, practice restricts network users' access through the use of USERNAMES (identification used to help a system match a user with a specific account) and PASSWORDS (words, phrases and numbers used to confirm that the person entering the username is genuine). Assigning usernames also allows a network administrator to use group policies to provide varying levels of access on a user-by-user basis – for example, an 'admin' password would give a user the ability to make changes to sensitive data whereas a 'user' password may just allow a user to view the data.

Practise

Imagine you are working as a junior IT support technician. You have been asked to set up some new users for the company's network. With user management tools, set up at least two new users. You should:

- provide a username
- set a unique password
- set rules for the password
- set different permissions for each of the users.

Pathway focus

Networking and Cybersecurity

In a networking and cybersecurity or IT support role, you may need to provide advice to others on how to ensure passwords are strong and kept secure.

Digital Applications

In a digital applications role, you may also need to configure or create validation routines that enforce the characteristics of a strong password.

Skills and knowledge check

- ☐ Can you explain the purpose of the main internal components of a computer?
- ☐ Can you select the most appropriate peripheral devices for a given task?
- ☐ Can you explain which connection type will be the most appropriate in a range of scenarios?
- ☐ Can you describe the role of different network components?
- ☐ Can you explain different network connection processes?

- ○ I can remove and replace a computer's internal components.
- ○ I can connect devices to make a simple network.

B Install, configure and test software in computer systems and mobile devices to meet user requirements

Software provides the data and instructions used to complete a specific task or to ensure a computer can function. Modern computers use what is called the 'stored program' model, which means that to enable the computer to perform different tasks you simply change the software. Before this concept was developed, computers that could only be used for a single particular task would have to be completely reconfigured if a different function was needed.

B1 Functions of an operating system

The operating system (OS) is probably the most important piece of software on a computer as it controls all the computer's major operations and ensures that it functions. Table 1.2 describes how the operating system supports different functions. Knowing how and why parts of an OS perform particular tasks will enable you to identify and diagnose problems and suggest solutions.

Function	How the operating system (OS) supports this function
Boot up	The initial boot check sequence is handled by the **UEFI/BIOS (UNIFIED EXTENSIBLE FIRMWARE INTERFACE/BASIC INPUT OUTPUT SYSTEM)**, a set of permanently stored data that specifies the order in which connected devices should be checked for an OS. Following this, the OS itself is responsible for starting individual processes and ensuring the relevant components are activated (or 'mounted') in the correct order, so that the system can start.
Central processing	A 'go-between' for the processor and any software. Any instruction or action performed by the software is converted by the OS into the relevant system instruction so that it is understood by the processor. In a system that uses multi-core and/or multi-thread processors, the OS will manage the load between the processors to ensure instructions are processed in the most efficient manner.

Table 1.2: How the operating system (OS) supports different functions

Table 1.2: *(continued)*

Function	How the operating system (OS) supports this function
Resource and device management	Device drivers provide the specific control instructions for each piece of hardware. They work like a translation program so any instruction provided by a program can be understood by the hardware in each computer. This removes the need for programmers to program software to include instructions for every possible make and model of hardware that might be used.
	The OS will also ensure that the instructions are sent to the correct piece of hardware and that this hardware has sufficient processor and memory allocation when needed.
Memory and sharing	The OS controls how much memory each active process is given. For example, if programs are running at the same time, the OS will monitor which program needs memory, when it needs it and for what. If one program is being displayed onscreen and is being actively used, this will be allocated more memory than a less active program that is running in the background.
Functionality monitoring	An OS can often provide two forms of functionality monitoring.
	1. Monitoring system processes and active programs – this allows users to monitor the resources being used and to identify any programs that are not performing correctly and take action.
	2. Diagnostic information on the components of the system – this may work in conjunction with the device drivers but is used to provide data on how well a system is performing, such as temperature readings of the processor or checking for damaged parts of a hard drive.
Directories for programs and storage	When data is stored on a hard drive, the data is placed in blocks and related data is linked or referenced using an index which tells the computer where this data is stored, how to find it and what it relates to.
	Finding data using the index system every time you want to load a file would be far too inefficient, therefore the OS provides directories that are a user-friendly way of finding any information you store. Directories are like virtual folders in which you can keep information and data so you can find it when you need it.
Displays and user machine interface	These provide a **USER INTERFACE (UI)** (screen that the user works with) for the system, translating the instructions and actions of the computer into a form of visual or audio feedback. Most modern OS use a **GRAPHICAL USER INTERFACE (GUI)**, an intuitive system for users to interact with and control a computer through a series of windows, icons, menus and pointers.
	The OS will also provide accessibility features so the interaction can be adapted to suit each individual's needs.

B2 Types of operating system

Operating systems come in many different forms and the OS you choose will depend on the hardware it is to be used on and the needs of the users. Selecting the correct OS is vitally important to the efficient running of an organisation. Choosing an inappropriate OS could lead to functionality, compatibility and security problems that could affect a company's efficiency and productivity. For example, an embedded system would typically have reduced computing resources, so a much more streamlined OS is needed. However, a workstation OS might not provide the correct level of user management and security configuration to be able to control a server and the workstations that would connect to a network.

The most common types of operating system are listed below.

- *Server*: operating systems designed to control a network or a web-based service and provide user, data and security management tools. It will communicate with and control a computer that uses a 'workstation' OS.
- *Workstation*: this is designed for use on a desktop or laptop, for stand-alone computers or ones that will be connected to a network. These are usually designed to be user-friendly.
- *Mobile*: similar to a workstation OS, these are designed for individual computers but optimised for use on mobile devices and touchscreens.
- *Embedded*: considered by some to be a sub-category of mobile operating systems, embedded operating systems are highly optimised control systems that are usually found in 'Internet of Things' devices (such as smartwatches and home-energy systems, for example Hive Active Heating™). They often have a highly streamlined UI (sometimes no GUI) and are saved directly onto chips inside the device.

All the different types of OS can be broken down into two further categories: open source and proprietary (commercial) (see Figure 1.3). **OPEN-SOURCE SOFTWARE** (free and in the public domain) is provided with access to the original source code, allowing the user to change or adapt the operating system to meet their needs. With **PROPRIETARY SOFTWARE** (usually paid-for and intellectual property rights claimed), the code is protected by copyright and the user is not allowed to access or change it.

Link it up

Networking and Cybersecurity

For more information on the Internet of Things, see Unit 11, C2.

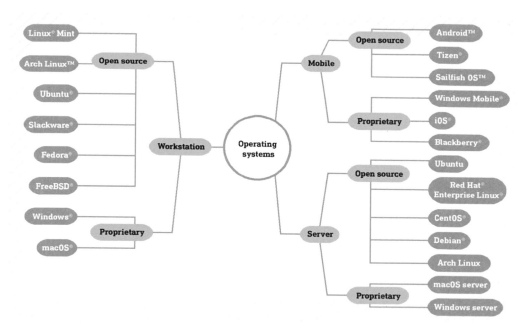

Figure 1.3: How many of these operating systems have you heard of?

B3 Software programs and their purpose

In an IT support role, you will be responsible for ensuring the software on a network or system is managed appropriately. This means ensuring it is maintained in a way that continues the good performance of the system as a whole.

Install/uninstall

Installing and uninstalling software is a key part of software management. It involves responding to a user's needs and identifying the correct

Link it up

Networking and Cybersecurity

For more information on open-source and proprietary software, see Unit 5, B1 'Do you own the software you use?'

software to install – finding out what will achieve the user's needs most efficiently and also comply with the organisation's policies and guidelines.

It is also important that currently installed software is monitored. Outdated or unused software should be reviewed and, if appropriate, removed as old software can cause issues of compatibility with hardware or other software, or even present security risks.

Version identification

As software is maintained and improved by its developers, new versions are released either in the form of a newly installable piece of software or as an update to the program. When using systems that will exchange data and work together, it is important that you can identify the version of a piece of software you have installed. Newer versions may include additional features or fixes to security bugs. Ensuring that systems that will work together are using the same version also reduces compatibility issues.

Identifying which version of a piece of software you use is important. Ensuring that your software is up to date will mean you will have the most current features to help limit security risks

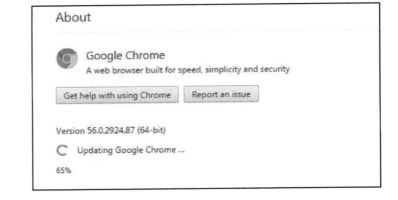

Licensing

When you purchase a piece of software you are not buying the software itself. Instead you are purchasing a LICENCE, a permit that allows you to use a version of that software. The licence specifies clearly defined parameters on how you can use the software, such as whether you can make changes to it or not (for example, with open-source software) or how many computers you can install the software on.

Large organisations will often purchase a SITE LICENCE. This tells you how many computers across the entire building can use the software. A licence such as this may typically be based on an annual fee and provide software updates and in some cases additional technical support.

Ensuring that the requirements of the licence are met is a key role of an IT support department, as failure to follow the terms and conditions could lead to the company facing legal action.

Updating

While all commercial software will be tested thoroughly before being released, it is impossible for the developers to test all possible situations that may occur when the software is used in the 'real world'. Therefore, it is common for updates to be released that fix problems that have been found by users. These may be compatibility issues with software and hardware or a security bug that needs to be removed. Ensuring that software is updated regularly and that a policy for doing this is adhered to is vital for a company's systems to work efficiently.

B4 Common application software features and functions

As you have already learned, computer software provides the data and instructions to allow a computer to perform a number of tasks. Software is usually grouped into types based on its primary purpose and there is an almost unending list of software for every common task. Identifying the features and functions will allow you, as an IT professional, to select software effectively to meet specific needs.

Productivity software

PRODUCTIVITY SOFTWARE is associated with tasks required in an office or similar environment. This includes word processing, spreadsheets, **DATABASES** and communication software such as email. (Databases are an organised collection of data used to store, manage and extract large amounts of information for a user.)

Browsers

A **BROWSER** is a piece of software designed to allow users to view web content. Browsers are designed to translate HTML code (and other associated scripting languages) into viewable content. Examples include Google Chrome™, Firefox® and Safari®.

Collaboration software

COLLABORATION SOFTWARE is typically implemented through the use of **CLOUD TECHNOLOGIES** (remote technologies that use internet-based resources to store and process data), and allows users to work more efficiently as a team. It may include the use of online storage to share documents, the use of cloud computing to work simultaneously on documents (for example, Google Docs™) or the use of web conferencing to communicate.

Messaging

The internet provides a number of ways to communicate with others. This could include the use of email, which provides a formal way of structuring communication and transferring documents and files. Alternatively, much more 'instant' forms of communications such as short messages or video chat can be used for real-time discussions (for example, Google Hangouts™).

Specialised software

Some tasks may require more specialised software. For example, many productivity suites provide a simple photo or graphic editor that allows a user to make basic alterations to an image they wish to include in a document (such as making it black and white instead of colour, or cropping out unwanted areas). However, if more complex processes are required, then specialist software may be needed. For example, Microsoft Windows® provides a simple video editor that is useful for editing basic home movies or creating a video for a school presentation. However, it would not be used to edit a major blockbuster movie.

Link it up

Data Applications

For more information on selecting software, see Unit 5, B1.

Link it up

Networking and Cybersecurity

For more information on cloud technologies, see Unit 11.

Link it up

Data Applications

For more information on selecting utility software, see Unit 5, B1 'How is software used in organisations?'

Utility software

UTILITY SOFTWARE is a set of tools that allow a user to maintain and optimise the performance of a computer such as **ANTI-VIRUS SOFTWARE**, encryption tools and diagnostic tools. (Anti-virus software protects a device from software that may be designed to damage or steal data.) Examples of these for common processes are likely to come bundled with your chosen OS but more specialised processes would need to be downloaded and installed separately.

Open-source and proprietary (commercial) software

When selecting software, as well as considering the features and functionality that the software offers, you may also need to consider whether it is more appropriate to use open-source software or proprietary (commercial) software. Open-source software is licensed in a way that provides users with access to the programming source code and allows them to modify the code to add functionality or develop a new piece of software. The programming code for proprietary software is protected and users are forbidden from accessing or changing it.

As with operating systems, there is a wide variety of choice of **APPLICATION SOFTWARE** (software that can be used to carry out a task or to produce products such as documents and presentations) and utility software in proprietary or open-source format. You should consider the implications of the license agreement before selecting a piece of software.

Link it up

Data Applications

For more information on open-source software, see Unit 5, B1 'Do you own the software you use?'

Common file types and purposes

When a piece of software saves or generates a file, that file is assigned a **FILE TYPE** (which can also be identified by its file extension). The file type tells the computer how the data in the file should be processed – for example, whether it is a document or an image. For many common uses, such as images, there is a range of different file types, each providing different functionality, benefits and drawbacks.

Table 1.3 shows some common file purposes and popular file types and extensions.

Table 1.3: Popular file types and extensions

Purpose	File type	Extension(s)
Word processing	Rich Text Format	.rtf
	Document	.doc, .docx
	OpenDocument Format	.odf, .odt
	Plain Text	.txt
Spreadsheets	Microsoft Excel	.xls
	OpenDocument Spreadsheet	.odf, .ods
	Delimited files	.csv, .tsv
Audio	MPEG	.m4a, .mp3,
	Open-source codec	.ogg
	Wave	.wav
	Windows media audio format	.wma
Image	JPEG (Joint Photographic Experts Group)	.jpeg, .jpg
	GIF (Graphics Interchange Format)	.gif
	PNG (Portable Network Graphic)	.png
	Bitmap	.bmp
Compression/archive	CD image	.iso
	ZIP files	.zip
	Tarball	.tar
	RAR	.rar

Link it up

Digital Applications

For more information on file extensions, see Unit 7, A3 'Simple editor programs, file extensions and syntax conventions'.

Pathway focus

Digital Applications

In an IT support role, you may have to select and install software to meet a user's needs or assess the use of currently used software and remove unused software to improve the performance of a computer system.

Networking and Cybersecurity

In a networking and cybersecurity role, you may have to assess the robustness of similar programs before installing them, to ensure that they meet the security requirements for the system they will be used on.

B5 Setup and configuration of mobile devices

In an IT support role, you may be required to set up and configure a variety of mobile devices. The tasks you will be required to complete will include those listed here.

Connection setup

The exchange of data between devices is a key part of the functionality of modern computer systems. Different devices, operating systems and tasks may require different methods of connecting and the choice of how these are set up will depend entirely on the required task.

Synchronisation

The development of mobile devices over recent years has made it possible to be much more flexible with how you work and access data and services. However, using multiple devices to access data and files can cause problems. For example, you might have been working on a document on your laptop but when you next need it, your laptop is not available and you have to use a desktop PC. SYNCHRONISATION allows users to use the same files and data across multiple devices by ensuring the most recent copy of the data or file is available on any of the connected devices.

Synchronisation can provide a way of backing up important data, as copies are saved on multiple devices, but it is best used for small amounts of data or tasks such as synchronising a calendar or contacts.

Synchronisation is not recommended for full system backups, as this is likely to cause performance issues. Typically, synchronisation across devices is linked to a server (such as a cloud service or office server). When setting up a system, for example, you may need to set up a worker's laptop so that when they are working away from the office, the document is saved in their 'Documents' folder on their laptop. At this point, only the local copy will be changed. The system may be set up so that when they next connect the laptop to the company network, or at a pre-set interval, the local 'Documents' folder is compared with the server copy and the most up-to-date version of the document is saved in both places, so that the worker can then access the latest version from any connected device.

Email configuration

When configuring an email account on a mobile device, many devices offer 'wizards' that make the process very easy. However, these are often designed to work for 'average' users and with popular email providers. If your employer uses an email system that they store on their own servers, you are likely to have to set up your connection manually.

When setting up email, one of the key decisions is the incoming mail protocol you will use. The following two options are available.

- *POP3 (Post-Office Protocol 3)*: when a user connects to their email, the emails are downloaded to the device and then deleted from the server, leaving only the copy on the user's device. This is best used when emails are required on only one device such as an office-based PC. POP3 is considered by some to be a good choice if emails are likely to contain sensitive information, as only one copy exists on a local machine, making it harder to obtain by criminals.
- *IMAP* (Internet Message Access Protocol): this protocol is used when a user wishes to have access to all their emails from a number of different devices. IMAP keeps a copy of the email on the server and synchronises received and sent emails between connected devices. This is typically used with web mail services such as Hotmail®.

Bluetooth® pairing

BLUETOOTH® is a low-powered, short-range (approximately 10 m maximum) wireless connection that creates a direct link between two devices to share data. Bluetooth provides a relatively small amount of **BANDWIDTH** (the maximum amount of data a connection can transfer at any one time) so is best used for small amounts of data such as synchronising calendars, transferring a small number of smaller files or connecting to headphones or speakers.

When connecting two devices using Bluetooth, the devices must be 'paired'. This typically requires both devices to be in 'visible' or 'discoverable' mode. The user(s) of both devices will then authorise the connection. These devices are then 'paired' so they can identify and communicate with each other in the future.

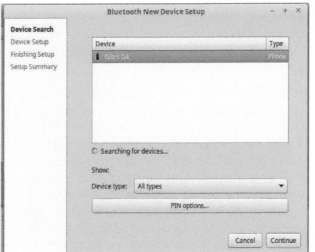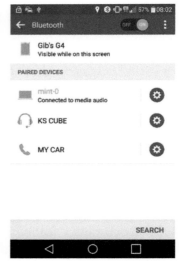

To improve security, devices often have to 'pair' when connecting using Bluetooth. The users have to agree to the connections and sometimes confirm a security code before they can connect

Locking/unlocking and security

Due to their portable nature, mobile devices can cause security concerns. As the ability of mobile devices to access and use a greater range of data increases, it is important that robust systems are in place on these devices to protect the data on them and the data on the systems they can access. Breaches to security can be detrimental to an organisation; failure to protect customer data can result in legal action being taken against the company and breaches can damage customer confidence, which can result in the loss of business.

Table 1.4 describes different security techniques that can be used to secure mobile devices.

Link it up

Networking and Cybersecurity

For more information on physical security, see Unit 8, B3 'Physical security'.

Method	Description
Restricting access	Challenge tests such as PINs, pattern locks and passwords can be used to restrict unauthorised users from unlocking the device and using it.
Biometrics	Similar to challenge tests, **BIOMETRICS** (the statistical analysis or measurement of biological data) restricts access to a device by using data relating to an individual's physical measurement. Common biometric techniques on mobile devices include fingerprint scanners and face recognition.
Encryption	Encryption uses a key to render data unreadable unless the correct key is entered. Encryption is a good way to ensure data is protected if the device is lost or stolen.
Restricted sources	Many mobile operating systems allow the option to only install apps via the integrated software management service (or the device can be configured to only allow software from this service), which can reduce the chance of **MALICIOUS SOFTWARE** (harmful programs that are intended to cause damage to computer systems) being installed.
Anti-virus	Installing and regularly updating anti-virus software will protect the device from malicious software that may be designed to damage or steal data.
Firewall	A **FIREWALL** monitors connections to a device and ensures that no connections are being made to the device by a malicious or unauthorised source.

Table 1.4: Different security options for mobile devices

Downloading apps

Software for many mobile devices (tablets and smartphones in particular) is provided through an integrated software management service or 'store'. These services often also provide a way of managing installed software.

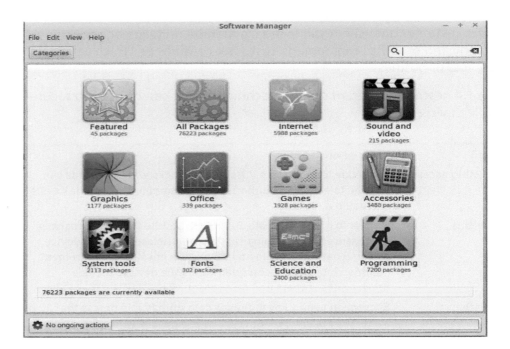

A software manager is used in smartphones to install software

Practise

The IT support department you work for has purchased a new laptop for use by one of the company's employees. You have been asked to prepare the laptop so it can be used on the company network. You are required to:

- install a suitable operating system
- connect the laptop to a Wi-Fi connection
- install appropriate productivity software.

Skills and knowledge check

☐ Can you explain the purpose of the operating system software?

☐ Can you select the most appropriate application software in a given task?

☐ Can you explain which connection type will be the most appropriate for a mobile device in a range of scenarios?

○ I can install and update operating system and application software.

○ I can configure a mobile device to connect to other devices or required services.

C Apply appropriate security measures to computer systems and mobile devices

When working with computer equipment, it is important to consider the safety of yourself and others. Organisations have a responsibility to ensure their customers and employees are safe.

C1 Safety measures

As an IT professional, you will need to ensure that appropriate measures are taken that enable the company you work for to consistently apply appropriate safety measures. There are a number of ways to improve safety that you should consider when setting up, using or disposing of computers.

Disposal methods

Many electrical products, and related items such as ink, toner and batteries, contain materials that can be hazardous to humans and the environment. When they are no longer needed, it is important to consider how to dispose of them in a safe and responsible way. There are a number of factors to consider.

- *Legal restrictions*: there are two main pieces of legislation to consider.
  - RoHS (Restriction of the Use of Certain Hazardous Substances) provides guidance to manufacturers about which materials they should or should not use, where they are permitted to use them, and the amount of that material that should be used when manufacturing the device. When purchasing equipment, companies should aim to purchase RoHS certified devices.
  - WEEE (Waste Electrical and Electronic Equipment directive) regulates how computing devices must be disposed of and sets targets and guidelines for different countries about which materials must be recycled.
- *Repurposing*: in addition to recycling the materials found inside electrical goods, there are some charities that specialise in repurposing old IT equipment that companies or individuals wish to dispose of. These charities recondition them so they can be used by those in need in the UK and in developing countries.

Power

Considering safe practices for power usage when using IT equipment is important for protecting both the user and the equipment.

- *Always use the correct power supply*: when using or charging portable IT equipment, it is important that you only use the power supply for that device to avoid damaging the battery or internal components.

- *International power differences*: some countries' mains power supplies provide different voltages from the UK. You should be aware of the following two main considerations when using equipment.
  - Always use an appropriate power converter if connecting a device (such as when charging a laptop) to the mains supply in a different country.
  - Some PC power supplies are designed for international markets and as such have a variable power setting, as shown in Figure 1.4. A PC's power supply should be set to the voltage that is correct for the mains supply it will be connected to, in order to avoid damage to the PC.

Cooling fan

AC power in

Power switch

Voltage switch

Figure 1.4: Selecting the correct voltage on a computer's power supply protects users and prevents damage to the computer equipment

Device placement

Where a device is placed can also have an impact on the safety of users. The following are examples of the factors you should consider when placing a device.

- *Airflow*: does the device have enough space/clearance to allow sufficient airflow to allow it to cool efficiently and avoid overheating?
- *Stability*: is the device on a level/stable surface or, if mounted on a wall, are the mounts attached securely?
- *Trip hazards*: is the device in a position where it, or related wires, could cause a tripping hazard?

Electrostatic discharge concepts

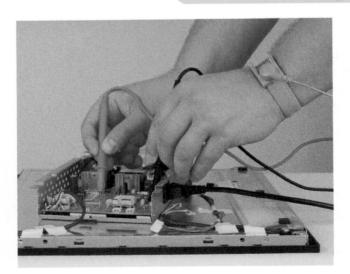

When removing or replacing internal components, it is important to consider the dangers of **ELECTROSTATIC DISCHARGE** (a sudden release of low-level electricity caused by friction from anything from clothing to human skin). This release of electricity can cause damage to the internal components themselves, which can result in loss of data or functionality, or in some cases cause injury to the user replacing the component. To reduce the risk posed by electrostatic discharge, you should always use an electrostatic prevention wristband that is appropriately grounded. You should also ensure that the products used when cleaning devices are certified to not cause, or even to reduce, electrostatic build up.

Wearing an electrostatic wristband prevents electrostatic discharge that can damage sensitive computer equipment

Ergonomic concepts

ERGONOMICS is the study of people and their working environment and how this affects their efficiency (see Figure 1.5). In terms of computer safety, ergonomically designed workstations and devices improve a user's efficiency, and their health and their safety. Ergonomics concepts to consider are:

- keyboard and mouse placement to avoid wrist strain and fatigue
- sitting positions (including adjustable and supportive chairs) to reduce back pain
- monitor placement to avoid neck pain and eye strain.

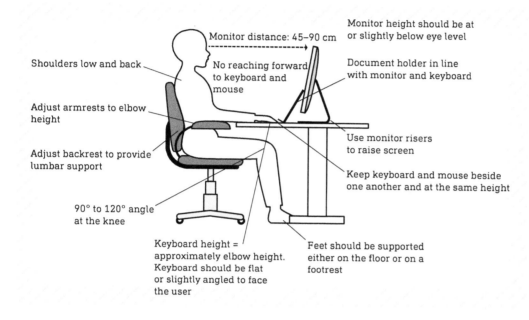

Figure 1.5: Compare this diagram with how you sit at a desk with a computer. Are you following all of the advice?

C2 Security and backup procedures

Ensuring the data on, and used by, computer systems is safe is a key consideration. Loss of data or breaches in security can be very damaging for an organisation. For example, the loss of data relating to products that may have given them a competitive advantage could be financially damaging, or the negative publicity that may arise from having their security breached may affect customer confidence, causing customers to go elsewhere.

Basic security threats

The threats to the data held by organisations can generally be categorised as accidental or malicious.

- *Accidental*: where data is lost or damaged by mistake such as accidentally deleting a file, overwriting data in a file or losing a device that contains sensitive or important data.
- *Malicious*: where data and/or systems are attacked with intent to cause damage, data loss, or to steal data. This can include hacking, the spreading of VIRUSES (once installed on a computer, a virus attaches itself to an existing program then copies itself) or the use of SOCIAL ENGINEERING (attempts by third parties to get users to reveal secure information such as passwords).

Basic security practices

In order to protect data, it is important that established good practice is followed. Ensuring device settings are robust and that users are aware of key dos and don'ts can drastically improve the safety of data.

Table 1.5 shows ways to improve security of IT systems and what to consider when applying these practices.

Table 1.5: Techniques for improving security in IT systems

Security practice	Considerations
Anti-virus	• Install robust and reliable anti-virus software. • Ensure it is regularly updated so that latest versions are used. • Schedule regular system scans to ensure system is actively protected.
Firewall	• Use of a blacklist to block specific connections. • Use a **WHITELIST** (a list of trustworthy sites) to allow specific connections.
Encryption	• Use encrypted connections when transmitting data (for example, https for websites, WPA when connecting to Wi-Fi). • Encrypt individual files or whole drive if storing sensitive data. • Use drive encryption on mobile devices, as these are at greater risk of being lost or stolen due to their portable nature.

Passwords	• Ensure a strict password policy is in use, detailing how passwords are utilised to keep data safe. It must be read by all users and may include advice such as:
	  ○ features of a strong password (minimum length, mix of lower and upper case, including numbers and other characters)
	  ○ how often a password should be changed
	  ○ password management (for example, use of password management software, not telling others, not writing it down).

Device hardening	• Remove all unnecessary software. • Disable unwanted/un-needed connection points (for example, disabling USB sockets, Bluetooth). • Regular updating and patching of software.

Link it up

Networking and Cybersecurity

For more information on security practices, see Unit 8.

Backup procedures

Even in systems where high-quality security is in place, it is not possible to prevent all possible threats to data. Data can get lost or damaged through human error or due to hardware or software failure. It is therefore important that effective backup procedures are implemented to ensure that the amount of data lost, in the event of a problem, is minimised and a company can resume normal activity as soon as possible.

There are a number of issues to consider when planning backup procedures.

Scheduling

When the backup will take place is important. Many organisations schedule the backup for the end of the day when business is concluded. However, what if you lose work you have done that day? Alternatively, what if a company generates so much data that leaving it until the end of the day would make the backup too large to manage?

You may also consider the impact of the backup procedure – for example, a batch backup may slow down the server or affect the available bandwidth if backing up to a cloud service. So you may choose to do it after standard working hours so as not to affect productivity of staff.

Frequency

As well as scheduling the time of day of a backup, you will also need to consider how often a backup will take place. Many organisations back up data every evening, but more sensitive information (such as banking transactions) may require much more frequent backup and instead use mirroring (creating duplicate copies) to ensure the data is backed up instantly.

Storage media

The choice of medium will depend on two main factors.

- *The amount of data to be backed up*: the storage capacity of a medium will drastically affect its suitability for particular uses. For example, a DVD may be suitable for backing up files from an individual's laptop but would not be suitable for backing up the work areas of staff and students in a large school.
- *The frequency and scheduling of the backup*: the read/write speeds of the medium is extremely important. For example, if data is being backed up overnight, then the read/write speed is less important, so a slower, but reliable and high capacity storage, such as magnetic tape might be used. However, if you need to back up instantly, then you would use mirroring on multiple hard drives.

Practise

Brian has bought a new laptop that he will use for work and for leisure. As part of his work, he often has sensitive client information, such as names, addresses and financial information, on his computer so would like to make sure that the data is protected.

Install and configure security software and settings on a laptop to ensure the device is secure. You should consider:

- anti-virus software
- firewall
- encryption
- passwords
- device hardening.

Skills and knowledge check

☐ Can you describe possible threats to data and systems?

☐ Can you explain the impact of not fully securing an IT system?

☐ Can you describe measures that can be used to protect IT systems and the data they hold?

☐ Can you explain the importance of appropriate backup procedures?

○ I can install, configure and/or update appropriate security features on a computer system.

○ I can use computer systems safely and ensure they are set up in a way that protects others.

○ I can select and configure appropriate backup procedures.

Ready for assessment

You have just been appointed as a junior IT support technician in a large office.

The company employs a wide range of employees with broad requirements. You will be required to provide technical support by installing, configuring and testing hardware and software to ensure the employees' needs are met.

This checklist shows the skills you will be required to demonstrate to complete this task.

I can:

- [ ] select and install appropriate internal components
- [ ] connect computer peripherals, including installing additional drives as required
- [ ] select appropriate connection types for specific devices and scenarios
- [ ] set up a simple network
- [ ] connect devices to wired and wireless networks
- [ ] install operating system software
- [ ] select, install and configure appropriate application software
- [ ] connect mobile devices to networks and services
- [ ] select, install and configure software for a mobile device
- [ ] work safely when connecting components and hardware
- [ ] ensure computer systems are set up and configured safely to reduce risk of injury to others
- [ ] apply appropriate and robust security measures to computer systems
- [ ] ensure appropriate backup procedures are followed to protect data.

When generating evidence for your assessment portfolio, you can use a range of evidence, including:

- screenshots/screen casts of processes carried out

- video and photographs (for example, of building a PC)

- witness statements from your tutor/assessor (useful for supporting video and photographic evidence)

- IT support logs detailing logged issue, when and how the problem was resolved.

WORK FOCUS

⌐HANDS ✋N

Imagine you are working on a technical support helpdesk in a large office. You receive a call from a member of staff stating that they 'cannot get onto the internet'. Role-play with a partner the questions you would ask to find the cause of the problem.

Were you able to:

- speak confidently

- use technical language appropriately in order to show knowledge but still be understood by a non-specialist

- systematically work through possible problems to achieve a solution?

You were unable to achieve a suitable solution over the phone so the device has been brought to you to be fixed. Your supervisor has said that there is a problem with the Ethernet socket and it no longer connects to any network.

The computer is a desktop PC. Describe how you would solve the problem in these two situations.

a) You must replace the motherboard as the Ethernet socket is integrated to the motherboard.

b) Install a network interface card using an expansion slot in the PC.

Were you able to remember all:

- appropriate health and safety procedures

- the steps of removing and replacing computer hardware?

NB: If you have access to equipment, you could demonstrate this in a practical manner.

Ready for work?

There are some key work-related skills that you will need to demonstrate in this unit. Developing these will greatly help you when looking for a job in an IT department and will allow you to be much more effective when in the workplace. You should take the opportunity to practise these skills as often as possible.

1 Communication

- Giving accurate information to help resolve problems.

- Using technical language accurately and in a way that is appropriate to your audience – for example, using different levels of technical language when explaining a problem to the head of the IT department compared with the member of staff who reported the problem.

2 Managing information

- Keeping track of support requests and maintaining records of how and when problems were resolved.

- Protecting and using sensitive information such as passwords appropriately.

3 Working with others

- Identifying needs and providing help and support in achieving aims. For example, identifying appropriate IT solutions.

2 Exploring Current and Emerging Technologies

Technology is the fastest growing and changing industry in the world. Every week there is news about the launch of a new device or new software.

How many new devices or software have you heard about or seen advertised in the last six months? How have you heard about them? Are these advances in technology designed to help whole organisations or individual users at work or at home? Perhaps they are simply new forms of entertainment? In this unit, you will explore a range of current and emerging technologies and the organisational contexts in which they are used.

How will I be assessed?

You will be assessed through a series of assignments that draw on the knowledge and skills you will develop in this unit. The assignment will focus on you demonstrating an understanding of current technologies in mobile, internet and cloud contexts. You will show that you can examine new technologies and understand how they will be used by organisations to support their activities. You will also investigate the technologies used by organisations and how these technologies help organisations meet their business objectives.

Analysing and evaluating technologies and their suitability for use in organisational settings is an important skill for an IT professional. This assessment will allow you to demonstrate both your technical skill and your creativity in how you promote particular technologies in business situations. When making recommendations, you should always be able to justify your reasons and evaluate how an organisation has benefited from recommendations made by you and others.

Assessment criteria

Pass	Merit	Distinction
Learning aim A: Explore current and emerging technologies and their purpose		
A.P1 Describe types of current and emerging technologies and their purpose.	**A.M1** Explain how current and emerging technologies are being used in organisations, giving detailed examples and identifying any future technological trends.	**A.D1** Analyse how current and emerging technologies are being used in organisations, using detailed examples and evaluating the impact of any future technological trends.
A.P2 Outline how current and emerging technologies are being used in organisations, giving outline examples.		
Learning aim B: Investigate how an organisation uses technology to meet its needs		
B.P3 Describe how an organisation has selected and used technology to meet its needs.	**B.M2** Explain how an organisation has selected and used technology to meet its needs, assessing the benefits and risks to the organisation.	**B.D2** Evaluate how an organisation has selected and used technology to meet its needs, analysing the benefits and risks and making suggestions for how it might be impacted by emerging technology.
B.P4 Outline how technology has benefited an organisation.		

A Explore current and emerging technologies and their purpose

Mobile technologies have made it increasingly possible for us to connect with each other, with organisations (including employers) and with the wealth of digital information that is available online.

A1 Mobile technology

One of the fastest growing areas in technology development in recent years has been mobile technology.

Mobile technology in different sectors

Mobile technology is a part of everyday life and widely used in different contexts such as:

- retail
- banking
- entertainment
- social media.

For example, managing your bank account has never been easier, as shown here.

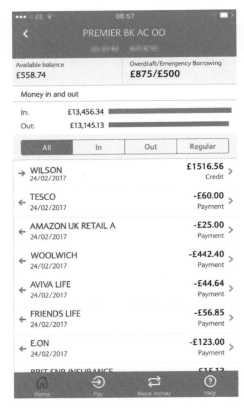

Banking apps allow you to see your balance and your recent transactions

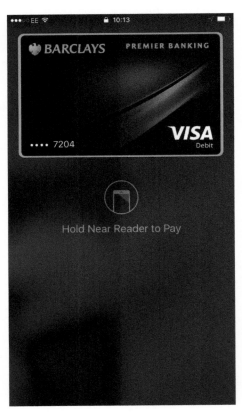

Smartphone apps have transformed the way you can pay for things

Smartphone apps such as Apple Pay® will store your card information, which can be used in shops and online to pay for goods and services. For example, you can use Apple Pay to pay for travel on Transport for London (TfL) services (such as the London Underground, bus and rail services). The service is activated by pressing the home button twice on an iPhone® in locked mode. This automatically activates Apple Pay, and you can then simply follow the instructions.

You can also stream media (such as music and video for entertainment) on your device. (**STREAMING** is when you listen to music or you watch videos on your device without downloading them.) If you want to use an online streaming service, you will need an internet connection. Paying a **SUBSCRIPTION** (paying regularly in advance for a purchase) will provide additional services, such as better quality or access to a wider range of streamable material. Streaming services include Spotify®, Apple Music®, Deezer™, Tidal™ and Google Play Music™.

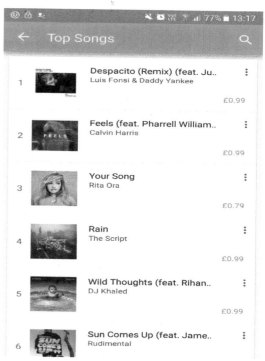

Music-streaming services can have both free and paid-for formats

Development and use of smart devices/smartphone apps

What does the 'smart' in smartphone mean? It means that your handheld device can now provide as much information as your PC or laptop. In fact, it could be argued that handheld devices are even smarter than a PC or laptop as they have extra features such as location services, which are not relevant to technology that is not mobile.

Link it up

Digital Applications

See Unit 1 to find out more on the ways in which emerging technology could be used in the form of innovative **SOFTWARE** or security applications.

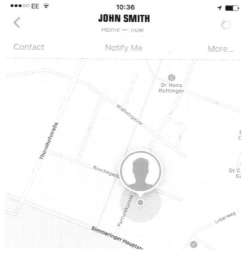

By zooming in you can see your friend at street level

Services such as Find My Friends® display the location of each of the friends that you have added to the app

Using the location services, the app will calculate the distance travelled, the time taken and the number of calories burned

Location services are also useful for tracking your progress, for example if you go for a jog or run. You can activate the app at the start of the run. You can still use other services while you run, such as listening to music.

Practise

If you own a mobile phone, write down:

- the names of the ten apps that you use most often

- how often you use them (for example daily, weekly, monthly).

Emerging mobile technology and its future use

We cannot possibly know yet what the future may bring in terms of mobile technology developments but we are already seeing paperless systems, as well as home and transport automation systems, being used in everyday life.

Smart home technology

The most rapidly growing area in mobile technology is currently smart home technology. This has an infinite number of possibilities for the future, such as those shown in Figure 2.1.

Figure 2.1: What other smart home technology do you think might be developed in the future?

Bedroom
- Clothes made with smart fabrics regulate your temperature and monitor your health.
- Lights come on automatically when you need to get up.

Kitchen
- Smart surfaces identify what is on them and react accordingly, keeping teacups warm and iced drinks cold.
- Smart plates identify what you are eating, including the calories and nutritional value.

Roof
- Power is collected through solar panels and stored in backup resources to power house and car.

Bathroom
- Water temperature automatically adjusts based on your body's temperature.
- Toilets analyse waste for medical problems such as colon cancer and diabetes.

Office
- See-through electronics, screens and touch panels deliver 3D holographic experiences.
- Contact lenses or glasses allow you to access information resources instantly before your eyes.

Living room
- All appliances are connected through invisible networking system.
- Automated robots carry out household chores.

Garage
- Camera at entrance has facial recognition software which is linked to a criminal database.
- Car is able to drive itself.

Travel

It is now possible to travel across the world with nothing more than your passport and your mobile phone. Take a look at the images below. This traveller was able to book both a flight and a hotel online, and could also make changes using an app or visiting the main website.

This screenshot confirms a flight with an airline

This is the boarding pass displayed on the traveller's smartphone – they can present their phone at the departure gate where it will be scanned

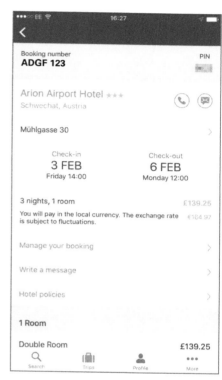

Booking in this way includes options for choosing a seat on the aircraft when checking in, and confirming special dietary requirements at the hotel through the 'Write a message' feature on the booking.com website

Pathway focus

Networking and Cybersecurity

In a networking and cybersecurity role, you will often be among the first IT specialists to see and use emerging technologies, as this is where many of the innovations will occur; for example, new cabling and wireless technologies to make connectivity faster and more responsive. You will connect new devices and new technologies to existing systems and you may even build whole new systems.

A2 Intelligent computer

The development of intelligent computers is creating many exciting possibilities in our working lives, as well as in domestic and leisure contexts. However there are also potential threats to our way of life as some tasks are replaced by intelligent computers.

An intelligent computer is one that is able to do many of the tasks that are currently carried out by people. For unpleasant or dangerous tasks, this is beneficial, but society is now asking the question: what will happen to our jobs if more and more tasks are carried out by a computer, device or app?

Link it up

Digital Applications

Go to Unit 10 to find out more about how multichannel solution systems can use emerging technologies to support an organisation's reliance on the digital world, enabling the organisation to operate in an increasingly complex environment.

Robotics

Automating manufacturing processes using robotics is one of the first areas where using computers has been found to give real benefits. Manufacturing processes are predictable, so using robotics is possible. Steps in the process can be programmed in advance and the technology can simply repeat the same processes over and over again.

Automated manufacturing processes have transformed the automotive industry

Online retail services such as Amazon® use robotic technology to pick orders. This means that the device moves to the location of each product in the warehouse and adds it to a basket.

People are still involved in the process, but the Kiva robots support much of the activity

Robots are also emerging in telehealth. This is the delivery of medical services remotely using telecommunications technology. An example of this is the use of a robot carrying a camera, microphone and speaker, which allows a medical specialist to interact with a patient. The camera enables the doctor to see the patient and ask questions, and allows them to monitor the patient after an operation.

Automation

Driverless cars are already being road tested. These rely heavily on sensor technology such as lasers, radars and cameras that are scanning in all directions and satellite navigation systems that control the position of the vehicle.

The technology for controlling driverless transport (such as cars, buses, lorries) is already well advanced where actions are predictable. Most of the development and testing is currently focused on creating systems that manage responses to what others do (for example, pedestrians stepping into the road, the actions of cyclists, managing poor road conditions such as snow, ice, rain, mud).

In a driverless car, the driver essentially becomes a passenger in the vehicle. These vehicles are capable of driving between destinations, as well as parking – both parallel parking and bay parking

Another consideration with driverless technology is the potential lack of privacy for users, as the location of their vehicle is always being tracked.

Practise

Investigate driverless technology and identify three types of business that could make use of this technology (for example, car hire and taxi services).

Global Positioning System (GPS)

GLOBAL POSITIONING SYSTEM (GPS) works by using the transmissions from a range of satellites to pinpoint the position of a device or object. The receivers in the devices or objects do not send any **DATA** to the satellite and, in order to work, a device needs a clear line of sight to the satellite (this means it must not be blocked by a building). Figure 2.2 shows how this works.

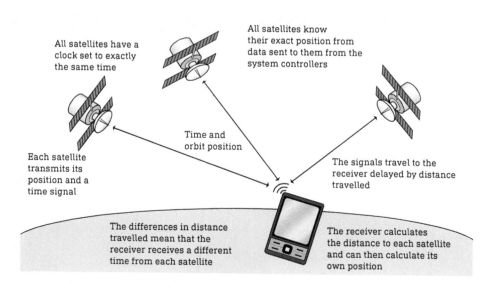

All satellites have a clock set to exactly the same time

All satellites know their exact position from data sent to them from the system controllers

Each satellite transmits its position and a time signal

Time and orbit position

The signals travel to the receiver delayed by distance travelled

The differences in distance travelled mean that the receiver receives a different time from each satellite

The receiver calculates the distance to each satellite and can then calculate its own position

Figure 2.2: GPS relies on a number of different satellite technologies working together reliably – typically a GPS receiver needs a minimum of four satellites to establish your position accurately

Reg EC-ILO   Flight No. BA524

London
LHR   00:36 AGO   IN 01:47   Madrid
MAD

15,447ft · 377kts · Airbus A321-211

The Plane Finder app updates in real time and you can see the aircraft moving across the screen

Using a combination of GPS and other location services, free apps such as Plane Finder™ display interesting information about both passenger and commercial flights. Clicking on any of the aeroplanes will usually display information about the flight, including:

- the flight number
- where it flew from
- where it is going
- its current height
- its current speed
- the type of aircraft.

Practise

If you have a smartphone, download the Plane Finder app. Wherever you are, open the app and if you can see an aeroplane above you, click on the plane on the app and it will give you the information about the flight.

Computer-aided design (CAD)

Designing objects used to be a lengthy process requiring SCHEMATICS (technical circuits) to be drawn on paper. Sometimes a number of engineers or designers would be working on one device or object and someone had to update a master drawing whenever changes were made.

CAD software has revolutionised design and, with collaborative versions of the software, multiple users can work on the same diagram in real time.

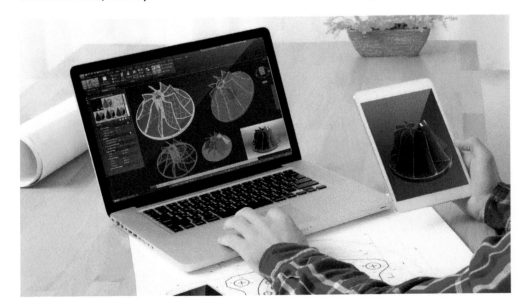

If the software is also linked to simulation software, the designs can be tested and, in some cases, prototypes can be printed using 3D printing technology

Table 2.1 shows how CAD technology can be used in many contexts.

Context for CAD	Description
Kitchen design	Once the dimensions of the room are known, objects such as cupboards and white goods such as washing machines, fridges, freezers and tumble driers, can be moved around the virtual room to find the most suitable positions for each object.
Bridge and building design	Bridges and buildings can be designed and the designs tested without any danger to life, before money is spent constructing a bridge or building that might be flawed.
Electronic design	Circuits can be tested and circuit boards designed for electronic devices.
Fashion design	Clothing can be designed and when combined with CAM (computer-aided manufacturing) systems, the finished product can be produced.
Prosthetic design	Using physical information about the patient, it is possible to manufacture prosthetic arms, hands, legs, feet or eyes to be a perfect fit.

Table 2.1: Uses for CAD technology

Voice control

There are many different ways that voice control is used in relation to technology. One of the most recent is the Amazon Echo® with its Alexa Voice Service, which uses voice commands to provide a range of services. Once set up, this device can control lights, switches and heating and can make diary entries, play music, provide food recipes, play the news, transmit audio content such as audio books and allow you to order takeaway food through services such as Just Eat®.

There is a variation of this on the iPhone called Siri® and another version on Windows® phones called Cortana®. Siri will carry out a whole range of tasks, including:

- scheduling reminders
- opening and closing apps
- reading your messages or emails to you
- searching for phone and internet content
- navigating with features such as 'take me home'
- texting or calling hands free
- setting a timer
- setting alarms
- checking the weather
- solving maths problems
- checking voicemails
- adjusting screen brightness
- adjusting volume
- searching Twitter®
- finding photos
- getting definitions of words.

With additional apps, other tasks can also be undertaken.

Practise

Investigate the commands that you can use with Siri or Cortana.

Use of drones

A **DRONE** is an unmanned aerial vehicle (UAV). They come in many shapes and sizes and are being increasingly used in different ways (see Table 2.2).

What are the advantages and disadvantages of drones?

Table 2.2: Uses for drones

Context	Use
Military	Drones are used by the military for surveillance because they are unmanned and can therefore be sent into hostile areas where flying a manned reconnaissance craft would be dangerous or too difficult for the crew.
Policing and crowd safety	Drones can be effectively used to monitor large crowds at public gatherings, at football matches or during police raids to capture film of the event or to provide a view of the wider context.
Weather	Drones are used to help scientists study climate and understand pollution. They can carry all kinds of scientific equipment, including devices to measure solar radiation and optical probes to measure the amount of ash in the air (for example, after a volcanic eruption).
Agricultural	Drones are very useful for producing maps for soil analysis. They can spray and monitor crops, identify areas of a field where the ground is dry and spot infections or other indications that crops are at risk. Some drones have been adapted so that they can plant crops by shooting pods with seeds and nutrients into the soil.
Aerial photography	Using drones to capture aerial images is a clear advantage of this technology, particularly as the drones can fly into areas that are less accessible for other forms of transport.
Transport systems (field maintenance)	As an alternative to employees walking railway tracks to check them physically, drones can fly over lengths of track, providing maintenance and safety data remotely. They can examine bridges and crossings, particularly after storms or other natural events and send back vital information. One of the more unusual uses includes a German rail company that is using drones to combat graffiti-spraying gangs. The drones monitor the railway lines and capture footage that can be used in prosecutions, as well as for alerting the police or other security professionals to activity in progress.
Retail	Amazon has been testing drones to make deliveries.

It is clear that drones can be used by organisations in many different ways. For this reason, they also come in a variety of shapes and sizes and with a range of accessories as shown in the photograph.

Why do drones need to come in different shapes and sizes?

The smallest camera drone currently on the market is 4.3 cm wide and has a fully working camera.

Artificial intelligence

New uses for artificial intelligence (AI) are being found every day, especially in areas such as medical diagnostics and fraud detection, making the processes much quicker and more effective.

Medical diagnosis

ARTIFICIAL INTELLIGENCE (AI) SYSTEMS are different from most computer solutions because they can make decisions and also be programmed to learn. It is not uncommon for computers to be used in medical diagnosis. For example, the Accident and Emergency departments at most hospitals run a triage service. This involves making some initial checks on the patient and then taking appropriate action. Using an AI system means that this initial screening can be undertaken by someone less qualified than a doctor. A qualified nurse will use the system to make an initial diagnosis by asking a series of yes/no questions that have a predictable outcome (see Figure 2.3). At any stage, a doctor can intervene.

One of the advantages of using an AI system is that it is unlikely that factors will be missed because the process to make all the checks has been set out in advance. It also benefits from the lack of emotion or personal connection to the patient, which means that the medical staff remain more objective. However, this could mean that other symptoms might get overlooked, which is why currently AI systems are not used where life or death decisions may need to be made.

Figure 2.3: Flow charts are used to design systems – this ensures that all possible routes through the system are encompassed in the solution

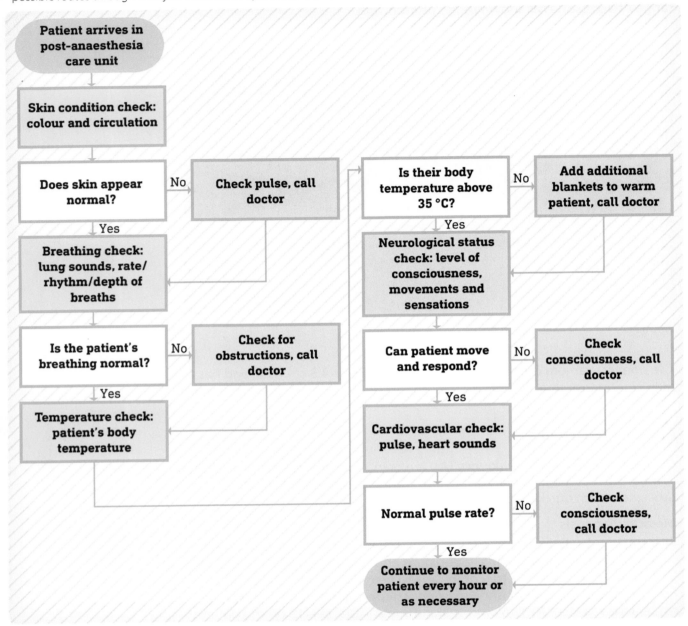

Link it up

Networking and Cybersecurity

See Unit 3 for more information on how innovations in security software and **HARDWARE** will help manage risks to network systems.

Refer back to Unit 1 for more information on how emerging technologies can be used to build and secure networks.

Finance

Another example of the application of AI is in neural network fraud detection. These systems use a range of information to identify unusual or suspicious activity that might be a sign of fraud. For example, if the profiles of card and account holders – how old you are, where you live and the amount of money you typically spend on technology – make the sudden purchase of new TVs, computers, laptops and devices unusual, this would trigger concern.

Profile and account information is combined with historical information about what tends to happen to lost or stolen cards, applications for credit and mail order accounts. Once this is in place, the software monitors activity and looks for common patterns that might indicate fraudulent activity. The system then sends alerts so that activity can be investigated.

Augmented reality (AR)

AUGMENTED REALITY (AR) is a technology that is used to overlay an image that has been generated by a computer onto what the user can see in the real world, providing a merged view.

An app being used in conjunction with a real view

Table 2.3 gives other examples of how organisations might use augmented reality.

Table 2.3: Uses for augmented reality

Sector	Description
Retail	An app on a phone could provide pricing information, ingredients or allergy advice on products on supermarket shelves. It can improve navigation in a warehouse so that staff can find stock more easily. **GAMIFICATION** (using game concepts and techniques outside a gaming environment) that has been added to products can help customers engage with a product by explaining what it is or how to use it. This may help them decide whether or not to make a purchase.
Medical	Augmented reality can provide assistance for surgeons during an operation.
Education	Augmented reality can be useful in education, for example to teach learners about different plants or animals, computer components, geography, biology or other sciences.
Gaming	The Pokemon Go™ game, launched in 2016, is a recent example of the use of augmented reality in gaming. The game superimposes characters on different locations and players have to find them and 'photograph' them using mobile phone cameras.

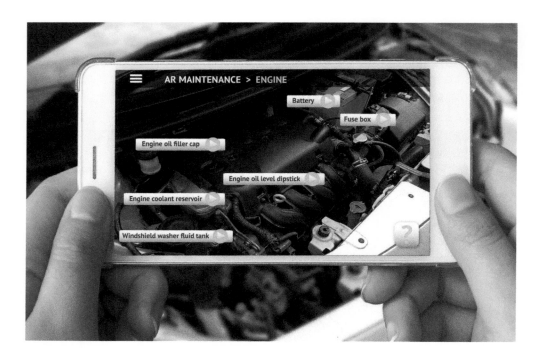

AR MAINTENANCE > ENGINE

Battery

Fuse box

Engine oil filler cap

Engine oil level dipstick

Engine coolant reservoir

Windshield washer fluid tank

Overlaying diagrams of car parts on to a captured image of an engine can help to teach basic car maintenance

Virtual reality (VR)

VIRTUAL REALITY (VR) is a computer-generated simulation that people can interact with in a physical way. It involves using a headset, but can also include gloves fitted with sensors. Table 2.4 shows some uses of virtual reality.

Table 2.4: Uses of virtual reality

Medicine	How virtual reality is used
Treatment for post-traumatic stress disorder (PTSD)	PTSD may be suffered by anyone who has been involved in a situation of extreme danger or stress. For example, soldiers can often experience PTSD after being involved in combat. People who have been involved in serious accidents or who have been victims of crime may also suffer from PTSD. VR technology is used to expose the patient to their experiences again in a controlled way and help them to develop coping strategies.
Pain management	In pain management, VR is used as a therapy to teach patients how to use distraction as a way of managing their situation.
Phantom limb pain	Amputees can suffer with pain in an arm or a leg that is no longer there. Using VR, they can 'see' the missing limb and can complete tasks. This fools the brain into thinking that the limb is still present and can help to control the pain.
Exposure therapy	VR can be used to treat phobias, such as the fear of flying, claustrophobia or the fear of spiders, snakes or insects. Using VR means that the patient can be exposed to their fear in steps and in a controlled environment.
Automotive	**How virtual reality is used**
Building better products	Engineers and designers can get inside the car in a virtual sense in order to experience and understand how their designs will be used by customers.
Education	Oculus Rift® technology (which completely immerses the user into a virtual world) can be used to teach parents and teenagers about the dangers of driving with distractions and why it is important to stay focused on the road.
Sales	Many car manufacturers now regularly use VR to help sell their products. VR is used to enable customers to try out different models. It has even been suggested that VR may one day replace the need for car dealership showrooms.

Table 2.4: *(continued)*

Construction	How virtual reality is used
Improving construction	VR is used to test out construction factors before any money is spent on building them. Construction workers and other employees can explore the building before it is built. The construction of the building can be simulated and tested for different situations and the design tweaked if necessary.

Aviation	How virtual reality is used
Manufacturing	New designs for aircraft are simulated and tested before the aircraft is manufactured. This helps to prepare pilots for actual test flights.
Training	VR is regularly used in training pilots using simulators; it is also used for training cabin staff in how to evacuate planes in an emergency.

Pathway focus

Digital Applications

In an IT support role, you will find that you will quickly become familiar with new technology as it appears in all areas of the IT sector. You will see innovations in security, IT service and the way that service is delivered, and in digital applications that will be designed for new contexts. You will become experienced in advising how organisations should use a range of technologies to support their business activities.

Use of social media

Organisations and businesses use social media in different ways to promote themselves and their services. For example, they might use Facebook® pages, Twitter feeds and YouTube™ channels.

BLOGS and **VLOGS** are also a part of the social media landscape. Blogs (short for weblog) are similar to a journal or diary written by an individual and made public for anyone to read; vlogs are weblogs that are largely made up of videos. A **VLOGGER** is a person who owns, runs or contributes to a vlog. They build up subscribers, and the more subscribers a vlog has, the more successful it is considered to be.

In February 2017, some of the most popular UK vlogs were:

- TheDiamondMinecart   14 million subscribers
- KSI   15 million subscribers
- Caspar   7 million subscribers
- ThatcherJoe   7 million subscribers.

These vlogs include prankster, comedy and gaming content. They are attractive to businesses for the following two reasons.

- If vloggers have a large number of subscribers, then businesses will target advertising that would interest a subscriber of that particular type of vlog. The business pays the vlogger to display their advertisements.
- Some vloggers become very well known and, as social media celebrities, any products they endorse should result in more sales.

Some vloggers are so successful that they earn their living from their vlog.

Practise

Use the internet to explore different organisations and the ways that they use vlogs.

A3 Internet of Things (IoT)

The **INTERNET OF THINGS (IOT)** is a term which groups together all technologies that have internet connectivity. This includes household devices, smartphones and smartwatches, tablets, and location devices.

Link it up

Networking and Cybersecurity

See Unit 11 for more information on the Internet of Things.

Connecting devices over the internet

The IT and computing industry generally agree that by 2020, there will be more than 30 billion devices connected to the internet. This will include significantly more handheld devices, such as phones and tablets, but is also likely to include an increasing number of devices in the home and both personal and public forms of transport. It is not possible to know what other technologies will be attached to the internet because these devices are currently in development.

Consumers

Consumers are becoming increasingly aware of the possibilities associated with the IoT and are finding more and more ways of using technology in their day-to-day activities.

Using smartphones and new smart fridge technology, the system monitors the food products in your fridge (including what you have, how much and the use-by dates). You use the app to decide what to eat (because it identifies what needs to be used first), and you can use the same app in the supermarket to buy products you are running low on.

Hive®, Nest® and tado° systems control the heating in your home and allow you to switch your home systems on and off, and change the temperature.

The next step is a home automation system such as Wink Hub 2™ or Logitech Harmony Elite that also controls the lighting and the locks in your home and can have surveillance functionality in various forms. The system can tell you when the members of the household leave and return to the home.

Enterprise deployments

ENTERPRISE DEPLOYMENTS are basic versions of software that have added functionality. They are designed for business use (rather than for an individual user). Two key factors that are considered when creating enterprise versions are additional security and **SCALABILITY** (this means that the software can support more users as necessary). Enterprise systems are often made up of a large number of PCs and servers, with a wide range of connected devices.

Link it up

Data Management

For more on managing risks to data systems using a combination of physical and logical devices, go to Unit 3.

Online connectivity

Connected devices that are not using a free Wi-Fi connection will be subject to data charges.

Practise

Investigate the technology in your home and make a list of all the devices that are linked to the internet.

Enabling technologies

There are three key communications technologies that make the IoT possible that are heavily used in different contexts. These technologies are **BLUETOOTH®, RADIO FREQUENCY IDENTIFICATION (RFID)** and **NEAR FIELD COMMUNICATION (NFC)** – see Table 2.5.

Table 2.5: Key communication technologies in the IoT

Technology	Description	Examples of use
	• Bluetooth is a short-range wireless connection used in mobile phones and other devices such as tablets. • This technology uses radio waves and sensors to enable devices to connect (for example, phones can connect to each other as well as to computers using this technology). • Bluetooth devices need additional power.	• Mobile phone headsets. • Using Bluetooth between devices to transfer files. • Tethering a computer to a smartphone, which allows the user to use the phone as a portable hotspot.
	• Radio Frequency Identification (RFID) is a short-range technology that is able to uniquely identify an animal, a person or an object using an electronic RFID label. • This technology is similar to barcode technology.	• Library books are fitted with RFID tags in their spines. The tags set off an alarm if you try to remove a book without checking it out. • Fast payment systems such as toll bridges (for example, the Severn Bridge). • Timing competitors in events such as a marathon race. Each competitor wears a wristband containing an RFID tag. When the runner crosses the line the tag reader makes a note of the competitor number and the time. • Animal identification – to stop the spread of diseases among farm animals, all farm animals are tagged with an RFID and each time they are moved their records are updated. This means that any subsequently diagnosed diseases can be tracked back to source.
NFC	• Near Field Communication (NFC) is a very short-range technology where the portable device needs to be within 1.6 inches (4 cm) of the receiving device.	• Pre-payment cards used for public transport (particularly the underground and bus services). • Smart cards used to open keyless smart locks. • Logging in and out at work, simply by walking past a sensor.

Development of wearable technology

One of the biggest growth markets currently is wearable technology, from the smartwatch to smart glasses and devices such as Fitbit® that are used in sport.

Fitbit

Data can be uploaded to Fitbit software that you can use to monitor your own health over a period of time. Fitbit uses sensors on the back of a watch to monitor a range of factors, such as your activity, your heart rate and your sleep patterns.

Fitbit trackers allow users to monitor their health around the clock

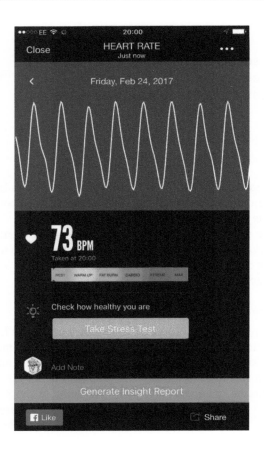

The Heart Rate app can be used to look after your heart's health

Smartwatches

An alternative is using an app such as Heart Rate on a smartwatch. To get a reading, you simply hold your index finger flat over the camera for approximately 10 seconds. Readings are stored in the app and allow you to build up a picture of your heart health over time and when you are in different states, such as during an exercise warm up or cardio session.

Smart glasses

Using augmented reality technology, smart glasses are a wearable technology that overlays what you can see with computer-generated information. For example, you could be wearing the glasses while walking through London and text or images would appear beside buildings, statues or other features you are looking at, telling you something about them. This technology is already being used in some museums as an alternative to tour guides. The advantage is that, in addition to not having to employ someone to show you around, this technology means that users can walk through the museum at their own pace. It also allows the information to be delivered to the user in their native language.

Goggles

Goggles that make use of virtual reality technology are used to enhance the wearer's gaming experience, or can be used in a range of training or therapeutic contexts such as teaching firefighters to cope in a house fire. Where previous training has relied on the use of real smoke-filled constructions, most of these effects can now be achieved through the use of VR goggles.

What kind of games do you think would benefit from virtual reality technology?

A4 Cloud technology

Historically, organisations were responsible for their entire IT systems and all the functionality that was needed by the organisation. This was called **LEGACY IT**. The emergence of **CLOUD TECHNOLOGY** has made it possible for IT services to make use of computing resources that are not physically present at the organisation's office. They are remote services that are accessed via the internet.

As there is no physical box on site, this reduces the amount of money that the organisation has tied up in technology. In addition, the business does not need to worry about maintenance and any faults are usually handled by the service provider. The servers tend to be a combination of physical and/or **VIRTUALISED SERVERS**. (A virtualised server is simply a server where storage has been split into different parts and each one behaves like a server in its own right. It is a physical server of virtual servers.)

Cloud servers tend to exist in larger data centres and warehouses so the physical conditions, the environment, the backup and the security are typically very good. Even if the organisation is using cloud services, it should still continue to make occasional backups. These will usually be scheduled automatically at off-peak times (when the organisation is closed, such as overnight). Cloud services can be split into four separate cloud technologies.

a. Software as a service (Saas)
b. Infrastructure as a service (Iaas)
c. Platform as a service (Paas)
d. Data as a service (Daas)

Each service provides different functionality and each is used for different purposes by different types of people. Some solutions that a company might use may involve more than one simultaneously, much in the same way as a car relies on petrol, electricity, coolant, air and so on to work properly.

Link it up

Networking and Cybersecurity

For more on how new tools are developed to manage network processes, go to Unit 11.

Pathway focus

Networking and Cybersecurity

In an IT support role, it is likely that you will be working with an existing network and you may be required to connect a device to the network or replace a component of that network such as a switch or **NETWORK INTERFACE CARD (NIC)**.

Software as a service (Saas)

This is a cloud-based application service, which replaces the more traditional installed software with applications that are provided by the service provider. These are used via an internet **BROWSER** (for example, web-based applications to create spreadsheets, word-process, complete online forms such as tax, interact with a customer relationship management database). A third party sells the organisation a licence that enables it to use applications it would previously have had to buy and install on its own machines.

Advantages of Saas are that:

- it is always up to date
- no installations or patches are needed on individual machines in the office
- technical support needs are reduced
- staff always use the same version of the application so there will be no incompatibility issues with files
- it can be used outside office hours and outside the office itself
- users will normally be able to collaborate online.

Commercial examples of the uses of Saas include:

- Google apps for Work™ (also known as G Suite™)
- Draw.io™ for creating flowcharts and diagrams online.

Infrastructure as a service (Iaas)

This service focuses more on the organisation's hardware. For example, the organisation will not purchase physical servers and machines, but will instead use cloud-based hardware and virtualised instances as its base platform.

This means that a remote 'box' provides an **OPERATING SYSTEM** (often Linux™ but MS® Windows Servers™ also exist). Iaas can be referred to as consumption based: the organisation can use the services in much the same way as it uses electricity. It pays for the amount of data it stores and the central processing or **RANDOM-ACCESS MEMORY (RAM)** it uses on an ongoing basis. One of the main advantages is its scalability.

The main benefit of this type of service is that the organisation no longer has to worry about the hardware and networking equipment as this is managed by the service provider, which also manages and maintains the servers. Commercial examples of the uses of Iaas include:

- Amazon Web Services®
- Microsoft® Azure™
- Google Compute Engine™.

Platform as a service (Paas)

This approach is often used in software development because it allows the programmers to work at a higher level with less complexity. It can be useful where multiple developers are working together on a single project.

The hardware infrastructure is provided and the development applications are managed by the organisation. Commercial examples of Paas include:

- Open PaaS
- Mobile PaaS
- PaaS for Rapid Development.

Data as a service (Daas)

In traditional systems, the format and structure of data was linked closely with the application that created and managed it. This meant that any changes in data or processing would affect each other. This required the code or the data to be restructured to keep everything working.

Daas involves separating the two and having data provided in a neutral way that multiple applications can 'talk' to. Then, even if the application changes, it can use methods that translate the data sources so that they can be used. Examples of data that could be used include:

- population data
- statistics
- consumer data.

Link it up

Data Management

Using new technology in data management was explored in Unit 1.

Skills and knowledge check

- ☐ Can you remember three different ways in which organisations make use of mobile technologies?
- ☐ Can you give three examples of smart devices/apps?
- ☐ Can you explain the concept of the IoT and list its key enabling technologies?

- ○ I understand the concept of an intelligent computer and can give examples.
- ○ I can distinguish between the four key cloud technologies.
- ○ I know what is meant by voice control systems.
- ○ I know how I could use augmented reality in daily life.
- ○ I can name three opportunities for emerging technologies in the home.

B Investigate how an organisation uses technology to meet its needs

There are many reasons why organisations invest in current and emerging technologies and these often mirror their activities and their general business strategies.

B1 Why organisations invest in technology

Because investing in technology can be expensive, organisations must be able to justify the choices they make as they might have to explain them to their **STAKEHOLDERS** (individuals or organisations who have an interest or a stake in something – this is particularly true of investors).

The following are some of the main reasons why an organisation will invest in technology to meet its needs.

Improving productivity

There are many ways that technology can improve productivity. Here are a few examples.

- *Collaborative working*: where a group of staff work together on the same document, graphic, or idea, in real time.
- *Using interoffice communication tools*: this can speed up the process of getting answers to questions (rather than the questions sitting in an email trail).
- *Connecting remotely*: this means having an ability to quickly organise virtual meetings so that decisions can be made. All relevant people could be included regardless of their actual location. This can save time.
- *Being organised*: ensuring that files are managed and sorted into appropriate directories will save time finding important files.
- *Financial tracking*: access to a wider range of faster and more accurate financial data and information will speed up decision making.

Meeting business goals

Most organisations understand the importance of linking their business strategy with their IT strategy. Meeting some of these goals might be achieved using technology – for other goals this may not be the case. Table 2.6 gives some examples for you to consider.

Link it up

Digital Applications

Unit 7 looks at how technology is used in different configurations to create digital applications for organisations to manage their activities.

Goal	How technology could be used
Improve customer service	Online support services like real-time chat, a Facebook or Twitter presence.
Grow sales by 20 per cent	A digital marketing campaign could contribute to a growth in sales. Improving customer satisfaction through better support will also result in enhanced sales due to the improved customer experience.
Improve employee retention	Employees might be leaving the organisation because the technology they use is old and slow (which can be frustrating) – the organisation might consider updating its hardware and software.
Access new markets overseas (for example, sell products to North Africa)	Depending on the product or service, it is likely that technology will be heavily used to deliver to new markets (possibly using online tools and resources).
Improve profitability from 15 to 25 per cent	This can be achieved through cutting costs (this could involve automation and a reduction in staff), or could be achieved through increasing prices. Organisations are more likely to try cost cutting before raising prices.

Table 2.6: Technology can be used to meet many business goals

Improving efficiency

Using technology to capture, examine and analyse the organisation's processes will help the business understand where it is inefficient, for example, using data about IT failures and time taken to resolve the issues can prove that existing hardware has become unreliable and outdated.

Many organisations are now using online functionality to improve staff training. Training sessions could focus on a range of topics such as customer service, health and safety, manual handling, Control of Substances Hazardous to Health (COSHH) Regulations 2002, export and international trade, analysing data, or cybersecurity.

The advantage of using online tools for staff training is that training sessions can sometimes be undertaken over a period of time, when the employee has less to do. Also, if you are using technology, you can track employee training performance and completion, identifying any areas where more work is needed.

Increasing cost effectiveness

Organisations can use data and statistical analysis techniques on a range of factors to calculate the return on investment (ROI). This is a recognised calculation and it looks like this:

$$\text{Return on investment} = \frac{\text{Net profit}}{\text{Total amount of the investment}}$$

If the answer to the calculation is 0 or is a negative value, it means the amount of extra profit that will be generated by the investment will not be cost effective.

What if...?

Due to an expanding workforce, the software company you work for is considering moving premises to a larger building. What advice would you give the company about the implications of an office move? What technologies might it be able to implement that will further improve the benefits of a move?

Consider how the organisation could use 'what if...?' analysis to determine the most cost-effective combination of factors to benefit it in the longer term. These factors could be any combination of: costs of premises, operational costs, logistics and plans for the future.

Achieving increased growth

Digital marketing is one of the most important strategies for increased growth and the two key technologies for use in this area are social media and blogs/vlogs. As mentioned earlier in the unit (A2 'Use of social media'), bloggers and vloggers can have a real impact on the sales of products and services.

Innovating

Collaboration is one of the key ways that organisations innovate. This is because sharing ideas often produces new ideas. Most organisations make use of multi-user software, collaboration software and real-time communication tools to manage creative processes, as shown in Table 2.7.

Table 2.7: Software for managing creative processes

Software	Description
Wrike®	Project management and tracking software that helps to manage any project or development.
Basecamp®	Software for conducting meetings using a range of technologies (voice, screen sharing, file sharing and video). Allows teams to communicate and share ideas around projects. Files can be uploaded and downloaded, and users can send a private message or post on boards.
Blackboard Collaborate™	Educational software that creates a virtual classroom where teachers and learners can collaborate.
FlockDraw	A collaborative drawing tool that allows contributors to simultaneously edit the same file in real time, with a chat function to discuss development. As each person draws on the pane, their name is displayed beside their contribution.

Improving agility and competitiveness

Developing designs faster through collaboration and using CAD/CAM systems to get designs into production faster is just one example of how organisations can improve their agility. Getting products and services to market faster will improve competitiveness.

Providing quick and easily accessible customer support is another example. Many businesses use technology to provide an additional level of more accessible service to make their products and services more attractive to potential customers.

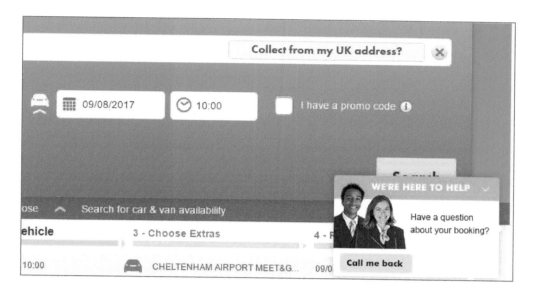

Often when you enter a website a 'We're here to help' box pops up. Through this, you can either chat directly to an agent, or you can request a call back

Global communication

One of the key benefits of today's fast, reliable communications technology is that it has become much easier to trade with the whole world. Many people believe that the negative impact of trading across time zones has been dramatically reduced through investment in new technologies, even in the simplest of ways, for example the use of mobile phones and apps.

With more than 95 per cent of organisations thought to have an online presence, customers can access them and their services 24 hours a day, 7 days a week.

Increasing promotion and sales

With an online presence, businesses are much more able to be responsive to what their customers want. They can also respond quickly to the activities of their competitors (for example, offering discounts if a major competitor is doing the same).

There seems to be some consensus in the business community that the amount of discount offered directly affects the amount of additional sales. Strategies to increase sales include:

- offering deals (such as buy one, get one free)
- sending out targeted e-vouchers by email to generate interest
- offering deals which involve free shipping.

However, offering deals and discounts does reduce the profitability of a product or service, so most organisations do not use discounting as a long-term strategy.

Having a wider consumer reach

Investing in new technologies helps organisations to access a wider and more varied range of markets using the internet. Customers can place electronic orders at any time of the day or night, reducing the need for expensive phone calls and saving them time.

However, there are consequences of trading with the wider world, for example other countries may have different laws about particular products or services that must be taken into account. There may be a situation in which you are not allowed to make a product available in a country or region.

Providing instant customer service

We have so far concentrated on how technology can improve access to customers, how customers can get faster support and how technology can be used to grow business. One additional way that technology can impact on the relationship between organisations and their customers is in the management of complaints.

Realistically, no organisation can claim to be completely complaint free, but some organisations take pride in their use of the internet and social media for managing complaints.

You should realise, however, that not all complaints will be managed in the public domain (where they are visible to everyone). Some complaints have to be taken offline (even if they started online). Remember to go back online once the problem has been resolved and be positive about the outcome. It is also worth keeping in mind that badly written responses to customer complaints can do as much damage as not responding to the complaint at all.

Practise

Investigate how your centre uses technology to support you as a learner. For example, do they provide computers with internet access so that you can carry out research?

How else do they use technology (for example, is your learning centre a cash-free environment, and do you use electronic registration)?

Write a short 200-word article about your findings.

B2 The types of technology that organisations use

To be able to recommend technologies to organisations, you should have a good understanding of how businesses use them.

How organisations select technology

Which technologies organisations choose to use will depend, to a large extent, on the product or service and the profile of their customers or clients.

What organisations consider and why

Table 2.8 gives some examples of the ways in which organisations use technologies and why they use them.

Table 2.8: How organisations use technology

Consideration	Examples
Type of business	• If the business is selling a product or service that has nothing to do with technology (for example, garden tools such as rakes, spades and hedge trimmers), it might only need the most basic support such as a website about their products with a range of **FAQS** (frequently asked questions are a predicted list of common questions that users are likely to ask).
	• If the business is selling a technology-related product or service, it will probably choose to use a wide range of technologies, including websites, blogs and/or vlogs, social media, online interactive customer support. The content is likely to be extensive and complex.

Table 2.8: *(continued)*

Consideration	Examples
Needs of customers	• There may be some products or services for which customers will need little or no support other than a telephone number or an email address. This is often the case with old products that are no longer sold but which consumers might still own. Most organisations will keep information about old or outdated products, but they might not have this information online all the time, so if they need it, customers will have to request it. • Organisations will also consider the profile of their customers, for example if the product is targeted at a particular type of user, then it would make sense to use the technologies that this type of customer will use.
Hardware/software and networking requirements	• Organisations have to be very careful as they will need to calculate the return on investment in comparison to the amount of money they are potentially going to spend. • Cloud technology has made many things possible and organisations will consider what cloud services could offer in their deliberations.
Particular security issues	• Organisations must never forget their responsibilities in relation to security, whether this is the security of their own systems, or the security of customer information (as captured by their technologies).

Each consideration must be carefully investigated and informed decisions made. Getting it wrong can have a negative impact on the organisation and its reputation or brand, as well as its finances.

Pathway focus

Digital Applications

In an IT support role, you may have to select and install software to meet a user's needs or assess the use of currently used software and remove unused software to improve the performance of a computer system.

How organisations make decisions

There are three common triggers that drive organisations to think about changing their use or application of technology.

1. A problem occurs or an opportunity arises: this is usually something that they have to react to, such as identifying that the business is running out of storage or that market research has identified a new business opportunity.
2. Actions need to be taken because of business strategy or an organisational policy: for example, needing a new website in a particular language because the organisation is seeking to trade in a new country, or fulfilling the organisation's policy to upgrade all mobile devices every three years.
3. Feedback from stakeholders: customers may have identified issues with the website (such as broken links or outdated content), or employees may complain that the DATABASE has become unresponsive so that it takes a long time to edit a record (this could be because the database contains a lot of old records which are slowing it down).

Link it up

See Unit 5 for more on how to make recommendations about an IT service and how it can help an organisation achieve its objectives.

Feasibility study

Whichever trigger causes the organisation to investigate its IT systems, the process it will go through follows the standard development life cycle shown in Figure 2.4.

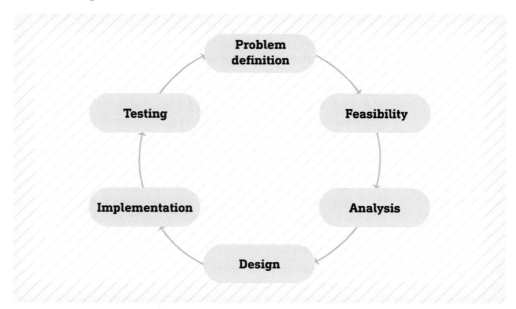

Figure 2.4: Life cycle models are used to manage developments and projects – there should be activity in every phase, although some methodologies place more importance on some parts of the life cycle than others

Link it up

Data Management

For more on making use of emerging technology to make data more accessible to an organisation (using dashboard visualisations) to help it meet its needs, go to Unit 9.

Once the problem or opportunity has been identified and defined, a feasibility study is carried out. The study investigates the problem or opportunity thoroughly to establish whether something needs to be done or not. If so, then the process moves to the next stage (analysis). If not, the problem might need to be redefined or the opportunity re-examined before the organisation decides that no action is necessary.

Digital strategy, policy or business plan

Organisations have to plan for the future. As part of this plan, they have to think carefully about what they want to do in the short term (six months to two years), medium term (three to five years) and the longer term (five to ten years). Organisations that do not think about the future will often fail because they are not planning resources, finance and technology that will help them meet their future goals. They become reactive (responding when something happens instead of thinking ahead) rather than proactive (making informed decisions, planning what will happen and then taking appropriate action).

One of the more recent and controversial digital strategies has been to allow staff to bring their own devices to work and allow them to connect to the organisation's own Wi-Fi. The **BRING YOUR OWN DEVICE (BYOD)** strategy has allowed some organisations to reduce the costs of the technology by making use of staff members' own devices. An additional benefit has been the improvement in staff morale.

Some organisations are also thinking carefully about their email policies because there is a consensus that emails are often unnecessary and time wasting. Whole groups of people are copied into emails 'for information only'. These do not require any action but do take time to read. For this reason, some organisations ban this practice and insist that emails are only sent to other members of staff when action is required.

Digital strategies, policies and business plans should be reviewed regularly. It is not sensible to create a strategy or plan and then stick to it without reviewing it. That means revisiting it regularly. For example, an organisation might be planning to start trading in a country that then suffers a natural disaster, such as the floods in Malawi and Mozambique in 2015 or Hurricane Katrina in 2005. Similarly, wars and civil unrest in countries such as Syria, Iraq, Yemen, Libya, Afghanistan and Turkey in recent years would impact on business plans in the same way as a natural disaster. Organisations need to think about their business in a much bigger context and change their plans if necessary.

Feedback from stakeholders

Organisations must continuously listen to their stakeholders because both customers and employees can identify problems early, which should mean that they can be dealt with before they become much bigger problems.

B3 How organisations assess if technology has met their needs

Organisations must always be able to justify the expenditure on technology by showing how they have benefited from this activity.

Benefits

In order to establish whether an organisation's use of technology has met its needs, it will need to evaluate the impact that the technology has had on its activities. This will, in part, be achieved through statistics, but should also involve talking to the people who have been affected by the changes and improvements made. Some of the benefits, and how to measure them, are shown in Table 2.9.

Benefits	How to check
Improved efficiency	There are a number of mathematical calculations that can be carried out by managers to assess improvements in efficiency. Other signs of improved efficiency include: • staff managing more work • sales orders being processed more quickly • faster production • databases that work faster • faster internet responsiveness.
Increased profit/ reduction in cost	Measuring the benefits of increased profit and reduction in cost are statistical exercises using mathematical formulae. • **PROFIT** is the difference between the amount of money you receive for a product or service and what it costs to provide that product or service. • A **GROSS MARGIN** is the difference between the price a customer paid and the cost of the actual resources (raw materials) used to create the product. • A **NET MARGIN** is the difference between the price a customer paid and the cost of the actual resources (raw materials) used to create the product added to a proportion of the **OVERHEADS** (the salaries and building costs that an organisation has to pay all the time whether it sells products and services or not).
Increased productivity/ reduction in time wasted	Are staff more able to do their jobs? This will be shown in better morale as well as in the results of the physical tasks they perform. Are there fewer distractions? For example, a reduced amount of email or fewer interruptions due to systems not working as they should.

Table 2.9: Establishing whether the technology has met the organisation's needs

Even if the system is working better, the organisation should keep asking: 'Is there anything else that could provide additional benefits?'

Risks and issues

When implementing new technology there are risks and issues you should be aware of.

Change management

Implementing change requires different parts of the organisation to work together (see Figure 2.5). Usually managers and project members trigger the change process, which is then filtered through to the employees. But change also carries risks and potential problems.

- Staff may need to be trained to use the new systems – this can be expensive and while they are training they will not be doing their usual job.
- Even with training it can take time for staff to become confident with new technology.
- Old systems need to be turned off as the new systems are turned on – this is often done overnight to cause the least disruption to the service.
- There is always a risk that data could be lost when moving activity from one system to another.

Figure 2.5: Deciding how change will be implemented requires developers to consider how all parts of the affected process interact

Link it up

Data Management

Go to Unit 3 to find out how innovations in security software and hardware can help manage risks to data systems using a combination of physical and logical devices.

Ethical considerations

Before changing systems or technologies, the organisation should undertake a consultation with the stakeholders. This will ensure that they feel part of the process and that they are involved in the process of change, rather than change just happening and them having to cope with it. Organisations that do this are much more successful in implementing change.

Change can cause stress, so organisations should make sure that employees are fully aware of how the change will affect them. For example, they might need to work different hours or even relocate (move to another department or even another town or city). If they have dependents, this might mean an additional level of understanding from the organisation while the transition takes place.

Data management

Changing technology is also a time when the ownership of data should be revisited. Data needs to be secure and kept private and organisations must make sure that changes they make to their systems do not compromise this.

Pathway focus

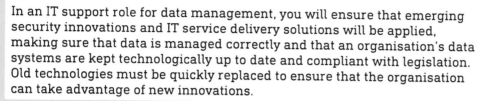

Data Management

In an IT support role for data management, you will ensure that emerging security innovations and IT service delivery solutions will be applied, making sure that data is managed correctly and that an organisation's data systems are kept technologically up to date and compliant with legislation. Old technologies must be quickly replaced to ensure that the organisation can take advantage of new innovations.

Legal considerations

There are rules and regulations that govern how data is stored and used, so any changes in the use of the data need to be checked for **COMPLIANCE** (working within the legal requirements) with these regulations.

The key pieces of legislation that affect data and systems are the:

- Data Protection Act 1998
- Computer Misuse Act 1990.

The Data Protection Act is designed to protect data by setting out how it can be used and how it must be stored. There are rules that must be followed by organisations and there are penalties for organisations that do not comply with the law.

Organisations that want to store data about people have to apply for permission to do so from the Information Commissioner's Office. They are then given a checklist of actions that they must take and evidence they must generate to prove that they can comply with the regulations. The application is then approved or declined. If an organisation is declined, it can prevent them from working with other organisations.

The Computer Misuse Act is designed to protect data and materials from criminal activity. This applies to individuals as much as it does to organisations, as in the following examples.

- **HACKERS**: unauthorised people who use network functionality to gain access to systems with the intention of stealing or destroying data or disrupting the operation of the system.
- *Theft*: did you know that you are committing a criminal offence if you upload and share copyright materials on the internet? **COPYRIGHT** means that the person who created the material is the only person who can assign other people the right to use it. This is why copying music or videos and giving them to your friends without the permission of the copyright holder is against the law.
- *Pornography*: in addition to copyright issues and other legal restrictions on pornography, and due to the rise in 'revenge porn', it is now illegal to share photographic images or videoed content of individuals without their consent and if you intend to cause them distress.
- *Identity theft*: this is using someone's personal information to create false profiles or to pretend to be that person for criminal purposes (such as acquiring loans or credit cards in someone else's name).

There are three key offences under the Computer Misuse Act.

1 Accessing someone's files without their permission.
2 Accessing their files with a view to committing other crimes.
3 Changing data without permission (this includes writing **VIRUSES** to destroy data).

Skills and knowledge check

- ☐ Can you remember the different ways in which technologies benefit organisations?
- ☐ Can you remember the key requirements of the Data Protection Act and Computer Misuse Act?

- ◯ I know my personal responsibilities and can advise others to make sure that they do not break the rules of the Computer Misuse Act when using computers.

Ready for assessment

This unit is assessed using two different techniques. Learning aim A focuses on the creation of a report in which you will have an opportunity to explore current and emerging technologies in the context of your pathway.

You should make sure that you consider all four key technologies (mobile, intelligent computer, IoT and cloud).

- Carry out your research using a broad range of sources to give yourself the widest possible range of examples to draw your evidence from.

- Think about different types of organisations and contexts (such as sport, education, health, hospitality and leisure, the arts – for example, developments in media and gaming, manufacturing).

- You should consider any trends that are emerging in how technologies are used and the impact that these have on the organisations that adopt them.

Learning aim B focuses on a case study. You will use your learning to explain how a particular organisation (or type of organisation) uses technologies to meet business needs.

- Explain in detail how the organisation has benefited from the technology or technologies. What were the key factors in the process?

- Were there any risks or negative effects?

- Consider how the organisation made the decision to select a particular technology.

- Remember to provide as much detail as you can to demonstrate that you really understand how technology affects organisational activity.

WORK FOCUS

⊣HANDS ⊙N⊢

There are some important occupational skills and competencies that you will need to practise which relate to this unit. Developing these and practising them could help you to gain employment as an IT technician or helpdesk worker.

- Employers will expect you to understand a wide range of existing technologies and to be aware of some of the emerging technologies.

- Read sector publications, such as *Computer Weekly*, so that you can stay up to date.

- Use the internet and search for information about emerging technologies.

- Find sources of apps (for both Apple® and Android™).

- Find out more about devices that are used by organisations.

- Find out more about enabling technologies and where they can be used.

- Get used to using features such as Bluetooth.

Ready for work

Take this short quiz to see if you are ready for a role as an IT technician or helpdesk operative. Do you know what the following terms mean?

1 What is streaming?
- ☐ A Uploading information
- ☐ B Downloading information
- ☐ C Accessing and using media remotely
- ☐ D Paying in advance for a service

2 Which of the following is most likely to be used in fraud detection?
- ☐ A Artificial Intelligence
- ☐ B Augmented Reality
- ☐ C Virtual Reality
- ☐ D Robotics

3 Which of the following enabling technologies is being described?

A short-range technology that is able to uniquely identify an animal, person or object using an electronic label.
- ☐ A Bluetooth
- ☐ B NFC
- ☐ C Wi-Fi
- ☐ D RFID

4 Which phase of the software development life cycle does feasibility follow?
- ☐ A Analysis
- ☐ B Problem definition
- ☐ C Design
- ☐ D Testing

5 Which of the following is NOT an offence under the Computer Misuse Act?
- ☐ A Accessing someone's files without their permission
- ☐ B Changing data without permission
- ☐ C Accessing someone else's files with a view to committing other crimes
- ☐ D Sending someone else a file which you know contains a virus

Answers: 1C, 2A, 3D, 4B, 5D

3 Security Protection and Risk Management

Try to imagine living your life without using computers, mobile phones or other types of information technology (IT) systems. How much information do these systems contain about you? Your personal information is valuable. You use it on websites to identify who you are and to make payments for goods and services. This makes your information valuable to other people who could use it to commit crimes such as identify theft and fraud.

In this unit, you will learn how the IT systems that you use are vulnerable to accidental or malicious (intentionally harmful) acts. You will also learn what you and the owners of these systems can do to protect these computer systems and keep your information safe.

How will I be assessed?

You will be asked a number of questions during a computer-based exam.

You will need to show that you know the main threats to the security of IT systems and how to manage the risk of accidental or malicious acts against them. You will need to show that you understand how to protect IT systems, as well as how these methods work. You will also need to judge the effectiveness of these methods and recommend ways to protect against specific types of security threat.

Some questions will test your knowledge by asking you to select the correct items from a list. Some questions will ask you to write longer answers explaining your understanding of the issues relevant to the question. Some of these questions will be based on realistic scenarios, including ones related to how organisations use IT systems.

Assessment outcomes

AO1 Demonstrate knowledge of security protection and risk management issues
AO2 Demonstrate understanding of security protection and risk management issues and the methods that can be used to manage and protect computer systems and data against security threats
AO3 Be able to assess or analyse information, make connections on the effectiveness of methods used to manage and protect computer systems and data against security threats
AO4 Be able to assess or evaluate information on the threats to computer systems, their impact and how they can be managed

What you will learn in this unit:

A Security threats and system vulnerabilities

B Methods used to secure computer systems and data

C Legal requirements and IT security policies and procedures

A Security threats and system vulnerabilities

A1 Internal threats

We use computers to carry out all sorts of useful actions, for example buying and selling products, or communicating with friends and work colleagues. In order to do this, computers need to store and process information. This information could include:

- **USERNAMES** and **PASSWORDS**
- names and addresses (postal and email)
- bank account and payment card details
- medical information (for example, illnesses and operations).

If not properly protected, this valuable and sensitive information could be accidentally deleted, **CORRUPTED** (damaged beyond use) or even stolen by a **HACKER**. Many daily activities we rely on can only happen if the computer systems that are used to control them are working properly. Examples include:

- transport systems (for example, trains and aeroplanes)
- electricity generation and distribution, including nuclear power stations
- medical equipment in hospitals
- the internet.

What might be the consequences if the computer systems used to control these activities suddenly stopped working? This is a very real threat, and can happen for many reasons, including power loss or equipment failure. The **DATA** that the computers contain can be stolen, deleted or corrupted. Sometimes the causes are accidental but sometimes they are due to deliberate actions by individuals, organisations or even governments.

Computer systems and the data that they hold are vulnerable to threats when data is:

- first entered onto a computer
- transmitted to another computer (for example, using a wireless network connected to the internet)
- stored on a computer or external **STORAGE DEVICE**
- being processed by a computer.

Internal threats to computer systems and data

Computer systems and the data they hold may be threatened by the actions of the people who are required to operate them. These people include the organisation's own employees and other people authorised to use the systems (such as visitors or **SOFTWARE** engineers). These internal threats could be a result of actions that are either accidental or malicious (where the computer user means to cause harm).

Accidental threats

Accidental threats are usually caused by careless or unsafe working practices. The user does not mean to cause harm but their actions can still leave the system vulnerable. Table 3.1 shows some of these possible threats and their consequences.

Threat	Examples of actions	Possible consequence
Damage to equipment	Dropping a laptop causing the hard drive to fail.	Data is lost if the hard drive is unreadable.
Accidental loss of power	Unplugging a desktop computer before saving work and closing down the **OPERATING SYSTEM (OS)**.	Any unsaved work is lost and software updates or data backups may not be completed.
Unintentional disclosure of data	Taking a photo in an office that shows confidential information on a computer screen – the photo is uploaded to a social media site.	Anyone viewing the photo could read the confidential information.
Authorised user action	A software engineer accidentally adds a website that should be blacklisted (avoided) to a **WHITELIST**.	The website can be visited by anyone on the system, possibly resulting in **MALWARE** (software designed to cause damage to a computer system or to steal its data) being downloaded.
Physical damage	A fire caused by an overloaded electrical socket destroys the **HARD DISK DRIVES (HDD)** of several computers.	Data is lost if the hard drive is unreadable.
Risk of **BRING YOUR OWN DEVICE (BYOD)**	Synchronising data from a work computer to a personal mobile phone that is not secure, then losing the mobile phone.	Anyone finding the mobile phone can view the confidential information.
Unsafe practices	Knocking over a drink left next to a desktop computer.	Water damage to the computer – possibly causing it to shut down unexpectedly.
Using external storage devices	Copying data to a **USB** drive, then accidentally losing it on public transport.	Anyone finding the USB drive can view the confidential information.
Visiting an untrustworthy website	Browsing the internet during a lunch break using a workplace computer results in a virus being downloaded onto the organisation's computer systems.	The virus could be used to access confidential information and transfer it over the internet to an unauthorised computer.
Downloading/ uploading files to and from the internet	An office worker checks a personal email account using a workplace computer and downloads a file sent by a friend. Unknown to either, the file contains a virus.	The virus could be used to access confidential information and transfer it over the internet to an unauthorised computer.
File-sharing applications	An office worker uses a work laptop to download music from a **PEER-TO-PEER FILE-SHARING SERVICE** (a site where files are shared directly between computer users and not downloaded from a legitimate business) – the music files contain malware.	The malware could be used to prevent the computer system from operating correctly.

Table 3.1: Possible accidental threats to a computer system and their consequences

You work for an organisation that is keen to reduce the risk of accidental threats to the security of its computer systems and data.

Describe five actions that computer users could take to reduce the risk of accidental threats.

Malicious threats

Sometimes employees may deliberately try to cause harm to their organisation's computer system or its data. Table 3.2 shows some of these malicious threats.

Table 3.2: Types of malicious threat

Threat	Examples of actions
Malicious damage caused by employee/ unauthorised user action	An employee at a power station deliberately installs a virus that is used to stop electricity generation. The resulting power cut affects thousands of homes.
Intentional deletion/ editing of data and intentional disclosure of data	An employee copies confidential information about a new product and sells it to a competitor.
DUMPSTER DIVING (the searching of rubbish bins in order to find confidential information)	A manager writes down their username and password on a piece of paper. The paper is thrown into a waste paper bin. The contents of the bin are searched and an employee uses the username and password to gain access to the manager's files.
SHOULDER SURFING (someone watches you at work and sees you using or entering confidential information)	A manager logs onto the office network. A colleague watches them, memorises their username and password, then uses this to view their files.
Theft of equipment or data	An employee steals an external hard drive containing backup data. As a result, data cannot be restored if the primary storage device fails.
Malicious damage to equipment or data	An employee at a train station installs malware that damages signalling equipment. Trains are unable to enter or leave the station.
Unauthorised access by employees to secure areas in a building	A server room is left unlocked. An employee is able to enter and copy data.
Unauthorised access to administration functions, security levels and protocols, users overriding security controls	A wireless **ROUTER** has a default password of ADMIN. If this is unchanged, an employee is able to log on to the router and use it to control network **HARDWARE**.
Risk of bring your own device (BYOD)	A family member views confidential work information on your mobile phone. An employee uses their own portable USB drive to connect to the office network. The device contains a virus that is transferred onto the network.

Why should you be careful when logging on to your computer?

A2 External threats

Computers and their data are vulnerable to unauthorised individuals, businesses or governments that wish to find out about them or control them.

Many of the threats listed in A1 are also external threats. For example, if the person doing them is not an employee of the business, then they are an external threat. Examples include shoulder surfing and dumpster diving (see Table 3.2) – if shoulder surfing happens when an employee is working on a train, then it is an external threat. Other threats to computers include fire and theft – these can be external threats if they have causes outside the organisation (for example, if the cause of the fire is in a building next door).

Two of the other main threats to both computers and their data are **MALICIOUS SOFTWARE** and social engineering.

Malicious software

The internet is used to distribute malicious software. This 'malware' can be distributed as code hidden inside:

- a document (for example, sent as an email attachment – see Figure 3.1)
- an html web page
- a digital image (for example, on a web page)
- an executable file (for example, a program downloaded from a file-sharing service).

Malware is also transmitted on storage media such as USB devices or DVDs. The main types of malware are as follows.

- **VIRUS**: once installed on a computer, a virus attaches itself to an existing program then copies itself. It can then infect other connected computers.
- **WORM**: unlike a virus, a worm is a piece of malicious software that can operate as a standalone program. It can infect other connected computers.
- **TROJAN HORSE**: this is a term for any malicious software that pretends to be something harmless. For example, you might receive an email offering you a new job with an attached application form. The attachment is a Trojan horse if it contains malware.

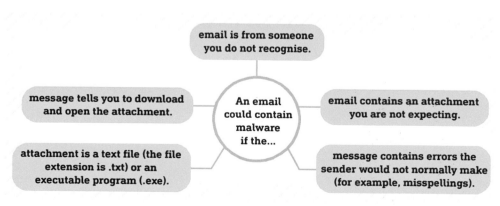

Figure 3.1: Beware of email containing malware

- **RANSOMWARE**: once downloaded the malware encrypts the user's data, and the sender then demands money in return for the data being decrypted back into useable information.
- **SPYWARE**: software that collects information about the user (for example, web-browsing history, keystrokes made on a keyboard) and then shares this information with other people. Spyware could be used to blackmail visitors to certain websites or collect usernames and passwords.
- **ADWARE**: software designed to impose unwanted adverts on the user. It can result in new windows opening that prevent **BROWSERS** from closing properly. The adverts can also send users to websites containing more harmful malware.
- **ROOTKITS**: software that reaches protected parts of an operating system. This can help other malware to operate undetected. Rootkits are sometimes used as part of **ZERO-DAY ATTACKS** (viruses or hacking attempts that exploit software weaknesses that have not yet been patched by the software company).
- **BACKDOORS**: a backdoor bypasses the security methods used to protect computers from unauthorised remote access (such as **FIREWALLS** and **ENCRYPTION** systems). As a result, an unauthorised remote user can use the computer.

Malware is used to create zombie computers that can be controlled by a remote individual (for example, a cybercriminal). A group of zombie computers can be connected to form a **BOTNET** (robot network). The botnet can then be used to send spam emails, attack other computers or host files that the cybercriminal wishes to hide from others.

Social engineering

Have you ever been sent an email asking you to reply with personal information such as your address, username and password? If so, you might have been the target of a **SOCIAL ENGINEERING** attack, where a third party aims to steal data from you by winning your trust and then have you give them the information they want. Social engineering scams can trick us into revealing confidential information in several ways.

- **PHISHING**: this is when many users are sent the same spam messages in the hope that at least some people will be tricked into replying with the desired information.
- **PHARMING**: this is when malware is used to direct the user to a fake website that requests information. For example, a fake bank website could look like the real thing but has been designed to capture account security information then use it to break into the user's account on the real website.
- **SCAMS**: these are more subtle and can involve individuals being targeted via friend requests on social media sites. The 'friend' aims to gain the user's trust and exploit this to get confidential information from them.

A3 Changing and evolving threats

As the number and use of computing devices has increased, so have the number of threats. Hackers are constantly on the look out for new vulnerabilities and new ways to exploit old ones. Many thousands of new computer threats are created every day.

New threats

New computer hardware and software results in new bugs and vulnerabilities that can be found and exploited. For example, the launch of a new operating system is an opportunity for malicious users to exploit loopholes that enable them to gain control of systems. New viruses are developed that can exploit these loopholes.

Existing threats

As existing viruses are detected and anti-virus systems are updated to protect against them, malicious users can edit viruses to use new ones. These new versions can overcome the security measures put in place to protect against earlier versions of the virus.

Over half of all threats come from viruses. New threats could come from new viruses or evolve from updated versions of existing ones. The best way to keep your computer protected against threats is to use security software and keep all software up to date.

ANTI-VIRUS SOFTWARE works to protect a computer by comparing the programming code in a virus with a library of code taken from all known viruses. If this library is not kept up to date, then the computer will not be protected against the newest threats.

Updates from manufacturers

A vulnerability could come from a weakness in an installed program. Software companies regularly release new versions of their programs or PATCHES (a small section of code designed to replace the vulnerable part of an existing program). Microsoft® regularly releases updates of its software on the second Tuesday of each month. This is known as 'Patch Tuesday'.

You can set your computer to receive updates either manually or automatically.

- Automatic updates are downloaded and installed without any action from the user (so long as the computer is connected to the internet).
- Manual updates require the user to give commands to their computer: to search for, download and install updates.

Pathway focus

Networking and Cybersecurity

As an IT support technician, your role may be to ensure that all software, including security software, is kept up to date. This might mean checking that automatic updates are enabled and that updates have been successfully installed.

Help facilities for hardware and software vulnerabilities

To find out about the latest vulnerabilities in any hardware or software, you can usually find a list of them in the following places:

- help or FAQ (frequently asked questions) pages of manufacturers' websites, on which the manufacturer provides information about common issues
- user forums (for example, of COMPUTER NETWORK managers).

Jamil Jackson runs a small business that prints documents received from clients sent by email using a file-sharing service. The business has anti-virus software installed but this is set to update manually only. Explain to Jamil:

- why it is important to keep anti-virus software up to date
- the benefits of updating software automatically.

A4 Vulnerabilities

There are many reasons why computers and their data are vulnerable. These vulnerabilities can be a result of how systems connect to each other to send and receive data. In this section, you will learn about the different factors that can make systems and their data vulnerable.

Types of systems

The main types of computing systems are:
- individual devices, including personal computers (PCs), laptops and mobile devices such as tablets and smartphones
- portable storage devices such as SD cards and external hard drives
- networks, including **LOCAL AREA NETWORK (LAN), WIRELESS LOCAL AREA NETWORK (WLAN)**, a network with wireless connection (see Figure 3.2)
- file servers used to exchange data between devices on a LAN
- **CLOUD** computing systems such as online storage (see below), remote servers and online software such as Google Docs™.

Connections between systems and storage devices

Any two devices can connect together in a number of different ways. For example:
- two or more PCs can connect to a file server in a LAN using wires or a WLAN
- a laptop can connect to a router using Wi-Fi in a coffee shop and so connect to the internet
- two mobile phones can connect using **BLUETOOTH®** to exchange photos
- two mobile phones can connect using a cellular network to exchange text messages
- a laptop can connect to an external **HARD DISK DRIVE (HDD)** using a wired USB connection or to a **CLOUD STORAGE SYSTEM** (a remote storage device where data is read-to and written-from via an internet connection).

Any of these connections is a potential threat. For example:
- a wired network could lose data if the wires become damaged by flood, fire or rodents
- Wi-Fi networks are vulnerable to hacking, especially if they are unencrypted – as are many public hotspots in railway stations and cafes
- data sent to and from internet browsers is usually unencrypted – so third parties can access the data while it is being transmitted
- Bluetooth can be used to connect with unknown devices – especially if one user is not careful to establish that the other device is safe

- mobile phone networks are unencrypted – voice and text conversations made using mobile phones can be eavesdropped on by third parties
- storage devices can contain data infected with malware. One organisation was hacked by an employee finding a USB memory stick in the office car park – the device had malware deliberately installed hoping that an employee would load it onto the office network!

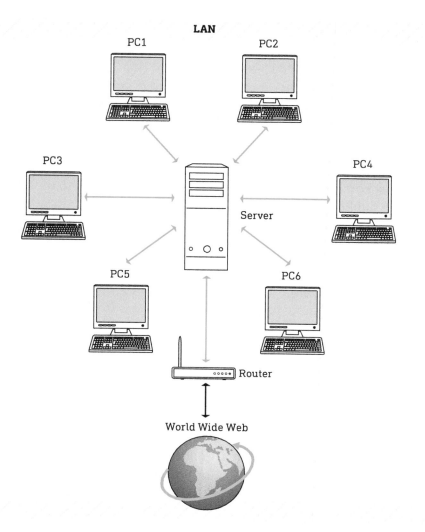

Figure 3.2: Computer networks can be vulnerable to malicious users

Operating systems

Computers can also be vulnerable because of weaknesses in their operating systems, which can occur for the following reasons.

- The system is old and so unsupported. Manufacturers support their OS by issuing patches and bug fixes to remove any new vulnerabilities. Eventually they stop doing this to old systems. Examples of unsupported OS include: Windows 95™ and Mac OS9®. Some hardware manufacturers stop supporting devices. For example, Google™ stopped issuing updates for the Android™ OS to its Nexus™ 9 phone in October 2016.
- Updates are available but have not been installed. Usually this is because automatic updating has not been allowed or a problem has caused it to fail.
- The responsibility for updating the OS lies with the OEM (original equipment manufacturer). For example, Android phones must have their OS updated by the mobile phone manufacturer (for example, Motorola®). This can sometimes happen months after Google updates the Android OS.

Link it up

Networking and Cybersecurity

For more on operating systems, refer back to Unit 1.

- The system is out of date because it is needed to run legacy systems (old hardware). For example, some banks use computer systems that are over thirty years old. These systems are no longer manufactured but work and so are still used. The OS is 'frozen in time' because if it were replaced, the new system would be unable to control the hardware. If vulnerabilities or bugs are found in such OS, they can be hard to fix.

Software

APPLICATION SOFTWARE can be vulnerable because it has:

- zero-day vulnerabilities – bugs that have been spotted that could compromise the security of the system have not yet been patched
- been downloaded from an untrustworthy or illegal source. For example, you do not have to download a mobile phone app from an official OEM, Android or Apple® store but **SIDE-LOADING** apps (getting them from unauthorised software hosting sites on the internet) is the most common way in which malware is installed onto mobile phones. Similarly, downloading a **PIRATE** (illegally reproduced copy of copyright material) version of PC software may be cheaper than buying it from the manufacturer but the pirated copy could have had malware added.

This is one reason why manufacturers have produced online software that can only work when connected to the internet. By controlling the source of the software, the manufacturer can ensure that it is free from malware.

Users

A user's own lack of understanding of system vulnerabilities may put systems at risk. For example, users may not:

- know the risks of using an unencrypted public Wi-Fi network to exchange confidential data
- check whether automated updates of software are working as intended, or may even set them to 'manual' to minimise data use
- know how to decide whether an email containing **EXTERNAL HYPERLINKS** (links to other products or websites) and attachments is genuine or from an untrusted source
- know how to check whether a website uses encryption to send and receive sensitive information.

Why should you be careful when using a Wi-Fi hotspot to connect to an office LAN?

Organisations can help their employees minimise risks by providing training. For example:

- online training courses with questions and feedback at the end
- help and support web pages for employees to view.

Pathway focus

Networking and Cybersecurity

As an IT technician, you might be asked to provide support to new staff, for example by supporting them during training and answering any questions they might have about how to operate the company's computers safely.

Organisations can also take active steps to ensure their employees operate safely. For example, organisations may:

- require employees to change their passwords at regular intervals
- send employees fake spam and phishing emails to check whether employees respond to them, so that training and advice can be offered to those employees
- use **POP-UPS** (windows that open up when the user clicks on a link) to offer advice and reminders (for example, to check that software and anti-virus definitions are up to date).

Assessment practice   A01 A02

Topps Toys has a head office that contains ten PCs connected by wire to a central file server that is kept in a separate locked room. Laptops can connect to the network using Wi-Fi. The business uses a legacy operating system. Each laptop user is responsible for keeping its security software up to date.

1 Identify two benefits of keeping the file server in a separate locked room.

2 Explain one drawback of keeping the file server in a separate locked room.

3 Describe two security risks of allowing laptops to connect to the LAN using Wi-Fi.

4 Explain two security risks of requiring that individual employees are responsible for the security of their own laptops.

What if...?

Your friend has recently started a new business making birthday cards. The business operates from home and has two laptop computers connected to the internet. Card designs are emailed to a local printing business by email. Neither laptop currently has any security software installed.

1 Why is it a security risk to have no security software installed?

2 Outline a series of actions that your friend should take to minimise the security risks of operating the computer system.

Skills and knowledge check

- ☐ What is meant by computer security risks and vulnerabilities?
- ☐ What are the main internal threats to computer systems?
- ☐ What are the main types of malicious software?
- ☐ What are the main methods of social engineering?
- ☐ Why should software and operating systems be kept up to date?

- ◯ I can list five things employees can do to minimise security risk when using a computer in an office.
- ◯ I can list five vulnerabilities of using a laptop or mobile phone in a public place.

B Methods used to secure computer systems and data

B1 Software- and hardware-based protection

In order to protect your systems against vulnerabilities, you can use a number of different methods, including:

- installing security software
- using physical protection methods
- using your system in ways that minimise the risk of unauthorised access.

Each method will work in different ways and will help protect you against specific threats. A well-protected system will use a variety of methods.

Link it up

Data Management

Your understanding of how to protect data will be useful in Unit 9.

Anti-virus software

Anti-virus software checks whether files contain viruses. It can check:

- existing files on the system or storage device
- new files entering the system (for example, downloaded from the internet or copied from a USB device)
- files that begin executing (for example, when a spreadsheet file is opened).

A **VIRUS SIGNATURE** is a short extract of code from a virus program. Anti-virus software has a library of virus signatures that are used to help detect viruses. Figure 3.3 shows anti-virus software comparing items in a user's file (target file) with examples of virus code stored in its library (virus definition file). When a match is found, the anti-virus software identifies that the source file contains a virus.

Link it up

Data Applications

For more on installing anti-virus software, refer back to Unit 1.

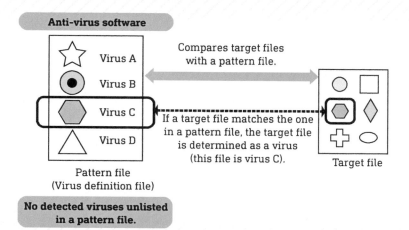

Figure 3.3: Why should you keep your anti-virus software up to date?

The two main detection techniques are as follows.

- *Detection*: this checks files that are not running by examining their code. Files are compared with the virus signatures in the library. Any file containing code that matches a virus signature is identified as a potential virus.
  - Simple detection looks for an exact match. This is best for identifying known viruses in an existing system.
  - Generic detection looks for patterns of code in different parts of the program: this helps to identify new versions of existing viruses.
- *Heuristic*: files are allowed to run and are identified as suspicious if they act in ways that viruses are known to behave. Sometimes this results in false alarms. Heuristic detection can happen in one of two ways.
  - *Real-time*: all files can execute and any that begin to act like a virus are stopped.
  - *Sandbox:* files are run in an isolated part of the system (virtual runtime environment) to identify which are safe and which are malicious.

Anti-virus software will stop a suspected virus from running. Then it will give the following options to the user.

- *Cleaning*: the infected parts of the program are removed. This may prevent the file from running properly.
- **QUARANTINE** (place in a safe place on the hard disk): the suspected virus is kept on the system but prevented from running. This allows the AV program or user to check if it really is malware.
- *Removal*: the file is deleted, even if it was a false alarm.

Link it up

Data Applications

For more on installing firewalls, anti-virus software and IP addresses, refer back to Unit 1.

Software and hardware firewalls

Firewalls protect computers by controlling the data transferred between them (traffic). Any incoming or outgoing traffic not allowed by the firewall is blocked.

Hardware firewalls sit between a router (connected to the internet) and the server that distributes data to the LAN.

- Updates to the firewall rules are made on the hardware firewall and not on each computer.
- Malicious data cannot reach a computer unless it can first get through the hardware firewall.

Software firewalls are installed on each computer.

- No additional hardware is needed to operate the firewall.
- They are easier to configure than hardware firewalls.

Data sent across the internet is split into **PACKETS**. A request for data should include the **IP ADDRESSES** of the computers sending and receiving the data. (Each computer has a unique IP address that works like a postal address. The IPv4 IP addresses currently used contain 32 bits of data. Current IPv6 IP addresses are much longer to allow more devices to be assigned an IP address.) Each packet should also list the **PORT** used to send the request. The data sent in response should contain the same information.

Firewalls use packet filtering to check each packet received to see whether it meets rules (see Figure 3.4). Rules can control inbound or outbound traffic. Outbound rules control data sent from a computer. Usually outbound traffic is allowed by default but you could block outbound requests to specific websites (blacklisting). The following are examples of inbound rules control data received from other computers (for example, from the internet).

- Does the data come from an IP address recognised as being safe? The IP address is allowed if it is on a whitelist of allowed computers or not on a blacklist of blocked ones.
- Was the request for the data sent by the user's computer? The port used to send the request should be correctly listed on the incoming packets.

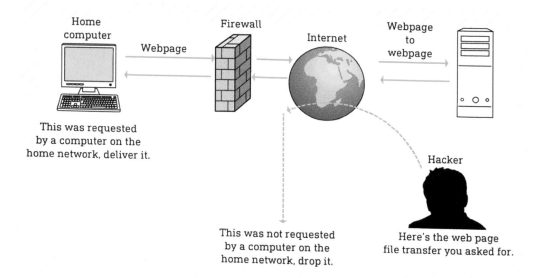

Figure 3.4: Why might a firewall not protect you when connecting to a website containing malware?

A firewall can protect a computer by assigning it a public IP address that is different from the private IP address used by the computer (like a false name). A LAN of 20 computers could all be assigned the same public IP address.

- Unrequested data cannot be sent to a computer on the network.
- There is only a single public IP address to manage.

User authentication

Usernames and passwords can be guessed or stolen. The following are alternative ways users can prove their identity.

Biometric authentication

Every person has features that are unique to them. Computer software can capture this data and then scan the person's features to compare them with the stored data. If there is a match, the software allows access.

Methods include using:

- fingerprints
- the retina (the back of the eye)
- facial recognition (for example, the shape, size and distance between specific features).

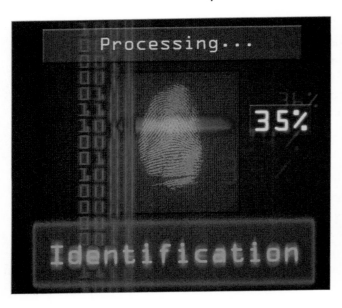

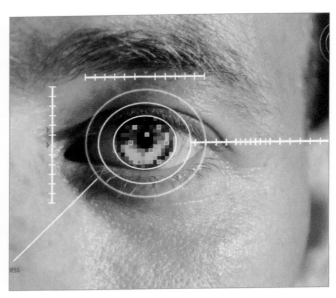

What are the advantages and disadvantages of biometric authentication?

Two-step verification

A two-step verification process could operate as follows.

- Step 1: username and password is entered on a device (for example, laptop).
- Step 2: a security token is generated on a second device (for example, mobile phone) then entered on the first.

USB-based keys

A laptop might have its contents encrypted unless a special USB key is connected to it.

Knowledge-based authentication

Some websites allow users to set their own questions and answers. For example, in order to reset a password, a user might be asked to state their place of birth or favourite pet.

Digital signature

A **DIGITAL SIGNATURE** is a code embedded within a document which confirms that the sender is genuine and the document has not been edited after being sent. The digital signature is generated using data contained in an electronic certificate.

Certificate-based authentication

Electronic certificates are issued by a certification authority and only last for a few months. They are used to help generate a digital signature and to identify a website as being genuine.

CAPTCHA

Have you been asked to enter data from an image on a website to prove that you are human? If so, then you performed a **CAPTCHA** (Completely Automated Public Turing Test To Tell Computers and Humans Apart) test. They help prevent automated systems from using the service.

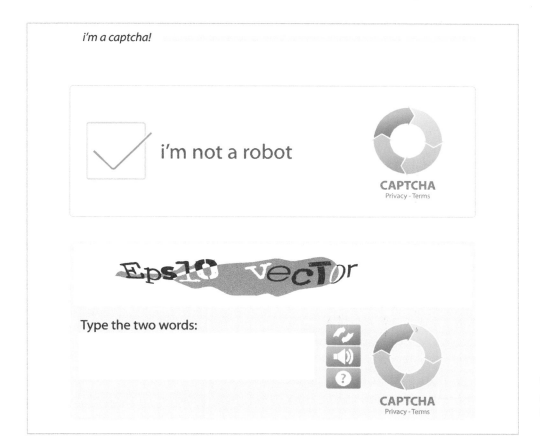

i'm a captcha!

i'm not a robot

CAPTCHA
Privacy - Terms

Type the two words:

CAPTCHA
Privacy - Terms

Why could a robot not complete this CAPTCHA request?

Assessment practice   A01

State two advantages and disadvantages of each of the following user authentication methods.

1 Facial recognition to unlock a mobile phone.

2 Two-step verification using a mobile phone as the second device.

3 A CAPTCHA form asking the user to read a word in a distorted image and then type the word into a text box.

Log-on procedures

Usernames can either be generated by the user or assigned to them by the system. Passwords confirm that the person entering the username is genuine.

Usernames and passwords

Passwords are not secure – they can be guessed either by a human or a computer program designed to hack into a system.

> **Rules for password security**
> - Use a different password for each account.
> - Do not write down passwords.
> - Passwords should be complex – so that they are not guessable.
>
> **How to choose a complex (strong) password**
> - Use a mixture of numbers, letters (upper and lower case) and special characters (such as % ~ +).
> - The longer the better – at least eight characters.

Use a graphical password

Rather than remembering a specific password, users select images that match a pre-set topic (for example, features of a country). The computer presents a range of images to the user, only one of which matches the user's chosen topic.

Change passwords frequently

Passwords should be changed frequently. This reduces the chance that someone will find out your password, and if they do, they will be unable to use the account after the password is changed.

Some accounts keep a log of previous passwords. These can be used to help identify if the user is genuine, for example by asking them to enter a previous password.

Locked out? Reset your password

Some systems will lock the account if an incorrect password is entered – usually more than three times. You must reset the password in order to log back in.

- Enter your account name or email address.
- Answer any security questions (knowledge-based authentication).

Then one of the two following processes occurs.

a. A weblink is emailed to the user. The user follows the link to enter a new password.
b. A new password is emailed to the user. The user is told to replace this password after they have logged back in.

Some systems prevent a previous or similar password from being reused.

Link it up

Networking and Cybersecurity

For more on applying password security when installing and maintaining computer systems, refer back to Unit 1.

Access controls to restrict users' access

Once you have gained access to the system, you may still find that parts of it are protected. Different users are given different access rights. Here are some of the main areas controlled in this way.

Applications

Users are only given access to the software they need to carry out their job role. Some parts of programs might be disabled, for example the ability to right click on a web page and download its content.

Folders/shared areas

An organisation might set up shared folders where specified users can view documents saved into it. Users have access only to folders they need, for example only managers have access to folders containing confidential information.

File access and editing rights

Staff might have access to files. But they might be able to do different things with them.

- *No access*: users are unable to view the file.
- *Read only*: users can open a file and view its contents.
- *Read/write*: users can open a file, view and edit its contents.
- *Full access (read/write/execute)*: as well as read/write access users can delete the file or change its properties (for example, by adding a new author name to a document file).

These rights are also called permissions.

Assessment practice · A01

Kate is a new employee who needs access to some folders and files.
For each scenario below, state what type of access is required.

1 Kate needs to view the contents of a shared folder but not edit or delete any files.

2 Kate needs to open a file in a folder and add new information. She is not allowed to delete the file.

3 Kate needs to be able to create and delete files and folders in a folder.

4 Kate must not have access to a confidential folder.

Access to peripheral devices

Users might have restricted access to some network resources. For example they might:

- only be able to print to specific printers and not be able to change printer settings
- have limited ability to transfer data using **PERIPHERAL DEVICES**, removable items such as USB memory sticks or SD cards.

Link it up

Networking and Cybersecurity

For more on how to control users' access to a computer system, refer back to Unit 1.

Protection of data during transmission

There are several ways you can protect data during transmission, including:

- encryption
- virtual private network
- digital signature.

Each of these methods is covered in the sections below.

Encryption

Encryption is used to ensure that hacked data is not useable by a malicious user. To do this, data is encrypted (converted into scrambled code) using an encryption key and encryption software. Then a **DECRYPTION KEY** is used with encryption software to restore the encrypted data back into useable data.

An encryption key is a long string of binary digits (bits). If the correct string is used, then the software will encrypt and decrypt the data. Two methods are possible.

- *Symmetric*: both sender and receiver use the same key to encrypt and decrypt the data.
- *Asymmetric*: the receiver shares a key with the sender (the public key) that is used to encrypt the data. The data is then decrypted by a private key known only to the receiver. The private and public keys are linked – the private key will only work with data encrypted using the public key (and the other way round).

This is like using two keys in a lock – one turns to the left and is used to close the lock (the public key) and one turns to the right and opens the lock (the private key). So long as the recipient never loses their private key, then the data is secure (see Figure 3.5).

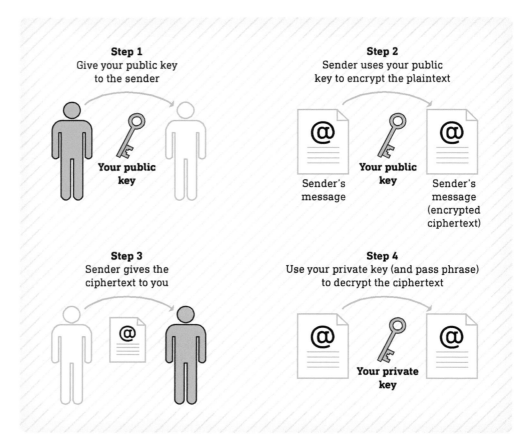

Figure 3.5: Why is asymmetric encryption more secure than symmetric encryption?

Encryption is used in the following ways.

- To protect files being transferred via the internet or a WLAN. Only the intended recipient will be able to decrypt the files to make them readable.
- To protect files stored in folders on a computer or external storage device. Encrypted files can only be decrypted by using a password that only the authorised account holder will know.
- To embed a digital signature within a file to confirm it is genuine (a private key is used to generate the encrypted signature, so if the signature can only be read using the public key, then only the sender could have created it).

Pathway focus

Digital Applications

As a developer of digital applications, you will need to think about how to design systems and media content that do not compromise the security of the system or its user's data. For example, your applications might use encryption technologies to transfer data.

Securing a wireless local area network (WLAN)

There are different ways of securing a WLAN.

Virtual private networks (VPN)

A **VIRTUAL PRIVATE NETWORK (VPN)** operates like a LAN but uses the internet to connect its users together. Data sent between users is encrypted, so then, for example, an office worker can connect to their office location securely while working remotely if they use a VPN (Figure 3.6).

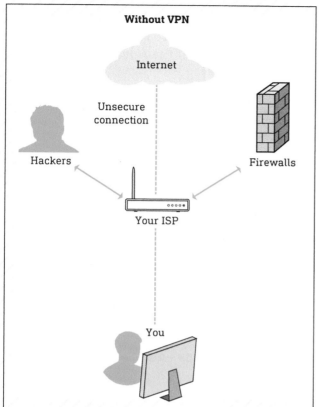

Without VPN

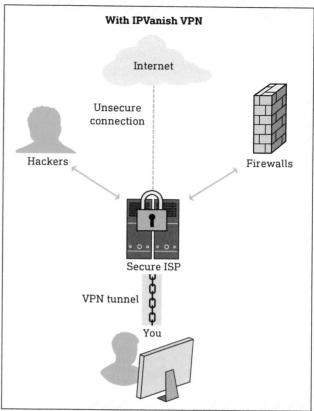

With IPVanish VPN

Wireless encryption methods

Wireless networks normally have two security measures: you need a passcode to join the network and all data traffic is encrypted.

To connect to a WLAN you need to know its **SERVICE SET IDENTIFIER (SSID)** (for example, CAFE_HOTSPOT) and its passcode. Select the SSID from the list of available networks then type in the correct passcode. Wi-Fi Protected Setup (WPS) is used to connect devices such as printers to a wireless network without having to manually connect using the SSID and passcode.

WLANs can be made more secure by hiding the SSID so it is listed as a 'hidden network'. After selecting this you must enter its SSID correctly before inputting the passcode.

Data transferred across the WLAN should be encrypted. The following two main encryption methods are possible.

- **WIRED EQUIVALENT PRIVACY (WEP):** this is the oldest and least secure method of encrypting

Figure 3.6: Why is it safer to connect to the internet using a VPN?

Which Wi-Fi network is the least secure?

a wireless network. It is possible to unlock WEP encrypted networks in minutes using specialist software.

- **WI-FI PROTECTED ACCESS (WPA2)**: this is the most up-to-date and secure method of encrypting a WLAN – especially if the Advanced Encryption Standard (AES) is used.

Be warned: **OPEN NETWORKS** are unencrypted networks, which means anyone can access the data you send and receive over an open network.

Restrict users by MAC address

Each device capable of connecting to a wireless network has a unique **MEDIA ACCESS CONTROL (MAC)** address. MAC address filtering can prevent access to specific devices based on their MAC address.

Securing transfer of personal information and payment details

Data transferred between a web browser and a recipient computer are normally sent using the **HYPERTEXT TRANSFER PROTOCOL (HTTP)**. HTTP is sent plain text (unencrypted). This is fine for non-sensitive information such as news articles or help advice. But what about when sending sensitive information when buying goods or setting up a new account?

A more secure standard is **HYPERTEXT TRANSFER PROTOCOL SECURE (HTTPS)**. You can tell if HTTPS is used because:

- the website address will begin with https:// (for example, https://uk.pearson.com)
- some web browsers will display a closed padlock symbol next to the website address in the browser's address bar.

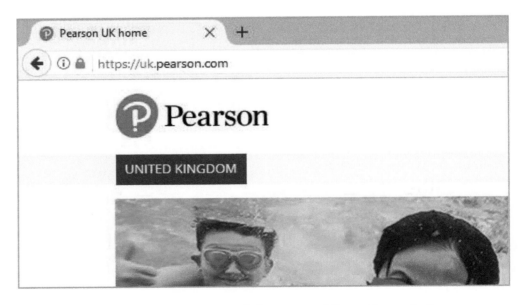

How can you tell that this website is secure?

HTTPS uses data encryption to send data to and from the website.

Digital signatures

HTTPS enables the use of digital certificates to verify that the website is genuine.

Digital certificates are issue by a certification authority (CA).

- The certificate declares that the website is genuine and used by the host organisation. For example, if the browser displays that the site is https://uk.pearson.com, then the certificate will confirm that this is the true address and is not being 'piggybacked' by a malicious site.
- The CA can confirm that the public key used to decrypt data received from and encrypt data sent to the website is genuine.

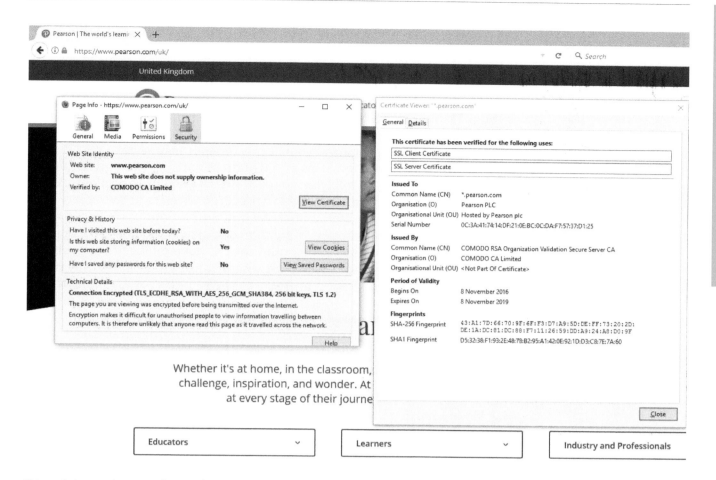

Whether it's at home, in the classroom, challenge, inspiration, and wonder. At at every stage of their journe

| Educators ∨ | Learners ∨ | Industry and Professionals |

This website can be trusted. How does this certificate prove this?

Assessment practice   AO3

You are using an online store's website and to make a payment you are taken to the website's payment page. You are about to enter your credit card information when you notice that:

- the website address begins with http

- your browser tells you that the digital certificate is out of date.

Explain why the above information makes the website unsafe to use.

Secure access to personal information

The following is a list of the main dos and don'ts when using the internet to send and receive personal information.

- Be careful when opening email attachments. Email attachments, even if they come from a trusted source such as a friend, might contain malware. Make sure that your anti-virus software offers real-time protection (so the file is scanned while it opens and begins operating). If in doubt, scan it before opening it. Be especially careful with attachments on emails if you do not recognise the sender or they look suspicious.
- Be careful when downloading web pages and following hyperlinks. Websites can be dangerous because they might:
  - be fake (some malicious websites rely on internet users not understanding how web addresses work: https://www.famousbank.co.uk is likely to be the genuine website for Famous Bank – the

electronic certificate will prove it – but http://www.famousbank.fakewebsite.co.uk or http://www.famusbank.co.uk will not be

- ○ have links to websites that contain malware
- ○ have content such as images or sound clips which themselves contain malware.
- Avoid using unsecured wireless networks. **TRAFFIC** (incoming and outgoing data) on unsecured networks is sent plaintext (unencrypted) so it can be eavesdropped by malicious users. Unlike web browsers (where you can look for https in the address bar), mobile and tablet apps make it hard to tell whether data is sent encrypted or plaintext – if in doubt, do not use an app on an unsecured wireless network.
- Use passwords wisely. Remember the guidance about using passwords in B1 'Log-on procedures'. If there is an opportunity to use two-factor verification, then do so. Some organisations have replaced passwords altogether with methods based on access to a second-device only (for example, giving permission on your mobile phone's social media app in order to log on to the social media website on a PC's browser). Consider using a password manager service – this will generate a different complex password for each account you access on your web browser, store the passwords (securely) and use them when you need them to log back into the account.

B2 Physical security

As an IT professional, your aim is to protect data by preventing unauthorised users from coming into physical contact with systems. Security measures are necessary for both computer rooms and the buildings in which they are housed.

Building and computer/network room security

The level of security will depend on how important the system is. File servers and backup systems in banks, hospitals and military bases are more heavily protected than PCs running applications software in a library.

Table 3.3: Advantages and disadvantages of security systems

All systems have their advantages and disadvantages, some of these are covered in Table 3.3.

Security method	Description	Benefits and drawbacks
Site security locks	Doors can be locked with padlocks or keys. A benefit is that only the keyholder can lock or unlock them. This method is used to protect a site when it is closed.	A drawback is that if the key is lost, then the lock must be replaced.
Card entry	A key card is credit-card sized and stores data that is read by a card-reader on a door or turnstile. If the data is valid, the card-reader will unlock the door or allow the card-holder to pass through the turnstile. Some key cards store the data on a magnetic strip so the card is swiped. Others contain a Radio Frequency Identification (RFID) chip that enables the card to be checked while in the user's pocket.	A benefit of card keys is that the card can be set as valid for a specific period of time, making it a suitable method to give to a temporary user. A drawback is that sometimes the data on the card can become corrupted (for example, by being left next to a magnetic device).

Table 3.3: (continued)

Security method	Description	Benefits and drawbacks
Passcode	The user enters a passcode, usually onto a keypad on the door. If the code is correct the door unlocks. Older systems allow only one code that is used by all authorised users.	A drawback is the possibility of a shoulder-surfer viewing and then using the code.
Biometrics	Fingerprint, retina and facial recognition systems are linked to door locks (see B1 'Biometric authentication'). An advantage is that each person has a unique finger, retina and face.	A drawback with facial recognition systems is that they can be fooled (for example, by using a photograph of an authorised user).
Security staff	Guards can either be placed at the entrance to buildings/rooms (to check users' identities before allowing them access) or they can patrol the room/building (to ensure only authorised users are present).	Security staff give an extra layer of security but they could be expensive to employ and may need to be away from their posts temporarily, leaving the system vulnerable.
Closed circuit television (CCTV)	Can monitor rooms when closed and record images that could be used in crime investigations.	A drawback is that they do not prevent access, merely record it.
Alarms	If unauthorised access is detected by any of the above methods (plus others such as motion sensors when a building is closed), then alarms can be set off – these could be a loud siren or an alert sent to security staff.	Alarms can be set-off accidentally and they cannot prevent unauthorised entry.

Data storage

Once data has been used it may need to be stored in case it is needed again.

Where will the data be stored?

Two main methods are possible.

- Data is stored where it is needed (for example, the data used by a hospital's DATABASE is stored in the main hospital building).
- The data is stored separately (for example, the hospital's data is stored in a separate town. Data is transferred using a VPN).

How will the data be protected?

There are some key questions that need to be asked.

- Should the data be encrypted?
- Should a portable storage medium be used?
- Where should the storage media be stored?
- Who should have access to the storage location?
- How should data be transferred between the storage location and the computers that use the data?

Backup procedures

Data can be accidentally deleted, or the device it is stored on could be damaged. It is important that organisations keep backup copies of their data in case the original data is lost or damaged.

The best backup system will be cheap to run and have limited impact on the organisation while it is running, offer secure storage of data and enable data to be restored almost instantly. In practice, all backup systems are a compromise between these aims. Here are the main things to consider when backing up data.

Which data to back up?

There are several aspects to consider when creating a backup.

- You can either back up files or files and system data. If just files are being backed up, then which ones? Should this include recently deleted files?
- You can either back up the entire file or just the blocks of data that have changed since the last back up.
- A complete backup would take a copy of the entire system (a system image) – files and operating system settings and logs. However, most backup systems focus on capturing files.

When is the best backup window?

This might be overnight or at weekends but this could be a problem if the organisation runs 24/7.

One solution is to have real-time backup: data is backed up continuously. A drawback is that it might not be possible to back up live (open) files.

How often?

Data could be backed up daily or weekly. But if the system fails, then any data created since the last backup will be lost.

What storage media to use?

Magnetic tape can store large amounts of data but restoring data from it can be slow.

Why might large organisations use a magnetic tape backup system?

Hard disks store less information than tape systems but read/write times are faster. CDs and DVDs store less data than hard disks and read/write times are slower but optical disks are a cheap backup solution for very small organisations.

When to trigger a backup?

Most backups are planned to happen at set days/times. Some systems are fully automated so no human intervention is needed, but if something goes wrong the data might not get backed up. You could have a fully manual system that must have a human operator. In practice, most systems are automated but humans check that the backup is running smoothly.

What type of backup?

There are three kinds of backup.

- *Full*: complete system images are made. This is beneficial if the whole system is damaged. It is time consuming to use as a method of restoring data if only some files need restoring.
- *Differential*: data is backed up if it is new or changed since the last full backup.
- *Incremental*: data is backed up only if it is new or changed since the last incremental backup.

Where to store the data?

There are several options to consider when choosing where to store backup data.

- *On-site*: same location as the original data. An advantage is that it is easier to restore but data is as vulnerable to damage as the original data.
- *Off-site*: potentially safer option but data may take longer to restore.
- *Cloud*: off-site storage where data is transferred via internet. This is useful for small organisations where data is not backed up but synchronised across several devices so that it can be used when working remotely. The cloud storage data serves as the backup.

Link it up

Data Management

For more about archiving, see Unit 9.

Pathway focus

Data Management

In a data management role, you will need to consider how database and spreadsheet-based systems should be stored. You may need to consider where the data should be stored, including storage media and security issues such as password protection. You will also need to consider how the data can be protected through designing appropriate backup systems, including the choice of storage location and media.

Individual actions

You should take actions to protect your data. This is especially important if you are working in a public place.

- Make sure you log out of applications after using them – especially web browsers. You might want to delete browsing history and disable the option for the browser to save data you entered onto forms and passwords.
- If you are going to be away from your machine for a short while, then lock the screen and require a password to unlock it. If you are going to be away for an extended period, then log off your computer to prevent someone else accessing your programs and files.
- Prevent shoulder surfing by thinking about who is behind you when working – if you are on a train, who else can see your screen while you work?
- Do not leave important printed documents lying around. Lock them away if you need them again and shred them if you do not.

Link it up

Data Management

You will consider the choice of on-site or off-site storage in Unit 9.

Skills and knowledge check

- ☐ How does anti-virus software work?
- ☐ How does a software firewall work?
- ☐ What are the main ways a computer can check the identity of a user?
- ☐ Can you explain the difference between a simple and a complex password?
- ☐ Can you explain how public-key encryption works?
- ☐ What is HTTPS? How can you tell whether a website is using it?

- ◯ I can list five ways to restrict physical access to a computer system.
- ◯ I can describe the differences between full, differential and incremental backups.

C Legal requirements and IT security policies and procedures

C1 Legal requirements

As an IT professional, you will need a solid understanding of the current UK legislation that applies to different computer systems and data.

Principles and requirements of the Data Protection Act 1998

The Data Protection Act (DPA) 1998 gives rights to individuals (data subjects) who have **PERSONAL DATA** (information about people, for example, name, contact details, interests and preferences) stored by organisations. The DPA states that data subjects own their own data but can give their permission to particular organisations to use it for specified purposes only.

The DPA states that:

- all organisations will have a data controller who is responsible for how the organisation uses personal data
- all data subjects have the right to view their personal data stored by an organisation
- organisations can use personal data if its use meets eight key principles (shown in Table 3.4).

Link it up

Data Management

You will explore the types of information that organisations may hold about individuals in Unit 9.

Table 3.4: Eight key principles for using personal data

Principle		Implications for organisations
1	Personal data shall be processed fairly and lawfully.	
2	Personal data shall be obtained only for one or more specified and lawful purposes, and shall not be further processed in any manner incompatible with that purpose or those purposes.	Organisations must have a valid reason for collecting personal data.
3	Personal data shall be adequate, relevant and not excessive in relation to the purpose or purposes for which they are processed.	Only relevant data should be collected (for example, if gender is irrelevant this data should not be collected).
4	Personal data shall be accurate and, where necessary, kept up to date.	Organisations must ensure that the data stored is accurate.
5	Personal data processed for any purpose or purposes shall not be kept for longer than is necessary for that purpose or those purposes.	Once no longer needed, the data should be deleted.
6	Personal data shall be processed in accordance with the rights of data subjects under this Act.	

Table 3.4: *(continued)*

Principle		Implications for organisations
7	Appropriate technical and organisational measures shall be taken against unauthorised or unlawful processing of personal data and against accidental loss or destruction of, or damage to, personal data.	The data should be protected using adequate security measures and policies.
8	Personal data shall not be transferred to a country or territory outside the European Economic Area unless that country or territory ensures an adequate level of protection for the rights and freedoms of data subjects in relation to the processing of personal data.	If an organisation also operates in another country, it can only send the data there if that country has a similar law to the DPA.

The main implication for organisations is that they need to think carefully about data security and design new systems that will enable them to meet the data protection principles.

Rights of data subjects

The DPA protects data subjects by allowing them to:

- see their personal data if they give a written request and pay a small fee if required
- object to the data being used in a way that is distressing
- prevent organisations contacting them with marketing or other communications
- object to decisions being taken by automated systems without a human reviewing the results (for example, loan applications)
- have inaccurate personal data corrected or deleted
- claim compensation for damages caused by a breach of the Act.

Organisations need to have systems in place to respond to requests for their data by data subjects and to deal with issues and complaints.

The Computer Misuse Act 1990

This law makes a number of malicious acts illegal. These include:

- hacking
- malicious use of computer systems
- deliberately spreading malware
- gaining access to a computer system (or unauthorised parts such as admin accounts) without permission
- editing data, including software and passwords without permission
- impersonating another user (for example, by using their username and password or on a social media site).

People found guilty of breaking this law can be fined or sent to prison.

The main implication for organisations is that they can be held responsible for the actions of their employees while the employee is carrying out their work. For example, an employee of business X uses their work computer to hack into the systems of business Y. Business X could be held responsible for the employee's actions if, for example, it failed to train the employee in how to use computers legally.

Link it up

Data Management

To learn how to set rules for the secure use of personal data, see Unit 9. To learn about the benefits and limitations of a proposed IT solution, including its security implications, go to Unit 5.

Digital Applications

You will learn how to consider legal constraints when developing a multichannel digital media system in Unit 10.

C2 IT security policies and procedures

Organisations need to make sure that all their employees fully comply with data protection laws. Organisations also have a responsibility for the personal digital security of their employees while they are at work. They must try to ensure that users themselves do not break the Computer Misuse Act. An organisation ought to have:

- *an IT policy*: a statement of how and why the organisation expects its users to use IT safely and securely
- *IT security procedures*: the actions that users and their managers should take to ensure that the policy is carried out.

Organisations often ask their staff to declare (by signing a form) that they have read and understood the policies and that they will comply with them. Users who fail to follow policies and procedures may be in breach of their contract of work and could be disciplined. You could lose your job for a serious breach of a policy.

The actual title and content of policies will vary from organisation to organisation but the main ones are outlined here.

Organisations and acceptable use policies

These policies set out how users should operate systems.

Internet and email use policies

These often include guidelines on:

- limiting use of the internet and email for personal purposes while at work
- what can and cannot be said in an official email
- what can and cannot be sent using a work email account
- the use of personal social media accounts to discuss work matters (most organisations ban this)
- examples of user actions that could be illegal (for example, the Computer Misuse and Data Protection Acts), such as stealing confidential data or knowingly damaging equipment
- the consequences for the individual of not following the policy.

Security and password procedures

Security and password procedures will explain how and why users should keep their equipment and the data on it secure, for example:

- the creation of strong passwords
- how to keep usernames and passwords secure
- systems for updating passwords (for example, the frequency of updates and whether or not the existing password can be edited or a new password be created, such as can you replace password 5t0k35A with 5t0k35B?).

Staff responsibilities for the use of IT systems

These will include:

- computer use in public places (some organisations ban work using confidential data in public places or at home)
- protecting equipment when not at work (for example, whether or not equipment can be left unattended in the boot of a locked car).

Staff IT security training

These policies should cover:

- the content of training (that is, the topics that should be covered)
- how often training should take place
- how the training should take place (for example, face to face with a trainer or remotely using a computer aided learning package)
- how the user will be tested (for example, a quiz at the end of the training or by monitoring their use afterwards).

Backup policies and procedures

These will set out how the organisation will ensure that data is protected against loss or damage. This will include:

- what and how data will be backed up (that is, all the issues covered in B2 'Backup procedures')
- the staff responsible for managing and implementing backups
- how and when the backup systems will be tested
- procedures for restoring data (for example, a written request from a manager is needed to restore data lost by a user).

Data protection policy

The main aim is to ensure that the organisation meets the requirements of relevant data protection laws such as the Data Protection Act. This policy will specify:

- what types of data count as personal data and so are covered by the policy
- who has responsibility for the organisation's data security
- how the organisation will keep data secure and accurate
- how data will be stored and processed and how this complies with the DPA
- the specific circumstances when personal data can be shared with others (for example, suppliers or branches in other countries)
- how to respond to requests by data subjects (for example, to view their personal data)
- how the organisation communicates with data subjects.

Disaster recovery policy

You can do everything possible to protect your computer system and data against threats but a fire, explosion, earthquake or other disaster can still happen. A **DISASTER RECOVERY POLICY** is designed to help an organisation recover quickly from such an incident. A typical disaster recovery policy will:

- identify potential risks
- identify how each risk will affect the computer system and data
- assess the impact of these risks on the system and data
- decide which systems are critical and must be recovered first
- decide on short-, medium- and long-term plans to recover the systems
- develop procedures based on these plans that key workers must follow when recovering from each disaster. These will include:
  - the key workers needed
  - how they will be contacted
  - their role in managing the disaster
  - their role in recovering from the disaster
  - explain how the disaster recovery policy will be tested to make sure it will work effectively.

Assessment practice — AO1

Gavin Jacobson owns an online pet food business. Gavin is struggling to ensure that all workers use the computer system correctly. Gavin has asked you to help develop IT policies.

For each of the following situations, state the policy that should be developed.

1 Staff need to know how to process personal data lawfully.

2 Staff need to be trained to deal with a fire in the server room.

3 Staff need to know what to do if they accidentally delete an important file.

4 Staff who take portable computing devices away from the office need to know how to use them securely.

5 Staff need to know if it is acceptable to use social media at work.

What if...?

Mega Phones 4U sells a range of mobile phones and provides contracts for all the leading UK mobile service providers. To sign up for a contract, users must provide the business with personal data, including name, address, date of birth, contact and payment details. The business would like to use a supplier based in Africa to handle customer support calls. Mega Phones 4U will need to share some of its customers' personal data with this supplier.

1 A customer has recently requested to be given a copy of their personal data. Is this allowed under the Data Protection Act?

2 Under what circumstances would it be against the DPA to share data with a supplier based in another country?

3 A customer has complained that collecting their address details is excessive collection of personal data. What reasons might Mega Phones 4U have for collecting this data?

4 Mega Phones 4U has a policy of keeping customers' personal data for ten years after they cease to be a customer. Is this likely to be allowed by the DPA?

Skills and knowledge check

☐ What is a data subject?

☐ What is a data controller?

☐ Can you list three different types of personal data that you might use to buy films from an online store?

☐ What are the main principles of the Data Protection Act?

☐ Can you list three types of computer misuse?

☐ What are the punishments if found guilty of breaking the Computer Misuse Act?

○ I can explain the difference between a policy and a procedure.

○ I can explain why an organisation should have a disaster recovery policy.

Getting ready for assessment

This section has been written to help you do your best when you complete the external assessment for this unit. Read through it carefully and ask your tutor if there is anything you are not sure about.

About the assessment

You will be assessed by a written exam. It will take place on a computer so you will not need to take a pen with you into the exam room.

There will be a number of different types of questions. Below are the main ones.

1. *Multiple choice:* you will be shown a statement and a number of possible responses. At least one will be the correct answer. You will be told how many responses to select.

2. *Match response:* you will be given a number of technical terms and must match each term to its correct definition by selecting each word and then the definition you think is correct.

3. *Short-answer questions:* you will type your answer to a question in the box below the question.

Some questions will test your understanding of the main technical ideas and issues covered in the unit – these will mostly be multiple-choice or short-answer questions.

Some questions will be based on a scenario. These are mostly short-answer questions.

The total number of questions may change from test to test, but there will usually be about 30 questions. The number of the question you are on and the total number of questions on the paper is shown at the bottom of the screen (for example, question 13/27). At the bottom of the screen you can also:

- move forward and back through the questions

- see how much time you have left.

Top tips

1. Make sure you plan your time so you can answer all questions.

2. Read each question carefully so you understand exactly how to answer it.

3. Check your answers carefully before moving on to the next question.

Command words

Short-answer questions are of different types. The first word in each question is the command word. The command word tells you what kind of answer is needed. Make sure you know what each command is telling you to do.

- *Identify/Give/State/Name:* the answer to these questions is usually a fact that relates to the item in the question. It could be the name or definition of something. For example: 'Name the software used to scan for malware in an email attachment' or 'State one purpose of a firewall.'

- *Describe:* a slightly longer answer that shows you understand the purpose or features of something. For example: 'Describe how anti-virus software could be used to prevent malware from infecting a computer hard drive.'

- *Explain:* here you will need to show you understand how or why something happens, perhaps by giving reasons to support a statement. For example: 'Explain why bt6*ge@ll7 is an example of a strong password.'

- *Analyse*: to analyse is to explore something in detail by breaking it down into parts and then showing how the parts fit together. For example: 'Analyse how data could be put at risk by a failure to update anti-virus software.'

- *Discuss*: to discuss something you will need to recognise that there are different sides to an issue; for example, benefits and drawbacks, or strengths and weaknesses. You will then need to explain or analyse these in detail. For example: 'Discuss the benefits and drawbacks of using a cloud-based service to back up customer data.'

- *Assess*: to assess something you need to discuss it then reach a conclusion or make an overall judgement. For example: 'Assess which method Meg's Nursery should use to back up its customer data.'

Sample questions and answers

Question 1

Dream Weddingz is a small company employing wedding planners who visit customers' homes to plan their wedding. The wedding details are recorded using spreadsheet software on the planner's laptop and at the end of the consultation they send a copy of the spreadsheet to the customer. This is done by email, Bluetooth or USB memory device if the customer has one. When back at home the planner connects to the internet to log on to the head office LAN.

State two security credentials the planner will need to log on to the head office LAN.

Sample answer 1

Username and password.

Verdict

This is a good response as it states two relevant security credentials.

Sample answer 2

Username and account name.

Verdict

This is a weaker answer because both credentials are the same thing, so the answer only gives one correct credential.

Question 2

Identify two risks to Dream Weddingz of using a customer's USB memory device to transfer files from the wedding planner's laptop.

Sample answer 1

One risk is that the customer's USB device could contain a virus that will be transferred onto the planner's laptop.

Another risk is that the planner could load the wrong files onto the USB stick – for example, confidential files from another customer.

Verdict

This is a good answer. Two relevant risks have been identified.

Sample answer 2

One risk is computer security.

Another risk is the USB stick could transfer a virus from the planner's computer to the customer's.

Verdict

This is a weak answer. The first risk is very vague – what kind of security risk is it? The second risk is in fact a risk to the customer, but the question asks for a risk to the business. It is important to read the question carefully!

Question 3

Explain one way that data on the wedding planner's laptop could be kept secure.

Sample answer 1

The planner could use anti-virus software. Each new file that is transferred onto their laptop is scanned to see whether it contains malicious code like the examples kept in the software's library. If there is a match, the software stops the file from running and can delete it if the user agrees.

Verdict

This is a good answer that gives a detailed explanation of how anti-virus software works.

Sample answer 2

The planner could use anti-virus software that will delete a file with any viruses that it finds.

Verdict

This is a weaker answer because although it identifies a correct method and it states that the software will delete the virus, it does not explain how the software decides whether the file has a virus or not.

4 Working as an IT Support Technician

What would the impact be on learners if they could not access their personal documents on the computer network? What would the impact be on patient care if the computer network in a hospital failed to work? What impact would the failure of an air traffic control computer network have on passenger safety?

Most organisations rely on their computer networks working correctly 24 hours a day. However, technical problems can occur at any time and IT support technicians need to be able to adapt to a range of problems quickly to minimise the disruption that can happen when a network fails to work.

How will I be assessed?

During this unit you will need to show that you can work by yourself and with others in order to solve problems. You will:

- explore the different types of problems that can occur within computer networks and the different methods that you can use to solve these problems
- use a range of different skills to carry out tasks that will require you to show initiative and use appropriate methods to diagnose different problems and resolve them
- create a report stating the work that you have carried out and the methods that you have used
- review your own skills and then make suggestions as to how these can be improved further in the future.

Assessment criteria

Pass	Merit	Distinction
Learning aim A: Explore the processes and procedures used by IT support technicians		
A.P1 Identify the types of task carried out by IT support technicians in an organisation.	**A.M1** Describe the IT issues across an organisation and the processes and procedures used by IT support technicians to address them.	**A.D1** Explain how IT issues across an organisation are addressed and the processes and procedures used by IT support technicians, making recommendations for improvement.
A.P2 Outline the processes and procedures used by IT support technicians.		
Learning aim B: Carry out IT support technician tasks using a range of skills		
B.P3 Demonstrate ability to log and prioritise IT tasks accurately.	**B.M2** Perform IT support technician tasks efficiently, diagnosing and resolving a range of technical problems while demonstrating the appropriate skills and behaviours.	**B.D2** Perform IT support technician tasks effectively, showing initiative when diagnosing and resolving a full range of basic and complex technical problems, confidently communicating and supporting team members.
B.P4 Perform IT support technician tasks to resolve basic technical problems, following the agreed processes and procedures.		
Learning aim C: Report on the work carried out as IT support technician, reviewing own practice		
C.P5 Identify the IT services that were provided and the processes that were used during a service period.	**C.M3** Assess how IT services were provided and how own skills were applied during the service period, reflecting on how own skills were developed and making outline suggestions for how skills could be further improved.	**C.D3** Evaluate how IT services were provided during the service period, analysing own skill development and making detailed suggestions for how skills could be further improved.
C.P6 Outline how own skills were applied and developed during the service period.		

A Explore the processes and procedures used by IT support technicians

A1 Types of service support

You cannot always prevent problems from happening. The key, however, is to ensure that correct processes and procedures are in place to deal with problems effectively when they do occur.

Service-level agreements

A **SERVICE-LEVEL AGREEMENT (SLA)** is an agreement that has been made between two groups, usually those accessing a service and those providing the service. For example, this could be an agreement that is made internally between departments, such as the IT support department and all other departments using the **COMPUTER NETWORK**. Or it could be an agreement between an internal department that is accessing a service provided by an external organisation.

IT support services keep modern businesses running smoothly

SLAs are used to ensure that the quality of the service provided is maintained. Within the agreement, there will be an outline of the procedures that will be put into place when the quality of service is interrupted. The SLA is outlined in organisational catalogues and portfolios, which are handed over to the service user when the service starts. Figure 4.1 shows what part of an SLA might look like.

Practise

Think of a device that you own or use such as a mobile phone. Research what service-level agreement the manufacturer provides. Note down the following.

1 How can you get in contact with the manufacturer if you need support?

2 What are their opening hours?

3 How long do they say it will take to replace faulty **HARDWARE?**

Service-level agreement

This service-level agreement is made between

Organistion A [Service user]

AND

Organisation B [Service provider]

Type of service	Level of service
Telephone helplines	A telephone helpdesk will be available from 9.00 a.m.to 5.00 p.m. Monday to Friday.
Initial troubleshooting	An initial attempt to fix the problem will be made within two hours.
Email responses	Emails will be responded to within two working days.
Replacement parts	Replacement parts will be ordered within three hours.
Engineer visits	An onsite visit will be made within three working days.

Figure 4.1: A service-level agreement defines the service the provider will supply and the performance standards they will meet

Link it up

Refer back to Unit 2 for more information about why organisations invest in technology, including meeting business goals, improving efficiency, increasing competitiveness and increasing sales. Service-level agreements can ensure that the impact on these areas is reduced if an effective plan is in place to deal with any disruption to services.

Levels of IT support

There is often a chain of different people who will attempt to fix a problem. This means that if a problem cannot be solved by the first line of support, then the problem can be moved up the chain to the next line, and so on, until the problem is solved. The number of different lines of support will depend on how large an organisation is. A small organisation with one IT technician may only have one line of support, while a large organisation may have several.

A high level of support may involve a site visit to resolve the problem

Figure 4.2 shows how a problem may move through the three most common lines of support.

Figure 4.2: A problem may move through different lines of support before it is resolved

1st line	2nd line	3rd line

```
┌──────────────────┐
│ Service provider is │
│   notified of the   │
│       problem       │
└──────────────────┘
          │
          ▼
┌──────────────────┐
│ The problem is   │
│      logged      │
└──────────────────┘
          │
          ▼
┌──────────────────┐        ┌──────────────────┐        ┌──────────────────┐
│ A script will be │        │ Specialist support is │    │ High-level support is │
│ followed to solve│──────▶ │ provided (e.g. over the│──▶│ provided (e.g. a site │
│small/basic problems│      │   phone remotely)   │      │        visit)        │
└──────────────────┘        └──────────────────┘        └──────────────────┘
          │                          │                          │
          ▼                          ▼                          ▼
┌──────────────────┐  No    ┌──────────────────┐  No    ┌──────────────────┐  No    There may be
│    Problem       │───────▶│    Problem       │───────▶│    Problem       │───────▶ further lines
│   resolved?      │        │   resolved?      │        │   resolved?      │         of support
└──────────────────┘        └──────────────────┘        └──────────────────┘         available.
          │ Yes                     │ Yes                     │ Yes
          ▼                          ▼                          ▼
┌──────────────────┐        ┌──────────────────┐        ┌──────────────────┐
│    Problem       │        │    Problem       │        │    Problem       │
│    resolved      │        │    resolved      │        │    resolved      │
└──────────────────┘        └──────────────────┘        └──────────────────┘
```

This line of support is usually provided over the phone or by email. At this point the problem is logged. The person who is logging the fault (for example, an IT support technician) will have limited technical knowledge. They will usually have a script to follow and may attempt to solve basic problems.

This line of support is provided by a group of people with a higher level of technical knowledge (for example, IT technicians). They try to solve specific problems that the service user has. This level of support is usually still provided over the phone. They may attempt to solve the problem remotely.

This line of support is provided by a group of people with a very high level of technical knowledge who can solve major problems (for example, network managers). At this level, the technician may visit the location to address the problem in person.

Methods of support

In-house

Most organisations have one or more full-time IT support technicians based within the organisation. They will be the first port of call when there is a problem. Smaller organisations may share a technician or may have no technician at all and may rely on getting support externally.

Table 4.1 shows how in-house support may be structured.

Table 4.1: In-house support

Job title	Responsibilities
Network manager	A person who has overall responsibility for the network and all the people who are maintaining the network. They will make all major decisions about the network, including purchasing new hardware and **SOFTWARE**.
IT technician	A person or group of people who perform jobs outlined by the network manager. They will carry out general day-to-day tasks to ensure the network is working and meeting the needs of the company.
Support technician	A person who is currently in training. They will usually work alongside an IT technician and perform low-level tasks such as fixing paper jams, changing ink cartridges.

Contracted out

If an organisation is not able to fix a problem itself or there is a problem with a service it is accessing externally, then it may contact another company to help. This contact is usually made by the network manager.

Table 4.2 shows some possible external services that may be contracted out.

External service	Support given
Internet service	Organisations will use a company to provide the internet. They may be contacted if an organisation is having internet connection problems.
CLOUD STORAGE	Organisations may use a company to store all their DATA online. They may be contacted if an organisation is having problems accessing its data.
Warranty	Organisations will often take out a warranty when they buy new hardware or software. The company may be contacted if an organisation requires new parts for a computer.

Table 4.2: External support

Service providers will often provide a basic level of support free of charge that guarantees to get the problem fixed. However, organisations may wish to pay extra money to upgrade this level of support in order to get problems fixed more quickly.

Table 4.3 shows the different levels of support a company may provide.

Type of support	Low	Medium	High
Cost	Free	£50 per month	£100 per month
Free phone support	8 a.m. to 10 p.m.	24 hours	24 hours
Free web support	Yes	Yes	Yes
Response time	24 hours	3 hours	30 minutes
Hardware replacement	24 hours	5 hours	2 hours
Onsite visits	Within 3 days	Within 24 hours	Within 3 hours

Table 4.3: Different levels of support

Methods of supporting employees internally

If IT technicians are based within the organisation, then they will be responsible for supporting other employees inside the organisation who use the computer network. This can either be done formally or informally.

- *Informally*: when an employee needs support, then any available IT technician will provide help.
- *Formally*: when an employee needs support, the case is logged and assigned to a specific technician to deal with at a particular time.

Methods of supporting customers

Table 4.4 shows some possible methods that may be used to provide support to customers.

Table 4.4: Methods of customer support

Type of support	Examples	Description
Hardware based	Voice calls/email	A call or email will be made to the company. The operator will try to fix the problem using a list of common problems and solutions.
Software based	Remotely	A technician may be able to log in to your computer from another location in order to fix software-related problems. Therefore they do not have to visit the site personally.
	Expert systems	Online expert systems may be available on the internet that will ask you questions about the problem you are having. They will offer you a recommendation on how to fix the problem.
	Online chat	Some companies have online chat facilities that you can access from their website. Here you can speak to an operator via instant messaging and they will deal with your problem.
Service providers	Onsite visits	An external IT technician may visit the organisation to sort out a problem. This is usually for major problems or hardware repairs that are not possible to solve over the phone.

Types of support requests

As an IT support technician, you will be expected to adapt to lots of different problems. In most cases it is not possible to predict the problems that users are going to have or when they might have them. Therefore you will need to adapt quickly to the different requests that you may receive.

Table 4.5 shows some types of support requests that you may receive.

Table 4.5: Types of support requests

Support requests	Examples
Hardware faults	• A printer may have a printer jam or require a new ink cartridge. • A set of speakers may not be producing any sound. • An employee may have run out of **STORAGE SPACE** (the space each user has to store their files).
Software faults and error messages	• An error message may keep appearing on the screen. • A piece of software may keep freezing.
Ability to use software features	• A user may have limited IT skills and may need some basic training. • A user may want help using a new piece of software. • A user may want advice on which software tool to use. • A user may have accidentally deleted their work.
Services or features that are not available	• A user may want their **PASSWORD** resetting. • A user may want their storage space expanding. • A user may not be able to access their personal documents.
Software installation and upgrade requests	• A department may want a piece of software installing or updating. • Hardware may need to be updated to support new requirements. • Security software such as **FIREWALL** or **ANTI-VIRUS SOFTWARE** may need updating.
Performance issues	• A user may have reported that their internet connection is running slow. • A user may have reported that a particular program is not producing the results they want.
Mobile technologies	• Users may bring in their own devices into the workplace and want support connecting them to the wireless or wired network. • A mobile device may have been damaged and need repairing. • A mobile device may have been lost or stolen and the insurance company may need to be contacted.

A2 Functions and tasks carried out by IT support technicians

Setting up new equipment and upgrading existing systems

As an IT support technician, you will be expected to set up new equipment and upgrade existing equipment for other people to use. It is very important that you follow the instructions that come with the new equipment to ensure both the safety of people using it and that the equipment works correctly (see Figure 4.3).

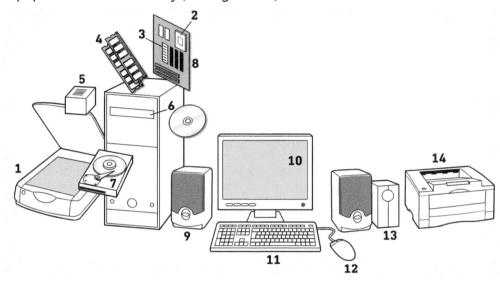

Figure 4.3: Setting up new equipment and upgrading existing equipment

External components you may be expected to set up.

Hardware devices and components

1   Scanner: to keep an electronic copy of paper documents.
9   Speakers: to listen to sound.
10 Monitor: to view documents and websites.
11 Keyboard: to type text or commands.
12 Mouse: to navigate around the monitor.
13 Wireless access point: to provide wireless access to the internet.
14 Printer: to create a paper copy of an electronic document.

Internal components you may be expected to upgrade.

Hardware devices and components

2   **CENTRAL PROCESSING UNIT (CPU)**: you may be asked to install a better CPU that can handle more advanced software.
3   Graphics card: you may be asked to install a more advanced graphics card that can handle high definition graphics.
4   **RANDOM-ACCESS MEMORY (RAM)**: you may be asked to install more RAM because a computer may be running slow.
5   Power supply: the power supply may be malfunctioning and may require a replacement.
6   DVD drive: the DVD drive may have stopped working and may require a replacement.
7   Hard drive: you may be asked to install a new hard drive to give a user more storage space.
8   **MOTHERBOARD**: the motherboard may have stopped functioning or a more advanced motherboard may be required to support more advanced hardware components.

Link it up

Refer back to Unit 1 for more information about the different types of internal computer hardware components and different types of **COMPUTER PERIPHERALS**. All of these are devices that you will be expected to set up.

Using a range of operating system security functions and features

As an IT support technician, you should make full use of the security functions and features built into **OPERATING SYSTEMS**. Ensuring that the correct security is in place will prevent disasters from happening that will cause disruption in an organisation. Table 4.6 summarises some of these security options and features.

Table 4.6: Security functions and features

Function or feature	Description	The IT support technician's role
Firewalls	A firewall will stop people from outside the organisation gaining access to the computer network. This will ensure that data about employees and the organisation cannot be accessed by a **HACKER**.	This software will create a log of all possible attempts that have been made to attack a network. You should review these logs regularly to identify weak spots in the network.
Anti-virus software	A **VIRUS** may enter the network. Users may accidentally visit an infected website, open an email attachment that contains a virus or bring in a memory stick that contains a virus. Anti-virus software will constantly scan the network and prevent viruses from entering a computer network.	This software will create logs of all viruses that have come into contact with the network. You should review these logs regularly to check whether users are repeatedly trying to spread viruses.
Passwords	Passwords can be given to all those who use the network. This should stop anyone from outside the organisation being able to log onto a computer easily.	Logs can record how many attempts it takes users to enter their password correctly. You should review these as it could indicate that people are trying to hack into the network.
Backups	Backups should be taken regularly of all the data an organisation uses. How often backups are taken will greatly depend on the amount of data that needs to be backed up.	Having a backup in place means that you will be able to recover the data if the data becomes unavailable, and minimise the disruption to an organisation.

Link it up

Refer back to Unit 1 for more information about security threats, including **MALWARE**, viruses and firewalls. By utilising operating system security functions and features you can reduce the risk of these security threats.

Testing and servicing equipment

It is important that you test new equipment before it is used and service it regularly. Health and safety regulations require organisations to ensure that their equipment is safe for employees to use.

Testing equipment

When testing equipment, you should:

- check the equipment is working
- check fault logs and check for recurring faults
- carry out a visual inspection of the equipment
- check flexible cables are in good condition
- check for bare wires that could cause electrocution.

When equipment has been tested, this should be reviewed regularly and there should be a plan in place that states how often the equipment will be tested.

Servicing equipment

Equipment is less likely to break down if it is regularly serviced. How often equipment needs to be serviced will vary greatly depending on how often it is used and the impact the equipment will have on the company if it fails.

Table 4.7 shows an example routine that may be carried out by IT support technicians.

Daily servicing	Weekly servicing	Monthly servicing	Yearly servicing
Replace ink and paper in the printer.	Remove dirt that has built up inside the mouse.	Check cables are firmly plugged in.	Ensure components are firmly connected into the motherboard.
Check anti-virus logs and check for updates.	Remove dust and fix broken keys on the keyboard.	Clean the ventilation grills to ensure air can be circulated around the computer.	Check the internal components inside the printers such as the rollers.
Back up data that has been changed since yesterday.	Empty the recycle bin and remove temporary internet files.	Remove dust from inside the computer case and the projector.	Carry out general room inspections to ensure equipment is visually safe to use.

Table 4.7: Service routine for IT support

Providing guidance for technical and non-technical users

Users who ask for guidance will have different experiences in using IT. Some users may be very confident and therefore you can use lots of technical language. Other users may have limited IT experience and therefore you may need to explain technical language. It is important that you know your audience to ensure you are giving them guidance they can understand.

Providing guidance to technical users is easier as the user is also technically minded. However, when providing guidance to non-technical users, it is important that you keep the following points in mind.

- *Break tasks down*: break the problem down into as many small parts as you can and then deal with each small part before moving onto the next. For example, if a user is having trouble with their printer, do not start by saying, 'Go into the CONTROL PANEL'. Instead you would start by telling the user the steps to access the control panel (the set of functions that allow you to change settings on a computer).
- *Do not make assumptions*: do not assume that the user you are giving guidance to already knows something. Do not assume that users have already used the hardware or software that they require help with.
- *Avoid technical language*: do not use technical language that is not essential to solving the problem. If technical language is required, keep it minimal and explain terms to the user.
- *Do not be condescending*: you may be asked to support a user with a very simple problem – do not make them feel foolish for asking for help.

Methods for logging faults

A company may use one single method or several different methods for logging faults.

- *In person*: there may be a dedicated helpdesk that users can visit if they have a problem. An IT support technician may be available at this point to deal with the user's query or they may write down instructions for the user to solve the problem on their own. Alternatively, the problem may be logged and dealt with at a later time.

- *By phone*: there may be an internal telephone system for the user to reach the IT support helpdesk or an IT support technician directly.
- *By email*: there may be a dedicated email address that can be used. The email may be picked up by a general assistant and forwarded on to the correct support technician who will then deal with the problem.
- *By post*: there may be an address that users can write to with details of their problem. Users may include a telephone number or their address so that you can contact them to help with their problem.

When you log a fault, you will record the details in a fault-logging system so that the job can be monitored.

A3 Processes and procedures used by IT support technicians

There are various processes and procedures available to IT support technicians to help them support users.

Compliance with service-level agreements

If a service that is being accessed fails, the SLA should guarantee the support that will be in place or the amount of time it will take to get the service up and running again. For example, an SLA may state that minor problems will be fixed within two hours and major problems will be fixed within two days. It is therefore important that you try to stick to this and that faults that are covered by an SLA are prioritised.

Prioritising incidents and service requests

Although faults that fall under an SLA should be given priority, all faults, including those that fall outside the agreement, need to be given priority, especially if there are multiple faults or requests to deal with.

Figure 4.4 shows the factors that you may consider when prioritising a fault or service request.

In B3 'Being able to prioritise jobs', you will find further information about prioritising incidents and service requests.

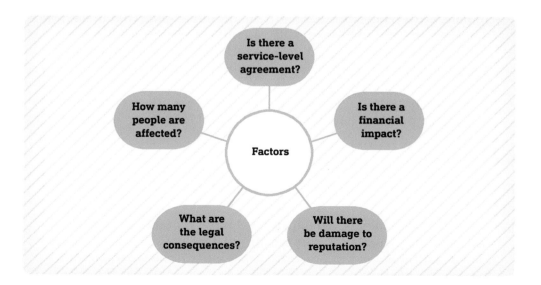

Figure 4.4: Considering the relevant factors will help you prioritise a fault or service request

Validating and assessing incidents and service requests

Before you start to fix a fault or allocate it to a different support technician, it must first be assessed to ensure that the fault is handled by the right person or the right department. Before handing over a fault, the following may be considered.

- *Which department is responsible?* The IT support team may be split into several different teams. One team may deal with giving advice, while another team may deal with fixing hardware faults.
- *Is the fault covered by a warranty?* Before you attempt to fix a fault or order a replacement part, you would consider if the equipment that contains the fault is covered by a **WARRANTY**. Most electronic equipment comes with at least a year's warranty, which means that if there are any faults with the equipment, the manufacturer will fix the faulty equipment and cover the costs. Some organisations pay extra money to extend the length of the warranty.
- *Is the fault covered by insurance?* If the equipment has broken due to an accident, then it may be covered by the organisation's insurance. For example, if there were a flood or a fire, then it could be covered under the company's contents insurance.

Ensuring continuity in service for IT users

Users should be able to access their IT facilities at all times, with the amount of disruption kept to a minimum. You can achieve this in a number of ways.

- *Setting equipment up correctly*: if the equipment has been set up correctly, then it should function correctly. It is important that you always read the instructions that come with new equipment.
- *Regular testing*: you should test new equipment to ensure it works correctly and you should then test it at regular intervals. To reduce the disruption, the equipment can be tested overnight or at a time when the user does not want to use the computer network.
- *Regular servicing*: you should service equipment regularly. Even if equipment is working correctly and not producing any faults, it is still important that it is maintained. This will reduce the chances of problems occurring that can disrupt the users.
- *Sandbox testing*: any new software or software updates should be tested first before being installed on a computer network. **SANDBOX TESTING** can be used to test new software or updates in a small confined area. This means that new software and updates can be tested without impacting on the whole computer network. If there is a problem with the new software or update, then there is no impact because it has not been formally installed. This will reduce the disruption to users if new software or updates do not work correctly.

Maintaining service management/ticketing and reporting systems

There are many stages you may go through when fixing a particular fault. These include:

- an initial assessment of the fault
- a visit to the location where the fault exists
- waiting for new parts to be delivered
- fixing the fault and putting the equipment back in service
- ensuring that fault logs are updated accurately.

The network manager may want to see an overview of all faults, including the stage they have reached. There are many pieces of software available, including service management, and ticketing and reporting systems, that allow faults to be managed. This software will allow the network manager to:

- see an overview of all faults
- receive automatic notifications if faults are close to time limits as stated in the SLA so they can be prioritised
- see what faults technicians are currently working on.

It is therefore important that you maintain the status of this software to ensure the network manager can see an accurate reflection at all times. A user may also call, email or visit the IT support department and want an update on the status of the fault. Therefore it is important to keep this system up to date so that the user can be given accurate details.

Escalating problems to different lines of support

After the problem has been logged, it will then be passed on to someone within the IT support team to handle. A problem may escalate upwards between each group of people until it is solved, as shown in Figure 4.5.

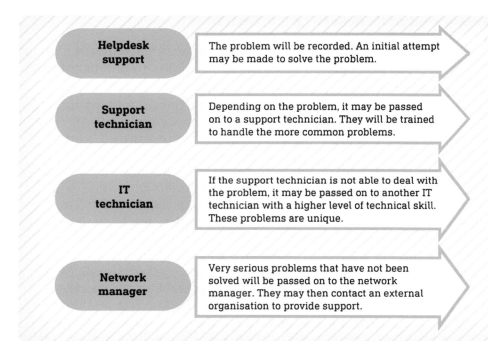

Helpdesk support — The problem will be recorded. An initial attempt may be made to solve the problem.

Support technician — Depending on the problem, it may be passed on to a support technician. They will be trained to handle the more common problems.

IT technician — If the support technician is not able to deal with the problem, it may be passed on to another IT technician with a higher level of technical skill. These problems are unique.

Network manager — Very serious problems that have not been solved will be passed on to the network manager. They may then contact an external organisation to provide support.

Figure 4.5: You may need to escalate a problem in order to resolve it

Complying with relevant legislation, regulations and external standards

Legislation and regulations

As an IT support technician, you must ensure that the organisation and all users of the computer network are following the correct legislation and regulations. You need to consider the following laws and regulations.

- *Data Protection Act 1998*: under this law, any stored personal data about individuals needs to be kept secure. You need to ensure that correct hardware and software is in place so that personal data cannot be accidentally or deliberately accessed. This can include making certain that **USERNAMES** and passwords have been set up and that a firewall is in place to stop people hacking into the computer network. This could also include checking that there is a lock on the door of the server room where personal data is stored.

- *Waste Electrical and Electronic Equipment Recycling (WEEE) 2013*: under this regulation, old equipment that is no longer required needs to be disposed of in a safe way. The regulation promotes the recycling of old equipment such as extracting the precious metals that can be used in new devices. Therefore when you need to dispose of old equipment, you should take the equipment to a site that will dispose of the equipment safely. Some companies will collect old equipment from you and will sometimes give you a certificate to confirm that it has been recycled and that all personal data has been destroyed.

- *Computer Misuse Act 1990*: under this law, it is illegal to use a computer system to carry out crimes. Therefore you need to ensure that the right practices are in place and that users are aware of their duties. This can be achieved by asking all network users to sign an **ACCEPTABLE USE POLICY (AUP)**, which states what users can and cannot do. For example it could include the following.
  1 You are not allowed to access data that you are not authorised to use.
  2 You are not allowed to access another user's account.
  3 You are not allowed to transfer a virus.

You could also use monitoring software to ensure that users are not breaking this law. You can monitor firewall and **ANTI-VIRUS SOFTWARE** reports to check whether users have been trying to access data they are not authorised to or attempting to spread a virus.

Link it up

Refer back to Unit 3 for more information on legal requirements, including the principles and the impact of the Data Protection Act 1998 and the definition and impact of the Computer Misuse Act 1990. Dumpster diving and its impacts if equipment is not disposed of safely are also covered here – all important areas to keep in mind if the company is to avoid breaking the law.

External standards

Standards allow hardware and software to work together and therefore you need to ensure you are using the right standards to allow hardware and software to communicate internally and externally.

- Natural standards that have occurred over time: this could be caused by one particular company that has played a big part in the industry and their hardware or software has become the set way of doing a task. Examples include:
  1 use of QWERTY keyboards
  2 use of Microsoft Office® for written documents.
- Standards that are set by governing bodies: a group of agencies have got together to agree a set way of doing something. Examples include:
  1 Wireless 801.11n
  2 TCP/IP Internet Protocol.

If you are not following external standards, then it may cause problems if users access the network from home as their computer at home may use different standards from the computers within the organisation. Users may also work on documents at home and then transfer them via a memory stick to the organisation and may not be able to open their documents in the workplace if the standards are different.

A4 IT support technician tasks

The IT support technician role can be diverse – the following section looks at the different tasks you might be expected to perform.

Recording details of faults

It is very important when you are logging details of any faults that the right amount of information is gathered. If not enough information is gathered about the problem, then it could increase how much time it takes to solve.

The information that you should record includes:
- the name of the user who is reporting the fault
- the room number or location where the fault exists
- the name of the device that contains a hardware or software fault
- details of the problem.

A2 'Methods for logging faults' gives more information about recording and logging details of faults.

Logging and recording requests

Figure 4.6 shows an example fault log. The details that will be logged will depend on the organisation and the size of the IT support team.

Fault ID	Location of fault	Device name/ID	Details of fault/request	Allocated technician	Work carried out	Priority
1	Room 1	Colour printer	The printer keeps getting jammed when attempting to print and an error message saying 'please clear jam' keeps appearing on printer screen.	Alan Green	Printer rollers have been replaced. Tested and working correctly on 3 June 2017.	Job completed
2	Room 3	Computer 6	Operating system is not loading. A message saying 'looking for operating system' appears and the computer freezes.	Vicky Jones	A new hard drive has been ordered and is due for delivery on 4 June 2017 before 2.00 p.m.	High priority Waiting for parts
3	N/A	N/A	Paul Foster has left the company and his account needs to be deactivated.	Pam Gibson	Account has been deactivated and data has been deleted.	Job completed

Figure 4.6: The details recorded in a fault log will vary from one organisation to another

Identifying issues with hardware and software

When a fault is identified, you will need to use all available information from the different parts of a computer system. On their own the different parts may not mean anything; however, when they are put together you may be able to work out the problem.

When fixing a fault, you should consider a number of issues.

- *Is the hardware non-functioning?* If so, this could indicate a possible power problem or a faulty component.
- *Are error messages showing?* This could give an **ERROR CODE**, a reference number for the type of problem that allows you to look it up.
- *Are there speed/performance issues?* This could possibly suggest the hardware is under stress or could indicate possible overheating of hardware components.
- *Are there compatibility issues?* Hardware and software may not be using the same standards to allow them to work together.

Resolving issues and incidents within the service-level agreement

When fixing a fault, it is vital that the time taken to respond, assess and fix the fault is within the agreed time stated in the SLA. However, there are some situations when SLAs cannot be met. This may include events that go beyond the control of the service provider such as a service being interrupted due to bad weather.

What if...?

A service-level agreement will usually contain a penalties section that states how service users will be compensated if the contract is not met. Therefore if you are not able to fix a problem within the time stated in the service-level agreement, then the service user may be able to claim compensation for the money they have lost during the lack of service. You may also lose your payment bonus for not meeting deadlines.

Imagine you are working in a school as an IT support technician. Staff and students are unable to access the school intranet. You have been assigned this fault to fix. However, you are not able to fix the fault within the service-level agreement time.

Consider the following questions.

1 What might be the consequences for you if you do not fix the fault on time?

2 What might be the consequences for staff and students if you do not fix the fault?

3 Who might you have to justify your reasons to?

4 Can you think of genuine reasons why the fault may not have been fixed on time?

Setting up new users and user passwords

As a technician, you may be asked to set up new users when they join the organisation. Often this will involve setting up a new username and a password for the user. If the users are temporary and only involved with the organisation for a limited amount of time, you may give them a temporary username and password. Permanent users may also be given a temporary username and password until you have set up their own username and password.

Providing advice and guidance

As well as assessing and fixing faults, you may get a request from a user who wants some advice or guidance. Users will all have different levels of IT knowledge and different experiences with using different computers and software packages. Therefore you will need to be flexible and able to deal with lots of different requests.

A user may need help with the following.

- *How to use a system*, for example they may want guidance on how to access and use:
  - the staff shared drive
  - their personal emails
  - their personal documents.
- *How to use a piece of* **APPLICATION SOFTWARE**, for example they may want advice on:
  - what is the best application software to use for a particular task. (Application software is software that can be used to carry out a task or to produce products such as documents and presentations)
  - how to transfer data from one piece of application software to another.
- *How to use a specific tool*, for example they may want guidance on how to:
  - arrange text a particular way in word-processing software
  - create a bar/line chart in spreadsheet software
  - send a group email in email software.

Monitoring traffic and data usage

As an IT support technician, you will need to monitor the activities that occur on the network. By effectively monitoring the **TRAFFIC** and data usage on the network, you may be able to spot problems before they occur and then put steps in place to reduce the impact they have.

Monitoring traffic
- The amount of time it takes for users to log in could be monitored. If this is slow at particular times of the day, then you may need to set up an additional login server.
- The websites that users visit should be monitored. If a lot of users are trying to access the same website that is blocked, then you may want to look at the website and check if it is safe to unblock.
- The number of attempts it takes users to enter their password should be monitored. If a lot of users are routinely making many attempts to enter their password, it could potentially indicate that someone is trying to gain unauthorised access to a network.
- User patterns should be monitored. For example, a user may log in around 8.30 a.m. and logout at approximately 5.30 p.m. every day. However, if that user logged in at 2.30 a.m., then this could potentially be a sign that a hacker is trying to access the network.

Monitoring data usage

- The amount of STORAGE SPACE on the STORAGE SERVER (the space available centrally that will be used to store all data that is used by everyone on a network) should be monitored. If the amount of storage space is close to being used up, then you may need to buy additional storage space or clear existing storage space.
- The internet BANDWIDTH should be monitored. If the bandwidth is low, then it could indicate a possible attack on the company from outside the organisation or it could indicate a problem with the internet connection and the INTERNET SERVICE PROVIDER (ISP) (the company that provides the internet to organisations and individuals) may need to be contacted.

Identifying issues arising from monitoring progress and completion of service operations tasks

When a fault or service request has been made, it should be monitored to ensure that deadlines are met. If an incident is given a high priority, it should be checked continually until the issue is solved.

If an incident has been given a low priority, it is still important to check this regularly. This is because the priority of a fault can change during the fault-fixing process. For example, a fault could start as a low priority but then if the time limit that is taken to fix the fault gets close to the time limit agreed in the SLA, the same fault could be given a high priority.

Skills and knowledge check

- ☐ Can you describe what is meant by the term 'service-level agreement' and explain why it is important?
- ☐ Can you describe what is meant by the term 'levels of IT support' and explain why faults may be given to different lines of IT support?
- ☐ Can you list the different requests an IT support technician may receive?
- ☐ Can you list the tasks that an IT support technician may carry out?
- ☐ Can you list the processes and procedures used by an IT support technician?
- ☐ Can you describe the different legislation, regulations and external standards that must be followed by an IT support technician?
- ☐ Can you describe different ways of logging faults from a user?

- ◯ I can take different factors into account and prioritise service requests.
- ◯ I can make recommendations on how an organisation can improve its IT system processes and procedures.

B Carry out IT support technician tasks using a range of skills

Practise

Imagine you work on a helpdesk that provides help and support to other users who are experiencing computer problems. As part of your role you are required to log these problems.

- Make a list of the top ten problems that you think people may ask for support with.
- Make a list of five problems that you think fewer people will need support with.

B1 Using fault diagnosis and logging procedures

When a user has a fault that needs to be addressed, you must make use of fault diagnostics to find the problem. When you are trying to diagnose a fault, it is important that you use the correct method.

Not using the correct **FAULT-DIAGNOSTIC PROCESS** (the staged process that is used to find out the fault with hardware or software so a solution can be found) can result in the following problems.

- *Misinterpreting the fault*: if the fault is misdiagnosed, this can lead to the actual fault that has been reported not being fixed. If parts need to be ordered, it could mean that incorrect parts are ordered that will not actually solve the problem.
- *Increasing the time it takes to fix the fault*: not fixing the actual problem to start with could mean further fault-finding assessments may be needed, increasing the amount of time it takes to fix the fault. This would cause more disruption in an organisation.

Using the correct fault-diagnostic process

There are many different ways to assess a fault. Sometimes the solution to a fault may be obvious and other times you may need to use your problem-solving skills to come up with a solution.

Examples of the methods that you could use to assess a fault or problem are shown in Figures 4.7 and 4.8.

- *Error codes*: some faults may produce an error code (see Figure 4.7). While the error code itself will not give you a solution, you can use it to see what the problem is. If you contact the manufacturer and give them the error code, they may be able to diagnose the fault for you. Often you can search for this error code on the internet to find the solution. You can also post the error code in **ONLINE FORUMS**, internet sites where you can exchange information and ideas and get advice from other experts.

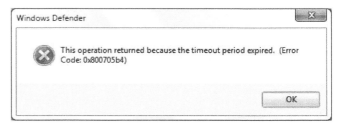

Figure 4.7: Example of an error code

- *Automated troubleshooting*: there are many troubleshooting tools that you can use to automatically locate the fault. The most common ones are used to find a fault with a printer (see Figure 4.8) or internet connection. If they are not able to diagnose the fault, they will attempt to search online **DATABASES** to check if other people have had the same problem.

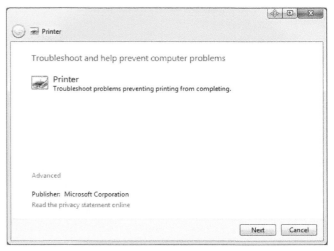

Figure 4.8: Example of automated troubleshooting

- *Manual troubleshooting*: you can read the **MANUAL** (the guide documentation that comes with the equipment when it is first bought). Often this will contain a troubleshooting section that will tell you how to solve the most common problems. If not, it may give you the manufacturer's contact details so you can get in touch with them for help.
- *Expert systems/program help tools*: many software packages have their own built-in help facilities. These are usually based on menus that will ask you various questions and, depending on your answer, they will respond with another question until they reach a recommendation. More advanced expert systems allow you to type in your problem and will detect certain key words in your answer.
- *Visual check*: sometimes a quick visual check will tell you what the problem is. For example, a visual check could tell you if unplugged cables are causing the fault.
- *On-board diagnostics/Stress testing*: some computer systems have **ON-BOARD DIAGNOSTIC SOFTWARE** that will detect faults. This software will test each individual component and then generate a report about the working status of each one. You could then look more closely at the components that have failed during the diagnostics tests.

Recording detailed incidents and service requests accurately

When you respond to a fault, you may need to visit the location of the fault. You therefore need to plan accurately to ensure you have everything you need to fix it. You will need to think about:

- whether you or another support technician have the right skill level to fix the fault
- what tools you will need to fix the fault
- the time and date to fix the fault in order to cause the least disruption
- whether replacement parts will be needed.

It is very important to record faults accurately and in as much detail as possible. This will allow you or other support technicians to plan effectively, reducing the amount of time it takes to deal with a problem.

Using ticketing systems

A **TICKETING SYSTEM** is a piece of software that can help you record and monitor the progress of fixing problems. There are many different types of ticketing system. The process of a ticketing system is shown in Figure 4.9, and Figure 4.10 provides an example of ticketing-system software.

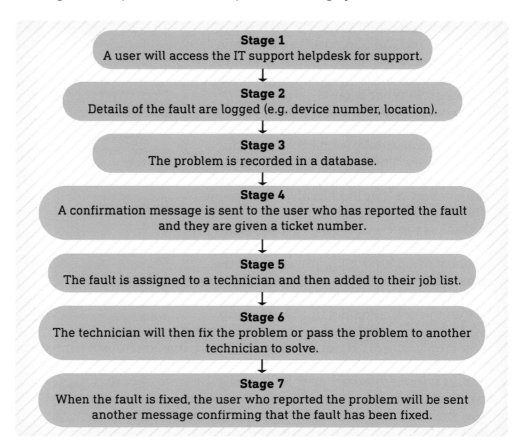

Stage 1
A user will access the IT support helpdesk for support.
↓
Stage 2
Details of the fault are logged (e.g. device number, location).
↓
Stage 3
The problem is recorded in a database.
↓
Stage 4
A confirmation message is sent to the user who has reported the fault and they are given a ticket number.
↓
Stage 5
The fault is assigned to a technician and then added to their job list.
↓
Stage 6
The technician will then fix the problem or pass the problem to another technician to solve.
↓
Stage 7
When the fault is fixed, the user who reported the problem will be sent another message confirming that the fault has been fixed.

Figure 4.9: A ticketing system process – what strengths of this process can you identify?

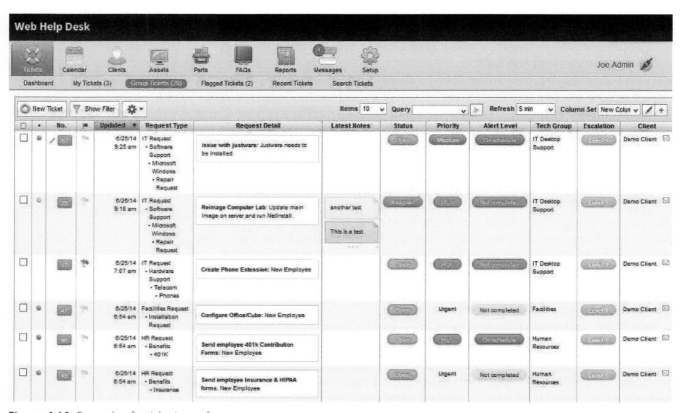

Figure 4.10: Example of a ticketing software screen

Communicating with clients

When a fault has been reported, it is important that the user who has reported the fault is given accurate information.

- *What the fault is*: by knowing what the fault is, if it happens again in the future, users will be able to go directly to the right team, which will speed up the process.
- *When the fault is likely to be fixed*: users may want to know when the fault is going to be fixed in case they need to let others know, including customers.
- *What caused the fault*: this is very important because the fault could have happened due to faulty or ageing equipment, but it could have also been caused by the user's actions. If the user knows what caused the fault, then they will be more aware in the future and put steps in place to try to stop the same fault occurring again.

Use of formal reporting

There are different methods of formal reporting.

- *Diagnostic sheets*: DIAGNOSTIC SHEETS will contain a list of initial questions/tests that can be carried out to see what the fault may be. This may include running tests on the hard drive or the computer's memory. They will allow you to identify a rough idea of what the fault could be so you can assess if you have the right skill level to fix the fault or pass it on to another support technician.
- *Ticketing systems/logging templates*: these will allow you to record the details of a fault. The features will usually:
  - allow you to enter details of a fault
  - give the fault a status (for example, Assigned, Not Assigned)
  - give the fault a priority (for example, Low, Medium, High)
  - give the fault a completion status (for example, Completed, Not Completed, Pending)
  - allow you to enter details of work that you carried out.

Reporting methods can either be paper based or electronic. The method that is used will depend on the organisation. Electronic methods may be preferred as these will:

- make it easier for the network manager to monitor the progress of all faults across all IT support technicians
- allow you and other support technicians to share ideas about faults more easily
- allow the user who has reported the fault to see up-to-date information at all times.

Link it up

Refer back to Unit 3 for more information about the different login procedures, including usernames, passwords, the rules for password security and the best practice for password strength. It is important that you enforce these rules to ensure that all users on the network create effective passwords.

B2 Resolving technical problems

As an IT support technician, you may be required to assess and fix a variety of problems.

Basic problems

Below are some of the basic problems you might come across.

Customisation

- *Changing default settings*: this may be done for many reasons, including personal preference or because the user has a particular disability or impairment such as an eyesight or hearing problem. Possible default settings that may be changed include:
  - changing icon/menu font sizes (see Figure 4.11)
  - adjusting the screen resolution
  - changing the cursor speed
  - changing system sounds.

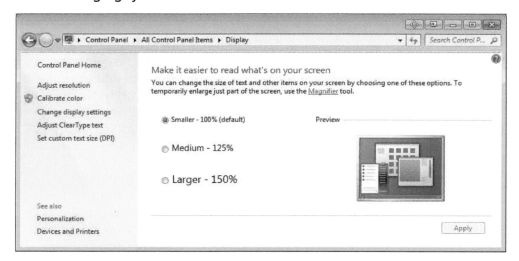

Figure 4.11: Why might you need to change the size of text and other items in the control panel?

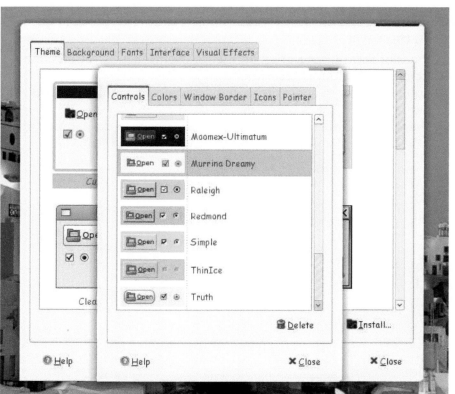

Figure 4.12: Changing desktop themes

- *Customising templates*: organisations use templates to allow several different users to work on the same document at the same time. This allows the document to be put together more easily. However, a user may want the template to be customised such as:
  - placing the items in a different position such as the logo
  - changing the font style and size
  - changing the page orientation
  - changing the page margins.

Configuration

- *Setting up new users*: when new employees join an organisation they need to be set up on the network so that they can access the network facilities. This may include:
  - setting up a username that will uniquely identify the user on the network
  - assigning the user a temporary password, which will usually be changed by the user when they log onto the network for the first time
  - assigning access rights to set which files and folders the user will be able to read, delete or edit
  - setting up an email address so the user can send messages both internally and externally
  - specifying whether the user is allowed to access their files and folders remotely from another location.
- *Password management*: passwords are one of the main security mechanisms on a computer network and this has to be managed centrally. A support technician will need to:
  - change a user's password if they have forgotten their password
  - reset a password if a user has entered their password incorrectly too many times
  - decide the complexity of user passwords across the network
  - decide how many attempts users should be given to enter their passwords.

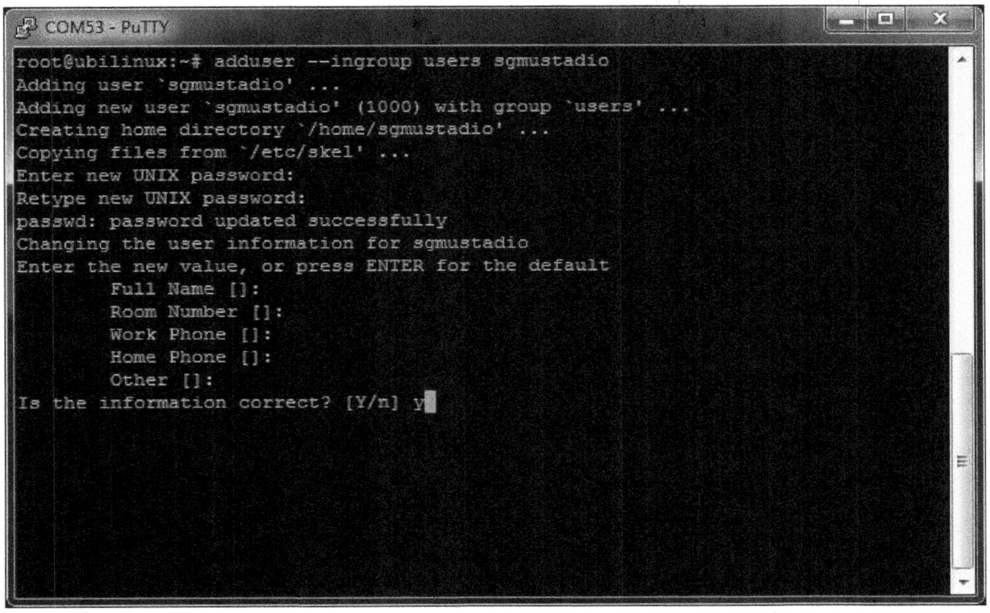

```
COM53 - PuTTY
root@ubilinux:~# adduser --ingroup users sgmustadio
Adding user `sgmustadio' ...
Adding new user `sgmustadio' (1000) with group `users' ...
Creating home directory `/home/sgmustadio' ...
Copying files from `/etc/skel' ...
Enter new UNIX password:
Retype new UNIX password:
passwd: password updated successfully
Changing the user information for sgmustadio
Enter the new value, or press ENTER for the default
        Full Name []:
        Room Number []:
        Work Phone []:
        Home Phone []:
        Other []:
Is the information correct? [Y/n] y
```

Figure 4.13: Setting up a new user and setting the password

Installation

- *Installing operating systems*: the operating system (OS) is the main piece of software installed on the computer and it allows you to interact with the hardware and other software installed. It is one of the most essential pieces of software needed in order to use the hardware. Computer systems generally come with an operating system already installed. However, an operating system may need to be reinstalled if the:
  - hard drive has been replaced and therefore requires the OS to be installed again
  - user wants to format their hard drive either because they want to pass the computer on to another user or they want to remove all the data from the hard drive
  - OS that is installed on the computer does not match the OS installed on other computers in the network.

Figure 4.14: Installing a Linux® operating system

- *Installing application software*: application software will need to be installed to allow users to complete tasks. Application software can either be general software or specific to the company. Examples include word processing, spreadsheet and presentation software. Application software will come with an installation wizard, a step-by-step set of instructions that will guide you through the process. The wizard will usually allow you to select the tools and features that you want to install.
- *Network connectivity*: additional software may need to be installed that will allow users on a network to use shared devices such as a printer or scanner. This software will allow these devices to function as well as handle requests from multiple users.

Complex problems

As an IT support technician, you may be required to assess and fix more complex problems that require more technical knowledge. Below are some of the complex problems you may come across.

Hardware, software and network faults

- *Loss of service*: a service that is run on the network may either not be performing as it should or not performing at all. Some services can have a big impact on the organisation if they stop the organisation from operating with its customers. Examples of **LOSS OF SERVICE** that you may have to deal with include:
  - ○ loss of internet connection
  - ○ users not being able to log on to the network
  - ○ users not being able to access their email services
  - ○ users not being able to access their personal or shared documents.
- *Hardware repair and replacement*: in order to fix a fault, you may need to replace hardware. This may be a **PERIPHERAL DEVICE**, which is any device that connects to, and works with, a computer to provide some form of additional functionality, such as a mouse or a keyboard, or it could be an internal component such as a hard drive or memory. After hardware has been replaced, it may require software to be installed so that it can be recognised by the operating system.

In order to fix a fault, you may need to replace an internal component, such as RAM

- *Recovery of lost data*: an organisation should always back up its data to another **STORAGE DEVICE**. This means that if the original data becomes unavailable, then you could restore its data from the backup. How often the data is backed up will depend on the organisation.

Sometimes you may install new software, change system settings or carry out a software update. However, these changes could create problems and therefore you may want to recover system and software settings. Windows System Restore (see Figure 4.15) will restore your computer to an earlier restore point as long as this software has been set up previously. You could therefore restore your system back to an earlier time before a particular problem occurred. This, however, will not restore files such as documents, pictures, music or videos. These types of files need to be backed up separately.

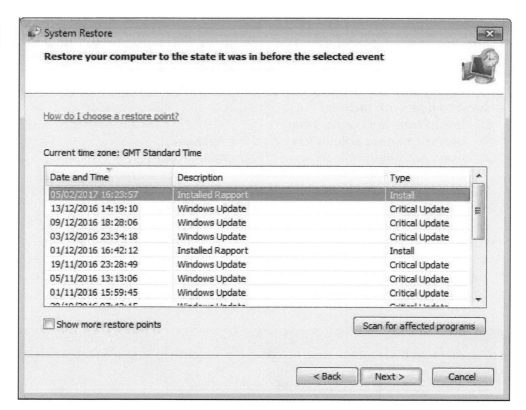

Figure 4.15: Restoring back to an earlier restore point in Windows System Restore

Installation of network services

- *Server software*: software may need to be installed on the server. This software could be used to ensure better management of the computers that it is connected to or it could be software that needs to be installed on all computers within the network, including security software such as firewalls and anti-virus software.
- *Shared resources*: in a network, the server will have overall control of a network. It will handle requests from all users and then respond with their request. You may be required to install additional software to allow users to use a new shared resource. This includes:
  - shared file access
  - shared printer or scanner access.
- *Allocating access rights for new services*: you may be responsible for ensuring that the users on the network have access to the data that they need. Therefore, ACCESS RIGHTS (the different permissions that are given to different users or groups of users on a computer network) can be set up to restrict the access that users have to files and folders. Common access rights include the following examples.
  1. *Read*: this will allow the users to access and read data such as documents. This does not allow any changes to be made.
  2. *Edit*: this allows users to access the data and make changes to it.
  3. *Write*: this allows the user to create new files and folders.
  4. *Delete*: this allows the users to delete any data.
- *Remote desktop software*: this will allow you to fix a problem with a faulty computer using a working computer on the same network. For example, you may receive a phone call from a user and you may be able to use REMOTE DESKTOP SOFTWARE to control their computer and fix the fault without having to visit the location.
- *Operating systems*: B2 'Installation' outlined reasons why an OS may need to be reinstalled. As well as installing operating systems on user computers, you may also need to install server operating systems on the server to manage USER ACCOUNTS on the network. User accounts are specific accounts given to individuals in an organisation so that they can log on to a network.

Using appropriate information sources to diagnose problems

Diagnosis tools

- *Control panel*: the control panel is part of Microsoft Windows. It allows you to view and make changes to basic system settings on your computer. This will allow you to do things such as:
  - change power settings
  - install new software
  - add new hardware devices
  - change the mouse and the keyboard settings
  - change the language settings.
- It also contains some basic diagnostic tools that will allow you to locate:
  - program problems
  - hardware problems
  - networking and internet problems
  - appearance and personalisation problems
  - system security problems.
- **REMOTE DIAGNOSIS TOOLS**: these allow you to monitor a computer system away from where the hardware or software is actually located. You can be sent automatic alerts if a piece of hardware or software is not performing as it should. For example, you could monitor the following aspects remotely.
  - *Bandwidth*: if the bandwidth speed starts to drop, this could indicate a connection problem that could turn into a bigger problem.
  - *Storage capacity*: if storage capacity is running low, you can buy more storage before the storage capacity runs out.

Other information sources

- *Manuals*: these are guides that come with new hardware or software containing instructions about how to operate it. They will often have a troubleshooting section that contains information about how to solve common problems. They will also have information about how to access support from the manufacturer, including a website address that may give more information or a telephone number or email address for you to get in touch with them.
- *Previous fault logs*: if the fault has happened before, then the solution to the fault will probably have been recorded in a **PREVIOUS FAULT LOG** (a list of faults that users of a computer network have reported in the past). By looking at previous fault logs, you can start by using a solution that worked last time before trying alternatives. If this works, this could save a lot of time.
- *Online support tools*: there are many online forums that will allow you to post a question on which other people can comment or provide answers. You can post technical details such as error codes, error messages or even photographs. Experts can then read the post and provide possible solutions to the problem.

Keeping to service-level agreements

When fixing a fault, it is vital that the amount of time taken is within the SLA. Often this will be monitored by the network manager, who may prioritise faults that are close to the time limits set within the SLA. If a fault is not fixed within the SLA time limit, then they may need to justify the reasons for this to the managers of an organisation.

Keeping customers updated

It is important that customers are kept updated at all times when fixing the fault. Customers need to be told:

- which stage the fault is at (assessment stage, waiting for parts to be delivered etc.)
- an estimated date and time of when the fault will be fixed.

The customer should also be told as soon as possible if these details change. Customers can be updated in the following ways.

- *The telephone*: if the customer is not available for a conversation, a voicemail can be left updating them on the progress of the fault.
- *Email*: written information such as an email can be sent to the customer containing the progress of the fault.
- *In person*: if the fault is internal, then a message can be given in person. Depending on the situation, it may also be appropriate to send confirmation of what was discussed via email.

B3 Skills and behaviours required when working as an IT service technician

Prioritising jobs

If you have to deal with multiple incidents or service requests at the same time, they need to be prioritised and dealt with in order. Apart from the SLA, incidents or service requests need to be given priority depending on the following.

- *Financial impact*: incidents that stop an organisation from providing a service or selling products to customers would result in financial loss and would therefore be given priority.
- *Damage to reputation*: if the fault would have an impact on customers accessing a service externally, then this may be given priority. If the fault has only occurred once, then the company reputation would be unlikely to change; however, if the fault happens several times, then this could impact on the company reputation and a loss in customers.
- *Legal consequences*: there are various computer-related laws that organisations must follow and failure to do so can result in a fine being issued. For example, the Data Protection Act 1998 states that personal data must be kept safe. Therefore if a firewall stops working correctly, this could mean that personal data can be hacked into and therefore should be fixed as soon as possible.
- *Number of people affected*: the more people that are affected by the incident, the more priority it will usually get. For example, a printer that is malfunctioning may affect a small group of people but no internet connection may affect a lot of people and therefore this would be given priority.

Being able to prioritise jobs is vital in ensuring that jobs are completed on time. However, you will also need to consider when you are going to fix faults. For example:

- it may only be possible to fix some faults at particular times of the day when equipment is not being used by anyone. Some faults may need to be fixed before an organisation opens in the morning or when users go home in the evening
- if you know that the start of the day is when most users will place a service request or report a fault, then this may not be the best time to fix major faults.

Accuracy in logging and reporting issues/faults

Accurate logs are especially important if faults are being passed over to other lines of support. They are also important because they could be accessed again in the future to deal with similar faults. The following details will need to be recorded accurately.

- *The date and time that work was carried out on a fault*: this could allow technicians to see if faults are occurring at particular times or days of the week.
- *Details of the work carried out*: this is useful because if the fault was fixed, a technician could look back at the logs in the future and use the same solution to fix a similar fault. However, if the fault is not fixed, this information is still useful because you can check what solutions a previous technician attempted so that you are not wasting time by repeating the same tasks.
- *Details about further work that needs to be carried out*: one support technician may have started to fix a fault on one day but then may be off work on the following day and therefore it could be passed on to another team member. The first IT support technician may have assessed a fault and then ordered replacement parts, and the replacements parts may be fitted by you. Keeping details of the work that still needs to be done allows you and other IT support technicians to pass jobs on to each other more easily.
- *The name of the technician who carried out the work*: this information is needed because you may need to contact a technician who has already worked on a fault.

Time management

- As a support technician, you will be expected to manage your time efficiently. Your network manager may give you a list of faults to fix and you will be expected to use your time effectively to ensure that they are all fixed within a certain amount of time.
- If you think that parts need to be ordered so a fault can be fixed, then this fault should be looked at first so that you can order the parts required. This will allow you to continue to complete other jobs while you are waiting for replacement parts. You also need to ensure that you give yourself enough time to update fault logs or ticketing software.

Communicating with others

When you are fixing a fault, you may need to communicate with many different people.

- *Internal colleagues*: this could include your line manager such as the network manager or another technician. You may be required to provide an update on a particular fault to the network manager or you may be passing a fault on to another technician to deal with.
- *End-user*: you may need to take details from the END-USER (the person who is using the hardware or software on a computer) who is reporting the fault or service request or they may request an update as to the progress of a fault or service request.
- *External stakeholders*:
  - manufacturers – in some cases, you may need to communicate with the manufacturers of the equipment. You may need advice from the manufacturer or you may inform them of faulty equipment that is still covered by a warranty

○ service providers – you may need to speak to external service providers such as internet service providers or cloud storage providers to report a fault or performance problem for them to fix

○ suppliers – you may need to order new parts in order to fix a fault and therefore need to communicate with suppliers that have the parts you require.

Remaining calm and supportive

While fixing a fault, it is essential that you are able to work well under pressure. You could be put under pressure particularly if:

- lots of users or customers are relying on the fault being fixed
- users or customers are demanding and putting increased pressure on you
- the organisation is losing money while the fault is not fixed
- the amount of time that it is taking to fix the fault is close to the amount of time stated in the SLA
- other IT support technicians have attempted to fix the fault but not managed to find a solution.

Therefore it is very important to stay calm during stressful situations. This will allow you to:

- think more clearly so that you are more likely to think of a solution
- create a positive environment for yourself and others around you
- communicate more clearly with others who may be supporting you while you fix the fault.

Supporting team members

Complex problems may require more than one IT support technician to work together to find a solution. When working on a fault, you may already have the technical knowledge you need or you may have experienced the fault before and therefore you can share your knowledge with other support technicians.

Skills and knowledge check

☐ Can you describe the different methods that can be used to diagnose faults with a computer system?

☐ Can you describe what is meant by the term 'ticketing software' and how it can be used to monitor the progress of faults?

☐ Can you identify information sources that could be used to help you fix a fault?

◯ I can communicate with others effectively and provide them with accurate information about a fault.

◯ I can work well in a team, support other team members and share my knowledge and ideas.

◯ I can resolve a range of basic and complex technical problems on my own and know when I may need additional support.

◯ I can show initiative when diagnosing and resolving faults.

◯ I can manage my time and prioritise tasks to complete them on time.

◯ I can remain calm and focused when under pressure to fix technical faults.

C Report on the work carried out as IT support technician, reviewing own practice

Practise

Think of two problems you have experienced with an IT device and two problems you have experienced with a piece of software you have used.

- Did you manage to diagnose the fault on your own? What strategies did you use?

- Did you need to ask for help from another person?

- How do you know when you could solve the problem and how did you know when you needed help from another person?

C1 Recording findings on common errors and system faults

When you have been working to fix a fault, you should keep a log of all activities that have been carried out.

Logging your activities

You will need to log what actions you have taken, regardless of whether the fault was fixed or not. If the fault was fixed, then the incidents that took place should be logged so that if the fault occurs again, you can look back at previous attempts to resolve the problem. You may be able to solve the same problem again by the same method, which will minimise the amount of time it takes to fix the problem. By doing this over a period of time, you can build up a knowledge base of problems and possible solutions.

Even if the fault was not fixed, it is still important to log the incidents that took place. This is because the fault could be passed on to another line of support or another technician.

Recording data on errors and system faults

The are several details that should be noted when recording faults.

- The username/employee number of the user who is reporting the fault. This will allow you to keep in contact with the user to keep them informed of the fault progress.
- The room number/general location of where the fault exists. This will allow you to know where to find the faulty device.

- The device type/number of the device that contains a hardware or software fault. This will allow you to research any specific information about the device (that is, from the device manuals) before you go to fix the problem. You can also use this information to check whether the faulty device is still in warranty.
- Details of the problem. This will allow you to have a rough idea of what the problem is before you attempt to fix it. You may need to carry out some preparation work before this visit and gather the necessary tools.

Analysing and reporting information

You will need to be able to analyse information. Additional information may need to be analysed when a fault is being fixed. The following are the types of information that you may need to analyse.

- *Error messages*: these are messages that appear on the screen that will tell you what the problem is.
- *Error codes*: these are codes that are generated by the device to show the type of problem. These codes can be looked up in a database to find additional information about the problem and its solution.
- *Sounds*: some computer systems may make sounds to indicate a problem. For example, when you turn your computer on it may make a series of bleeping noises. Note that two bleeping noises could indicate a problem with the computer's memory.
- *Resource monitoring*: this is software that will give you information about a computer system such as the CPU usage, memory usage, disk space usage and network usage. This information could be used to indicate a problem with a particular section of the computer system.

C2 Reviewing information

Reviewing information will enable you to identify common faults and prevent a recurrence of the problem.

Identifying trends or patterns in common faults

If the same fault keeps recurring, you should identify if there are any trends that are also recurring. Consider the following factors.

- *Day/time*: are the faults recurring at the same or a similar time of day or at a particular time of the week?
- *Users*: are the faults that are recurring reported by the same user or by the same group of users? Is there a possibility that they keep accidentally causing the same problem?
- *Technicians*: are the faults that are recurring being fixed by the same technician? Could they be misdiagnosing the problem?

Reviewing methods used

After a fault or service request has been dealt with, you should review the methods used to:

- record the fault or service request
- resolve the fault.

Reviewing these methods could make the way that you deal with future faults or service requests more efficient. When reviewing the methods used, you should consider the following.

- Time allocated:
  - how much time did you first allocate to the incident
  - how much time was actually spent on the incident
  - how could the amount of time spent be decreased?
- Proficiency of the service:
  - how did the initial recording of the fault or service request improve the efficiency of the incident
  - was the incident dealt with within the agreed SLA time
  - which team members have shown effective teamwork that contributed to deadlines being met or excellent end-user feedback
  - which team members caused a delay in meeting the deadlines or poor end-user feedback and how could this be improved in the future?

When reviewing the methods used, you could also ask the end-user for their feedback, using a range of questions.

- How easy was it to log your fault or service request?
- How well did the service desk understand the nature of your problem?
- How satisfied are you with the length of time it took to resolve your issue?
- How effectively were you kept up to date with the progress of your request?
- What are the good things about the service you have experienced?
- How do you think the service could be improved in the future?

Removing the root cause

If a fault keeps recurring, then it is good practice to look at what is causing the problem. You can then remove the **ROOT CAUSE** (the basic cause) of the problem, which may then stop the same fault from recurring. For example if:

- the printer keeps getting a paper jam, then in order to remove the root cause you could change the type of paper or clean the inside of the printer to remove any old bits of paper that may be causing the jam
- the internet bandwidth keeps dropping, then you can possibly remove the root cause by stopping users accessing video and music websites that use up a lot of internet bandwidth
- viruses keep being detected on the network that have come from memory sticks, then you can stop the root cause by setting up a rule to scan all memory sticks before they can be used.

Preventing recurrence of problems

When a fault has been fixed, you may need to recommend ways to stop the same problem from recurring. Consider a range of factors.

- *Staff training*: do users need better training? If so, which users? What areas of training do they require?
- *Better monitoring*: do you need better monitoring in place? If so, what needs to be monitored? Who will carry out this additional monitoring?
- *Additional equipment*: do you need additional hardware or software? If so, what do you need? How will this stop the recurrence of the problem?
- *Removing the root cause*: what was the root cause of the problem? Has this now been removed?
- *Update procedures*: does the acceptable use policy need to be updated? If so, what needs to be updated?

C3 Reviewing your practice

Working in IT support requires a mix of technical and transferable skills. You have to diagnose and resolve technical problems and you also have to be able to prioritise tasks, work well with people and manage your time effectively.

Carrying out a skills audit and identifying areas for improvement

Carrying out a skills audit is a good way to look at the skills you already have and the skills you need to develop. Once you have completed the skills audit, you will then be able to set yourself targets to improve your performance.

Table 4.8 shows an example skills audit that you can use to gain a greater understanding of your technical skills.

Table 4.8: Technical skills audit

Skill	Not confident	Fairly confident	Very confident
Hardware skills			
I am able to clean computer equipment (for example, both external and internal computer parts/components).			
I know the tools that can be used to diagnose a hardware fault.			
I know how to install a peripheral device (for example, keyboard, mouse or digital camera).			
I know how to change basic internal components inside the computer case (for example, hard drive, graphics card).			
I know the safety procedures that I should take *before* I carry out work on a computer system.			
I know the safety procedures that I should take when working on the inside of a computer system			
Software skills			
I know the tools that can be used to diagnose a software fault.			
I know how to change basic default computer settings (for example, icon size, background picture).			
I know how to change complex default computer settings (for example, change anti-virus and firewall settings).			
I know how to set up new usernames and passwords.			
I know how to set up access rights for network users.			
I know how to back up and recover data from a backup.			
I know how to install an operating system.			
I know how to install application software.			

Table 4.9 shows an example skills audit that you can use to check your transferable skills.

Table 4.9: Transferable skills audit

Skills	Not confident	Fairly confident	Very confident
Transferable skills			
I am able to communicate with others effectively (for example, end-users, other internal colleagues and external stakeholders).			
I can accurately record the details of a fault that a user has reported.			
I can work as part of a team, provide advice to others and I am open to taking advice and ideas from others.			
I am able to manage my time efficiently and prioritise tasks to ensure that work is completed on time.			
I am able to keep accurate logs of the work I have carried out.			
I am able to work well under pressure.			

When you have carried out an audit of your technical and transferable skills, you will need to make suggestions for how you can improve them.

Figure 4.16 shows an example improvement plan that you can adapt for your own use.

Figure 4.16: Think about what you would put in your own improvement plan

Target number	Target description	Methods	Deadline
1	Learn more about the tools that can be used to diagnose a hardware fault.	• Research diagnostic tools on the internet. • Speak to others in my team and ask them which one to use. • Speak to my tutor or the IT technicians if I am unsure.	2 May 2017
2	Learn more about the safety measures that could be taken when working on the inside of the computer.	• Research safety measures on the internet. • Always read the instructions when handling equipment I have not used before. • Speak to my tutor if I am not sure about anything.	3 June 2017
3	I would like to work better as part of a team.	• Take up opportunities to work in groups. • Make sure I listen to others. • Be willing to try other people's ideas. • Be open to taking advice from others.	1 July 2017

Skills and knowledge check

- ☐ Can you list the details that should be recorded when logging faults?
- ☐ Can you describe possible trends or patterns that could be looked at if faults keep recurring?
- ☐ Can you describe different factors that should be considered when trying to prevent a problem from recurring?

- ○ I can keep logs that give details about the activities that I have carried out in order to fix a fault.
- ○ I can review the methods that I have used to fix a fault and describe how these can be improved further.
- ○ I can carry out a skills audit and set targets for how my skills can be improved.

Ready for assessment

For your assessment, you may be asked to work in the context of an IT support team in a medium-sized company. You may be asked to produce a report in which you will need to outline:

- the types of service support the team provide and the service-level agreements
- the processes and procedures that the support team use
- the common tasks the team carry out
- how the processes and procedures used can be improved.

You may be observed carrying out IT support activities such as:

- using a ticketing system to log incidents and service requests
- filling in documentation to track requests
- resolving any reported faults/requests
- escalating faults when appropriate to another member of your team
- communicating with end-users and team members.

You will produce a review of your work, reflecting on the feedback given, your own performance and the technical and transferable skills that you developed while providing IT support, and highlighting the skills that you need to develop further.

WORK FOCUS

HANDS ON

Imagine you are working in an office as an IT support technician.

You are based on the ground floor. You have received a phone call from another employee called Alison who works on the tenth floor. She is trying to insert an image into a company report using word-processing software.

You have tried to help Alison but she has limited understanding of what you are saying and she is not able to carry out your recommendations by herself. As a result of this she becomes increasingly frustrated. You are not able to solve Alison's problem over the phone and therefore you record details of her problem for a technician to visit her.

Role-play with a partner the recommendations that you would offer to Alison over the telephone and how you would communicate with her, taking into account her limited technical knowledge.

How did you:

- offer suggestions that were relevant to Alison's problem
- break tasks down into small chunks to aid Alison's understanding of what you wanted her to do
- manage to not be condescending towards Alison for having limited technical knowledge?

Questions

- What details did you record?
- How will the details that you recorded help the technician who is going to visit Alison?

Ready for work?

You will need to demonstrate that you have the skills and behaviours required to work on your own and with others to solve simple and complex problems. Being able to practise these skills and behaviours could help you gain employment as an entry-level support technician in a range of organisations.

Problem solving

- Are you able to stay calm and supportive and think of creative solutions to problems?
- Are you able to use the right diagnosis tool to find the cause of a problem?

Communication

- Are you able to communicate with different people, including people with and without technical knowledge?

- Are you able to talk to clients and explain the reasons for faults, giving them accurate information?

Managing information

- Are you able to accurately record the details of faults and service requests from users?
- Are you able to read error codes and user manuals to diagnose simple and complex technical problems?

Working with others

- Are you able to support team members who may be trying to fix a fault that you have experienced before?
- Do you know your own strengths and weaknesses and are you able to delegate jobs to other people appropriately?

5 IT Service Solutions

From sending an email to a colleague to controlling a complex manufacturing process, information technology (IT) plays a vital role in the running of most organisations. Ensuring that the correct IT service is selected and used effectively to meet the needs of customers and employees, as well as the organisation as a whole, is key to the success of any organisation.

In this unit, you will learn the importance of effective IT service design and how it can impact on an organisation and its stakeholders. You will learn how to analyse the needs of organisations in different contexts and sectors, to identify IT requirements and to plan appropriate IT solutions.

How will I be assessed?

You will be externally assessed using a task that is set and marked by Pearson. The assessed task will take place during a window timetabled by Pearson. There will be no pre-release material for this task.

During the assessment task, you will be required to respond to a given scenario by applying your understanding of the IT service life cycle and IT systems to plan an IT service solution that meets the needs of a given organisation. You will be required to consider the impact of IT solutions on the given organisation and compare these to possible alternatives.

You must complete the assessment under supervised conditions within the timetabled window. Your outcomes will be submitted in a format specified by Pearson.

Assessment outcomes

AO1	Demonstrate knowledge and understanding of IT solutions through recall and selection of facts, terminology and processes
AO2	Apply understanding of terminology, information technologies and procedures to make IT recommendations
AO3	Review IT needs and recommendations to make reasoned judgements, justify decisions and present conclusions

What you will learn in this unit:

A Analysing the IT needs of organisations

B IT systems used by organisations

C IT service delivery

D Impact and implications of an IT service delivery solution

A Analysing the IT needs of organisations

A1 IT service life cycle

The **IT SERVICE LIFE CYCLE** (a way of identifying, defining, planning and evaluating a solution to meet the IT service needs of an organisation) is used by IT professionals to help match the needs of an organisation to suitable **IT SERVICES** (any activity or process performed by an organisation that requires IT systems to achieve its aims). For example, your centre (the organisation) may have a need to provide facilities for learners to submit work to tutors and receive feedback. The IT professionals in your centre would look at this need and use the IT service life cycle (see Figure 5.1) to analyse this need, identify IT services that would meet this need, consider alternatives and then implement the solution.

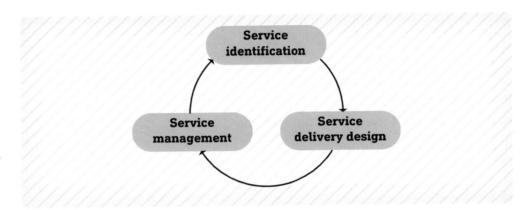

Figure 5.1: Use the IT service life cycle to help you to identify the IT service needs of an organisation

Service identification

The most effective IT service solutions exist when the IT services are dictated by the needs of the organisation, the users of the IT systems and the organisation's customers.

Identifying the needs of organisations, users and customers

An organisation will choose a technology because of its ability to perform specific tasks effectively and not because the technology is currently the 'must have' gadget. For example, a worker in an organisation may like the idea of having a small tablet computer, and while this may meet some of their needs (such as, portability, accessing emails and the internet), if their job requires working with files that require large amounts of storage, or more extended periods of typing, then ultimately a laptop computer may be more appropriate. Therefore, at this stage of the cycle, it is important to identify all the needs of the organisation and **STAKEHOLDERS** (any person or group with specific interest in, or dependence on, an organisation and/or its services) in order to ensure that when the final decisions about IT services are made, this can be done so effectively.

Using outline service catalogues

In most organisations it is highly likely that some IT services will already exist, and it is good practice to keep a record of an organisation's IT services in an **IT SERVICE CATALOGUE** (a document where all IT services for an organisation are identified and their requirements described). This will list all the IT services used and provide a description of the purpose and intended use of the IT service. Every organisation's catalogue will vary slightly and in some organisations, the service catalogue may also provide information about who is responsible for maintaining the service and what they must do to ensure the service functions appropriately and meets requirements. This is particularly useful if an organisation does not have its own technical IT staff and relies on a paid-for service from an outside company. Figure 5.2 shows an example from a simple IT service catalogue from a college.

Service name	Service description
Virtual Learning Environment (VLE)	Used by learners to: • submit work to tutors and receive feedback (see description of marking and assessment system) • access course materials provided by tutors • check timetable, college 'public' calender dates.

Figure 5.2: It is good practice to keep an IT service catalogue as a record of an organisation's IT services

Interpreting an IT service catalogue

As technology progresses or the needs of an organisation change, new services may need to be identified and introduced. In order to do this, start by looking at a company's IT service catalogue to identify what systems and needs it currently has, and to identify if any of its current systems could be utilised to meet its changing needs without having to spend large amounts of time and money completely redesigning the system. It is important that any new IT services identified take into consideration what is already there so that they can be integrated.

Service delivery design

Identifying the requirements for IT service delivery solutions

Once the needs of an organisation are identified, you can start to design a solution that will meet these needs. At this stage you will identify the specific technologies that can be used and plan a complete solution.

When producing a design, you will need to produce a range of documents detailing how the organisation will use the system and how each of the IT services will meet the identified needs. The documents you produce may include:

- IT service catalogues
- data flow diagrams
- **NETWORK**/system diagrams.

See C2 for more about designing solutions.

Service management

Why do organisations regularly review their IT solutions?

In order for an organisation to continue to be successful and serve its stakeholders well, IT services must be continually monitored, evaluated and improved. To do this, you will have to continually review the benefits and drawbacks of a system in terms of how it meets the organisation's needs. You might argue that after spending a large amount of money, time and effort designing IT service solutions that meet the needs of the organisation, to then review and change the system would be a waste of time and resources. You will need to consider any changes carefully and only implement them if absolutely necessary. Updates and upgrades to systems can sometimes cause compatibility problems between the old and new systems, therefore if a system that is in place meets the needs of an organisation effectively, you should not alter it just because a new piece of technology has been released.

Considering alternatives

The rapid development in technology can mean that alternative solutions become available that provide more efficient ways of completing tasks or additional functionality. This may be beneficial to the organisation, and would allow them to be more productive with significantly less effort and reduced cost. It may also be that a piece of **SOFTWARE** becomes outdated and is no longer supported by the publisher, so continuing to use this may cause security problems for the organisation. A change would therefore be essential.

Implications of solutions and possible alternatives

No matter what solution is chosen, it will have either positive or negative implications for the organisation and its stakeholders that you should consider carefully. These can be quite minor, such as getting used to a slightly different interface, or more significant, such as the need to replace all computers within an organisation's office. As an IT professional, it is your job to be aware of these implications, and to be able to explain them to the owners and management of an organisation so that decisions can be made.

See D2 for more about reviewing IT service solutions.

Updating the service catalogue

Once you have found a solution, the IT service catalogue will be updated and the solution implemented. It is usually the job of an IT service manager, or other designated person within the IT department, to keep the IT service catalogue up to date. At this point the cycle will begin again and the effectiveness and appropriateness of the organisation's IT systems will be reviewed at regular intervals.

Assessment practice	AO1 AO2 AO3

In April 2014, Windows® withdrew all technical support for XP and stopped providing updates for the **OPERATING SYSTEM**. Windows XP® was estimated to be running on 24.34 per cent of computers.

Between 2016 and 2017, Windows XP was estimated to still be running on 9.94 per cent of computers. While many of these are owned by individuals, it is thought that many organisations are still reluctant to move away from Windows XP.

In a small group discuss the following questions.

1 What are the benefits and drawbacks for these organisations of continuing to use the older operating system?

2 What are the alternatives?

3 What are the implications for organisations of:

   • keeping their current operating system

   • upgrading to a newer operating system?

A2 The purpose of organisations

Every organisation exists to fulfil a particular role; this role is its purpose and is the key driving factor in informing the IT services and the solutions that are designed to fit its needs. While every organisation will have its own unique needs, which will affect the specific details of the IT services used, an organisation exists to provide:

- *a service* – for example, the NHS is a service organisation as it operates to provide specific services rather than to sell a physical product
- *a product* – for example, the electronics firm Sony® provides physical products to its customers in the form of electrical goods such as smartphones, games consoles and digital cameras
- *both services and products* – some companies, such as Google™, provide both.

How does the purpose of an organisation relate to its IT service requirements?

All organisations have a main purpose (to provide a service or product) and each organisation has specific IT service requirements to allow it to operate effectively. For example, many organisations provide a 'service' but the service provided by each will vary, as will the people who make use of the provided service. Table 5.1 shows some of the questions that you should ask when analysing how the purpose of an organisation will inform its IT service requirements.

Table 5.1: Analysing how the purpose of an organisation relates to the IT service needs

Product organisation	Service organisation
• What is the product?	• What is the service?
• Is it a physical or digital product?	• Who will access the service?
• How will it be provided to customers?	• How do customers access the service?
• Where is it produced?	• When must the service be available?
• Who is the product for?	

Key tasks carried out by organisations and individuals

When analysing the needs of an organisation, you will need to consider the key tasks that should be carried out by the organisation as a whole, or by groups and individuals within the organisation. Figure 5.3 shows some IT services that relate to some key tasks of an organisation.

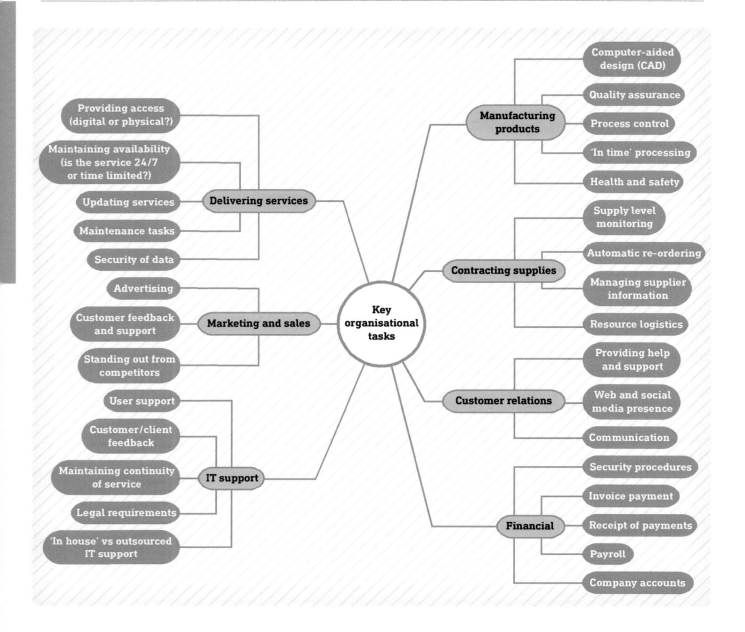

Figure 5.3: Establishing key tasks is essential to ensure you have sufficient information to identify appropriate IT services and to design appropriate solutions

Using information in different forms

Organisations generate information and display it in many different forms. In order to analyse the requirements of an organisation effectively, you will need to be able to interpret the information in different forms. Some examples are given here.

- *Business outlines*: these give a written description of the purpose of the organisation and relevant information about its needs. The outline may also provide information relating to the company's stakeholders.
- *Functional specifications*: most typically used to outline the features of a product or digital service. It may provide technical details of how the product/service will look and work.
- *Data flow diagrams*: used to show how data is used within an organisation and how the data (and information) flow between different parts of an organisation and/or its stakeholders.
- *Building/floor plans*: graphical plans that show the layout of a building and/or room. These provide a location context for IT services and help make decisions on what may or may not be possible.
- *IT system diagrams*: visual plan parts that make up an IT service solution. These show the devices and connections to be used and how they will integrate.

Assessment practice   A01 A02

Parvinder owns and runs a small courier service that provides a door-to-door delivery service.

Customers can use the company's website to book a collection date along with selecting morning or afternoon collection. Alternatively, they can telephone the office.

The company has eight delivery vans with IT equipment that allows the office to determine their location so pickups and deliveries can be organised efficiently. The office can forward new collections to the drivers in the vans.

Describe some of the key tasks that will need to be carried out by different groups or individuals in the organisation.

Use these headings to organise your ideas:

- delivering services
- customer relations
- contracting supplies
- IT support
- marketing and sales
- financial.

Skills and knowledge check

☐ What is the IT service life cycle? State the three main stages.

☐ Why is the IT service life cycle used?

☐ What is an IT service?

○ I can explain the two main purposes of organisations.

○ I can list five key organisational tasks.

B IT systems used by organisations

In the previous section we learned that an IT service is any task or process that requires IT to achieve its aims. Therefore, IT services are often linked with, and defined alongside, the **HARDWARE** or software that is needed to facilitate them. To effectively design solutions you will need to understand the features and characteristics of different IT services used in organisations.

B1 Software and hardware

How and why software and hardware are used in organisations

As an IT professional, you should understand the difference between how and why something is used. By understanding 'why', you can consider the needs of an individual or organisation, which is the main factor in deciding the IT services to use. Understanding 'how' something is done allows you to consider whether the software or hardware is suitable for the intended task and to compare different ways of achieving an aim. You can then decide what is most appropriate for a given situation. Often there can be many ways to meet an identified need that may be equally useful. Table 5.2 shows a small number of examples of how IT hardware and software are used.

Table 5.2: How hardware and software are used in organisations

Why IT services are used in organisations	How IT services are used	
	Software	**Hardware**
Communication	• Composing messages • Creating documents • Extracting and presenting **DATA**	• Sending/receiving documents and messages • Making phone calls • Video conferencing • Displaying data and information
Collaboration	• Online office applications/document editing • **CLOUD STORAGE** • Video conferencing	• Local area networks • Mobile internet connections • Webcams
Product production and/or service provision	• CAD/CAM (computer-aided design/computer-aided manufacturing) • Website hosting • Mobile applications	• 3D printing • CNC (computer numerical control router, for example, computer-controlled lathes) • Web servers • Individuals' digital devices
Financial transactions	• Third-party payment systems (for example, PayPal®) • Accounting software • Webstores	• Servers • **FIREWALLS**
File storage and/or transfer	• Cloud file sharing/storage services • Email	• Local and remote servers • External hard drives • Optical media

Table 5.2: *(continued)*

Why IT services are used in organisations	How IT services are used	
	Software	**Hardware**
Productivity	• Office suites/document production • Graphic-editing software • Image rendering engines	• **INPUT DEVICES** (for example, keyboards, graphics tablets) • **OUTPUT DEVICES** (for example, large-screen displays, printers)
Remote access	• Virtual private networks • Remote desktops • Cloud storage	• Servers to host/hold site or data • Infrastructure (for example, mobile networks, Wi-Fi connections) to allow connection
Creativity and/or innovation	• Emulation and virtualisation for prototyping • Modelling • Rapid application development • Augmented reality	• Prototype boards • Single-board computers (for example, Raspberry Pi®) • Wearable technology
Customer access to product and/or service	• Downloading/accessing a digital product • Customer/client portals (for example, appointment booking systems, order management) • Order tracking	• Infrastructure (for example, mobile networks, Wi-Fi connections) to allow connection • Specialised hardware (for example, Google Chromecast™, Amazon TV Fire® Stick)

How is software used in organisations?

Computer software is a term used to describe either data or instructions (or often both) that are needed by a computer or digital device (the hardware) to complete a specified task. Computer software allows users to interact with computer hardware in order to meet specific needs or solve problems. Software also provides the instructions necessary for a computer to operate. Computer software can be grouped into several different types.

Operating systems

The operating system (for example, Microsoft Windows, Mac OS®, Android™) is vital to the operation of any computer or digital device. While many operating systems provide users with other types of software, an operating system's key purpose is providing instructions to allow a computer to perform its basic instructions (for example, task scheduling, memory management, controlling peripherals).

Utility software

UTILITY SOFTWARE is a set of tools that allows a user to maintain and optimise the performance of a computer. There are many different types of utility software, each of which provides a user with control of a specific task, process or component of a computer. The following are the more common utilities.

- **ANTI-VIRUS SOFTWARE**: protects systems and data from **MALWARE**.
- *Backup software*: used to schedule what data is to be backed up and specify the location to back up to.
- *Compression tools*: used to reduce the size of files to make more effective use of available storage.
- *Disk analyser*: a diagnostic tool that checks the available space and the condition of a computer's hard drive.
- *Disk defragmenter*: a tool that reorganises data on a hard drive so related data is grouped together.
- *Encryption software*: improves the security of data by making it unreadable unless the correct key is used to decode it.
- *Firewall*: security software that protects a computer or network from unauthorised access.

- *Network utilities*: a group of programs that allows a user to monitor and log activity on a network and alter network settings.
- *Package managers*: used to keep track of installed software and allow users to update or install/uninstall additional software.
- *Password managers*: use to store and organise a user's **PASSWORDS** for different services.

Application software

APPLICATION SOFTWARE is a general term that is most commonly applied to any computer software that is not considered to be **SYSTEM SOFTWARE** (software specifically designed to provide access to, or control of, a function of a computer or device, such as operating systems and utilities).

Application software is what most people associate with the term computer software. Some common application software is given here.

- *Office software*: designed to facilitate typical 'office' tasks such as writing letters, creating invoices, organising information. Office software often comes in a suite of related programs that include a word processor, spreadsheet, presentation and **DATABASE** software.
- *Database management systems*: used to create and manage complex, relational databases.
- *Graphic-editing software*: used to create and/or edit digital images.
- *Computer-aided design (CAD)*: software used to produce highly detailed technical drawings such as building plans or when designing a car's engine.
- *Accounting software*: a type of database software that is specifically designed to help organisations manage data relating to their finances such as issuing and paying invoices, monitoring cash flow and payroll.
- *Communication software*: includes email, instant messaging and video conferencing.

Practise

Can you think of any other types of application software?

Investigate other uses of application software and make notes on the types of software that are used.

Different ways of accessing software

When you have chosen which software to use, you will need to choose how users will access the software or where it will be stored. **HOSTED/CLOUD COMPUTING** is a method of deploying or providing access to application software. Whereas traditionally software was installed directly on the computer it was to be used on, hosted/cloud computing software has the application installed on a remote server and users access the software using the web **BROWSER** in their chosen device.

The increase in availability of network connectivity and improved **BANDWIDTH** has meant that, in recent years, the use of cloud computing services has become more commonplace. For example, products such as MS Office® now provide online subscription services allowing you to access the software from any computer with a browser and internet connection.

Table 5.3 shows the many benefits and drawbacks of using hosted computing for organisations and users.

Link it up

Data Management

See Unit 9 for more information on how and why software is used in organisations.

Hosted/cloud computing software

Benefits	Drawbacks
• Software updates are done by the hosting company • The same software can be used by users with different operating systems • Can be more easily linked with cloud storage and file sharing services • Often provides collaboration tools • Reduces the amount of local storage space required • Can be used by computers with lower performance specifications (typically just need an up-to-date internet browser)	• Can appear less responsive than locally installed software (due to the delay in communicating with the server) • Typically have fewer features than locally installed versions of similar applications • May not be able to use/access features if no internet connection is available

Table 5.3: Benefits and drawbacks of hosted/cloud computing

Link it up

Networking and Cybersecurity

For more information about hosting/cloud computing go to Unit 8, A3.

Mobile applications

MOBILE APPLICATIONS are software that is optimised for use on mobile devices such as tablets and smartphones. They can take the form of conventional applications and utility software, though these may have reduced features to compensate for the less powerful specifications of a mobile device. Mobile applications are often designed to provide a more user-friendly experience when accessing web-based information, compared with using a full website.

Do you own the software you use?

Software such as Microsoft Office is what is known as **PROPRIETARY SOFTWARE**. That is to say, the program, its design and the programming code that made it is the intellectual property of Microsoft. When you pay for and install this software, you are paying to be able to have a copy of the software that you can use. **OPEN-SOURCE SOFTWARE** is different, in that it makes the programming or 'source' code available to users and other programmers, allowing them to alter the code in order to customise the software, improve it or make a different version of their own.

Open-source software is often provided free of charge, although many larger open-source providers provide paid-for versions of software. These are often cheaper than proprietary equivalents and the fee may include continued technical support rather than just the software.

Some people are wary of open-source software and are concerned that having the source code available for anybody to see makes it more likely that it will be attacked, as **HACKERS** can see the code and find vulnerabilities. However, advocates of open-source software argue that because the code is visible, the code is checked by more people so any problems are identified quickly and fixed before hackers can exploit them.

As with any IT service solution, as an IT professional it is your job to analyse the needs of the organisation and evaluate the benefits and drawbacks of a suggested solution, as shown in Table 5.4.

Table 5.4: The benefits and drawbacks of open-source software

Open-source software	
Benefits	**Drawbacks**
• Often cheaper than equivalent proprietary software • Software can be modified to meet specific needs of an organisation • Errors or vulnerabilities in code can be spotted and fixed • A wide selection of operating systems, system and applications software available • Popular programs have a large and active community support base	• Updating of smaller projects may be sporadic (as programmers may be working on it as a hobby) • Some projects do not provide direct support and help can only be found in the user community • May use file formats that are not compatible with the software used by customers • Staff may require additional training as software may be less well known. • There may be fewer staff available with the skills and experience to use or modify open-source software.

How is computer hardware used in organisations?

Technology systems

TECHNOLOGY SYSTEMS is a general term that is used for any complete computing system and is often what people think about when they say the word 'computer'. Technology systems within organisations come in many different forms.

- *A server*: a large central computer on a network that controls access to the network and its resources.
- *Clients*: a term that refers to any device that connects to a server. These could be traditional desktop PCs, laptops or even mobile devices (for example, tablets).
- *Independent digital devices*: any digital device that does not link directly to, or is directly controlled by, the organisation's network. For example, an employee may be given a smartphone which may occasionally use the company Wi-Fi network to access the internet but is generally used separately.

Multiple servers are sometimes contained within a large server room

Storage devices

STORAGE DEVICES are used to hold data for use by the organisation and its stakeholders. Within an organisation, data storage may be for different purposes, including data, that is actively used and worked on, backing up/ protecting data, archiving or transferring data to other users. The devices used may include the following.

- HARD DISK DRIVES (HDD) and SOLID-STATE DRIVES (SSD): data is stored directly on a device and unless these drives are located on a server, the data is typically only available to the device on which it is stored.
- *External HDD/SSD*: connected to computers using UNIVERSAL SERIAL BUS (USB) or ESATA connections, these hard drives are often used for small-scale backup (for example, when only one or two devices need backing up) or to transfer large files from one computer to another.
- *USB flash drive*: a small, portable external storage is used to store relatively small amounts of data (compared to HDD/SSD), and typically used to transfer files from one device to another.
- *SD/micro SD cards*: small, highly portable, solid-state storage that is used to increase the storage capacity of smaller digital devices such as tablets, smartphones and digital cameras and typically provides less storage space than USB flash drives.
- *Optical media*: storage discs that include Blu-ray, DVD and CD. Due to their relatively small storage sizes when compared to other storage methods, and because the surface of the disk where data is stored can be easily damaged, optical media has become less common in recent years. However, it is often still used for distributing copies of programs or other media due to the relative low cost of the media.

Peripheral devices

A PERIPHERAL DEVICE is any device that connects to, and works with, a computing device to provide some form of additional functionality or to make the device easier to use. This can include:

- input devices such as keyboards, pointing devices (mouse, stylus, touchpad), scanners and graphics tablets
- output devices such as screens, printers and projectors
- external storage devices such as USB flash drives and USB hard drives.

Link it up

Refer back to Unit 1 for more information on peripheral devices.

Accessibility devices

ACCESSIBILITY DEVICES, sometimes referred to as 'assistive technology', are peripherals designed to enable users, who would otherwise have difficulty, to use an IT system. These can include the following.

- *Alternative keyboard*: a keyboard that is modified to meet a user's particular need. This may involve removing the standard 'qwerty' layout and instead providing fewer and or larger buttons that are programmed to perform set functions.
- *Sip-and-puff system*: an input/control system for people with limited or impaired motor skills. The user has a straw, which they either suck or blow into in order to operate a switch. The computer is programmed to respond to different lengths and strength of 'sip' and 'puff'.
- *Wands* and *stick*: allow users to interact with a computer or device by using a stick that is operated/controlled by the head or the mouth. Typically used by those who have limited function in their arms.
- *Braille embosser*: an output device that outputs onscreen text, in a similar way to a printer but uses 'impact printing' to make indentations on the page in the form of braille.
- *Refreshable braille display:* an output device that provides braille output by mechanically controlling plastic pins that raise and lower to form braille characters.

Refreshable braille displays enable visually impaired computer users to read text output

Organisations have a legal responsibility to provide support and make provision for workers with additional needs. The IT professionals in an organisation must consider the needs of the user and choose appropriate accessibility devices to enable access.

For more on accessibility and legal responsibility, see D on the impact and implications of an IT service delivery solution and D2 on legislation.

Multifunctional devices

Most modern computing devices are considered **MULTIFUNCTIONAL**, in that they can perform more than one specific task. For example, you can use a smartphone as a communication device in the form of SMS messages and phone calls but it can also be used to take photographs, access the internet or watch a film, or used as a control device for a larger system.

This is very convenient for users and selecting multifunctional devices can be very cost effective for organisations. However, the application of **CONVERGENCE TECHNOLOGY** (the combining of multiple technologies into one device such as providing a camera, GPS (Global Positioning System) and internet capabilities in a smartphone) has some disadvantages. For example, while you can take photographs using a mobile phone and the quality of these may be good enough for some purposes (such as posting on social media), the camera on a mobile phone would not be used by a professional photographer for taking advertising shots, as it will not produce the high-quality image of a dedicated camera.

As part of an IT solution you would need to consider the role the hardware will play and how important that role is. For example, if your employees only occasionally need GPS and satellite navigation, then providing a smartphone with this capability may be appropriate. However, if it will be used constantly and greater precision is needed, you may provide dedicated GPS systems.

Mobile devices

As technology has progressed, systems have become smaller and more powerful. Mobile technology is now capable of performing fully fledged, general computing tasks as well as more specific activities. Mobile devices may include:

- wearable technology (for example, fitness trackers)
- smartphones
- tablet computers
- laptops.

While the power of mobile devices has improved, they still do not possess the powerful computing specifications of more traditional PCs. The increased power and functionality of mobile devices has also had a negative effect on the amount of power that they consume.

B2 Connecting IT systems and transferring data

When planning an IT service solution, the way in which the component parts of the solution communicate and exchange data and information is an important part of the success of the solution. The methods you choose should be influenced by a range of factors, including the task that is to be performed, the devices to be used and the location of the user.

Wired or wireless? Which one should I choose?

Wired and wireless connections come in many different formats. A number of types have become commonplace and support of them is provided by many digital devices. See Table 5.5, which shows some common connection methods.

Connection methods

Wired	Wireless
• Ethernet	• Bluetooth®
• USB	• Wi-Fi (including Wi-Fi Direct)
• FireWire	• Infrared
• Thunderbolt	• Cellular/Mobile network (3G, 4G, LTE, etc.)
• eSATA	
• **HDMI**	• NFC (near field communication)
• Stereo jacks	

Table 5.5: Common connection methods

Practise

Research the features, benefits and drawbacks of each of the listed wired and wireless connection methods.

Present your findings in the form of a **WIKI** (a user-generated information site).

These websites provide free resources for producing wikis.

• www.wikispaces.com

• www.pbworks.com

The choice of wired or wireless will entirely depend on the device being used, and the type and amount of data to be communicated. Typically, wired connections provide a more secure connection and greater bandwidth and allow for data to be transferred over greater distances as wireless signals degrade the further they travel from their source. Wireless connections are usually thought of as being more convenient (as you are not always having to find the correct cable or install large amounts of wires in a given location). Wireless also allows transfer between a greater range of devices, and the equipment is generally cheaper and easier to set up. Table 5.6 outlines what to consider when choosing the wired or wireless connections for different uses.

Table 5.6: Uses of wired and wireless connections

Use	Use wired if...	Use wireless if...
Audio/video data	• Video/audio is being streamed in high quality to avoid buffering • It is a large distance to the target device • Images/sound need to be displayed/heard in 'real time'	• Sending data to a nearby device such as Bluetooth headphones or speaker • You need the device to be portable • Only small amounts of data are being sent (for example, streaming one song at a time)
Communication	• You need to reduce lag/delay • Multiple users will be using the same access point • Large amounts of data will be exchanged	• You need to use a device that does not support Ethernet (for example, a smartphone) • You wish to move the device around during use • Video is to be lower quality • Communication will be voice only
Device control	• Large amounts of graphical data are to be shared during control (for example, remote desktop software) • There is potential for interference from other devices	• Device to be controlled is 'mobile' • Only one-way data transfer is needed (for example, control commands)
Data collection and monitoring	• Large quantities of data are collected at once (for example, a large array of sensors in a weather station) • Data is to be collected in an area of high interference	• Installing wired technology is dangerous or problematic • Low quantities of data are collected (for example, a single temperature reading is taken every hour over a period of time)
File transfer and backup	• Large or 'complete' backups are to be completed (for example, backing up all user data from a company server at the end of each day) • A large number of files or particularly large files are to be transferred (for example, transferring a large number of HD pictures)	• A small number of amended files are being synchronised to cloud storage • Sharing individual files, such as photos or contact information between two devices

Common networks used by organisations

From enabling a range of options for communication between stakeholders to being able to access data and IT systems from almost anywhere in the world, networks and their associated technologies have had a significant impact on the way organisations are able to make use of information and resources.

Mobile/cellular

A **MOBILE/CELLULAR NETWORK** is one that uses a data connection provided by a mobile phone (for example, Three®, Vodafone®, EE®). The advancements in mobile/cellular networks, and the increases in data-transfer speeds they have provided, have made significant changes to the way organisations can conduct their business, and how stakeholders access systems and perform their roles.

Local area network

A **LOCAL AREA NETWORK (LAN)** is one that is based in one geographical location such as an office building or school. Networks of this type will usually follow the **SERVER–CLIENT MODEL** (a network model in which a central computer (server) controls access to files and data on the network; any connecting device is referred to as a client). A LAN enables the sharing of data and resources with any connected device. The organisation can monitor and control who accesses the server and on which device.

Wide area network

A **WIDE AREA NETWORK (WAN)** (see Figure 5.4) is one that is spread across a larger geographical area and will typically make use of other infrastructures to connect networks in two locations. For example, a company might have an office in London and Paris. Each office may contain a LAN and these two individual networks would be connected using a secure connection over the internet.

Link it up

Refer back to Unit 1, A3 for more information on connecting devices and systems.

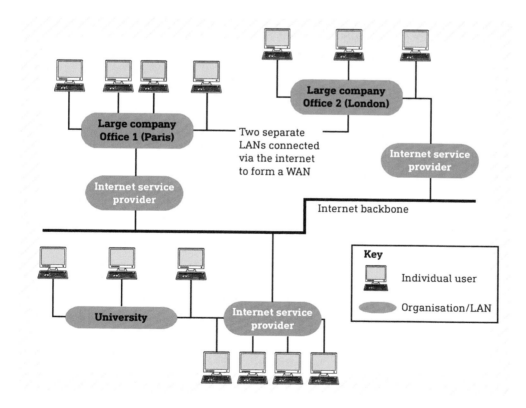

Figure 5.4: The internet is made up of lots of smaller networks and is considered to be the largest possible WAN

Personal area network

A **PERSONAL AREA NETWORK (PAN)** is one that is made up of a single user's devices such as their laptop, smartphone and wearable technologies (for example, fitness tracker). Devices on the network are likely to be connected, and kept in sync, using wireless connections such as Bluetooth or Wi-Fi, although other connections such as USB may also be used.

Which network or connection should I use?

As with selecting hardware and software, the network or connection type that will be used should be dictated by the specific need of the organisation and its stakeholders. It is unlikely that any IT solution will rely on just one network or connection type. It will combine the use of multiple networks and connections, depending on the task to be performed and the location of the user.

Factors affecting the performance of communication methods

There are a number of factors that affect how well a given communication method will perform. Understanding the potential impact of these can help you select, and justify, the most appropriate communication method for a given task. The factors to consider in selecting a communication method are as given below.

Volume of data

Consider how much data is to be transferred. For example, if the given task requires constant connection to a company server with large numbers of files being uploaded and downloaded, you would choose a different connection method than if you just needed to synchronise a calendar between a smartphone and laptop.

Bandwidth

Bandwidth is the maximum amount of data a connection can transfer at any one time. This often translates to the speed at which a task/data transfer can be completed. Different connection types offer different maximum bandwidths and choosing the correct one can greatly affect the efficiency of a solution.

Latency

LATENCY is the delay between when a signal is sent and when it is received. When latency is greater than expected, this is perceived by the users as 'lag'. Latency can be caused by a number of factors, including the distance the signal has to travel and the infrastructure that is being used. While latency is present in all communication, it is most noticeable when completing 'real-time' actions such as video chatting or playing online multiplayer games.

Hardware

The hardware used when communicating can have an impact on user experience. For example, a user may make use of the same video chat software on their smartphone (which has quite low specifications) and on their traditional high-powered PC. The user may notice that they have a smoother experience when using the PC as the higher specification machine can process data more quickly, or because it is connected using a high-speed network SWITCH rather than a Wi-Fi access point.

Software

The software used can drastically alter a person's experience when using communication systems and networks. It may be that a particular piece of software has been programmed more efficiently or is more compatible with/designed for a specific device or platform. Alternatively, especially in audio and video communication, the CODEC (Coder-Decoder) used can have a dramatic effect on the quality of the sound/image and the latency experienced.

Skills and knowledge check

- ☐ Can you explain a number of different ways hardware and software are used by organisations?
- ☐ Can you describe the features and characteristics of common hardware and software used in organisations?
- ☐ Do you understand how data can be shared between systems and the benefits and drawbacks of different connection methods?
- ☐ Can you describe the factors that affect the performance of systems and communications?

- ○ I can describe how hardware and software can be used for specific tasks.
- ○ I can explain why a specific piece of hardware or software is most suitable for a given scenario.

C IT service delivery

For your assessment, you will be required to make recommendations to an organisation for an IT service solution. You will need to apply the principles of the IT service life cycle, and be able to:

- identify the current (and possibly future) needs of an organisation – service identification
- make recommendations for an appropriate IT service solution – service delivery design
- review both current IT provision and your suggested solution – service management.

C1 Service identification

As part of the service identification phase, you should make use of a range of documents that will provide you with information about the company. You should use this information and your knowledge of IT systems to inform your solution. For more on the documents you might use as part of service identification, see A1 IT service life cycle for using information in different forms in the IT service life cycle.

What are the organisation's IT service needs?

You can only design an effective solution if you fully understand the organisation and its stakeholders. Having a clear understanding of the organisation will ensure that you can make recommendations that are appropriate to their needs.

What is the purpose of the organisation?

An organisation's purpose defines its primary function and will influence all other areas of the business. For example, does the organisation exist to provide a service or to produce a product? For more information on the purposes of organisations, refer back to A2.

What are the aims and needs of the organisation?

An organisation's aims and needs will relate to its purpose. For example, a company that provides IT support services may have a need to provide an online appointment booking service or to be able to update a technician's appointment schedule throughout the day.

Which tasks will be performed by the organisation or individual?

Understanding the tasks that the organisation or its stakeholder must perform as part of their role is key to helping understand how to meet the needs of an organisation. There may be many tasks performed by a number of individuals in order to achieve one aim. For example, the online retailer Amazon's primary function is to sell goods to customers, but in order for the customer to receive an order, other individuals must get the item from the warehouse, box it up and label it and so on.

What are the services or products provided by the organisation?

Generally an organisation can be thought of as a 'product' business, in that it provides or manufactures a physical or digital product, or it provides a service. For example, Microsoft provides digital products in the form of computer software, whereas an organisation such as a school or college provides a service in the form of education. Although organisations may fall under either banner (or sometimes both), the actual products will vary and this will create different needs and require different tasks. For example, a service organisation such as a college may have very different IT service needs when compared with an online file storage service.

| **Assessment practice** | **AO1 AO2 AO3** |

Investigate an organisation to find out its aims and the task that would be performed to allow the organisation to achieve these aims and provide services and/or products. An example is provided but you should do your own investigation into an existing organisation.

Organisation: Tom's Toys

Purpose: Retail outlet for toys

Aims	Tasks to be performed
Provide local 'high street' store	• Track current stock • Manage sales figures • Manage store finances
Provide online store	•

NB: This is just a guide as to how to start. It is likely your investigation will be much longer.

You could expand this further by considering:

- customer experience
- staff needs and working styles
- location.

Customer experience

Every organisation has customers – individuals or groups who purchase or use the services/products that it provides. The customers are the main reason an organisation exists, so it is important that you consider them when planning IT services. Table 5.7 shows some of the many factors that a company may consider in order to ensure a positive customer experience.

Table 5.7: Customer experience considerations

Consideration	What should the company consider?	Examples
Customer needs	Providing suitable IT support to allow all customers to access the product or service in a way that is efficient and effective.	• Providing alternative product interfaces for customers with additional needs. • Providing mobile and desktop versions of a site. • Providing help and tutorials.
Expectations	Ensuring that the user gets the type of experience they expect from the product or service.	• Delivering a product within a given time frame. • Ensuring a digital product provides all the features that a user expects. • Ensuring access to a product is consistent and down time is minimised.
How product/service will be delivered and consumed	How the customer will interact with the product or service.	• Ensuring delivery of a physical product. • Providing online access to allow customers to book face-to-face appointments. • Providing alternative access methods for different devices (for example, a mobile app as well as a website).

Staff needs and working styles

In the same way you consider customer needs, the needs of staff also dictate the IT services you provide. When deciding on an IT service solution, you need to consider how the organisation's staff complete their key tasks. For example, do staff need to move around a warehouse or is the task completed at a desk? Do they interact with customers? Do they work remotely or in the office?

Location

An organisation may wish to allow a staff member to work from home. However, their job requires regular access to the organisation's server and the user lives in an area where they are unable to get a fast broadband internet connection. It may mean that either this provision cannot be made or an alternative may need to be sought.

When considering the impact of location you should consider the needs of, and implications for:

- staff
- customers
- premises
- market/service delivery point (see also how product/service will be delivered).

How will the IT services be used?

IT service solutions are designed by IT professionals but the decisions to implement them are made by an organisation's management, who may not be IT experts. Therefore when designing a solution it is important that you can describe how IT will be used to complete tasks and contribute to meeting the needs of the organisation. In some organisations, this may take the form of a written report or proposal, or an IT service catalogue.

For more on the IT service catalogue, see A1 on service identification.

Is it information or data?

Information

This may be informed, or even generated, by the data that is produced but will have a context and be meaningful. For example, a supermarket knows that it needs to order more barbecue food in summer than in winter. This is information that will have been informed by sales data. Information can also be generated in other ways such as through emails and phone calls.

Data

Data can be thought of as facts and statistics about a subject that have not yet been put into a meaningful context in order to make them information. All organisations generate large volumes of data (for example, sales figures, manufacturing statistics, data from loyalty cards) so it is important that this is managed correctly so it can be used effectively and changed into information as required.

Link it up

Data Management

See Unit 6 for more information on how organisations use data from large data sets to analyse customer and user behaviour.

C2 Recommend an IT service solution

Once you understand the needs of an organisation you can start to make recommendations for a solution that will meet its IT service needs (IT service design). For more on the IT service life cycle, see A1.

Identify known IT service issues

Identifying possible issues that will impact on the organisation's effectiveness and the needs of its stakeholders will allow you to design a more effective solution. There are many different sources of information within an organisation that you can look at to identify these issues.

Stakeholder reviews

Feedback from stakeholders is a measure of the effectiveness of an organisation and its current systems. For example, customers may be able to provide feedback on the quality of a company's product or the effectiveness/ease of use of an order management system, whereas an employee will be able to give feedback on how easy it is to complete their role using the current systems or if a particular feature needs to be added.

Current IT service catalogue

It would be very rare to find an organisation that makes no use of IT at all, therefore it is important to consider the current use of IT within the organisation and to what extent it meets the needs of the organisation. Changing a company's IT services can be time consuming and costly so change should only happen if the current systems are no longer effective. It may also be the case that the current systems are still partially effective and just need improving or developing.

An organisation's needs

It is likely that as part of your service identification phase you will already have found a number of needs for the organisation. As you develop your recommendations into a solution, it is vital that you revisit these initial findings. As you increase your understanding of an organisation, you might discover others flag potential issues that need addressing. For example, the organisation's management may have said that they want to remove a feature from their customer portal, but stakeholder feedback identifies this as a popular feature that they would like to see developed. Alternatively, you may notice that an identified need is remote collaborative working but that current IT services do not support this, or that a more secure version would be beneficial to the organisation.

Identify affected stakeholders

Identifying the affected stakeholders in terms of IT service needs or potential issues is essential to recommending an effective solution. For example, just deciding that you will use email for all communication within an organisation may work if all employees sit at a desk with their email running all day. However, if you have some members of staff who do not work at a desk (for example, somebody who works at a machine manufacturing a product), this may not be an effective choice.

System diagrams – which should I use?

As mentioned previously, while the solution may be planned by an IT expert, the decisions about implementing the solution will be made by people who may not be experts. IT system diagrams are an effective way to present technical information in a way that is easier to understand. IT system diagrams can take many forms, but for your assessment you are most likely to use data flow diagrams and network/system diagrams.

Data flow diagrams

DATA FLOW DIAGRAMS show how data and information flow through an IT system, including data required or generated and the stakeholders involved. The diagram may even summarise how the data is converted to information. For more on the difference between information and data, refer back to C1.

Network/system diagrams

NETWORK/SYSTEM DIAGRAMS show how all the component parts of a solution will work together as a complete solution. This is likely to include the devices used by stakeholders, the connections that will be used to communicate between devices and systems and annotations explaining the software being used and the data/information that may be transferred.

See the 'Getting ready for assessment' activity at the end of this unit for an example of a network/system diagram.

Skills and knowledge check

- [ ] Can you identify the IT services needed for a given scenario?
- [ ] Can you describe how IT services would meet identified needs of a given scenario/organisation?
- [ ] Do you understand the difference between data and information?

- ( ) I can plan an IT solution for a given scenario/organisation using both written information and diagrams.

D Impact and implications of an IT service delivery solution

As part of the IT service life cycle, an organisation will continually review the effectiveness of its IT service solutions so that they continually improve the quality of its systems and the efficiency and effectiveness of the organisation.

D1 Reviewing a solution

When a solution is planned (or even when a new system is implemented), it must be reviewed to see if it meets the organisation's needs. In terms of a recommended solution, this review helps the management of an organisation to make decisions as to whether they should invest time and money in implementing the recommendations.

What are the factors that affect the choices made?

In your assessment, you will need to consider not only general factors, such as if an organisation provides a product or service, but also factors that are unique to the organisation for which you are planning a solution. These are known as contextual factors, as they are specific to that scenario (they are 'in context'). You may use communications with stakeholders and other documents and information sources to help you identify them (see Figure 5.5). For more information on the types of documents organisations use, see A2.

Figure 5.5: Contextual factors are those specific to a scenario

How does the solution address the needs of the organisation?

The management of an organisation will want to know why they should invest significant time and money in a recommended solution. As the IT professional, it is your job to ensure that the people who make these decisions have all the information they need. It is important that you can explain clearly how any part of a solution will meet the needs of the organisation and that you have taken into account the contextual factors that are specific to that organisation.

Can it be achieved any other way?

When justifying your recommended solution, it is important to demonstrate that you have considered possible alternatives.

For example, why have you chosen to provide members of staff with expensive laptops if much cheaper alternatives are available? Or why do they have a laptop instead of a tablet? In these cases you should clearly explain how your choice is the most effective in meeting the needs of the organisation and its stakeholders.

D2 Benefits and limitations of a proposed IT solution

Reviewing a solution is essential and it is important that the people who run the company are clear about how the organisation will benefit from the solution. It is unlikely, however, that any system will provide only benefits, but this does not mean that a particular IT service should not be used. Being aware of the benefits and drawbacks allows an organisation to make an informed choice and to allow for the potential drawbacks.

Benefits of a proposed IT solution

Impact on productivity

The primary focus for any IT service is an increase in productivity. However, a review should be more rigorous than just saying 'it will improve productivity' and the organisation's management may want to know how or why productivity is improved. Also, a system may provide mixed results, for example productivity for office-based workers may be increased significantly by a proposed solution but this may not be the case for remote workers. Providing suggestions for alternatives to these types of problems will help stakeholders make decisions.

Availability of service and/or products

One of the key benefits to organisations of IT is the ability to make products available to those who may not have previously had access to them due to location or other factors such as opening times. You should clearly consider this in terms of the benefits and drawbacks of a chosen IT service. For example, you may choose a digital platform that is extremely reliable and rarely breaks down; however, if the platform is not compatible with the devices the organisation's stakeholders will use, then the availability of the product or service is questionable.

Customer satisfaction

An organisation cannot function without its customers, so ensuring they are happy and will continue to use your product or service is key. You should consider multiple aspects of customer satisfaction, for example a change to a new system may cause some level of reduction in customer satisfaction due to customers being unfamiliar with the system. However, once they have adapted to the change, the new features offered may improve customer satisfaction.

Reduction in operational costs

The goal of many IT systems is to make a company more efficient, reducing the cost of running the business. However, there is often a trade-off, for example a computer-controlled manufacturing process may result in less wasted raw materials but the cost of setting up and maintaining the system may be high. The introduction of some IT systems may increase operational costs, but it may be that this investment leads to higher-quality products, improved customer satisfaction and, eventually, increased revenue.

Impact on security

A key aim of any system must be to ensure the security of the data that is held. There may be an option to use a system that is extremely secure but extremely expensive, requiring all staff to be retrained. In this situation, you may look for a solution that makes the current system more secure without major changes to what most staff must do. Another example may be that the system you choose improves the security of the organisation's data but the drawback is that it will change the way in which the organisation's employees perform day-to-day tasks. This may have an impact on productivity while they get used to the new system.

Accuracy of data and information

Data and information are vital to the running of an organisation and any system you choose should aim to improve the accuracy of data. You should consider what impact the resulting benefits and drawbacks of the system chosen have on wider aspects of the organisation. For example, a system may improve accuracy but reduce productivity as it takes longer to enter data.

Disaster prevention and recovery

Disaster prevention and recovery covers a number of systems and processes that ensure that an organisation's data is protected. As with other factors, you should attempt to provide a balanced consideration of how the chosen processes will provide benefits for the organisation. The processes and systems you consider may include, but are not limited to, the following points.

- How often data is backed up.
- Who is responsible for doing the backup.
- Where backed-up data will be kept.
- Policies for the use of external devices such as USB flash drives.

What if...?

Janet runs a care company that provides in-home care for the elderly. She collects and stores information about her clients, which includes personal and medical information.

In a pair or small group, discuss the following.

- Why would it be important that data is accurate?
- What might be the consequences if Janet does not have appropriate disaster prevention and recovery systems in place?

Limitation of features of chosen hardware/software

Although a single piece of hardware or software may not meet all the needs of an organisation, it is important to show that you have considered the limitations of a chosen IT service and why, despite the limitation, this is still the best option. It may be that one particular feature is not provided by a piece of software but it is not vital to the running of the company or it can be accomplished using a slightly different way of working, or by using an additional piece of software, such as the use of text-to-speech for partially sighted users.

Analysing the potential impact of a proposed solution

In addition to the benefits and drawbacks above, there are some factors when implementing a new system that cannot be categorised as 'good' or 'bad' but will nonetheless have an impact on the organisation, its stakeholders and the decisions made for the proposed solution. It is important that these are considered and planned for. While every scenario is different, there are a number of general considerations you can use as a starting point for your analysis. However, remember to ensure they are applied to the specific scenario and solution.

Number of users

A system must be able to allow all current and potential users to perform the required tasks without significant loss in performance. This may impact on choices relating to delivery platform, devices used or connection methods.

Location

The location of the systems that are to be used and the users and customers themselves can have a dramatic effect on the choices made in a solution. For example, it may not be possible to provide remote access to systems if a user does not have a reliable internet connection with sufficient bandwidth to perform the tasks.

User experience

Many systems may provide the same level of functionality but may perform in different ways. A key factor to consider is the experience of the user. If the organisation's employees are using a piece of software every day, for example you may choose a slightly more complex/difficult-to-use piece of software because, once learned, it can perform tasks much quicker. However, if a customer will be using a piece of software, but only rarely, you may choose ease of use over speed of performance. Another consideration may be the provision of accessibility features to support users with additional needs, such as the use of text-to-speech for partially sighted users.

In-house vs outsourced/third-party systems and services

When designing a solution, you may need to choose between using systems that are kept in-house (systems owned and maintained by the organisation) or outsourced/third-party systems (systems owned and maintained by another organisation). Outsourced/third-party systems may include physical network and IT components or cloud/hosted services. There are a number of considerations when choosing between these two options.

- *Expertise of staff*: a small organisation may not employ technical IT support staff and so may choose to outsource its IT services. However, one thing that may need to be considered is the cost. An organisation would need to compare the cost of renting equipment and paying for provided services against the cost of employing additional staff and purchasing the equipment.
- *Training*: ensuring staff can use systems is vital. Some third-party providers will include staff training as part of their service fee, while others will charge additional fees. Also, as new technologies and systems become available, current IT staff may need training to make sure they can continue to deploy and maintain a system or service effectively. An organisation may have to choose between paying for additional training for current IT staff or outsourcing.
- **SERVICE-LEVEL AGREEMENT (SLA)**: an SLA is a contract between the third party and an organisation that outlines what services will be provided and the terms on which they are supplied, such as how quickly issues will be resolved and procedures for reporting and fixing errors. An SLA may also include clauses that outline penalties the service provider will incur if it does not provide the service promised.

Link it up

Refer back to Unit 4 for more information on SLAs.

Implementation/deployment of the solution

When considering the implementation of a new system, an organisation must consider a large number of factors that impact on time and money.

- *Down time*: how long will the organisation be without a working system as data and systems are changed?
- *Compatibility*: how a new feature or system integrates or communicates with other/current systems is vital to ensuring a smooth implementation and continued productivity for the organisation. It does not matter how good a solution may appear in terms of the features it offers, if it does not work with the systems the organisation has, it may have a detrimental effect on the organisation as a whole.
- *Training*: a new system may require that staff are retrained, which may mean a loss in productivity while staff learn to use the new system effectively. Training may also incur costs if external companies have to be hired to provide the training.
- **SCALABILITY**: the ability to alter the capacity of an IT system to meet demand is key to efficiency when using IT systems. If an organisation is successful, it may need to add additional IT services and rapidly improve the capacity of its system. Conversely, should an organisation see a down turn, it may wish to contract its systems to reduce operational costs.
- *Legislation*: there are a number of laws that apply directly to the use of IT and govern what an organisation can and cannot do. An organisation must ensure that appropriate systems are in place so that its IT systems and practices are compliant with the law. This may include ensuring that the health and safety of people using its systems is considered or that it provides adequate protection for customer data.

Practise

Investigate the features and purpose of legislation relevant to the use of IT in organisations. Consider:

- Data Protection Act 1998

- Copyright, Designs and Patents Act 1988

- Computer Misuse Act 1990

- Health and Safety at Work etc. Act 1974.

Information on these can be found by visiting: www.legislation.gov.uk

- *Maintenance*: ongoing maintenance of an IT system is crucial to ensure it stays functional and that security is not compromised. The implications relating to maintenance should be considered when choosing IT services. For example, if an organisation provides desktop PCs for users, software updates can be rolled out across a network and can be scheduled to happen overnight when people are not working. However, if a laptop is provided for a member of staff to take home, it may not be as easy to schedule the update or guarantee that the laptop will be connected to the network when the update is needed.

What maintenance considerations are there for devices that staff take home?

Assessment practice　　　　　　　　　　　　　　**AO1 AO2**

Case study: Warwick Chemicals

Name of organisation: Warwick Chemicals (http://warwickchem.com)

Purpose and type of organisation: manufacturing washing powder additives (product-focused organisation)

Organisation's needs

Office, sales and management staff

Key needs	IT service description
Office staff • Payroll management • Order management • Financial • Communicating with customers	• Provision of desktop PCs connected to a site 'server'. • Server – use of SAN (storage area network) to create a shared-disk file system connected to a series of storage drives with built-in redundancy (RAID). • Enterprise resource planning (ERP) software to manage orders, payroll and company finances. • IP phones and email for communication.
Sales staff • Access to latest product pricing (must be kept secure) • Communication with customers • Mobile working (world travel to visit customers – sales managers only) • Remote/at-home working	• Access to Ultrabook laptops/tablet-laptop hybrid for use when travelling. • Standard laptop equipment for at-home-only workers. • All data on portable devices **ENCRYPTED** to keep sensitive information (for example, pricing, technical details about products) secure. • Smartphones provided for sales managers. • Remote sales work – Session Initiation Protocol (SIP) phone technology provides access to the same phone/extension number that would be used if working in the office, at home or on a smartphone. • Remote access to company network via **VPN (VIRTUAL PRIVATE NETWORK** – enables users to send and receive data across shared or public networks).
Management staff • Access to management-level information, including production figures, sales figures etc. • Mobile working • Communicating with customers	• Access to Ultrabook laptops/tablet-laptop hybrid for use when travelling. • SIP phone technology. • ERP software to manage and provide overviews of key company information. • All data on portable devices encrypted to keep sensitive data secure. • Remote access to company network via VPN.

Warehouse and manufacturing

Key needs	IT service description
• Control of manufacturing process • Track quantity and type of product produced	• Production process control system – allows control of the process from outside the manufacturing plant (improved safety for workers) and allows monitoring and control of all stages of the process (for example, adding raw materials, changing temperatures). • Production control is a closed system (that is, no connection to any other outside network) to ensure system is secure – incorrect control of process could be dangerous. • ERP software allows staff to record the amount and type of product produced using a unique product ID. • Final stage of production (drying/granulation) – each batch is given a unique Batch ID so product can be tracked at all times in the factory and for quality assurance when sent to customers.

Read through the case study on Warwick Chemicals. Practise the skills you will need for the assessment by completing the following activities.

1 Identify other IT service needs for each of the departments mentioned.

2 Describe alternative ways that the IT needs of Warwick Chemicals could be met.

3 Draw IT system/data flow diagrams for some or all of the IT service solutions.

4 In pairs, discuss the implications that the IT service needs and IT service solutions create for Warwick Chemicals. Report the key points of your discussion back to the rest of you class.

You can find out more about Warwick Chemicals at http://warwickchem.com

Skills and knowledge check

☐ Do you understand the contextual factors that affect the needs of organisations?

☐ Can you explain how specific features of a solution meet the needs of an organisation?

○ I can describe the benefits and drawbacks of an IT service delivery solution.

○ I can analyse the implications to stakeholders of a proposed solution.

Getting ready for assessment

This section has been written to help you do your best when you complete the external assessment for this unit. Read through it carefully and ask your tutor if there is anything you are not sure about.

About the assessment

This unit is externally assessed using an unseen task-based assessment. Pearson sets and marks the assessment. The assessment must be taken under exam conditions. You will have access to a computer to complete the activities. You will be given a template to complete some parts of the task, for others you will need to select appropriate software. The task contains three main activities.

Activity 1: IT service catalogue

Activity 2: IT recommendations

Activity 3: Impact and implications analysis

Sitting the assessment

The task-based assessment will be based on a simulated organisation. You will be given two scenarios that provide you with the information you need to complete the activities. The first scenario will be used with Activity 1 and the second will be used for Activities 2 and 3. These will be related to the same organisation but may look at different parts of the organisation or be based in different points in time. Read the scenarios carefully, as marks are often lost by misunderstanding what is required.

Understanding the activities

Activity 1: IT service catalogue

You will be given a service catalogue that will detail some IT services that the organisation is currently using. You will be expected to provide explanations of the benefits and drawbacks of the way the IT services are being used.

Activity 2: IT recommendations

You will be required to produce some IT recommendations for the given organisation to meet its IT service needs. You will need to provide explanations and/or descriptions of current issues, the stakeholders that are affected and the suggested improvements. You will be required to produce an IT system diagram of your proposed solution.

Activity 3: Impact and implications analysis

You will be required to analyse the recommendations that you have made in terms of how well they will meet the needs of the organisation in the scenario, the benefits and drawbacks of your proposed solution and any potential implications of the solution.

Sample questions and answers

Activity 1: IT service catalogue

Scenario 1

Organisation

Fizaan owns a small organisation that makes and sells ice cream.

The organisation is based in a small industrial unit, which contains the kitchen where the ice cream is made, a small warehouse where the product is kept before delivery to customers and an ice cream shop.

Its customers are supermarkets and restaurants who buy their ice cream in large quantities and 'walk-in' customers who buy individual servings from the shop.

Fizaan employs:

* one member of staff to work in the shop
* one member of staff to work in the kitchen and storage facility
* one delivery driver.

Fizaan shares his time between managing the organisation and working in the shop and kitchen.

The organisation's needs are to:

* manage financial tasks (payroll, invoices, shop takings)
* manage stock and customer orders
* manage information about staff and customers
* communicate with customers.

Sales, stock, manufacturing information (for example, quantity made) and incoming and outgoing cash for the shop are recorded using handwritten ledgers and later transferred to a spreadsheet.

Using the IT service catalogue given, you have been asked to provide Fizaan with a summary of the IT services that the business could adopt.

Explain the benefits and drawbacks of the way IT services are currently being used to meet the organisation's needs.

Note – in the assessment you will most likely be given between three and five IT services to consider.

Sample answer

Service name	Service description	Benefits	Drawbacks
Spreadsheet software	Used to keep track of: • staff payroll • money in/money out/profits • order and delivery information about customers.	• A spreadsheet would allow Fizaan to use formulas and functions to calculate pay and other related numerical information. • Date/time formatting in spreadsheet cells would allow Fizaan to track the date of delivery and dates of payments.	• A spreadsheet is not appropriate for storing the order and delivery information. A database would be more useful as this would reduce the chances of duplicated data. • It is difficult to link the different but related data (for example, customers, orders, payments) in a meaningful and effective way. • A spreadsheet does not provide the same 'query' features as a database so it may be difficult to keep track of paid/unpaid invoices or to complete incomplete orders.

Verdict

The learner has considered some benefits and drawbacks of the current IT services used. They have related their answers to the scenario and used suggestions of alternatives to provide meaningful explanations for the points they make. The response could be improved further by considering benefits and drawbacks for all the listed tasks, for example a drawback of using the spreadsheet for payroll is not included.

Scenario 2

Organisation

Fizaan's organisation is doing well and he would like to expand his business.

He is planning to move the organisation to new premises that include a:

- warehouse and commercial kitchen where the ice cream is made
- building that contains an office and the shop.

The warehouse and office/shop are in different locations.

Organisation's staff

- 4 staff in the shop
- 2 office staff
- 2 staff in the kitchen
- 2 staff in the warehouse
- 2 delivery drivers
- 1 IT specialist

Organisation's work locations and key tasks

Fizaan (home- and office based)

Responsible for the success of the company and management of other staff, including:

- managing the company's budget
- company payroll
- checking and monitoring work of staff
- advertising organisation/public relations.

Administration staff (office based)

General administration duties, including:

- organising staff rotas
- supporting customers (including order management)
- communicating with suppliers
- answering phone calls from current and new customers and suppliers
- keeping central records about staff and customers.

Shop staff

General sales duties, including:

- keeping track of stock in the shop
- contacting the warehouse to organise restocking
- keeping track of daily takings (money in).

Warehouse staff

- Manage orders forwarded by office staff.
- Prepare orders ready for delivery.
- Check warehouse stock levels.
- Communicate with kitchen as to current stock levels to plan what needs to be made.

Note – this example provides only an extract from a scenario. In the test your scenario would provide information about all workers and their tasks.

Organisation's key IT service needs

The demands of the organisation have resulted in these key IT service needs.

- Data storage for customer and staff records.
- IT access for staff to support their work.
- Allow accurate tracking of stock to assist with:
  - monitoring stock in the shop and assisting reordering from the warehouse
  - informing kitchen staff what products need producing and when
  - allowing warehouse staff to prepare orders for delivery to customers.
- Portable digital devices for the delivery drivers to:
  - record order contents coming on to and off the delivery vans
  - make and receive calls to warehouse/office
  - help finding delivery locations.

Stakeholders' feedback

- Customers would like to be able to place orders without having to call the office.
- Delivery drivers have noticed that the delivery locations and client contact information can be out of date.
- Delivery drivers find it difficult to schedule their deliveries.
- Delivery drivers say that it is not always easy to tell which boxes in the van are for which delivery.
- Kitchen staff have complained that they are not being given enough notice of what products to make.
- Warehouse staff have noticed that they do not always have the correct products in stock to complete orders.
- Fizaan states that he finds it difficult to monitor staff due to being in different locations.

Additional preferences

- An online platform that allows supermarket and restaurant customers, and members of the public to place and amend orders.
- A method for members of the public to make suggestions and provide feedback.

Activity 2: IT recommendations

Provide IT recommendations that will meet the needs of Fizaan's organisation.

Your recommendations must cover:

- the information and data required by the stakeholders
- the hardware and software to be used
- how hardware and software can be connected and/or will communicate.

Sample answer

Current IT issues	Stakeholders affected	Recommended improvements	Software and hardware
• Accurate tracking of stock	• Customers • All staff	• Provision of a central stock tracking system that will provide information to all staff based on their job role, for example monitoring of stock in the shop through tracking of individual sales.	• Central database software • Desktop PCs in shop, office and warehouse • Portable handheld devices for delivery drivers
• Communicating with customers	• Office staff	• Provide multiple ways of communication to suit the preferences of the customer, such as email or phone.	• Desktop PCs • Access to internet and email addresses • Landline telephone

Verdict

The learner has provided some recommendations that show some awareness of the scenario. They have identified and described some improvements that could be made as to how data and information is handled and the software and hardware suggested are appropriate for their recommendations. However, the learner has not shown a wide enough consideration of the organisation's needs. For the first IT issue identified, for example (accurate tracking of stock), the learner should have addressed each of the bullets provided in the scenario in turn.

Sample answer

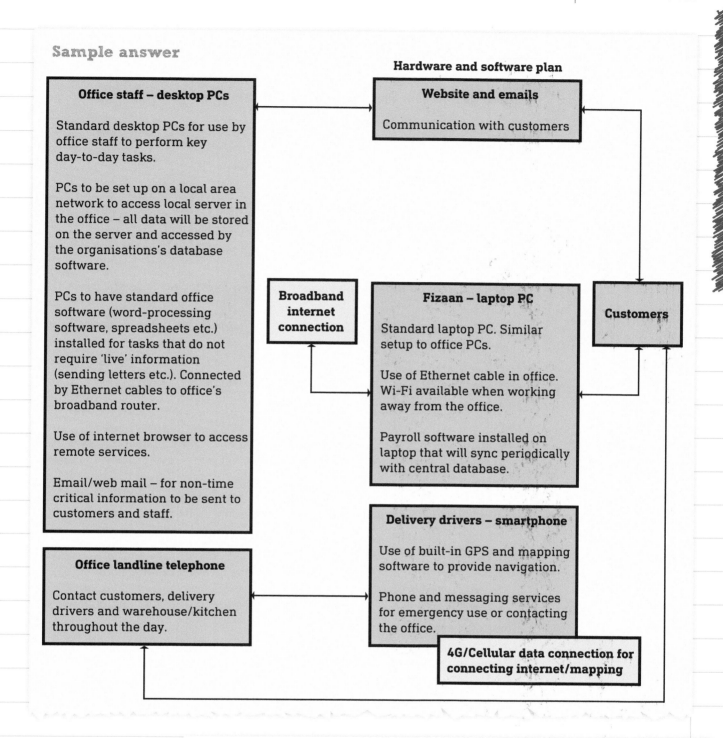

Hardware and software plan

Office staff – desktop PCs

Standard desktop PCs for use by office staff to perform key day-to-day tasks.

PCs to be set up on a local area network to access local server in the office – all data will be stored on the server and accessed by the organisations's database software.

PCs to have standard office software (word-processing software, spreadsheets etc.) installed for tasks that do not require 'live' information (sending letters etc.). Connected by Ethernet cables to office's broadband router.

Use of internet browser to access remote services.

Email/web mail – for non-time critical information to be sent to customers and staff.

Website and emails

Communication with customers

Broadband internet connection

Fizaan – laptop PC

Standard laptop PC. Similar setup to office PCs.

Use of Ethernet cable in office. Wi-Fi available when working away from the office.

Payroll software installed on laptop that will sync periodically with central database.

Customers

Office landline telephone

Contact customers, delivery drivers and warehouse/kitchen throughout the day.

Delivery drivers – smartphone

Use of built-in GPS and mapping software to provide navigation.

Phone and messaging services for emergency use or contacting the office.

4G/Cellular data connection for connecting internet/mapping

Verdict

The learner has provided a diagram of a partial solution that covers some of the IT requirements of the scenario. They have shown some technical understanding and when combined with the first part of the task (the table) it shows more understanding of the scenario. However, the learner has not addressed a number of the organisation's key needs and made only implied reference to the additional preferences.

Activity 3: Impact and implications analysis

Analyse your recommendations and how they meet the needs of the organisation.

Sample answer

How the solution will address the needs of the organisation

The solution meets all needs of the organisation by providing:

- a central database system and 'calendar' that can be managed remotely by the managers
- smartphones for drivers so they can locate the delivery locations and contact customers and the office
- a laptop for Fizaan, which allows him to work from home or the office and to work when visiting customers
- the local server to hold the database and other files
- emails and landlines to communicate with customers.

Benefits to the company and its stakeholders

Database

- Using a centrally stored database system that will ensure all data is always up to date on all connected devices, and the data can be reviewed and used in real time.
- A relational database will reduce duplicated data and mean stock levels and order information are more accurate (compared with using a spreadsheet).
- Use of a local server may improve security as hosted solutions are often targeted by hackers due to their high-profile nature.
- Hosted services for business can be very expensive and require complex contracts/agreements so having the organisation's own network maintained by its own IT staff allows the organisation to be more flexible with how staff use it.

Smartphones

- GPS and location features on the phone can be used to track location and movement of drivers during the day and estimate order delivery times for customers and allow Fizaan to monitor staff performance and efficiency.
- The smartphones' converged technology provides an effective and cost-effective solution. The one device can be used to provide multiple services (phone calls, internet connection, navigation, etc).
- The smartphones provide multiple ways of accessing data, so if one signal is unavailable (for example the mobile phone does not have a signal from the provider), other wireless networks could be used.

Drawbacks of the solution

Using a central self-maintained server solution has some drawbacks.

- The initial cost of purchasing the equipment and ongoing running costs.
- IT specialist staff may need regular retraining to ensure their skills are up to date.
- The company only employs one IT specialist, so maintenance, updates and repair may be difficult to manage or may be slow to implement.
- The use of smartphones to provide multiple services (GPS and contact) may mean battery life is very short and will need constantly recharging.
- Drivers may not feel comfortable being tracked. This may cause bad relationships between management and workers.
- Mobile devices such as smartphones are at risk of being lost or stolen. As they provide access to sensitive information, this would be a concern for the company.

The implications that your solution will have for the organisation

- Due to the risk of loss or theft of the smartphones, specific and robust security measures are needed to ensure that the sensitive data that they can access is kept safe. This may include:
  - use of encryption to secure any locally stored data
  - use of passwords to restrict access to the device.
- As the company will be storing personal data about customers and staff, it will need to ensure that it has systems in place that provide adequate protection and comply with UK requirements and laws.
- The company will need to register the fact that it keeps personal data (and what this data is) with the appropriate authorities (Information Commissioner).

Verdict

The learner has provided a good review of their solution. They have considered benefits and drawbacks of their solution and suggested some of the implications. The review could be developed further through clearer justification of their choices in the 'benefits' section and suggestion of some alternatives in the 'drawback' section.

6 Database Tools and Techniques

Have you ever considered what life would be like without databases? Or how data is being continually captured in our everyday lives? Databases are an integral tool for individuals and organisations, as they are able to store information in a way that allows it to be searched, retrieved and organised easily.

In this unit, you will learn how to use data collection methods and how to use database tools and techniques to design, create and test relational databases to be presented to different audiences.

How will I be assessed?

You will be assessed through an activity that will be practical in nature and will provide you with a realistic scenario in which you can draw on previous learning from the unit, including transferable skills such as communication, developing practical and technical skills, and managing information. You will need to assign a set period of time in order to complete the assessment and to ensure it is delivered on time.

Assessment criteria

Pass	Merit	Distinction
Learning aim A: Use data collection methods to gather data from a range of sources		
A.P1 Create and use a basic data collection document to gather data for a given purpose, using limited formatting.	**A.M1** Create and use a customised data collection document to gather data for a given purpose, using some structure.	**A.D1** Create and use a fully-customised data collection document that has clear structure and is easy to use, allowing data to be easily transferred to the database.
Learning aim B: Use database tools to design, create and test a simple relational database		
B.P2 Create outline design documentation for a given database using the design documentation, create the database.	**B.M2** Create detailed design documentation for a relational database using at least three tables and using the design documentation, create the database.	**B.D2** Create comprehensive design documentation for a relational database using at least three tables and using the design documentation, create the database.
B.P3 Create and use a basic test plan that tests some functions of the database.	**B.M3** Create and use a detailed test plan that tests most functions of the database and uses some appropriate test data.	**B.D3** Create and use a comprehensive test plan that tests all functions of the database using fully appropriate test data.
Learning aim C: Apply techniques to analyse and present data to different audiences		
C.P4 Apply basic database techniques to analyse and present data.	**C.M4** Apply a range of advanced database techniques to analyse and present data for given purposes.	**C.D4** Apply a wide range of advanced database techniques to analyse and present data that is suitable for different audiences and for specific purposes.

A Use data collection methods to gather data from a range of sources

Organisations make use of databases in a variety of ways. As a starting point, consider what a database is, and what it is used for.

A1 The purpose of databases

A **DATABASE** is an organised collection of **DATA** that uses tables, records and fields to store data.

- **TABLES**: these are used to store raw data for a particular category.
- **RECORDS**: a record is a complete set of fields, for example a student's school record.
- **FIELDS**: a field is a single piece of data, such as a name, date of birth or a telephone number.

There are different **SOFTWARE** applications available for developers to use. For example, Oracle®, IBM DB2® and MySQL™ are all types of database applications. In this unit, you will be using Microsoft Access®, which is known as a Relational Database Management System (RDBMS).

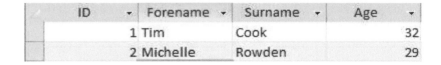

ID	Forename	Surname	Age
1	Tim	Cook	32
2	Michelle	Rowden	29

Records can be considered as rows, and fields can be considered as columns

Link it up

Data Management

Refer back to Unit 2 for more information on why organisations invest in technology (including databases).

Benefits of databases

Organisations use databases because they can store vast amounts of information efficiently as they require little space. In addition, they are more secure than traditional data storage, such as paper files, which are hard to protect. With electronic data you can secure data, for example with **ENCRYPTION** such as a **PASSWORD**. However, there are several other advantages for using a database. They can:

- improve productivity by allowing the user to search for key information quickly and efficiently
- aid decision making by looking at key information and making informed decisions
- be used to present information to a variety of stakeholders that can be shown in all different kinds of reports
- be used to interpret data by performing queries that can be used to filter information
- perform calculations to help managers' decision making
- be used to manage large data sets.

Where databases are used

There are many examples of where databases are used. You will find databases in numerous public and private organisations. For example, the Police National Computer (PNC) is used extensively by law enforcement organisations across the United Kingdom. It holds millions of records on individuals who have broken the law, and can be used to identify all known criminals. Schools also use a database to store details about their students.

For example, it can easily show staff how many days' absence a student has had, what their test results are, or how many achievement awards they have.

Below are some more examples of where databases are used.

- Hospitals store patient details, including history of any health issues they have reported and appointments they have attended.
- In any workplace, employers hold information such as your name, payroll information and what department you work in.
- The government uses a database to store records of people's income tax payments.
- Social media websites such as Facebook® use a database to store information on all registered individuals.
- Libraries use databases to store information on members. They can use this information to determine who has a book on loan and who has outstanding fines.

A2 Data collection methods

Data is the collective name for information that is recorded for statistical purposes so that sets of data can be compared and analysts can look for meaningful trends and changes.

Data requirements

There are two main forms of data, which can be categorised as qualitative data and quantitative data. Quantitative data is also known as discrete and continuous data (this is defined further in the section 'Gathering the data' below).

- **QUALITATIVE DATA**: this is data that can only be written in words (not numbers) – for example, 'What were your thoughts on the usability of the database?'
- **QUANTITATIVE DATA**: this is data that can be written in numbers – for example, 'What is your age?'

Primary and secondary sources of information

You can categorise information into primary information and secondary information.

Primary information

PRIMARY INFORMATION is when you gather new data that has not been collected before. For example by using surveys, questionnaires or interviews to collect information within a **FOCUS GROUP** (a small discussion group of users) or from the general public.

There are other types of primary information as well, for example sales employers can check availability of their existing customers using online tools such as Doodle polls and SurveyMonkey™. Phone use is another type of primary information source – researchers can look at an individual's phone use and ascertain how long they are spending on specific apps, and which apps they are using the most.

Secondary information

SECONDARY INFORMATION is existing data that has already been produced that you gather for your own use. For example, you might conduct research using the internet, newspapers and television. The largest store of information is the internet. For example, you might use published information from a website and collate it with your own findings (primary research).

It is important to consider that secondary information can be **BIASED** (biased information is written to provide one particular opinion or to influence people's views in a certain direction). In order to avoid using biased information, consider the following questions.

- Who produced the information?
- What is the purpose of the information?
- Is the text trying to be persuasive?
- Does the text consider other points of view?

Link it up

Data Management

See Unit 9 for more on data collection methods.

Gathering data

When you are gathering data for a questionnaire or a survey, it is important to understand how to develop qualitative and quantitative questions.

Qualitative questions are more influenced by personal feelings and opinions, and the value of the information you obtain will depend largely on the quality of questions you ask. For example, if you ask the question, 'Do you like food?' the answer is likely to prompt the response, 'Yes'. This does not tell you what the respondent likes about food or what types of food they prefer. An open-ended question such as, 'What type of food do you like best?' will provide a much more informative response.

Quantitative questions are easier to measure and easier for survey takers to answer. Quantitative questions typically start with 'How' or 'What'.

- How many?
- How often?
- How much?
- What percentage?
- What proportion?

When developing questionnaires or surveys, some users categorise quantitative data into discrete or continuous data. Discrete data is numerical data that can only be counted in whole units, and cannot be shown in decimals or fractions, for example the number of individuals attending a concert. Continuous data is numerical data that can be shown in decimals, for example the temperature outside.

Another method of gathering data is through observation, which you can use when you want to view or record a consumer's or customer's behaviour. For example, did you know that supermarkets often observe the patterns of how shoppers navigate around the store? This can help the supermarket identify the aisles that customers visit most often.

Practise

You have been recruited by a software development company to overhaul an outdated database system that is no longer fit for purpose. You are to develop a questionnaire that is to be used to elicit primary information from users. The data you provide will help the database developers shape the new and improved database.

1 Develop a list of five qualitative questions that could be asked.

2 Develop a list of five quantitative questions that could be asked.

Restrictions on data collection

In order to gain information from an individual you must have their consent. However, it is also important to consider that data processing is needed in order for a contract to be legally binding, for example for billing, job applications or loan requests. There is a legal imperative on any organisation collecting personal information to protect it. Failure to comply with this will lead to a BREACH (breaking of) of the Data Protection Act 1998. This was designed to protect sensitive data held in databases. It was originally passed in 1984, with an update in 1998 that was brought into effect in 2000. Every organisation that stores data (for example, information concerning customers) must register and state the data that it plans to hold. There are eight principles in the Data Protection Act (see Figure 6.1).

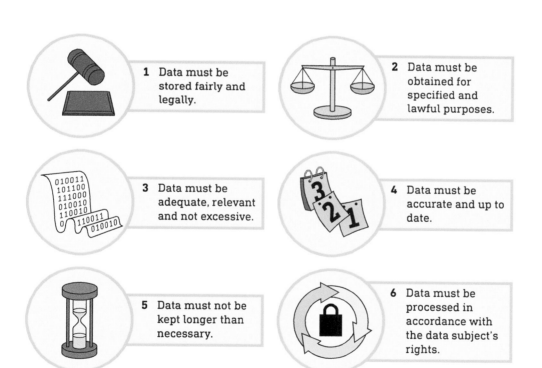

1 Data must be stored fairly and legally.

2 Data must be obtained for specified and lawful purposes.

3 Data must be adequate, relevant and not excessive.

4 Data must be accurate and up to date.

5 Data must not be kept longer than necessary.

6 Data must be processed in accordance with the data subject's rights.

7 Data must be reasonably securely kept.

8 Data must not be transferred to any other country without adequate protection in place.

Figure 6.1: The Data Protection Act 1998 is integral to protecting a person's right to have their personal data stored securely

Link it up

Data Management

For more on the Data Protection Act, including the eight principles, refer back to Unit 3.

Under the Data Protection Act, the data subject has several rights, including the right to:

- compensation for unauthorised disclosure of data
- compensation for unauthorised inaccurate data
- access data, which includes the removal of data if it is inaccurate
- compensation for unauthorised access, loss or destruction.

Therefore a considerable amount of responsibility is placed on the organisation that holds the data. Keeping the data secure is of significant importance and keeping it secure costs money. For example, a database administrator might be employed to look after the data and ensure the organisation is complying with the Data Protection Act.

What if...?

Tim works for the Metropolitan Police and is responsible for administrating the Police National Computer (PNC). The police use the database to provide intelligence to police and other criminal justice or law enforcement agencies by holding extensive information on people, vehicles, crimes and property. It is accessible over a secure network, within seconds and from thousands of terminals across the country at any time.

The PNC is used by different law enforcement agencies and is used for a whole variety of crime detection. For example, database analysts can use the PNC to identify patterns and links in crimes across the UK and use that information to aid in the detection of criminals, particularly in serious serial-type crimes.

1 One of Tim's jobs is to ensure that data is kept secure and not used irresponsibly, for example he is not allowed to use the PNC database for his own personal use. Why do you think this is the case?

2 What implications would there be for Tim and the police if he was shown to have broken this rule?

3 What would happen if Tim was negligent in his duties and information regarding criminals was revealed to someone who had no right to the information?

Skills and knowledge check

- ☐ What is meant by tables, fields and records?
- ☐ What is the difference between qualitative and quantitative data?
- ☐ What is the difference between primary and secondary information?
- ☐ What is discrete data?
- ☐ Which type of information has the potential for being biased?
- ☐ 'On a scale of 1–10' is what type of question?

- ◯ I can state which year the Data Protection Act was passed.
- ◯ I can name a possible consequence of storing inaccurate information on a customer.

B Use database tools to design, create and test a simple relational database

As with all creative activity, every database needs to be designed on the basis of a full analysis of requirements. Moreover, databases are always part of wider systems and, as such, database design activity should be seen as and be part of a system's analysis process.

B1 Design a simple relational database

In order to design a relational database, it is important that you first understand the fundamental concepts of relational database design. Once you have understood these concepts, you can then start designing the database.

Data dictionary

A **DATA DICTIONARY** is a set of information that describes the content, format and structure of a database and the relationship between its elements. In this section, you will explore this further, as well as looking at the tools necessary to design, create and test a relational database.

- Field names: a data dictionary will include information on a field name. A **FIELD** is a single piece of data, such as name, date of birth or telephone number. It is important to remember that when you design a database you should give a meaningful name to a field, for example use 'Date of Birth' rather than abbreviations such as 'DOB'.
- **DATA TYPES**: each field name will have a data type. This will determine how the data within the field will be stored, for example if you are storing someone's age, you will use a 'Number' data type.

Table 6.1 is an example of data types available in, for example, Microsoft Access.

Data type	Description	Comment, including field sizes
Text	Text or combinations of text and numbers	Up to 255 characters. Microsoft Access only stores the characters entered in a field. You can control the maximum number of characters that can be entered.
Number	Numeric data	Can be used for calculations but calculations involving money normally use currency type.
Date/Time	Dates and times	Uses 8 bytes only. Different formats can be chosen.
Currency	Currency value	Use the currency data type to prevent rounding off during calculations. Accurate to 15 digits to the left of the decimal point and 4 digits to the right.

Table 6.1: Data types in Microsoft Access

Table 6.1: *(continued)*

Data type	Description	Comment, including field sizes
Autonumber	Unique number incrementing by one each time	Automatically inserted when a record is added. Uses 4 bytes only. Can also choose random numbering instead of sequential.
Yes/No	Field to contain only one of two values	Appropriate for fields storing 'Yes/No', 'True/False' or 'On/Off'. Only uses 1 bit.
OLE (Object Linked Embedded)	Objects	Examples might be documents, spreadsheets, pictures or sounds. This can use up to 1 gigabyte.
Web (Hyperlink)	Fields that will store a hyperlink	Can store up to 64,000 characters.
Lookup Wizard	A field that allows a user to choose from another table or from a list of values	The same as the field that is also the Lookup field. Choosing this option in the data-type list starts a wizard to define the lookup table for the user.

- **FIELD SIZES**: a field size determines how much memory space should be set aside for a particular field. This can be important for the database to run smoothly, because if you allocate too much memory, this can slow down the database. For example, let us assume you create a name field. This would not require the default amount of 255 characters as no one's name is that long. So you would amend the 255 to be something that is more appropriate.

Table 6.2 shows the different field sizes of each data type.

Table 6.2: Field sizes of different data types

Data type	Size
Text	The text data type is used for short text fields of limited length, and can contain up to 255 characters.
Memo	A memo field is a virtually unlimited text field. It can store up to 1GB of text.
Byte	A single byte number can hold between 0 and 255. This uses 1 byte.
Integer	An integer can hold a number between −32768 and 32767. This uses 2 bytes.
Long integer	A long integer can hold a number between −2 billion and 2 billion. This uses 4 bytes.
Single	This is used for floating point numbers and uses 4 bytes
Double	This is used for large floating point numbers. Due to its sheer size this uses 8 bytes of memory.
Decimal	Decimal numbers are so called fixed point numbers. They can have a fractional part and can be either positive or negative. A decimal number uses 17 bytes of disk space.
Currency	The currency type is a special kind of decimal, with up to 4 digits on the right of the decimal point and up to 15 on the left. It was introduced for financial data and is available in all versions of Access. This type uses 8 bytes of disk space.

- **FIELD FORMATS**: within Microsoft Access and other database applications, you have the ability to change the field format. This means you can change how the data is displayed. This does not affect how the data is stored in a Microsoft Access database.

In the following example, you can see how the 'Date/Time' field has different field formats that you can select.

Field Properties

General	Lookup		
Format			
Input Mask	General Date	12/11/2015 17:34:23	▼
Caption	Long Date	12 November 2015	
Default Value	Medium Date	12-Nov-15	
Validation Rule	Short Date	12/11/2015	
Validation Text	Long Time	17:34:23	
Required	Medium Time	05:34 PM	
Indexed	Short Time	17:34	

American short date format differs from European short date format as the day and month are reversed (month appearing first)

In the following example, you can see the different formats of **INTEGERS** (whole numbers) including fixed and currency. You also have the ability to state how many decimal places are introduced.

General	Lookup		
Field Size	Integer		
Format			
Decimal Places	General Number	3456.789	▼
Input Mask	Currency	£3,456.79	
Caption	Euro	€3,456.79	
Default Value	Fixed	3456.79	
Validation Rule	Standard	3,456.79	
Validation Text	Percent	123.00%	
Required	Scientific	3.46E+03	

The E within scientific integer format means 'exponent (power or index)'. For example, if you multiply 10,000,000,000 x 10,000,000,000 the answer is too big so you will see 1.e4-20

- **DEFAULT VALUES**: this means a value placed within a numeric data field prior to a user inputting information. Typically, the value tends to be zero, although you can change this from the field properties, as seen in the following example.

General	Lookup
Field Size	Integer
Format	
Decimal Places	Auto
Input Mask	
Caption	
Default Value	0

Default values are a useful tool for database developers because they ensure that a record has data within it

- **PRIMARY KEY**: a primary key aims to uniquely identify every record. Sometimes the primary key is a single field but in other situations you might need a combination of fields to always uniquely identify each record. In many situations, there will be a natural choice for the primary key, but where this is not the case, database designers set an **AUTO-INCREMENT** (adding a value automatically) so that each new record receives a primary key that is just the next one on a sequence.
- Often the primary key of one table is found in another table when it is used to link the tables together. In this situation, in the other table it is called a **FOREIGN KEY**, as shown in the example in Figure 6.2. It is important that the tables related in this way are kept consistent and it should not be possible to add a record to the second table that does not exist as a primary key in the first table. When all the tables are consistent in this way, the database is said to have **REFERENTIAL INTEGRITY**.

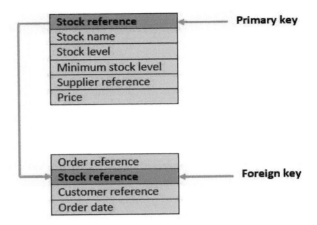

Figure 6.2: Using primary and foreign keys helps a database developer speed up queries and searches

Data validation

VALIDATION is the process of checking that data that is entered into a database (or system) is reasonable and in the correct format. For example, assume you are designing a database and one of the fields you need to create is called Mobile Number. A mobile number has 11 digits. A database developer can validate this to ensure that only 11-digit numbers can be entered. If a user tries to enter a value with fewer or more than 11 digits, then this will be registered as incorrect.

Below are some examples of validation.

- *Lists*: a list offers a user a choice of options. This is sometimes referred to as a combo box, and allows the user to simply select an option that appears from the list, for example a title field, with list options restricted to Mr, Mrs, Miss, Ms or Dr.
- *Rules/Text*: a validation rule and text are used together. A rule first sets out the condition of what values may be input. Text will appear on the screen as a form of message box that will inform the user if they have entered data incorrectly.

Link it up

Data Management

See Unit 9 for more information on the integrity of data and how to validate data.

Field Properties

General	Lookup	
Field Size	255	
Format		
Input Mask		
Caption		
Default Value		
Validation Rule	"M" Or "F"	
Validation Text	You must only type in M for Male, or F for Female	
Required	No	
Allow Zero Length	Yes	
Indexed	No	
Unicode Compression	Yes	
IME Mode	No Control	
IME Sentence Mode	None	
Text Align	General	

It is important when using a validation rule that the validation text is meaningful and relevant

- *Presence check*: a presence check is the simplest method of validation. A presence check can be used on any field in a database and simply checks that some data has been entered into the field, and that the field has not been left blank.
- *Range check*: a range check is commonly used when you are working with data that consists of numbers, currency or dates/times. A range check allows you to set suitable boundaries, for example only allowing ages to be entered between 18 and 100.
- *Format check*: a format check ensures that entered data is in a particular format. The format that data must be in is specified using an **INPUT MASK** (this is used to control what users are allowed to enter as input in a text box). The key purpose is to improve the quality of input data. The input mask is made up of special characters that indicate what characters may be typed where.

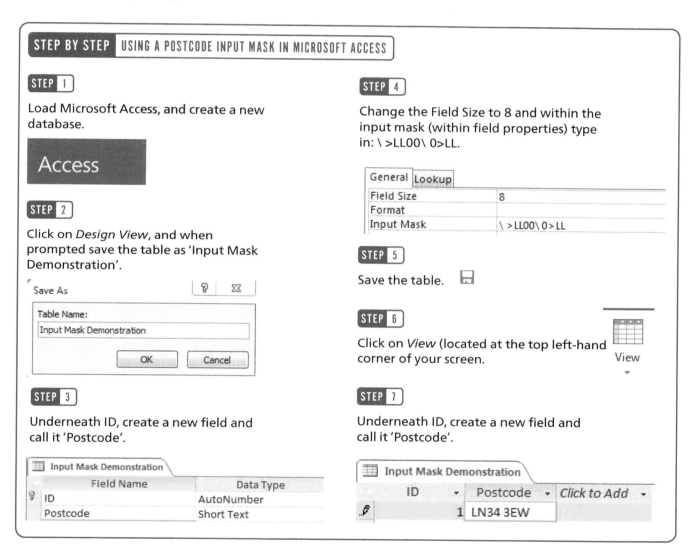

STEP BY STEP USING A POSTCODE INPUT MASK IN MICROSOFT ACCESS

STEP 1

Load Microsoft Access, and create a new database.

Access

STEP 2

Click on *Design View*, and when prompted save the table as 'Input Mask Demonstration'.

Save As

Table Name:

Input Mask Demonstration

OK   Cancel

STEP 3

Underneath ID, create a new field and call it 'Postcode'.

Field Name	Data Type
ID	AutoNumber
Postcode	Short Text

STEP 4

Change the Field Size to 8 and within the input mask (within field properties) type in: \ >LL00\ 0>LL.

General	Lookup	
Field Size		8
Format		
Input Mask		\ >LL00\ 0 > LL

STEP 5

Save the table.

STEP 6

Click on *View* (located at the top left-hand corner of your screen.

View

STEP 7

Underneath ID, create a new field and call it 'Postcode'.

ID	Postcode	Click to Add
1	LN34 3EW	

Entity relationship diagram

In this unit, you have learned about the relationship between primary and foreign keys. However, this does not necessarily show you everything you need to know about the nature of the relationship. Within databases, there are three types of relationship that can exist between tables. These are known as one-to-many, one-to-one and many-to-many relationships.

In the example that follows, each item in the 'Stock' table can be ordered by many customers, so for every record in the 'Stock' table, there may be more than one record in the 'Orders' table. For this reason, it is described as a one-to-many relationship. The tables actually relate to entities. The relationship is shown in Figure 6.3.

Figure 6.3: One-to-many relationship

In many situations, there could be a relationship which is many-to-many. For example, if a number of products could be put in any order, then the relationship becomes a many-to-many relationship. Many-to-many relationships are difficult to implement in a database. Therefore, to deal with this type of relationship, another intermediate table is created that breaks the many-to-many relationship into two one-to-many relationships.

In some situations, the relationship is one-to-one (Figure 6.4). For example, in the 'Patient details' table and the 'Patient medical details' table shown below, in both cases 'Patient' reference is the primary key.

Patient details table

Patient reference
Forename
Surname
Address
Patient date of birth

Patient medical details table

Patient reference
Blood group
GP
Gender

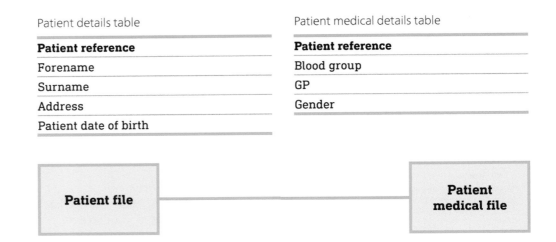

Figure 6.4: One-to-one relationship

Input forms

Once a table has been designed, a form can be generated using the form wizard feature. A form allows a user to enter data into the database. The wizard feature has a number of different layouts that allow a user to select their preference. Once a user has finished with the wizard and a form is presented, they can modify the form using the toolbox if necessary.

Output screens/reports

A report outputs the information. For example, if you have entered data within the database and would like to display the records in an appealing format, then a report can achieve this. Similarly, a web user can select the wizard function to use this. They go through the step-by-step options, such as what data they would like to display and the format it is presented in. Once this is completed, the data is presented onscreen.

It is sometimes easier to consider forms as the input method, and reports as the output method.

Report Example

PersonID	Surname	Forename	Age	Salary	County
1	Grajek	Dorota	34	£23,000.00	Lincolnshire
2	Rowden	Michelle	32	£34,000.00	Bedfordshire
3	Smith	Mick	56	£23,600.00	Yorkshire
4	Choudhry	Adil	41	£32,980.00	Lincolnshire
5	Bean	Cameron	39	£50,020.00	Buckinghamshire
6	Smith	Linda	65	£32,000.00	London
7	Green	Matthew	27	£43,567.00	Bedfordshire

A report outputs the information in a more appealing format

Test plan with test data

Test planning should identify the lists of tests that, if performed, will identify whether the database meets the business and technical requirements that guided its design and development and works as expected.

The test plan records the overall approach to the test. It shows how the tests will be organised, and outlines all the tests that are needed. When developing the series of tests, you must take full account of the original set of user requirements, as this will connect it to the fundamental purpose of the wider developmental activity. Furthermore, the customer should be given some access to the test results, as it will require them to formally sign off on the testing.

You should discuss the test plan and agree it with the wider development team.

A typical test plan is presented here in table form.

Test number	Purpose of test	Test data	Expected results	Actual results	Comments

- *Test number*: a unique number is assigned to a test.
- *Purpose of test*: a description of what is being tested.
- *Test data*: steps that describe the specific steps which make up the interaction.
- *Expected results*: this should describe the expected state of the database after the test case was executed.
- *Actual results*: citing what happened.
- *Comments*: this is an opportunity to comment further on the test, for example if a test did not perform as expected, but worked on remedial action, what steps were taken to fix the issue?

B2 Create a simple relational database

The design of the database must be finalised before you begin to implement it. Later changes made to the underpinning design could mean that you may have to start again from the beginning.

Creating tables

An ideal table:

- has a field that uniquely identifies each record (the primary key)
- does not contain unnecessary duplicate fields
- has no repetition of the same type of value
- has no fields that belong in other tables.

Creating fields

An ideal field:

- represents a characteristic of a table subject
- contains a single value
- has an appropriate name.

Validation rules

In Microsoft Access, there is a feature called 'Validation rule'. To enter a validation rule, a user must first go to the table properties and enter the rule and text they want to appear. The example below represents a field type where the user is forced to only type in 'M' for Male, or 'F' for Female. If this rule is broken, the database will force the user to try again.

Field Properties

General	Lookup	
Field Size	255
Format	
Input Mask	
Caption	
Default Value	
Validation Rule	"M" Or "F"
Validation Text	You must only type in M for Male, or F for Female
Required	No
Allow Zero Length	Yes
Indexed	No
Unicode Compression	Yes
IME Mode	No Control
IME Sentence Mode	None
Text Align	General

Entering a validation rule ensures you get the information you need

Practise

Using the steps shown previously, create the following database for a vet's surgery.

1 Create three tables, called 'Customer Table', 'Pet Table', 'Appointments Table'.

2 Create the following fields within each table:

Customer Table:

- Customer ID, Title, Surname, Street, Town, Mobile number

Pet Table:

- Pet ID, Pet name, Animal type, Age

Appointments Table:

- Appointment ID, Customer ID, Pet ID, Date of appointment, Time of appointment

3 Use appropriate data types for each field.

4 Use an input mask for 'Mobile number', 'Date of appointment' and 'Time of appointment'.

5 Set a validation rule that permits a pet's age to be between 1 and 50. Appropriate text should be displayed if the rule is broken to prompt a valid input.

6 Build the relationships.

7 Populate the database with five records in each table.

Importing data from external sources

If data that is to be used in a database is already available in another form, it makes sense to import the data electronically, thus avoiding the possibility of errors made when re-entering the data. However, it may be complex to do so. Importing can be a dangerous and sometimes time-consuming job. Things can go wrong and, if the file is large, it will not be possible to check the accuracy of every single entry. Small tests should be carried out on a limited number of records to make sure that the technique chosen is working.

Some files are stored as text but with a DELIMITER (a character used to separate fields when data is stored as plain text) to separate the files and a hard return to separate records. In the example shown, the delimiter is a comma. The delimiter most often used is the comma, hence the term comma-delimited file.

STEP BY STEP   HOW TO IMPORT DATA INTO MICROSOFT ACCESS

STEP 1

Open Microsoft Excel® and create six fictitious records for ID; Forename; Surname and Age. Save the file as test data and close Excel.

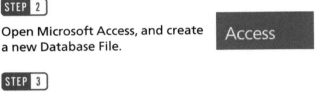

	A	B	C	D
1	1	Dorota	Grajek	32
2	2	Michelle	Rowden	33
3	3	Mick	Bean	55
4	4	Mark	Andrews	22
5	5	Barry	Douce	44
6	6	Heather	Miller	43

STEP 2

Open Microsoft Access, and create a new Database File.

Access

STEP 3

Click on *External Data*, and then *Microsoft Excel*.

FILE   HOME   CREATE   EXTERNAL DATA

Saved Imports | Linked Table Manager | Excel | Access | ODBC Database | Text File | XML File | More

Import & Link

STEP 4

STEP 5

The wizard will take you to the next part, click on *Finish*.

Field1 ▼	Field2 ▼	Field3 ▼	Field4 ▼	Click to Add ▼
1	Dorota	Grajek	32	
2	Michelle	Rowden	33	
3	Mick	Bean	55	
4	Mark	Andrews	22	
5	Barry	Douce	44	
6	Heather	Miller	43	

STEP 6

The imported data is available to view in Sheet1.

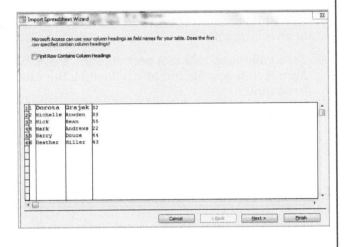

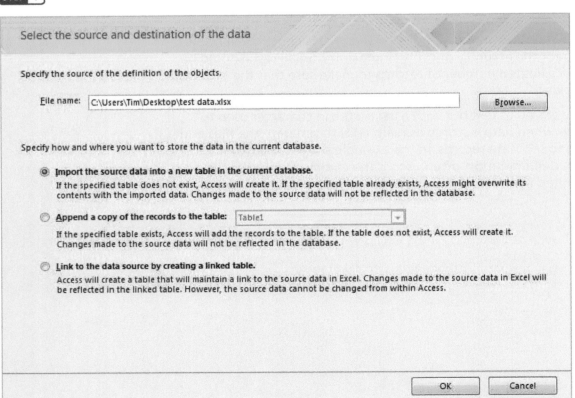

Select the source and destination of the data

Specify the source of the definition of the objects.

File name: C:\Users\Tim\Desktop\test data.xlsx   Browse...

Specify how and where you want to store the data in the current database.

○ **Import the source data into a new table in the current database.**
If the specified table does not exist, Access will create it. If the specified table already exists, Access might overwrite its contents with the imported data. Changes made to the source data will not be reflected in the database.

○ **Append a copy of the records to the table:** Table1
If the specified table exists, Access will add the records to the table. If the table does not exist, Access will create it. Changes made to the source data will not be reflected in the database.

○ **Link to the data source by creating a linked table.**
Access will create a table that will maintain a link to the source data in Excel. Changes made to the source data in Excel will be reflected in the linked table. However, the source data cannot be changed from within Access.

OK   Cancel

Relationships

You must ensure that the relationships between the tables are correct. As database designer, you must also ensure that, as changes are made to the content of the tables during routine use, the integrity of the database is not compromised. Referential integrity is needed in order to achieve this. Referential integrity ensures that relationships between records in related tables are valid and that users do not accidentally delete or change related data.

Creating, editing and deleting relationships

To create a relationship, you must first click on Relationships within the Design tab. From here you can add all your tables, and create relationships between the tables. Simply click on the link you want to provide (for example, primary key to foreign key), and drag this to the table where you want the relationship.

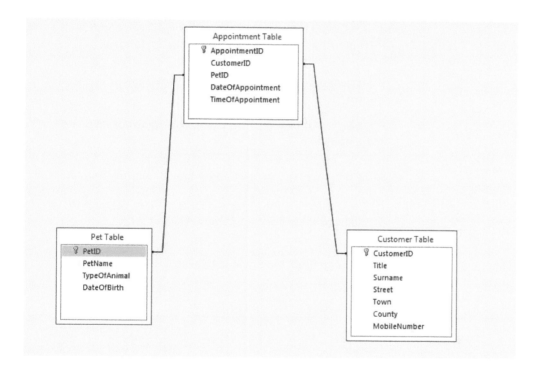

A primary key in Access is represented by a small key symbol next to the field name

Once this has been completed, you can edit the links by clicking on them and pressing delete, or by double clicking on the links to edit them.

Data entry forms

A **DATA ENTRY FORM** is viewed onscreen and a report that is created from the form is designed to provide printed output. Data entry forms are designed to make it easier to enter information into a database (as opposed to using tables). A report is used to present information in a more appealing way.

Wizards can be used to design basic forms and reports in a limited number of styles and can be modified to suit a particular need. It is possible to create a form or report from scratch. However, most database users opt to use a wizard alongside the Toolbox in order to modify it.

The Access Toolbox is a toolbar. When you choose one of the buttons that appear in the Toolbox, you add or influence a control, represented by that tool's symbol (see Table 6.3).

Table 6.3: Controls available in the Access toolbox

Control wizard	Logo	Description
Label	*Aa*	Control that displays descriptive text, such as a title or a caption.
Text box	|ab|	Used to display, enter, or amend data in the underlying record source of a form. Also, a text box can be used to display the results of a calculation or accept input from a user.
Option button	◉	Used to provide a true or false response (for example, yes or no).
Check box	✓	Used to provide multiple options for a user response (for example, bold, italic or underline).
Combo box		Used to control data entry by providing the user with a number of options to select from.
List box		Displays a scrollable list of values.
Command button	xxxx	Used to create buttons with actions attached.
Image		Used to display a static image within the form.
Page break		Starts a new screen on a form or a new page in a printed form.
Tab control		Creates a tabbed form with several pages or tabbed dialogue box.
Subform/ Subreport		Used to display data from more than one form or table.
Line	/	Adds a graphic line to help visual layout.
Rectangle		Adds a graphic rectangle to help visual layout.

STEP BY STEP **HOW TO CREATE A FORM IN MICROSOFT ACCESS**

STEP 1

Load Microsoft Access and open any saved database with a table.

Access

STEP 2

Click on *CREATE*, and then *Form Wizard*.

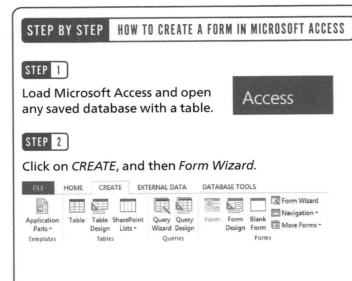

STEP 3

Select the table, and the fields you wish to place within the input form (simply highlight the field and click on >; alternatively if you wish to select all the fields click on >>). Click *Next* once you have finished.

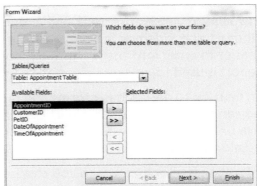

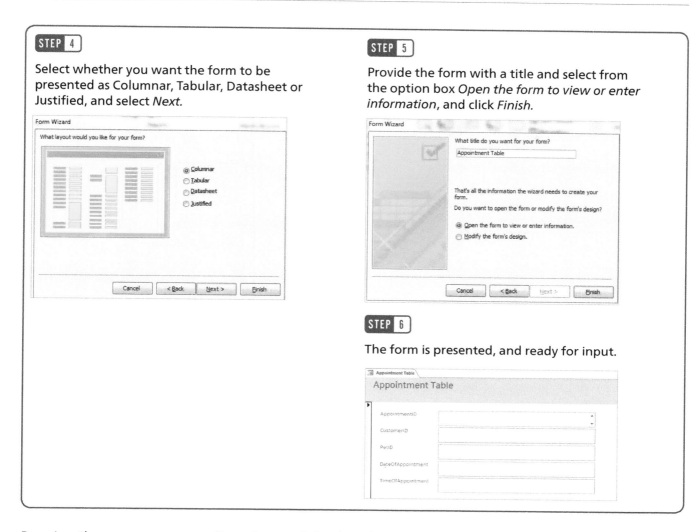

STEP 4

Select whether you want the form to be presented as Columnar, Tabular, Datasheet or Justified, and select *Next*.

STEP 5

Provide the form with a title and select from the option box *Open the form to view or enter information*, and click *Finish*.

STEP 6

The form is presented, and ready for input.

By using the menu, you can edit and amend the data form. By clicking on *View* (located in the top left-hand corner of the menu) and selecting *Design View*, you will be presented with the design layout of the form. From here you have the ability to add controls, amend the layout, style, colouring and alignment.

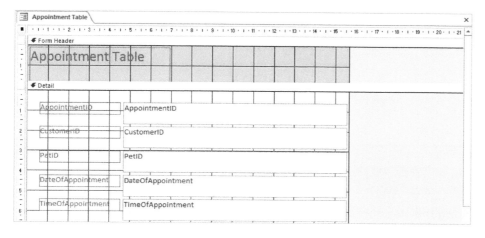

A form header is useful for giving a form a title. This is often emphasised to make it clear to a database developer what the form entails

Customising forms

Most database application packages are generic and designed to be used in any and all situations. When a particular application is designed for a specific purpose, it can be very useful to customise it in order to remove unnecessary options or provide specific front ends to support the intended users.

One of the features of forms is that you can customise the form to provide additional functionality. For example, you can create a button to scroll through records, print a record, amend a record, or search a record.

STEP BY STEP | **HOW TO CUSTOMISE A FORM BY ADDING A NEW RECORD**

STEP 1

Load Microsoft Access and open your previously saved form.

STEP 2

Double click on *Form* (in this instance it is called *Appointment Table* – you may have called yours something different).

STEP 3

Click on *View*, and then *Design View* from the dropdown list.

STEP 4

From the *Menu* click on *Button* (rectangle box with *xxxx*), and drag this onto your form (wherever you wish this to appear).

STEP 5

From the Wizard Options Click on *Record Operations* and select *Add New Record*, and click on *Next*.

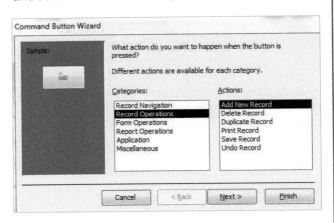

STEP 6

Select whether you want the button to have text or an image (to represent your *Add New Button* feature), and click on *Finish*.

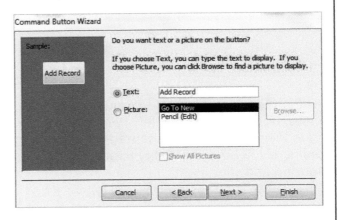

STEP 7

Your button is created, and you are now able to *Add Record*.

Practise

Using the steps shown previously, create the following features within your database form.

1. A 'Print Record' button.
2. A 'Delete Record' button.
3. A 'Search Record' button.
4. A 'Navigate to First Record' button.
5. A 'Navigate to Last Record' button.
6. A 'Navigate to Next Record' button.
7. A 'Navigate to Previous Record' button.

B3 Use a test plan to test a relational database

One of the most important aspects when evaluating a completed database system is whether it meets the user need. In order to find this out, a testing strategy is required.

Purpose of testing

Testing your completed database system will enable you to:
- identify whether the requirements have been met and if there are any further development needs (functionality)
- evaluate its ease of use (usability).

Testing data

There are different testing methodologies that a database developer can employ to ensure that the completed database fulfils these requirements.

BLACK BOX TESTING is commonly used by database developers and programmers. It uses pre-prepared test data that produces the expected results. (Black box testing is when a database or program is tested without taking into consideration the code. The database or program is the 'box', which is 'black', as the tester does not see anything inside it.)

Black box testing utilises a test plan (see B1 'Test plan with test data') to test various aspects of the database to ensure it works as expected. When you are developing a database, you will need to populate the test plan with the different aspects of functionality that you would like to test. You will then record the results to ensure the database works as expected. If some part of the database does not work as intended, then you will need to repeat the test (with a record of what went wrong), making any necessary amendments. Repeat the test until the desired outcome is met.

Making amendments following testing

Table 6.4 presents various testing data and results to show the process you will adopt as a database developer to test the functionality of your database. It is important to note this is just a small extract, and you could test much more to ensure your database works as intended.

Table 6.4: Testing data

Test number	Purpose of test	Test data	Expected results	Actual results	Comments
1	To ensure the input mask within the table 'Personal' works correctly for phone number.	01205 432123	The input mask should allow only the correct number of figures and no letters.	Worked as expected	N/A
2A	To ensure the validation rule within the table 'Personal' works correctly for 'Age', ensuring that a number equal to or over 18 can be entered.	18	The database should accept 18.	FAILED	The database prompted a message box stating that this number is not permitted.

Table 6.4: *(continued)*

Test number	Purpose of test	Test data	Expected results	Actual results	Comments
2B	To ensure the validation rule within the table 'Personal' works correctly for 'Age', ensuring that a number equal to or over 18 can be entered.	18	The database should accept 18.	Worked as expected	The issue was resolved as the validation rule omitted the '=' from >=18. It was only reading as >18 (see Table 6.5 for more information on the logical operators =, <, <=, >, >=).
3	To ensure the validation rule within the table 'Personal' works correctly for 'Age', ensuring that a number equal to or over 18 can be entered.	5	The database should prompt the user to try again, as the number entered is not equal to or above 18.	Worked as expected	N/A
4	To ensure the combo box within the table 'Personal' for the field 'Title' works correctly.	Click on the combo box and select Mr.	The database should allow the dropdown box to accept Mr when clicked on.	Worked as expected	N/A

As you can see, test 2A did not work as intended, and there was a fault in the database. This was clearly documented within the comments section. Amendments were made and it worked on the second test (test 2B), with the comments highlighting what amendments were made following testing.

Test data

There are three main types of test data to be created and included in the test plan for each table.

- *Normal*: this is data that can be considered the ordinary/typical (normal) type of data you would expect to be input to the field and that should be accepted.
- *Erroneous*: this is data that is incorrect for this field (for example, a text value in a number field) and should be rejected with a suitable error message.
- *Extreme*: this is data that is at the limit of what should be accepted. This might be in terms of the maximum and minimum acceptable values in a numeric field, or a value with the maximum number of characters for a text field. Extreme values (for test data) should include those on the limit of what is acceptable (and so should be accepted) and just outside the limit (which should be rejected).

Feedback from others

Finally, it is necessary to confirm that the system is fit for purpose by asking the client to formally 'sign off' the finished system. The act of asking a client to sign off typically encourages a more detailed check than would otherwise be made.

Within the feedback process, it might well be that the client will have several people testing the database to ensure it works as expected. Questionnaires and interviews can be used to elicit feedback from the user, asking questions such as 'What parts of the systems worked?', 'What didn't work?' and 'Are there any changes that are required?'. Once the client has signed off the system, it means that they accept it as it is.

Skills and knowledge check

- ☐ What is meant by a primary key and a foreign key?
- ☐ What is the difference between a form and a report?
- ☐ What is an ERD?
- ☐ How is a wizard useful to a database developer?
- ☐ What is the difference between a table and a field?
- ☐ When would you use a range check?

- ◯ I can describe at least two methods of data validation.
- ◯ I know what does black box testing is.

C Apply techniques to analyse and present data to different audiences

Databases are remarkable tools for many different reasons. They allow any user to analyse information in a variety of ways. For example, this is useful for the National Health Service (NHS) because it is able to search a database to find out which patients are due their annual flu vaccination. There are different techniques that make it possible to present data to different audiences. You are going to explore this next.

C1 Use techniques to analyse data

There are many different techniques that database applications such as Microsoft Access can use in order to analyse data. Perhaps one of the most common techniques is queries (see below). However, it is important to recognise that there are further techniques which can be utilised as well. In the next section, you will explore this further and learn how to apply these techniques.

Queries

Link it up

Data Management

See Unit 9 for more information about queries and how to design them for a given purpose.

Perhaps one of the strongest features that databases have is the ability to analyse data quickly and efficiently. The way in which they can achieve this is through designing a **QUERY** (used to select data from fields that you, as a database developer specify, and with the criteria that you set for those fields).

Queries allow users to see different views of the information in a database. Once a query has been created, it acts as if it is a new table, although the underlying information is not duplicated. Instead, it is used to present useful information that someone such as an administrator would need to know. For example, in an NHS surgery, letters might be sent to all patients who have not had their flu vaccination by the end of October. If an administrator did this manually (for example, by checking through the physical records in a filing cabinet) it would take a long time. However, using a query in a database, this information can be generated in seconds.

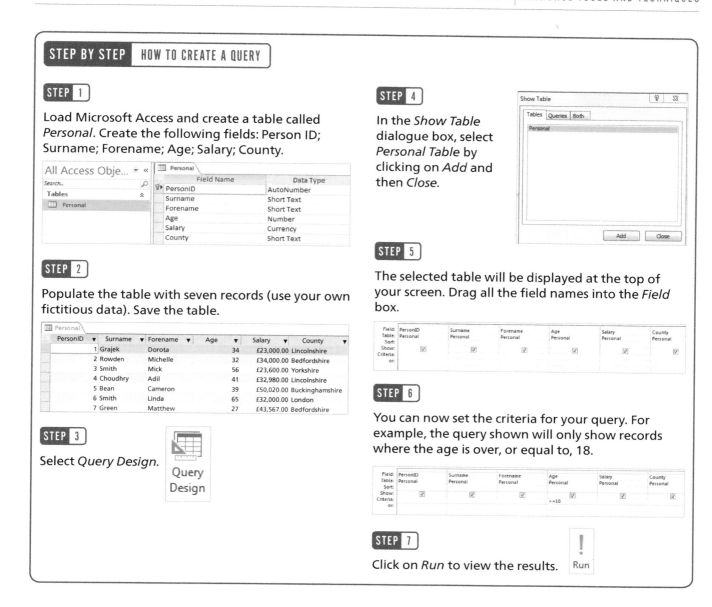

The exercise above gives an example of a single criterion in use. However, it is possible to generate queries that make use of multiple criteria linked to different tables. To achieve this, a database developer must make use of logical operators (see Table 6.5).

Table 6.5: Logical operators and their descriptions

Logical operator	Description
=	Equal to
Not	Not equal to
<	Less than
<=	Less than or equal to
>	Greater than
>=	Greater than or equal to
Like	Matches a prescribed character pattern. The * symbol is used as a wildcard

Practise

Based on the table you have developed, create queries for the following scenarios.

1 Find all records of people who have a salary over £17,000.

2 Find all records of people who were born before 1 January 1980.

3 Find all records of people who have the surname 'Smith'.

4 Find all records of people who are older than 50 and live in Lincolnshire.

Sorting data

The data that is returned from your query search can also be sorted. It is possible that this can be done across single and multiple fields. When you sort records, you are putting them into a logical order, with similar data grouped together. As a result, sorted data is often simpler to read and understand than unsorted data. Sorting it is achieved though either **ASCENDING ORDER** or **DESCENDING ORDER** (ascending means going up, so an ascending order will arrange numbers from smallest to largest and text from A to Z; descending means going down, so an descending order will arrange largest to smallest for numbers and Z to A for text).

It is important that primary fields are sorted to make it simple for a database user to find data easily

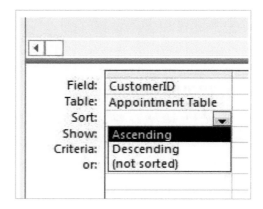

Calculations

Microsoft Access has several functions that allow for the use of calculations to take place. For example, within a query it is possible to calculate the total value of a field within a table or query. To do this you must first click on *Totals* within the query. Once this has been done, another row within the query called *Totals* appears.

'Avg' means average and gives you the mean average of a list of numbers

- *Sum*: this function is used to calculate the total value of a field in a table or query.
- *Average*: this function is used to calculate the mean average of a field that has a data type of number, date/time or currency.
- *Max*: the maximum value of a field can be calculated using the *Max* function. This could be a number, date/time, or currency, for example you could use this to calculate the highest unit price of all products sold.
- *Min*: the minimum value of a field can be calculated using the *Min* function. This could be a number, date, time or currency, for example you could use this to determine the smallest unit price of all products sold.

Data cleansing

DATA CLEANSING is the process of changing or removing data in a database that is incorrect, incomplete, improperly formatted, or duplicated. The aim of data cleansing is to make the data more accurate and consistent, thus also saving on storage space.

In an organisation where there are vast amounts of data within a database, it is inevitable that there will be some errors within the data, such as duplication of records. Within a database there are tools that can correct a number of specific mistakes such as inconsistently formatted text and duplicated records. These tools are very useful because without them it would take a lot of time for a database administrator to go through all the records and correct the mistake manually.

There are several data cleansing tools online, and companies that specialise in their use. Quite often organisations will utilise specialists in data cleansing to make their data more accurate and consistent. This costs the organisation money. However, it is important to consider that it is the responsibility of an organisation to keep the data accurate. Moreover, having a database administrator complete the task manually would take a lot of time, which is also expensive.

Data mining

DATA MINING is the process of analysing data, in an attempt to discover meaningful information that can be used by an organisation to predict future outcomes, discover new opportunities and improve their performance.

Data mining techniques automatically search large amounts of data to discover patterns and trends that may not be obvious with simple analysis. There are many different sophisticated mathematical techniques that can be used to analyse the data. Some of the common ones are listed below.

- *Cluster analysis*: this involves attempting to divide the data into groups or clusters. For example, a supermarket may divide its customers into groups according to whether they are interested in a particular product or based on their previous purchasing history. This information can then be used to target advertising at particular demographic groups.
- *Anomaly detection*: this type of analysis looks for data that is outside the norm (for example, values which are significantly different from the usual range of values). Typically applications include credit card fraud detection, where transactions are flagged up as possibly fraudulent because they involve far larger amounts of money or take place in a different location from where the account holder normally shops.

- *Association rule mining*: this attempts to identify dependencies in the data. The technique was originally developed to allow retailers to analyse customer shopping baskets and identify items that were commonly bought together. For example, the analysis might identify that when customers purchase one item, they very commonly also purchase another, otherwise unrelated item. This data can be useful for deciding how to adjust store layouts (which items to place close to each other), for choosing promotions and optimising catalogue design. The technique can also be used for other applications such as medical diagnosis and weather forecasting.
- *Data visualisation*: this involves presenting the data in charts or graphs to allow users to understand the data more easily and identify pattern that may exist within it.

Although data mining is primarily used by retail companies to identify customer preferences and use this information to inform decisions about pricing, promotions and product placement, it is also used in a wide range of other applications such as banking. For example, to assign a credit score to a customer when deciding whether to lend them money or not, scientific research and network intrusion detection are required.

There are many data mining tools available, comprising both open-source and proprietary software. Examples of well-known proprietary software include IBM SPSS® modeller, SAS Enterprise Miner™ and Microsoft SQL Server Analysis Service™.

C2 Use techniques to present data

Within databases you are presented with lots of data in different forms, for example this could be data that is presented in tables or queries. Sometimes you need the data to be displayed differently in order to present this information to different audiences. A **DATABASE REPORT** is the best way to achieve this.

Reporting

A database report presents information from a database. Information is displayed simply and efficiently in different formats and layouts.

This simple database table shows information very clearly, but database developers often use reports to display information in a more vibrant way

Customer Table		
CustomerID	Title	Surname
1	Mr	Cook
2	Mrs	Rowden
3	Mr	Annan
4	Miss	Wells
5	Mr	Smith
6	Mr	Brown
7	Mrs	Andrews
8	Mr	Benson
9	Miss	Chen
10	Mr	Lexy

STEP BY STEP HOW TO CREATE A REPORT

STEP 1

Load Microsoft Access and open a previously saved database (with populated data).

STEP 2

Click on *Create*, and *Report Wizard*.

STEP 3

Choose the *Tables/Queries*, and select the fields you wish to present and then click on *Next*.

STEP 4

Select any groupings you require, and then click on *Next*.

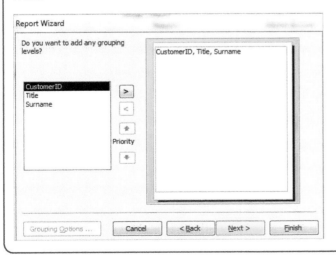

STEP 5

Select the sort of order you want to use to present your records.

STEP 6

Choose the layout you require, and click on *Finish*.

Customising and editing a report

In Access, the design of a report is divided into sections. In a client database, you can view your report in 'Design' view to see its sections. To create useful reports, it is important to understand how each section works. For instance, the section in which you choose to place a calculated control determines how Access calculates the results.

- *Report header*: this section is printed just once, at the beginning of the report. Use the report header for information that might normally appear on a cover page, such as a logo, a title, or a date. When you place a calculated control that uses the *Sum* aggregate function in the report header, the sum calculated is for the entire report. The report header is printed before the page header.
- *Page header*: this section is printed at the top of every page, for example use a page header to repeat the report title on every page.
- *Group header*: this section is printed at the beginning of each new group of records. Use the group header to print the group name, for example in a report that is grouped by product, use the group header to print the product name. When you place a calculated control that uses the *Sum* aggregate function in the group header, the sum is for the current group. You can have multiple group header sections on a report, depending on how many grouping levels you have added.
- *Detail*: this section is printed once for every row in the record source. This is where you place the controls that make up the main body of the report.
- *Group footer*: this section is printed at the end of every page. This is used for printing page numbers of page information.
- *Report footer:* this section is printed just once, at the end of the report. This is used to print report totals or other summary information for the entire report.

To edit the report, you must first go into the 'Design' view. From here you are able to change the alignment, colour and all the other aspects of the sections outlined above. For example, if you wanted to move the title (in report header Customer Table) into the middle, you would simply select it and drag it to the middle. You can then click on Report View to see the changes.

A report design view is important for a database developer to move and manipulate data to make it more intuitive for a user to view the information

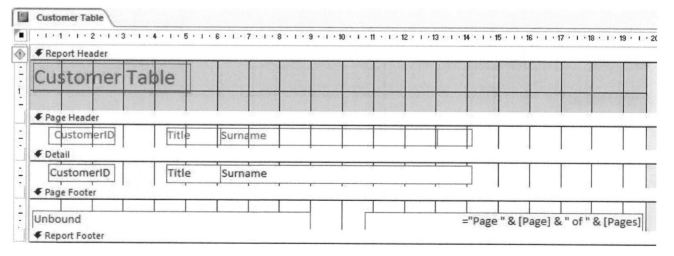

Presentations

Perhaps the most widely used presentation program is Microsoft PowerPoint®. This software package makes it easy for presenters to create a visual presentation package that will help to engage the audience. Within the presentation there are slides that convey information, which the presenter can communicate to the audience.

Many people like to add text, which can help to support their talking points and ensure that the audience takes away the key elements from the presentation. In addition, further elements can be embedded within the presentation to help engage with the audience. For example, images, sound clips and videos can be used to help the presentation become more engaging and interesting.

Diagrammatic displays

When presenting information to audiences, it is always advisable not to confine yourself to one type of medium. Presentation packages are a useful tool to communicate to audiences. However, diagrammatic displays are also a useful means of presenting information. There is a saying that 'a picture paints a thousand words'. This is true and there are packages such as Microsoft Visio™ where a user can present:

- flowcharts
- storyboards
- rich pictures
- data flow diagrams
- entity relationship diagrams (ERDs).

These are all useful methods that can be used to present to audiences.

Presenting to different audiences

Presentation is perhaps one of the most difficult skills to master. However, it is a skill that all computing professionals should try to develop. For example, in most computing jobs (including database development), you will be required to present data to different audiences. Also, when you apply for a computing position, the chances are you will be asked to undertake some form of presentation.

Presenting to an audience can be a daunting prospect and can cause nerves that may result in a confused demonstration. To combat your nerves, try adopting some of the techniques below.

- *Stay calm*: try to remain calm, and remember to breathe. Take a couple of slow, deep breaths just before your presentation to help focus your mind and steady yourself.
- *The presentation*: once you begin your presentation, try to project your voice and speak more loudly and slowly than usual. This may seem unnatural, but it will make your presentation easier to understand and will help to calm your nerves.
- *Field questions*: perhaps one of the most important points to consider when presenting is rehearsing. Rehearse your presentation multiple times, and research possible questions that could be asked. Managers will want to know as much information as possible, and will ask searching questions. The key is to prepare as much as possible and put yourself in the place of a manager.
- *Know your audience*: it is important to know your audience (this could be your peers, managers or customers), and acknowledge the people you are presenting to. This means that when you are communicating key information, look people in the eyes and try to make a connection.

Skills and knowledge check

- ☐ Can you sort data into single and multiple fields?
- ☐ Can you describe what a wildcard is?
- ☐ Can you sort data to represent different calculations?
- ☐ What is meant by the term 'data mining'?

- ○ I can describe how organisations use data mining techniques.
- ○ I can explain how data mining benefits an organisation.
- ○ I can produce and edit reports in Microsoft Access.
- ○ I can recognise techniques that are essential to presenting to different audiences.

Ready for assessment

In this unit, you will be assessed by a single assignment that includes a number of assessed tasks set by your tutor. Throughout this unit, you will find practice activities that will help you work towards your assessment. Completing these activities will not mean that you have achieved a particular grade, but that you will have carried out useful research or preparation that will be relevant when it comes to your final assignment.

In order for you to achieve the tasks in your assignment, it is important to check that you have met all the Pass criteria. You can do this as you work your way through the assignment.

If you are hoping to gain a Merit or Distinction, you should also make sure that you present the information in your assignment in the style that is required by the relevant assessment criteria. For example, Merit criteria require you to create detailed designs, whereas Distinction criteria focus on comprehensive designs.

The assignment set by your tutor will consist of a scenario with a number of tasks designed to meet all the grading criteria set out within this unit. For example, you may be presented with a scenario that places you in the role of a junior database technician, who has been given a number of practical tasks to complete. Your role in this organisation is to gather data on current and potential customers to use for a marketing campaign to promote the product or service. Once the data has been gathered, you will design, create and test a simple relational database with two tables to store data for the organisation. This will be used to make decisions on organisational matters using a range of database tools. You will also present information from the database into reports for a given purpose. (Tutors can decide on the purpose of the reports.) You will make your manager aware of the different techniques used to ensure accurate data is collected, stored and used.

Working towards a scenario and practical tasks will provide you with a realistic expectation of what it would be like if you were working for an actual organisation.

WORK FOCUS

┌ HANDS ON

Imagine you are working for a new doctors' surgery as an IT manager

A new small, rural surgery has opened and is currently deciding which IT application it should use to store all its patient information. The practice manager wants you to use Microsoft Excel because she is already familiar with spreadsheets. She is aware of the importance of verifying and validating the information stored.

However, there has been some suggestion that a database application program would be more suitable. Your practice manager is not keen on using a different application package and would like to know more about the benefits of Microsoft Access before any final decision can be made.

Role-play with a partner the reasons why your practice manager should use Microsoft Access and how you would communicate with her, taking into account her limited technical knowledge.

How did you:

- explain the benefits of Microsoft Access

- explain the limitations of Microsoft Excel when using it is a database

- communicate to your practice manager without being condescending to her?

Questions

1 What communication style did you adopt when communicating?

2 How will the details that you presented help the practice manager make her final decision?

Ready for work?

You will need to demonstrate that you have the skills and behaviours required to work on your own and with others to solve simple and complex problems. Being able to practise these skills and behaviours could help you gain employment as an entry-level database administrator.

1 Problem solving

- Are you able to design an effective database solution?

- Are you able to use the tools to validate data entry?

- Are you able to use queries effectively in order to search for data?

- Are you able to use reports to present information clearly?

- Are you able to use forms to facilitate easy data entry?

2 Communication

- Are you able to communicate with different people, including people with and without technical knowledge?

- Are you calm under pressure and able to communicate clearly to managers?

3 Managing information

- Are you able to accurately input records into a database with no errors?

- Are you able to decipher referential integrity errors and to develop a solution?

4 Working with others

- Are you able to support team members who may be trying to fix a fault that you have experienced before?

- Do you know your own strengths and weaknesses and are you able to escalate jobs to other people?

7 Digital Applications Development

Think about the digital applications you use each day. These could be applications on a computer or device, or could be hidden applications inside technology you use, such as games consoles or even your fridge or satellite TV box. Can you imagine a world without technology?

In this unit, you will learn how to design digital applications for a range of business contexts. You will study the principles of user interface (UI) design and explore the impact this has on the user experience as a whole. You will learn how to consider the end-user when you plan, create and test an application using a wide variety of digital components.

How will I be assessed?

You will be internally assessed through a series of assignments which draw on the knowledge and skills you will develop in this unit. The assignment will focus on the design and creation of a digital application that is required to solve a business problem.

You will need to show that you understand the useful features and any limitations in the hardware and software available, particularly in relation to how this may impact on your choice of interface design components.

Planning, creating and testing applications is one of the key skills required of an IT professional and this assessment will allow you to demonstrate both your technical skill and your creativity in problem solving for a business situation.

Assessment criteria

Pass	Merit	Distinction
Learning aim A: Develop skills to produce a digital application for an organisational purpose		
A.P1 Produce digital content for an application and identify digital applications suitable for the creation of digital content considering both hardware and software requirements to meet an organisational need.	**A.M1** Explain digital applications suitable for the creation of digital content considering both hardware and software requirements to meet an organisational need and produce a range of digital content within a content management system to meet organisational needs.	**A.D1** Justify choice of digital applications suitable for the creation of digital content considering both hardware and software requirements to meet an organisational need and produce a range of interactive digital content within a content management system to meet organisational needs.
Learning aim B: Create a user interface design		
B.P2 Create a UI design, identifying the key usability and accessibility features included.	**B.M2** Create a UI design, explaining the key usability and accessibility features included.	**B.D2** Create a UI design independently, justifying the design against user requirements, highlighting the key usability and accessibility features and providing alternative solutions.
Learning aim C: Create and test a digital application for an organisational purpose		
C.P3 Create a digital media within a content management system.	**C.M3** Create a range of interactive digital media to produce a functional digital application within a content management system, making an improvement based on user feedback.	**C.D3** Create a range of interactive digital media to produce a multi-functional digital application within a content management system, making significant improvements based on user feedback.
C.P4 Test a digital application, providing feedback and a completed test plan, including two positive comments and one area for development.		

A Develop skills to produce a digital application for an organisation's purpose

A1 Uses of digital applications

Organisations use **DIGITAL APPLICATIONS** (**SOFTWARE** used on computers or electronic devices) to be competitive and to keep their customers satisfied.

Digital application types

Digital applications help organisations to refine the services they provide and to improve how they communicate with their customers. Typical uses include the following.

- *Online help*: 24/7 (24 hours a day, 7 days a week) support for products and services that can usually be accessed from anywhere in the world.
- *Digital marketing*: through various communication channels, including email and social media, to find new customers.
- *Loan calculators*: to help customers make decisions about the money they borrow and who they borrow from.

Practise

Select at least six digital applications that you use (these could be social media sites, or apps on your tablet or phone). Write down:

- the name of each application
- how often you use it (for example, daily, weekly, monthly).

The features of digital applications

Digital applications that have been well designed and carefully developed can add to an organisation's image and brand. For example, Pepsi® or Pizza Hut® and Apple® are well-known brands.

How an organisation behaves, how it represents itself and how it responds to its customers are all part of an organisation's reputation and anything it does wrong can affect the brand.

If a brand has been positively affected, customers will usually buy more. If it has been negatively affected, customers will often buy less. This is why organisations look after their brands.

Practise

Select three digital applications that you would miss if they did not exist. Write down:

- the name of each application
- why you would miss them.

Digital applications and their use

Here are some examples of how digital applications can be used for a variety of business purposes.

- *Marketing*: display advertising on social media and gaming sites that use visual content such as images and videos to attract customers' attention.
- *Sales*: online brochures that use a combination of media content, including text, videos and images to enable customers to fully explore products and services (for example, looking at a product from all sides – a 360° view).
- *Information*: websites that provide technical information or **FAQS** (frequently asked questions are a predicted list of common questions that users are likely to ask) and which provide regularly updated content.
- *e-commerce*: online portals with efficient and easy-to-use functionality so that customers can purchase goods and services 24/7.
- *Support services*: animations or other **INTERACTIVE** content that help customers to use the products or services (such as putting together flatpack furniture). Interactive means that software or a product responds to a user's actions or inputs.
- *Financial*: services such as PayPal®, Worldpay® or Sage Pay® that have a reputation for reliability and security to enable customers to pay for things.
- *Collaboration*: online 'chat now' functionality so that customers can talk to company staff.

Practise

You are trying to set up a pre-owned mobile phone (which means there is no user guide to work with). You need help, but what sort of help do you want? Discuss with a partner which of the following you would prefer, and why.

- 'Chat now' functionality with the manufacturer of the phone.
- Video or animation that walks you through the setup process.
- A list of instructions with FAQs.

Real-world digital products and their effectiveness

For digital applications to be effective you have to think about how they are put together (Figure 7.1).

Figure 7.1: What do you need to consider when creating a digital application?

Target audience: the users that the digital application is for – for example, small children, teenagers, older people, business people, the less able, people of a particular religion, males or females, learners, computer users who are beginners or advanced users. It is likely that a target audience may well be complex – for example, a 68-year-old learner with limited vision.

Purpose: this is the reason why the digital application is needed. A digital application is usually created to solve a business problem – for example, to increase sales of a product or to give advice.

Aesthetics: this is the way that the digital application looks – its content, the quality of the content and the way the content is organised in the space available.

Copyright: before you publish any media content (sound, video, images and even text) you have to make sure that the **COPYRIGHT** (a legal term that gives a particular person or organisation the authority to make decisions about how materials are used) does not belong to someone else. If it does, you can be prohibited (stopped) from using it, or you could get into legal problems.

Multimedia: this is where you consider using lots of different media (sound, images, text, video, etc.) to communicate your content.

Interactivity: digital applications can be interactive or passive. Passive means that the user just looks at the content – reading text or looking at images. Interactive means that some of the content requires the user to input information, to click buttons or links, or to choose options from menus or submenus.

Accessibility: in order for a digital application to be considered fully accessible, any type of user should be able to use it, regardless of any disability or level of experience (such as a novice or advanced user).

Proofing content: no digital application should ever be made available for use unless the content has been fully proofed. This means you should check visual appearance, spelling and grammar. You must also check that all links work and any other errors that could impact on the effectiveness of the application have been corrected.

A2 Digital content systems

Organisations will require different types of content for different purposes.

Different types of content used by organisations

There are two main media types for content:
- printed
- digital.

Media for printed visual products include posters, packaging, brochures, leaflets and flyers.

Media for digital products include film, animation, interactive media, **AUGMENTED REALITY (AR)**, digital advertisements and CGI.

Link it up

Digital Applications

Refer back to Unit 5 for more information about **HARDWARE** accessibility devices and benefits in relation to how they are used in different solutions.

Practise

What does CGI mean? Find out and write down a definition.

The purposes of visual products

Table 7.1 gives some examples of both printed and digital media that are used for different business purposes or activities with ideas about the sorts of visual products that might be relevant.

Table 7.1: Print and digital media

Business purpose	Printed media	Digital media
Entertainment and leisure	Posters for films or events, brochures for club membership, sheet music	Web pages with activity timetables at a gym, computer games, health and fitness apps
Communication and socialising	Newspapers and magazines (both general and subject specific such as *Computer Weekly*)	Social media sites and chat applications for you to keep in contact with your friends
Education and training	Books and journals to support courses, newsletters for parents	Video tutorials
Marketing	Flyers for new products or services delivered by post, inserted into newspapers or under the windscreen wipers on your car	Rolling digital advertisements on the London Underground or on billboards, web banners
Virtual reality simulations		Applications for training, particularly for dangerous jobs such as bomb disposal, for surgeons to learn new procedures, or to teach pilots how to fly different types of planes and to handle complex situations
Publishing	Brochures and book listings to use with libraries, schools and colleges	e-books, including optional narration, electronic bookmarks, animated pictures, etc.
Sales, service and support	Packaging for products, posters for special offers	Web-based help content, chat now applications
Science (including social science)	Research papers	Applications to capture DATA or analyse data that has been captured
The Arts		CGI in films and TV programmes such as *X-Men*, *Star Wars* and *Doctor Strange* (among others), applications to create graphical images or to edit videos or images
Transport and logistics	Road maps	Satellite navigation systems that update in real time to provide a warning about traffic issues or show you exactly where your parcel is when it is with the courier service
Manufacturing		CAD/CAM (computer-aided design/computer-aided manufacturing) applications which can be used to design the product and control the manufacturing process
Project management		Applications to enable employees to work together to collaborate on activities

Practise

Think about how you interact with printed and digital media and answer the questions below.

- Can you list examples of printed media that you use?
- Can you list examples of digital media that you use?
- Which type do you use more of?
- Which type do you prefer?

Design fundamentals of creating digital media

Creating visual digital media relies on you understanding the components that make up the digital product. The following outline some of the design fundamentals for creating digital media.

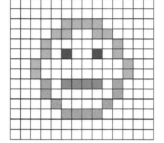

Example of a bitmap

- *Raster*: a **RASTER** is a grid of coordinates that maps a display space. Two-dimensional images are displayed on the *x* and *y* coordinates, and if it is a three-dimensional image, there is also a *z* coordinate.
- *Bitmap*: **BITMAPS** are made up of a grid of tiny dots called pixels – each pixel is a different colour and these pixels can be changed individually. Images are often made up of thousands of pixels. Bitmap files are large as the files contain information about every single pixel that forms part of the image. A colour bitmap stores the binary colour codes for each of the pixels in the image.
- *Vector*: **VECTORS** are graphics which are made up of objects. Each object can be changed. You can change the colour of an object, its size, its shape and its position on the display. In a mathematical comparison with bitmap files, vector files are small because the file contains the description of objects, rather than information about every pixel that makes up the image. This means that if the image is enlarged, the quality of the picture will stay the same.
- *Dimension*: the dimensions of an object are things that you can measure – for example, length, width, height, depth.
- *Resolution*: **RESOLUTION** refers to the amount of detail that can be seen in an image. The lower the resolution, the fewer pixels the image contains. This means that if you enlarge an image that has a low resolution, the picture will look blocky.

What can you say about the framed rose?

- *House style*: most organisations develop their own **HOUSE STYLE**. This means the way that their printed documents or digital screens look: the font type, size and styles and the colour combinations that are used.
- *Layout*: when you design a digital application you have to decide how you want to set out the content. You can use templates which put content in particular places, or you can decide where each bit of the content should be placed one at a time.

- *White space*: every document or screen should have some white space. This is space where there is no content. White space in both printed media and digital media helps to break up the content. It makes text easier to read and makes the various elements stand out.
- *Typography*: **TYPOGRAPHY** refers to the techniques you use to arrange text and make it readable and appealing when you are displaying it in printed or digital media. It means the style and approach that you take.
- *Colour modes*: the more colours you store in an image file, the greater the size of the file. You may have noticed colour modes before, particularly when you are printing something. The main colour modes are colour, greyscale, and black and white.
- *File types*: bitmap files in their native format are .bmp files, but similar files include .dib, .jpg, .gif, .tif and .png. Native vector files are .svg, although similar files include .cgm, .odg, .eps and .xml. Audio files come in different formats, including .wav, .aiff, .flac and .mp3 and video file formats include .mpg, .avi, .mov and .wmv. Animation formats include flash and animated GIFs.

Practise

Find an image file and save it in different formats.

Identifying organisational needs

The content that will be needed for a digital application will depend on a range of factors as shown in Table 7.2.

Factor	Explanation
Audience	In addition to the other possible characteristics of an audience you have already thought of, there are other factors that you might need to take into consideration, such as the occupations of your target audience, their level of education, the size of their family (known as the size of the household), the location of the audience and their personal preferences (such as attitudes, values and lifestyles).
Message	What is the content trying to say? Maybe it is an advertisement that is trying to persuade someone to buy something, or perhaps it is trying to provide some information about something. You need to be clear what the message is and who it is aimed at.
Design fundamentals	Will you need to use the house style? In some organisations, if you want to create something without using the house style, you will need to get permission from managers first.
Budget	How much money is available to support the development of the digital application, especially if you need to buy some of the content (such as images or film clips). It is likely that the budget will be fixed so you will have to work within it. You must make sure you work out how much you will need before the budget is set.
Deadlines	How soon will the content be needed?
Existing branding	Will the organisation's current branding be used or does new branding need to be created?
Delivery platform	Will the content be viewed through printed media or digitally using computers, devices, websites, wearable technologies, etc?

Table 7.2: Factors affecting content

Selecting appropriate software and hardware for creating digital media

The reality is that to create digital applications, you will need to use a variety of hardware and software, depending on what content you are trying to create.

Identifying appropriate software

Table 7.3 gives examples of software you might want to use along with the types of products you would need.

Table 7.3: Identifying software and products you need

Software	Examples
Vector graphics software	• CorelDRAW® • Visio® • Serif® DrawPlus • Adobe Illustrator®
Raster graphics/bitmap software	• PaintShop Pro® • GIMP™ • Microsoft® Paint® • Adobe Fireworks®
Dedicated manipulation software	• Photoshop® • Photoshop® Elements • Serif® PhotoPlus
Web authoring	• Adobe Dreamweaver® • Microsoft Visual Studio®
Video editing	• Adobe Premiere® • Windows Movie Maker • Corel VideoStudio®
Animation packages	• Adobe Flash® • Blender™ • GoAnimate™
Sound-editing software	• Adobe Audition® • Audacity® • WavePad®

Identifying software considerations

The software you choose will depend on different considerations.

- *File sizes*: the size of a file is often dictated by the software that is used to create the file. This means that you have to consider the amount of storage that will be needed for your content, and how long it will take to send your files or to download them from the internet.
- *Compatibility*: did you know that Apple Mac® software and file formats are not the same as those for Windows-based systems? You need to make sure that the software you use will create content that works with the operating system, web technologies and hardware that you will want to use to run it.
- *Compression*: to make a file smaller for storage or transfer you can COMPRESS it. This means that you allow the computer to modify the content to make it smaller. Unfortunately you cannot choose how the computer does this, you simply choose a compression format and the computer will use an algorithm to make the changes. Compressed files are much more suited to streaming than non-compressed files (because there is less data to transmit).

There are two types of compression:

1 *lossy compression*: the data is compressed in such a way that some of the original data and detail is lost. An image might seem a bit blurry, or the colours might not be quite the same

2 *lossless compression*: the original quality of the data is not changed.

Identifying appropriate hardware

Think about the hardware that will be used to execute the digital application.

What sort of **TECHNICAL SPECIFICATION** will it need? (The technical specification outlines the components and processes required to solve a problem using a digital application.) This means what sort of processor, memory, graphics card and sound card will be needed to display the content.

Link it up

Digital Applications

Refer back to Unit 1 for more information about the types of internal computer hardware components.

Practise

Use the internet to find out the technical specification requirements for the current versions of Dreamweaver and Microsoft Visual Studio.

- How do they compare?

- Check both specifications against the specification of your in-class computer. Could your machine run either, both, or would it not be able to run either software?

What types of devices will you need? What type of **STORAGE MEDIA** will be required? (Storage media are devices that can be used to store data.) Devices and storage media are essential in the development of digital applications. Table 7.4 gives some examples of what you might need to think about.

Device	Description	Considerations
PC (including processor, graphics card, sound card and **RANDOM ACCESS MEMORY – RAM**)	A basic desktop PC or notebook with interchangeable components (this often comes with onboard capabilities, but might need to be upgraded to support a digital application)	Processing speed Sound capabilities Graphics capabilities
Monitor	Outputs digital content onto a screen	Refresh rates Size of the monitor The resolution will impact on the visual quality of the image
Printer 2D	Printing text and images onto paper	Colour or black and white
Printer 3D	Printing in layers to create physical objects that can be handled	Cost
Digital camera	Capturing photographic images and video	Storage capacity (this can usually be extended with interchangeable **EXPANSION CARDS** – currently the largest size is 512GB)

Table 7.4: Devices and storage media

Table 7.4: *(continued)*

Device	Description	Considerations
Scanner	Useful for capturing content that only exists in paper form	Quality – particularly if the original images are damaged in any way
Mobile phone	A portable device that is capable of taking photos and capturing sound	Storage capacity (this can sometimes be extended with interchangeable expansion cards)
Tablet	A portable device with many uses – for example, using a stylus to draw	Storage capacity (while some tablets support expansion cards, others have a fixed storage capacity)
MIDI keyboard	A musical keyboard connected through the sound card, a MIDI 5-pin DIN plug (or sometimes a USB port) which allows music played to be captured directly into software on the PC so that it can be stored as a file	These can be very complex to set up
Webcam	Streams live images in real time and is often used for communication applications such as Skype®	Quality can be poor
Microphone	Capturing voice, but also capturing music from instruments using a microphone clipped to the instrument	It can be difficult to capture sound without background noise
CD-ROM	Optical storage that can store various types of data – once used, the ROM cannot be used again	Capacity – maximum capacity is 700MB and cannot be expanded
DVD-ROM	Optical storage that can store various types of data – once used, the ROM cannot be used again	Capacity – maximum capacity is 4.7GB and cannot be expanded
Hard drive	Electronic or physical versions that can be written to and rewritten to many times	Come in a variety of sizes with the maximum capacity currently 16TB
The **CLOUD**	Digital storage in a remote location that is accessed through the internet	Modern cloud storage is relatively reliable and secure but there may be a charge
USB thumb drive	Small flash **STORAGE DEVICES** that can be written to and rewritten to many times	Easy to lose Currently the largest size is 512GB

A3 Content management

You can use **CONTENT MANAGEMENT SYSTEMS** (software which allows users to create and modify a range of digital assets) for developing digital applications.

Content management systems

There are many content management systems (CMSs) available for you to try or to use with different functionality. Some systems can be used by novice users, others are more advanced. Here are three examples that are popular.

- *WordPress®*: this is probably the most popular system because it is quick to install and is easy to access. It has a large community of users and developers which means that it benefits from an extensive range of enhancements and templates libraries.
- *Drupal®*: this is a more basic system to install, but has many optional modules which can be installed to add a range of features.
- *MODX®*: this system requires users to have only the most basic understanding of coding. It means that both technical and non-technical staff can create content and use its features. It can also manage situations where multiple styles may be needed on the same page.

Creating and modifying components of digital applications in a CMS

Developers use a range of tools to help them create content and modify components that are being imported into the CMS from other places. Formatting and editing tools make it possible to adapt the components for the situation. The tools are common to most applications and the icons for each function or feature are also relatively standard.

(1): font tools

(2): paragraph tools

(3): styles

(4): editing tools

Formatting and editing techniques

Text

The font tools allow changes to be made to the type, colour and size of the letters and numbers in the text. **Bold**, *Italic*, <u>Underscore</u> or ***<u>All three</u>*** can be used together. You can also ~~strike through characters~~ or make them appear as _{subscript} (below the main line) or ^{superscript}(above the main line). They can be highlighted or the colour of the font can be changed.

The paragraph editing tools enable the developer to make different types of lists:

- bulleted

or

1 numbered

Line spacing, background colour and position can also be automatically adjusted, as shown opposite.

Single line spacing:
Single line spacing is where each line is displayed under the line above with no spaces.

Double line spacing:
Double line spacing is where each line is displayed

under the line above with a clear empty line in

between.

Single line spacing - with colour fill:

Text in single line spacing where the background has been filled with a colour.

Text can be left aligned

        Text can be centred

             Text can be right aligned

Text can be fully justified (against the margin on both sides like in the pages of a book) - this means that all of the lines are exactly equal and the text is adjusted automatically.

Styles are particularly useful for making changes to whole paragraphs. This means that developers can experiment with them until they get a style that looks right, but still allows them to change their minds.

Editing tools such as Find and Replace make it very easy to search for a specific word or phrase and then change it – for example, if the name of a product in a brochure has changed. It could take a long time to find each time the product is mentioned so that the name can be changed, and there is always the risk that one will be missed. Using Find and Replace means that the developer can be reassured that all the instances of the product name have been dealt with.

Graphics

①: adjust tools

②: picture styles

③: arrange tools

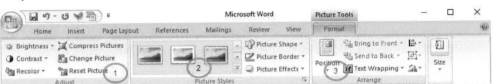

Adjust tools work directly with the picture, changing features like brightness and contrast. If mistakes are made, the picture can be Reset, which means that all the changes will be removed and the picture will be restored to its original state (including its size and position in the application).

Original

Brightness

Contrast

Recolour

Image files can be large in terms of the amount of storage they need. This is because the more detail and quality that they need, the more pixels will be stored. Once an image is in the right position in an application it can be compressed. This means that some of the detail that is not needed because of the size of the image in situ is removed. The image will then need less storage space.

Picture styles options are largely about borders and the shape of an image when it is displayed.

Original

Double frame black

Soft edge oval

Relaxed perspective white

The Arrange functionality is used to position the image in the application. It can also be flipped and rotated.

Original

Flip vertical

Flip horizontal

Simple editor programs, file extensions and syntax conventions

There are numerous editing programs, some that cost money and some which are free. Each one has different options in terms of the **FORMAT** that the image will be saved in. For example, Microsoft's Paint application saves in the following formats: PNG (.png), Monochrome Bitmap (.bmp, .dib), 16 Colour Bitmap (.bmp, .dib), 256 Colour Bitmap (.bmp, .dib), 24-bit Bitmap (.bmp, .dib), JPEG (.jpg, .jpeg, .jpe, .jfif), GIF (.gif), and TIFF (.tif).

However, an editing application called PicPick™ only offers the user the choice of the following formats: Portable Network Graphics (.png), Bitmaps (.bmp), JPEG Image File (.jpg, .jpeg), CompuServe GIF Image (.gif) and Adobe PDF (.pdf)

The format of a media file is obvious because of the file extension. This is the string of characters after the dot in the filename – for example, image20.png is a .png file (Portable Network Graphics).

The digital application may well, in fact, use a range of image file formats (maybe a .bmp, a .jpeg and four .gif files). While it is possible to remember the different media categories such as text, image or sound, with so many formats in each category it can be difficult to keep track.

As digital applications are likely to be made up of a large number of different media files and formats, it makes sense to use agreed syntax conventions when applying file names. For example, it is very clear what sort of files these are because of the first three characters in the filename.

Image files	Movie files	Text files
IMGRose.bmp	MOVArticle.mp4	TXTHeading3.rtf
IMGFace.gif	MOVNewsClip.avi	TXTMainText.txt
IMGPlace.png	MOVRunning.mov	TXTSubText1.doc

Using these naming conventions also means that all the files of a similar type (regardless of the format) will be displayed together in a directory. Creating file names without spaces will also make sure that the conventions are used consistently. Organisations may well have a house style for syntax conventions that should be observed.

Interactive elements

An **ASSET** is another term for a component of a digital application. Other assets that are usually involved in the creation of a digital application will include the following interactive elements:

- submit buttons
- email forms
- hyperlinks
- rollover images (which open other content).

Optimisation techniques

When using media assets in a digital application, you should use **OPTIMISATION TECHNIQUES** to make the assets as efficient as possible in terms of size, quality and so on. The assets should be optimised for the context. For example, when you watch YouTube™ videos in a standard screen, the video window may well take up between a quarter and a third of the screen. The video itself appears to be of reasonable quality, until the video is expanded to full screen. This is because, to optimise the application, the video was saved in the right format for the screen resolution being used.

The same is true of images. Look at the image below created in Word. The image was then saved as a vector image (.pdf) and as a raster image (.jpg). It is not until the .pdf and the .jpg images are expanded that the difference between the formats becomes obvious. Compare the images below (middle and right).

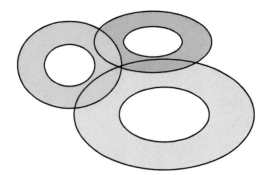

An image created in Word

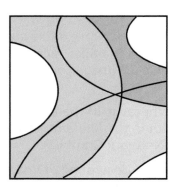

The .pdf at 800%

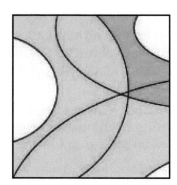

The .jpg at 800%

At original size, however, both images looked exactly the same.

When working with digital applications, you will use optimisation techniques on all the media assets. For example, you would use an image resolution which is appropriate for the size of the image in relation to the page. Adding pixels that will not even be seen because the image is too small unnecessarily uses up valuable storage space. In terms of a website, this can make a real difference in how long the page and the components take to load.

Practise

Just as images can be stored in different formats, the same is true of video formats. Think about which formats are the best.

Good practice

The following shows four good practice techniques when developing digital applications.

1 Using a **DATABASE** to organise the images (this is particularly useful if you are using the same image in different locations as it is easy to track).

2 Applying sensible **FILE-NAMING CONVENTIONS** to files, folders and directories, as stated earlier in A2. (This is a method of allocating file names in a consistent way – it is usually agreed by technical staff in an organisation and is applied to all files.)

3 Documenting the application so that the development process can be understood by others.

4 Ensuring that the application that is developed is accessible (appropriate accessibility aids, colour schemes, etc.) and will reach the widest range of potential users.

Skills and knowledge check

- [ ] Can you define at least five digital applications that you use, explaining what they are for and how you use them?
- [ ] Can you explain why digital applications must be made accessible for different types of users?
- [ ] Can you list five different ways that digital applications are used to support the activities of an organisation?
- [ ] Can you name the three key digital media formats?
- [ ] Can you explain image compression?

- ○ I can identify different uses for digital applications.
- ○ I can explain the difference between printed and digital media.
- ○ I understand how to make digital applications effective.
- ○ I can convert images between formats.
- ○ I understand the importance of file sizes in relation to available storage.
- ○ I can use the basic functionality of a CMS (content management system).
- ○ I can identify a range of digital assets.

B Create a user interface design

B1 Usability

Usability and how this applies to mobile, web and desktop applications

When creating a **USER INTERFACE (UI)**, the two key factors that need to be considered are **USABILITY** (whether it is fit for the purpose for which it was intended) and the user experience. These are linked, as poor usability design will usually lead to a poor user experience. This section explores these concepts and how they work together to create user-friendly digital applications.

> **Practise**
>
> Think about the applications you use and then answer the following questions.
>
> - Do you like using some applications more than others?
>
> - Can you think why that is?
>
> - Have you stopped using an application because you did not enjoy using it?

But what is usability? Usability is the degree to which a user is able to use something. If you look online to find the use over time for the word 'usability', you will see that its use has increased dramatically in the last 30 years. This is because today it is often linked to technology.

Designing products that are usable is extremely important because it can provide a **UNIQUE SELLING POINT (USP)** that makes people want to use it. To make the application usable, developers need to think about usability characteristics in relation to the development. These include:

- visibility
- control
- feedback
- consistency
- error prevention
- flexibility.

You will notice that none of the characteristics listed above is about the content of the application or what it looks like. So, what are these characteristics?

- *Visibility*: this is how well something can be seen by the user. This is impacted by the developers' choices of font types, font styles, text sizes, text colours, background colours. For example, using a small font to get more content on the screen will make it more difficult for the user to read. The user might need to magnify the screen to be able to read it.

Practise

Have you experimented with the accessibility settings on your computer? Find out what the operating system you use can do to support visibility.

- *Control*: this is about how easy it is to navigate and move around the application.
- *Feedback*: this is about how responsive the application is when being used – for example, if a link is clicked or a button is pressed, how long does it take for something to happen?
- *Consistency*: this means that each component of the same type behaves in the same way.
- *Error prevention*: this means validation to catch any incorrect inputs to prevent the application crashing because of something the user typed in (such as typing letters into an input box that is expecting numbers).
- *Flexibility*: this focuses on the number of functions the application has. If you have lots of functions to make the application more flexible, it can become more difficult to use because there is more for the user to navigate.

The best way to assess usability is to ask a range of potential users. Letting them input into the design process (by commenting on content features) and allowing them to try a prototype will give invaluable feedback. This will give the developer time to change aspects of the application early if problems are found.

Although most developers will consider usability characteristics when they create applications, this is not always the case. Operating systems like Windows have a feature called the Ease of Access Centre (or accessibility settings), which enables the user to magnify or narrate (speak) the content. This is obviously important for anyone who is visually impaired.

User interface content features

There are many different tools and approaches that developers can use in design. Below are some of them.

- *Pointers and icons*: icons are quick to create and easy to use because users can point and click. It should be very clear either from the image or the word on the icon what it actually does.
- *Desktop options*: for example, grouping icons, using menus, importing images, formatting text, colours and general appeal. Organising the desktop is very important. What do you think of the desktop shown in the photograph on page 234?

A cluttered desktop can be hard to navigate

The user would find it difficult to find anything on a desktop that was this cluttered and disorganised. In the same way, icons in applications should be organised in a way that makes sense. Older versions of applications used a series of dropdown menus to group functions together. Modern applications now use tabs rather than menus because so much more of the functionality is instantly visible and accessible to the user.

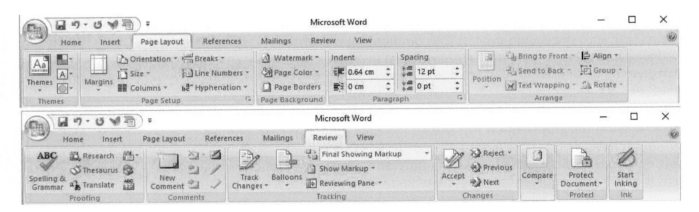

- *Text size, colours (with no background), colour clashes:* What do you think of this layout? Imagine this is a computer screen and the text is in the top right corner. Is this good use of space? With all the space available, the developer should have chosen a more appropriate size for the text to make better use of the space.

Backgrounds behind text also play a part in usability. This is known as a colour clash because the colours are too similar for the text to be legible. What do you think of this? What might improve it in terms of legibility?

- *Sounds*: these are especially useful for drawing attention to features in the application or for warning the user that something is not as it should be.
- *Timing*: if something takes too long to happen, then users will get bored and may even quit the application.
- *General styles*: there are many templates for applications that developers can use which provide a range of functionality so that the content just needs to be added. The key is for the developer to experiment with the environment they are using to see what is available. It might save time in the long run.
- *Provisions for ease of access*: developers have to be able to explain which tools or techniques they have used to promote ease of use and why they have used them. In most situations, you try to accommodate as many different user types as you can without compromising the content by trying to do too much.
- *Sourced assets*: where possible you should make use of assets that already exist even if you have to make some changes to re-purpose them. You should always know where every asset has come from (in case there are ownership or copyright queries).

Other useful features

Input controls

In addition to the input controls such as dropdown lists and buttons that have been discussed already, other controls that could be used in the development of the application include the following.

- **CHECK BOXES**: these make it possible for users to easily select items from a list. The user has the option to choose more than one.
- **RADIO BUTTONS**: these work in a similar way but force the user to choose only one of the options as only one of the buttons can be selected at a time.

- **TOGGLES**: these are often used in settings to switch a function on or off.

- **DATE FIELDS**: these mean that users will input dates in a consistent format – for example:
  DD/MM/YYYY   would produce   19/05/1999
  DD/MM/YY   would produce   19/05/99

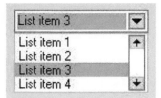

- **LIST BOXES**: these are very similar to **DROPDOWN BOXES** in terms of how they look. The difference is in how they work. List boxes show the users a range of options from which they can choose any number. A dropdown box will display the same list but will allow the user to choose only one.

Navigational components

The following features could be used to aid navigation.

- **BREADCRUMBS**: these are controls that show users where they are in an application. It is easy to go up and down through the levels by clicking on earlier crumbs.

- **SLIDERS**: these are often used to quickly limit a range – for example, if you want to limit the results of a search to all items between £20 and £50, the slider can set the upper and lower values.

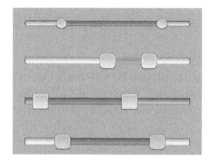

- **SEARCH FIELDS**: these allow users to input words or phrases so that they can quickly find what they are looking for within the application.

- *Pagination*: this is simply using page numbers to navigate.

Informational components

The following can be used to provide the user with information.

- **TOOLTIPS**: these are messages that can be added to components to give the user hints about how to use the feature. Tooltips can take many formats such as speech bubbles or sticky notes that appear when a mouse hovers over a component.

- **PROGRESS BAR**: there is no way to avoid situations where time is needed for components to load. To make this experience better for users, add a progress bar. This helps users to see how much more time is needed before the component is loaded and they then know that something is actually happening.

- **MODAL WINDOWS**: these are pop-up windows that temporarily suspend the active window and force the user to interact with the process. This is an example of a modal window and is something you will have seen many times without necessarily knowing what it is called.

B2 User experience

When you are designing a user interface you should always consider the impact that the interface will have on the user's experience of the application.

Graphical elements of UI design

The key factors to consider when designing a user interface are summarised in Figure 7.2.

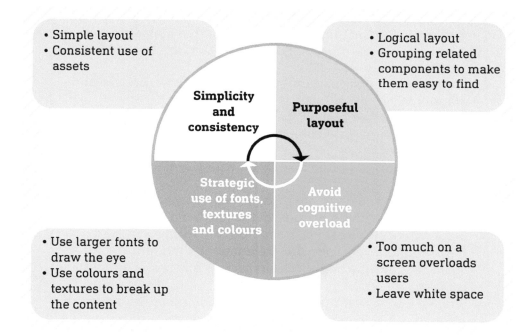

Figure 7.2: Key considerations for user interface design

The concept of visual appeal

Do you like the same things as all your friends or siblings? The chances are that what appeals to you will not appeal to everyone else.

However, there are some tricks and tips that can be learned to make your system appeal to your target audience.

Practise

Images used as part of a marketing campaign have to convey an upbeat (happy) message as they are supposed to encourage customers to buy the product.

Use the internet and a shopping site and investigate clock and watch images.

What time are the clocks generally set at?

How does this convey a positive message? You might like to compare the images you have found with the image opposite.

Answer: Clocks are generally marketed showing the time ten to two. This is because the hands pointing up look positive; visually twenty past eight makes a sad face. Buying patterns for clocks and watches over the years have identified that the sad-faced clock or watch sells less than a happy-faced clock or watch.

Here are some other considerations that will help your system to have a strong visual appearance.

- *Logos*: these should look professional. They should be prominently placed on your application. If the logo is for a well-known and respected brand, this immediately inspires confidence in the user.
- *Colours*: use colour intelligently. Think about the impact certain combinations have – for example, some colours are considered angry, others peaceful, and so on.
  - Warm colour combinations include reds, yellows, browns and oranges.
  - Colder combinations will include blues, some greens and purples.
  - White is an important colour as it is the most effective at giving the impression of space.
  - Yellow colours are often associated with warnings and red with danger.
  - Silvers, blues and greys are often linked to technology subjects.
  - Green is for anything to do with the outdoors.
  - Black, white and cream combinations are formal.
  - Neutral colours are considered elegant and modern.
  - Small children like bright colours such as reds, blues, greens and yellows.
  - There is also a view that certain colour combinations are more attractive to men or women. Women tend to like blues, purples and greens, while men tend to like blues, greens and black for websites. Blue is a colour that both sexes trust.

Practise

Look at the colours used on different digital applications (websites or application programs). Compare them with the list above.

Although there will be exceptions, is the list above relatively representative of what you have found?

- *Photos*: like logos, photographs in particular should be of good quality and if possible should be professional. This is because a photograph is not just about resolution and colour, but also about composition (how the features in the photograph relate to each other).
- *Fonts*: if your digital application is likely to be used across devices, you should use fonts and colour combinations that look appealing on mobile devices as well as when viewed on a PC.
- *Layout*: do not overload a screen. If necessary, use multiple screens and spread the content over a large number of screens.
- *Navigation*: make navigation as simple as possible. Having to click through menus and links to other menus is frustrating for users. Use tabs, icons, scrollbars, toggles and lists.
- *Level*: remember to accommodate both novice and advanced users.

Designing the user experience is essential if you are going to make a digital application that is usable by its intended users. A poor design will have a negative impact on users – novice users will become frustrated if the interface is too hard to use and advanced users will become bored if there are no advanced features. A successful application will use a combination of both.

Think back to the start of this unit where you considered the concept of brand and how digital applications that have been well designed and carefully developed can add to an organisation's image and brand. In the same way, a poorly thought-out design will also have a negative impact on the business it represents.

B3 User interface design

Designing an interface for a given scenario

Principles of UI design

Before starting to build a digital application, the interface has to be designed. Investigate this further by looking at the following scenario. Then compare your findings with the notes below.

What if...?

A group of developers has been commissioned to create class-based web pages for your centre's intranet – one for each year group (not class) at your centre.

The developers have produced the following initial design. Based on your understanding of digital applications so far, assess this design. You may think that some aspects are good but that others need work. To help you decide, read the questions and note down your thoughts.

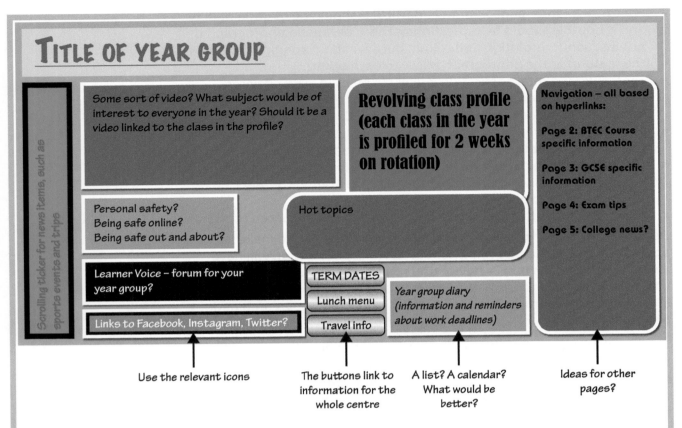

TITLE OF YEAR GROUP

Scrolling ticker for news items, such as sports events and trips

Some sort of video? What subject would be of interest to everyone in the year? Should it be a video linked to the class in the profile?

Revolving class profile (each class in the year is profiled for 2 weeks on rotation)

Navigation – all based on hyperlinks:

Page 2: BTEC Course specific information

Page 3: GCSE specific information

Page 4: Exam tips

Page 5: College news?

Personal safety?
Being safe online?
Being safe out and about?

Hot topics

Learner Voice – forum for your year group?

TERM DATES

Lunch menu

Travel info

Year group diary (information and reminders about work deadlines)

Links to Facebook, Instagram, Twitter?

Use the relevant icons

The buttons link to information for the whole centre

A list? A calendar? What would be better?

Ideas for other pages?

1   What do you think of the controls that have been used? Remember, input controls should be appropriate for the target audience.
    What might you change to improve them to make this aspect more appropriate for your year group?
2   Have any navigational components been used? If so, what are they? Are there opportunities to make changes or better use of them? What would you recommend?
3   What do you think about the information content and how it is planned? Is there something that you would not include, or something that is missing?
4   What do you think of the visual aspects of the home or landing page?
    - Is it a simple page? Is it consistent?
    - What do you think of the layout?
    - What about the use of colour and texture?
    - Is there any evidence that communication has been considered (providing users with feedback when the computer is processing in the background)?
    - How have shortcuts been achieved?
    - Would the planned content suit both an advanced and a novice user?
    - How many of the media formats have been used effectively (audio, image, video, animation)?

Here are some points you could have observed.
- Inputs have been limited to buttons.
- Button text is inconsistent.
- There is no search facility (is one needed?).
- The navigation bar on the right could be replaced with a dropdown menu. The text is too small to read at the moment.
- There is wasted space at the bottom of the navigation pane.

- Although a video is planned, the only other images planned for this page appear to be the icons for Facebook®, Instagram® and Twitter®. Maybe add some other images?
- There is poor use of colour and texture – only the buttons have texture so there is little consistency (some black borders, some white).
- Some of the boxes overlap.
- The screen feels cluttered.
- There is no white space.
- The idea of the revolving class profile initially could be a good idea but why would it rotate on a two-weekly cycle? Could this be used for another feature after one rotation?
- There is a lack of clarity about the subject for the proposed video.
- The idea of a scrolling ticker for news is good, and the subject is good, but blue on red is a bad colour combination.

In part, design is a personal thing because we are not all the same. Some people might like the design, but the reality is that many would not. Digital applications should be designed to appeal to the maximum number possible in the target category.

Justifying decisions made

Whether working for your manager or for a client, you should always be prepared to justify the decisions you have made in terms of your designs. You must be able to do the following.

1 Explain how your design meets the requirements of users. To do this you should say which features you have used and why you have used them and show that you understand your users and their needs.

2 When designing a user interface you may also be asked to create a series of alternative solutions from which the user (or client) can choose. This will give you an opportunity to be creative and explore a range of features that you can use in different combinations. You may find that the solution that is chosen may still be tweaked.

Skills and knowledge check

- ☐ Can you describe the key components of user interface design?
- ☐ Can you identify usability features in applications?
- ☐ Can you name colours that are classified as 'warm'?
- ☐ Can you name colours classified as 'cold'?
- ☐ Can you name the colours associated with danger or errors?
- ☐ Can you identify the key principles in relation to interface design?
- ☐ Can you identify which media group each of these file formats belongs to?
- ☐ .avi ☐ .jpeg ☐ flash ☐ .wav ☐ .wmv ☐ .flac ☐ .gif ☐ .mp3

Answer (in order shown) is: video, image, animation, audio, video, audio, image, audio.

- ◯ I can use a range of navigational components and input controls.
- ◯ I can set up usability features in applications.
- ◯ I can identify the key features of a range of file formats.
- ◯ I can explain key usability and accessibility features and how they are used in screen design.

C Create and test a digital application for an organisational purpose

C1 Planning the application

To create a successful digital application, you need to spend time planning your development.

Planning methods

The planning process is split into three parts:
- allocating time to each part of the development
- deciding how navigation through the application will flow
- designing the interface.

Using Gantt charts

Experienced developers know that when you are planning the development of a digital application, you need to make sure that you allocate enough time for each of the activities and that you include catch-up time for when things go wrong (which they often will). If you are going to involve users (during design, testing), time needs to be allowed for these activities to take place.

One of the best ways to allocate time is using a **GANTT CHART**. (This is a technique used when different tasks need to be planned out over time – it is easy to see which tasks can run concurrently (side by side) or which have to be completed before the next task can begin.) Gantt charts allow developer groups to break down the activities that will be needed and show how much time has been allocated in a visual way. You can also see exactly which day you are on because of the vertical black arrow.

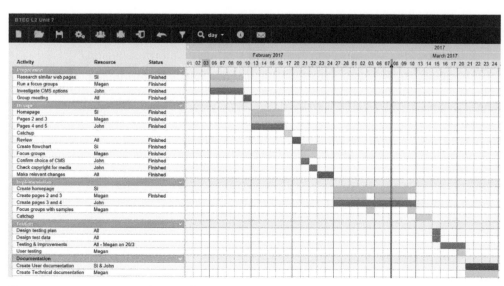

Figure 7.3: Using a Gantt chart to show the allocation of time
Source: www.tomsplanner.com

Figure 7.3 shows an example of a Gantt chart created using software that does not charge for personal use. It is very easy for the novice to use and has intuitive POP-UPS (new windows that open when you click on a link) that make it easy to learn. You can add, remove and colour time blocks by right clicking. Note the facility to use different colours for individuals, pairs and the group, and an additional colour for the catch-up sessions. This makes it very easy for the developers to know who is doing what and when.

Creating flowcharts

FLOW CHARTS (diagrams that are created to communicate the steps of a process in a visual way) are also widely used in application development as they are a visual way of demonstrating how different parts of the application will fit together. You can use formal software such as draw.io or graphics software such as Microsoft Paint or you can just draw your chart in Microsoft Word.

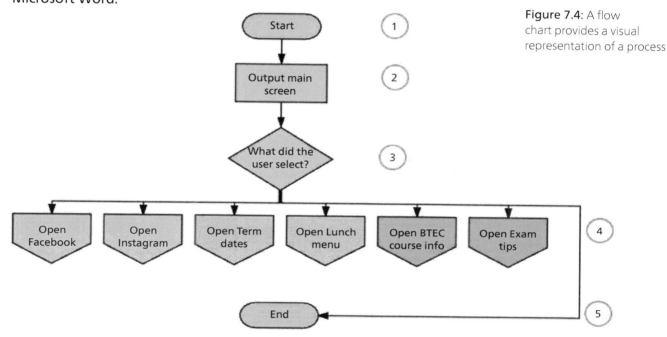

Figure 7.4: A flow chart provides a visual representation of a process

Figure 7.4 shows a flowchart for the home page of the digital application for the year group in your scenario. This is what each line means.

1 Start.

2 Display the main screen (which is a process).

3 Decision box in this context means check what the user does.

4 Go to something on a different screen. Notice the use of colours in this diagram: the gold boxes are social media icons, the grey boxes are the buttons and the red boxes are the hyperlinks listed in the navigation pane.

5 End.

You could then create a flowchart for each of the boxes on line 4.

Screen layout design

When you have planned your development, you will need to draw layouts for each of the screens. You do not have to use a computer to do this. You can create pen and paper drawings and then scan them (so that they can be stored).

This stage should include decisions that have been made about how data will be input. For example, consider the following.

- Will inputs be captured with free text input boxes or one of the dropdown list options (such as list or combo boxes) to limit the potential for incorrect input (as the user chooses from a list rather than typing in data that could contain errors)?
- What sorts of screen prompts will be needed? Is it really obvious what input is required? Imagine the prompt 'Input weight' – would this need to be in kilos, pounds or stones and pounds? Without an appropriate prompt the user may well not know.

The design should communicate how the output of information will be achieved. For example, the colour, position, font of text, as well as the actual content that will be output.

The usability features should also be included on the design – what will be used and how? This ensures that these important features are not forgotten.

At times it can be helpful if the development team work on aspects of the design together using software like FlockDraw, which allows multiple people to work on the same file at the same time.

C2 Creating a digital application

To demonstrate the process of creating a digital application you are going to consider a new scenario, as detailed below. The following text will then walk you through the development process. For this demonstration, we will be using WordPress as the content management system.

What if...?

Your group has been asked to create a small website as a digital application, which can be used by a digital artist to showcase their work. You have been briefed to develop a site that can display a range of images and will also invite the user to join a mailing list via an input form.

Developing the media

When you start creating the digital application you will either need to create the media you use from scratch, or you will need to acquire it. There will be no copyright issues if you create the images, sounds and videos yourself, but if you use any media that you have not created, there might be a copyright issue and you will need permission to use it.

Creating a digital application: a demonstration using WordPress

Begin by creating a user account in WordPress by following the instructions onscreen. Once you have done this, you can get going.

Start by choosing one of four basic WordPress templates as shown on the next page. Think about the scenario you are working with. You would not use the 'Online store' in this context as you are building an application to manage an electronic portfolio. 'Website' is a good choice for the digital artist's portfolio.

One of the main advantages of using software such as WordPress as your content manager is that, unlike starting from scratch, you can choose from preset themes and layouts and the software organises your content for you, making the best use of the space.

Choosing a theme

Once you have selected your template, you will be asked to choose one of nine themes. Do not worry about this too much at this stage as the theme can be changed later if you decide it is not right.

You will then be asked to decide on a domain name. For this demonstration, the domain name is BeanyArt.

When you key in the domain name, a range of available domain names or .wordpress.com addresses are listed. Some are free, for others there will be a charge. Usually the domain name you type in will be available as the first item in the list and it will be free.

Step 2 of 5

What would you like your homepage to look like?

This will help us figure out what kinds of designs to show you.

A list of my latest posts

A welcome page for my site

A grid of my latest posts

An online store

If you pick the free option, you can confirm this on the next screen by choosing the 'Free' plan.

Choosing a plan

You will notice that the free plan includes support, themes, design customisation and 3GB of storage space.

Once you have confirmed the free option, you will receive an email and be asked to confirm the account.

Toggling between the views of the site

There are two ways to view the BeanyArt site: from the user's perspective and from the developer's perspective.

To view the site, simply type in 'beanyart.wordpress.com'.

To make changes to the site you will need to log into the admin part of the system. To do this, simply add /login after the initial address. This allows you to access the Dashboard.

To change the features of the home page (or landing page), use the settings link at the bottom of the navigation page.

You can then create the site title, a tagline and choose an icon (that will represent the brand) by uploading an appropriate image.

Remember to check the date and time settings are accurate for where you are, and make sure you Save the changes.

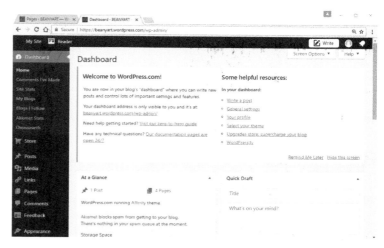

As mentioned above, one of the big advantages of using software such as WordPress is that you can flip between the views. To go to the view that the user sees, you click on the MySite link in the top left of the screen. You will now see the reader view, but you will also see additional icons in the bottom right-hand corner. This is useful as you can 'see' how things look and then still go back and 'customise' or 'edit' without extra navigation.

Click to edit the home page and then provide a new image for the background, and change the welcome text.

To make further changes, go back to the Dashboard.

Using plugins

There are lots of **PLUGINS** that you can use free in WordPress that provide different functionality. (A plugin is a prewritten module that has a particular function that you can choose to add to your software.) To view the plugins, select the Plugins link on the main navigation panel. There are four categories.

- *Engagement*: includes plugins for social media, setting up email subscriptions and inviting your readers to Like your content.
- *Security*: includes security scanning, backup and anti-spam security.
- *Appearance*: includes preset galleries (for displaying slideshows of images) and extended widgets (these are very small pre-programmed features such as Google™ Calendar).
- *Writing*: includes a Form Builder so that you can invite your readers to get in touch, and do polls and surveys and video uploads. Video uploads is a chargeable plugin so when you create your own digital application you may or may not have this feature available.

Adding media

The next step is to add the media that will be used. To do this use the Media link in the navigation pane. At the top of the screen you can Add New media library. When this is selected the developer can drag and drop any content into the library.

You can edit the media once you have uploaded it to your library. The image can be flipped, scaled or cropped and the orientation can be changed (between portrait and landscape). You can add a caption, additional text and, at the bottom of the screen, you can choose to invite your users to Like the individual image.

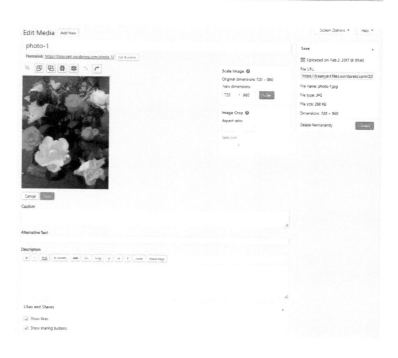

Your library will now contain a mixture of video and image files that need to be organised on the pages. For this example, each **BLOG** post will contain a different collection of images.

Adding a post

To add a post, click on MySites then on Blog Posts and Add.

For this post use the title Places.

You can now add your media. To create a gallery you need a range of images. Hold down the CTRL key and click on each of the images to add multiple images.

Next, decide how the images will be presented by choosing from the layout options. For this example, choose Thumbnail Grid – 4 columns. You can add text to support these images.

When you view blog posts, WordPress automatically adds a Header image at the top of the post. This can be changed by using Customised and selecting your own header image – simply click on Add new image under the Current Header heading.

The Contact page gives the user the opportunity to communicate with you directly and is generated by WordPress.

Input form

When you have made any final changes to the About page, the last component you need to add is the input form that offers the user an opportunity to sign up for email alerts.

Make sure that you are logged in to the admin interface and have clicked onto the site. To create this content, you will create a new page.

Change the title to Email alerts then select the + symbol so that you can Add Contact Form.

You will now be given some standard input fields to use, but you can delete these and/or add some of your own.

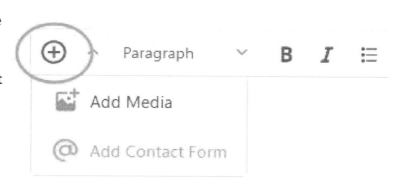

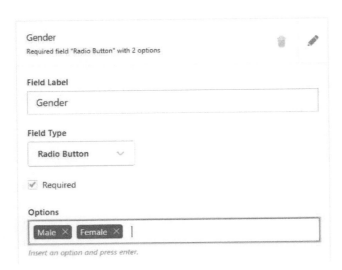

Name, Email, Website and Comment are automatically included. In this example you will need to delete Website and Comment.

You might want to know more about your subscriber – for example, gender, age (or age range) or general location. Once you have created one input field, you can repeat the process for the other fields you want on the subscription form.

The image on the left shows the screen for choosing radio buttons (for male and female) – note how ticking the required button means that your subscriber has to provide the information.

You can add the Male and Female options by typing where the cursor is shown in Options and deleting the default Option 1 and Option 2 tags.

Age range provides four options.

Finally, you can use the same process to set up input fields for Location – this has five options of England, Ireland, Scotland, Wales and Other.

The button to submit the information occurs automatically.

There are clearly many more settings that you can change, and you can add, delete or update content as required. For more guidance, there are many good tutorials online that can help you learn to work with the WordPress environment.

Even though the WordPress environment is largely automated, as a developer you can inspect the underlying code at any time. If you are using Google Chrome™, it just means right clicking on any object and then choosing Inspect. The image (below right) is an example of the code that controls the Contacts page on the BeanyArt website. Note: most (but not all) **BROWSERS** allow you to Inspect.

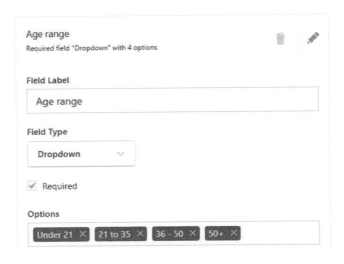

C3 Testing applications

Testing is one of the most important areas of application development but its importance is often underrated and even overlooked.

The concept of testing applications

Testing occurs at the end of a development when there may be two pressures.

- Trying to make up for lost time when earlier activities took longer than expected.
- If the deadline originally agreed with the client is imminent, to ensure it is not missed developers will often try to squeeze all of the planned testing activity into a shorter period.

This means that at times developers can be tempted to cut corners with testing and this can have a negative impact on the product itself, the satisfaction of the client and the user experience.

Why test?

Thorough testing of a program or application, and fixing any faults before users begin to use the system, will save time in the long run. It will also make it less likely that the client and users will be disappointed.

Stages of testing: alpha, beta and user acceptance testing

As with many computer-related activities, there is a well-documented process of stages that developers should work through to ensure that the testing phase of a development is undertaken correctly and thoroughly.

Alpha testing

Although you might think that **ALPHA TESTING** (in-house testing of a product to detect any design flaws) is done early in a development, it is actually carried out when the development is almost complete. Table 7.5 summarises the alpha testing stage, which is undertaken by the developers before it is released for beta testing.

Table 7.5: Alpha testing for application development

Stage	Activity
Requirements review	This means checking what the application or program does in relation to what was expected.
Planning the tests	Deciding what to test and how much testing to do.
Designing the tests	What each test will involve (for example, if testing an input, the developer would test by inputting correct values and incorrect values; if testing that a button moves between pages or that a hyperlink works, it might be clicking on the button or link at least twice and checking that the correct page loads).
Executing the tests	Working through each test one at a time and writing down what happens.
Reporting the results of testing	The outcomes of the tests are written into a document that the developers can use to make corrections.

Beta testing

When alpha testing is complete and the application needs to be tested in a more real-world environment, this becomes **BETA TESTING**. This is where the intended users of the application begin to try it out. The process puts some of the normal user stresses on the application.

User acceptance testing

When the application has been through alpha and beta testing and any issues that have been found have been resolved, the final process is USER ACCEPTANCE TESTING. This is where users carry out a final test to confirm that the application is working as it should.

Tools and techniques

For some applications that developers test, there are built-in tools and techniques that are available to help in the testing process.

Alternatively developers can use DEBUGGERS, which are programs used to test and debug other programs.

The following are the techniques most commonly used in debugging.

- *Step through*: this is where each line of code is executed slowly, one at a time with the developer controlling when each line is run.
- *Watch*: the developer can then add a Watch to a variable to see what happens when the code is executed. For example, the application includes a calculation and the calculation does not appear to give the right answers when they are checked with a calculator. The developer watches the inputs and checks the calculation using a Watch to identify where the process is breaking down.
- *Break points*: a break point is like a flag that can be placed on any line of code. When the code is then run, the program executes normally but stops when it gets to the flag. The developer can then step through the next few lines more slowly. Break points are very important in applications where there are thousands of lines of code.

Functional and non-functional testing

FUNCTIONAL TESTING is when you compare the solution provided by the application to the business requirements – does it have the expected functionality (and does it all work)? It is about checking whether all the requirements of the proposed solution have been created. This is also known as BLACK BOX TESTING. The tester does not need to know anything about the code. He or she will use a list of all the functions that the application is supposed to have and will check that each one is present and that it works.

NON-FUNCTIONAL TESTING is more focused on how the application behaves – how it performs on the system it is loaded on or how it manages lots of users using it at the same time.

Most programs contain SELECTION AND ITERATION TECHNIQUES ('if' statements and loops) and the tester should test every part of the code. Does the loop run again when it is supposed to? Does it stop when it is supposed to? Does the 'if' execute when the condition is met?

Developing the test plan

Good testing means making sure that the test plan has been created properly and that it is testing everything that it should be testing. But the plan itself will be very different depending on the application that is being tested. For example, for a program that adds two integer (whole) numbers the tests will check that the:

- first input accepts whole numbers only – no numbers with decimal points, no characters or symbols
- second input accepts whole numbers only – no numbers with decimal points, no characters or symbols
- answer is calculated correctly – the developer should have provided some test values such as 3 and 9 and the answer 12. This is known as a test case.

When testing inputs and calculations, the data that is used should be:

- *normal*: sensible data that is what the application expects the users to input
- *extreme*: this is still sensible data but would be high or low, but the application should be able to work with it
- *erroneous*: this will be values or inputs that are incorrect, such as characters where numbers are expected.

There should be a button on a web page that opens another page: when clicked does the correct web page load?

Creating a test plan

The test plan itself consists of a series of headings. It usually is presented as a table because it makes it easier to organise the tests and the results of testing.

Sometimes, particularly with coded programs, there is an additional column that identifies the line of code being tested.

Figure 7.5 shows an example of what a test plan might look like.

Figure 7.5: Sample test plan template

Test	Purpose	Expected result	Actual result	Errors	Actions
Main page About button	Check button functioning	Open About page			

Practise

Create a test plan for a program you have already created. Test the logic as well as the outputs.

Make sure you identify the test (what data you are going to use in the test), the purpose of the test and what you expect the result to be.

Use the test plan to test the program and complete the actual result, errors and actions columns.

Test plans for functional and non-functional testing

Some developers create two test plans – one for the functional testing and one for the non-functional testing. Table 7.6 summarises what should be included in a test plan.

Table 7.6: What to include in a test plan

Type of test	What is being tested? What would be checked?
Functionality	Navigation between pages (internal to the application). Navigation between the application and external websites or files. Content loads as expected. Features work.
Usability	Navigation is clear (users really know what they are supposed to do). Application is easy to use. Navigation is quick (if navigation is slow it tends to frustrate users).
Accuracy	Content is accurate – this is not just about proofreading (although that is obviously very important), it can also be about checking that the content is correct. Why? There could be a situation where a developer who does not understand the subject might have picked the wrong file and included content that was made for a different application. It is rare, but can happen.
Readability	Check that the text is legible, that the font chosen and the font size are legible and that there are no issues with colour combinations.
Accessibility	One of the advantages of software such as WordPress is that it automatically adjusts the content to suit the device it is being viewed on. But this is not the case with all application development environments. Therefore, applications should always be checked on the devices they will be viewed on where screens will potentially vary in size and resolution.
Overall performance	The final part of the process is to assess whether the product does what it is required and designed to do across all the platforms where it will be used.

Exploring the role of a software tester by testing peers' developed products

During development of programs and applications, it is common practice for peers to test each other's products while they are in development. This practice means that some faults and issues can potentially be identified before they seriously impact on the development work.

This can take place formally (using a checklist of aspects you want someone to look at) or informally, such as simply showing someone something you have done and asking them what they think (even looking over your shoulder).

Obtaining test feedback from peers

Feedback

Feedback should always be constructive. Just because you do not like something does not necessarily mean that it is wrong. You might choose to question it, but you would not flag it as an error. If you are going to be involved in giving and receiving feedback, then the following points may help you with this process.

If you are giving feedback:

- make sure you feed back on good aspects of the application, not just on the bad ones
- be specific and concise
- be kind and try to use objective and impersonal language (not accusing or getting personal).

If you are receiving feedback:

- try not to get defensive – assume that the person who is feeding back to you has good intentions
- ask for clarification if you are not sure you understand the feedback you are receiving.

Making improvements

There are many reasons why improvements need to be made to designs (and even to live systems). Here are some examples.

1 Part of the functionality is not needed anymore and needs to be removed.
2 New functionality is needed.
3 There is an error – for example, the tab order on input boxes could be incorrect which means that users have to move up and down a page, or it could be that the position of an input box is too low issue which means that users have to scroll unnecessarily to access content.
4 A new type of user needs to use the system and it therefore needs some adjustment.
5 The organisation changes its branding.

The need to make improvements is often triggered by user feedback and is no reflection on the developer's designs – it is sometimes simply personal choice.

Skills and knowledge check

- ☐ Can you explain why screens should be designed rather than moving directly to implementation?
- ☐ Can you identify the reasons for the choice of a particular theme?
- ☐ Can you identify how plugins can be used to provide additional functionality?
- ☐ Can you name the phases of testing?

- ○ I can create a digital application.
- ○ I can use the features of a content management system.
- ○ I can create a post.
- ○ I can use common debugging techniques.
- ○ I can develop a test plan.

Ready for assessment

This unit is assessed through the development of a Portfolio of Digital Evidence and it focuses on the learner producing a range of content in different formats that can be used in the development of a digital application.

You should make sure that you select or create content that is appropriate for the application and is of a high quality. You should also make sure that you can explain your reasons for your choices.

- Check that you know the different media formats and the key factors about them (such as how much memory they need because this has an impact on how quickly components of your application load).

- Make sure you think very carefully about the amount of time you have to design, create and test your application and try to make sure that you do not spend so much time on some of the earlier tasks that you run out of time at the end.

- You will design a solution against a brief and you should make sure that you consider all potential user types and that what you create is appropriate for them and is not simply something you personally like. Remember to talk to other people and find out what they like too.

- Concentrate on the design, because if the design is not correct, you will waste time later if you find you have to change components of the application.

- When you implement your design, keep checking that your development is moving in the right direction.

- Thoroughly test your solution.

WORK FOCUS

HANDS ON

There are some important occupational skills and competencies that you will need to practise that relate to this unit. Developing these and practising them could help you to gain employment in a digital applications role.

- Employers will expect you to demonstrate that you can work effectively with other people. Next time you work with others, practise your listening skills. Really listen to what they are saying and try not to interrupt.

- Contribute creatively to projects. This means coming up with ideas and being prepared to share them. In your next group activity, make sure you contribute at least one idea.

Ready for work?

Take this short quiz to see if you are ready for a role as a digital applications developer.

1 What does CGI stand for?
- [ ] A Computer graphic image
- [ ] B Computer generated image
- [ ] C Compressed graphic image
- [ ] D Compressed greyscale image

2 Which of the following definitions describes the term 'raster'?
- [ ] A A graphic made up of spaces on a grid.
- [ ] B A graphic that can be made up of objects.
- [ ] C A graphic made up of pixels.
- [ ] D The amount of detail that can be seen on an image.

3 Which of the following input controls should be used if input data needs to identify a range?
- [ ] A Toggle
- [ ] B List box
- [ ] C Radio button
- [ ] D Slider

4 Which of the following lists is largely made up of warm colours?
- [ ] A Blues, greens, purples and reds
- [ ] B Black, white, blues and greens
- [ ] C Reds, yellows, browns and purples
- [ ] D Black, purples, reds and greens

5 In relation to CMS systems such as WordPress, what does this describe: Introduces additional functionality to the development interface.
- [ ] A Gallery
- [ ] B Plugin
- [ ] C Embedding
- [ ] D Posting

If you found this quiz hard, go back over the unit to refresh your understanding of the uses of digital applications and content management systems, the theory of user interface design, and the planning, creation and testing processes.

Answers: 1B, 2A, 3D, 4C, 5B

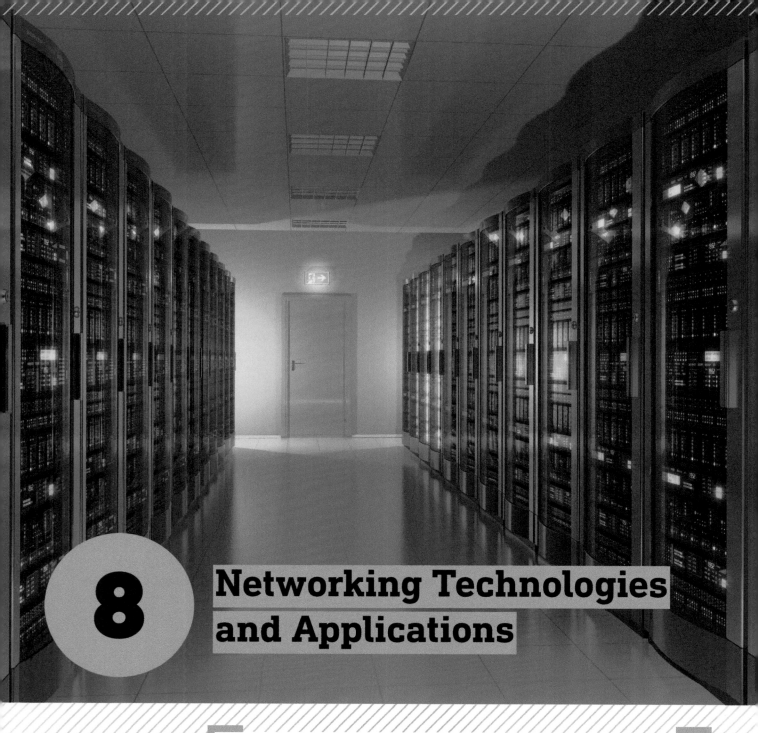

8 Networking Technologies and Applications

Do you ever think about why stories about networks and hacking are often in the news? This is because computer networks are at the very heart of modern workplaces and our homes. We work, learn and play using a variety of online devices that are constantly transmitting and receiving complex data from servers across the world.

Network connections, wired or wireless, are often critical for the key applications we use at work and in our leisure time. Under normal circumstances, networks operate quickly and reliably, but threats to their security and function increase every day. Have you ever experienced difficulty when trying to connect to a network? If you have, you probably appreciate how important it is to have engineers dedicated to keeping them working properly.

This unit helps you to explore network construction and standards, encouraging you to discover how they operate. You will also investigate how they can be made secure and the risks and repercussions for organisations and individuals when this fails.

How will I be assessed?

You will be assessed through a series of class assignments focusing on different parts of the unit.

Your tutor may give you a set of assignment briefs that you will be expected to complete individually, asking you to produce a report outlining the key components, services, topologies and protocols used in networks. In addition, you will be expected to develop a secure network solution, test it and modify it according to the needs of an organisation. Once the network has been developed you will be asked to review and troubleshoot a network solution, justifying the decision you have made to meet the user requirements and citing its current performance levels and room for potential improvement.

Assessment criteria

Pass	Merit	Distinction
Learning aim A: Understand protocols and applications used in networking		
A.P1 Produce an outline of key components, services, topologies and protocols.	**A.M1** Explain how directory services support networking.	**A.D1** Evaluate differing component types used in networks and recommended components for a solution to a given scenario.
Learning aim B: Develop a secure network		
B.P2 Configure and test a network solution to a given situation.	**B.M2** Modify a network solution according to organisational requirements.	**B.D2** Produce a robust and effective network solution that has security features appropriate to the organisational requirements.
B.P3 Secure a network to meet requirements.		
Learning aim C: Review and troubleshoot a network solution		
C.P4 Review a network against given requirements.	**C.M3** Explain how the network should be managed.	**C.D3** Justify the produced network against all user requirements, with reference to performance and future improvements.
C.P5 Troubleshoot a given network solution.		

A Understand protocols and applications used in networking

A **COMPUTER NETWORK** consists of a number of different components and applications. You will need to have a good grasp of them in your work as a network technician.

A1 Understand components and applications used in networking

It is important that you understand the terminology associated with networking. Being able to identify the basic terminology used is a good starting point.

Types of network

Think about the different types of network that are available. You can categorise network types as follows.

- *Client–server*: this is a network where a typically more powerful computer (a server) controls the operation and security of the network. Less powerful computers (called 'clients') connect to this network and are managed by the server.
- *Peer-to-peer*: this is a network where each network client has no more importance or responsibility for the network's operation or security than any other; all are equal.
- *Internet*: this is the worldwide network consisting of countless servers and clients. Many of the devices you use every day – for example, tablets, videogame consoles, televisions, home security systems, or baby monitors – have connectivity contributing to the **INTERNET OF THINGS (IOT)**.
- *Mobile*: this is a network where clients are connected together using wireless technologies.

Link it up

Networking and Cybersecurity

Go to Unit 11 for more on the Internet of Things. For how emerging technologies are being used in the Internet of Things, refer back to Unit 2.

Interconnection devices

Networks use a range of different devices. Those that are used to connect clients and servers together are called **INTERCONNECTION DEVICES**. Below are some of the common interconnection devices available.

- **HUBS** *(wired and wireless)*: a cheap device that connects clients together by repeating all network traffic through each port (even if not needed).
- **WIRELESS ACCESS POINTS (WAP)**: these plug into a wired network and provide additional wireless access.
- **SWITCHES**: physically similar to a hub but intelligently knows which device is connected to which port and whether it should send network **DATA** to it. It is therefore more efficient than a hub.
- **ROUTERS** *(wired and wireless):* devices which connect one network to another, for example joining your home's **LOCAL AREA NETWORK (LAN)** to your **INTERNET SERVICE PROVIDER (ISP)** and the internet beyond. A wireless router includes WAP functionality.
- **FIREWALLS**: a device (**HARDWARE** or **SOFTWARE**) that screens network data to stop harmful **TRAFFIC** entering or leaving a network.

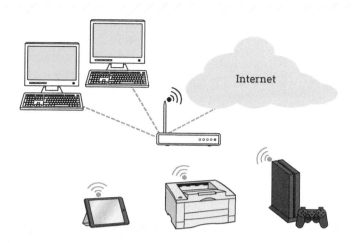

Figure 8.1 shows a typical home or small office network with a number of computers wired to a switch. The switch is connected to a wireless router that has an external connection to the internet via an ISP. Printers and mobile devices can easily be added to this type of network via the router's wireless support. Modern routers often have basic firewall functionality and similar software can be installed onto a desktop computer or tablet to improve security.

Network interface cards, cable types and connectors

Any device connected to a network is usually equipped with a **NETWORK INTERFACE CARD (NIC)**, although in modern technology these are often integrated into the device as a single chip. It is the NIC's job to transmit and receive network data to and from the device. Network interface cards may be wired or wireless.

Wired networks may use different types of media. The three most popular are shown in Figure 8.2.

Category 5/6	Coaxial	Optical fibre
• Often abbreviated to Cat 5/6 • Sometimes called an Ethernet cable • Thin and flexible, easy to work within confined spaces • Has eight different coloured copper wires, twisted into four pairs to reduce outside interference • Cat 5e was superseded by Cat 6 • Use an **RJ-45 (REGISTERED JACK)** connector	• Familiar to most people as a TV aerial cable • Has a single thick copper core • Can carry high-speed network signals over long distances • Not as flexible as Cat 5/6, which makes it difficult to install • Insulated and shielded from outside interference • Often used to connect a router to an ISP – for example, broadband internet • Uses a BNC (Bayonet Neill-Concelman) connector	• Thin strand of high-quality glass • Data travels as light or infrared signals • Signals do not weaken over distance as much as electrical signals on copper wires • Carries more data as the equivalent thickness of copper wire • Exists in two common types: single-mode fibres (SMF) and multi-mode fibres (MMF) • Unaffected by traditional forms of electromagnetic interference

Figure 8.2: Each cable type has different construction, uses and features

The popular and instantly recognisable RJ-45 connector used on Cat 5/6 cables

Wired networks typically use Cat 5/6 cables to connect devices to a switch or router, but these are not used for transporting data over longer distances because of **ATTENUATION** (when the data signal loses strength over distance). Instead, coaxial or fibre optic cables are often used to transport data over longer distances because they are less susceptible to interference and can carry higher volumes of data (also known as **BANDWIDTH**).

Types of network services

A network provides its users with a number of different services. There are three basic categories of network service to consider, as shown in Figure 8.3.

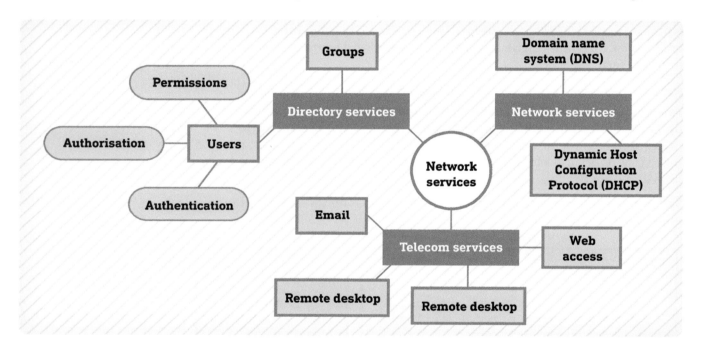

Figure 8.3: Network services are often categorised by technical use

Directory services

DIRECTORY SERVICES (an information store about network users, resources and services) appear as a single **DATABASE** that provides a global catalogue of objects that exist within the network. This provides information on organisational groups within a business, different users and connected devices. The database is highly searchable and can be accessed from many different operating systems using a vendor-neutral protocol called LDAP (Lightweight Directory Access Protocol). This means it is possible to query a server running Microsoft® Active Directory™ (AD) from Linux® for tasks such as authenticating a user's log-in credentials.

Telecom services

TELECOM SERVICES provide popular facilities such as email, web access, remote access and remote desktop.

Network services

NETWORK SERVICES chiefly provide services to clients connected to the network. Two popular examples include **DOMAIN NAME SYSTEM (DNS)**, which translates domain names (for example, www.google.com) into **IP ADDRESSES** (for example, 62.252.191.212) and DHCP (Dynamic Host Configuration Protocol), which allows a client to request its network unique IP address from an available 'pool' of addresses allocated by the server.

Link it up

Networking and Cybersecurity

For more on network connections and IP addresses, refer back to Unit 1.

Using appropriate tools to make and test networking cables

Many different tools are used to make network cables and test them. Common tools you may find in a network engineer's toolkit are shown in Figure 8.4.

Crimper

A tool used to cut Cat 5/6 cables and physically '**CRIMP**' (compress into small ridges) RJ-45 jacks onto Cat 5/6 cables

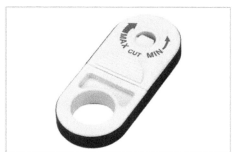

Cyclops cutter

A tool used to cut the sheaf from a Cat 5/6 cable to expose the individual twisted pairs

Punchdown tool

A tool used to 'punch' the wires of a Cat 5/6 cable into a **PATCH PANEL** (a rack-mounted wiring panel used to connect cables directly to a network)

Cable tester

An electronic tool that tests the connectivity of wires in a Cat 5/6 cable and whether they have been grouped correctly

Figure 8.4: A network engineer's toolkit contains a mixture of mechanical and electronic tools

Making a Cat 5/6 network cable

The best way of learning to use networking tools is to try to create a simple straight-through Cat 5/6 cable. This uses either T568A or T568B wiring diagrams (see Figure 8.5 and the Step by Step instructions). The process is intricate and will require patience. In time and with practice, most people are able to build their own network cables and test them successfully.

Note: if you have deuteranomaly (red–green colour blindness) or protanomaly (red colour blindness), you may need assistance identifying the differently coloured pairs.

STEP BY STEP | MAKING A CAT 5/6 NETWORK CABLE

CHECKLIST

Personal protective equipment (PPE)
- [ ] First-aid kit (for cuts)
- [ ] Protective mat

Tools and equipment
- [ ] Cyclops cutter
- [ ] Crimper
- [ ] Cable tester
- [ ] Tape measure

Consumables
- [ ] Cat 5/6 cable
- [ ] 2 × RJ-45 jacks and boots
- [ ] Cable tag/label

Source information
- [ ] T568A or T568B wiring diagrams

STEP 1

Cut the cable to the correct length in metres using tape measure and crimper.

STEP 2

Strip outer sheath from one end of the cable, exposing the twisted pairs.

STEP 3

Re-order pairs to match T568A (or T568B) wiring diagram and cut wires to correct lengths (see Figure 8.5).

STEP 4

Push each wire carefully into the RJ-45 jack and crimp it firmly to ensure a good connection.

STEP 5

Slide the two connector boots on the cable, one at each end and facing the correct direction.

STEP 6

Repeat steps 2–4 at the other end of the cable.

STEP 7

Test the cable using a cable tester. If the cable is not OK, check each end of the cable and retry until successful.

STEP 8

Push the boots firmly over each jack to protect them and label the cable as straight through.

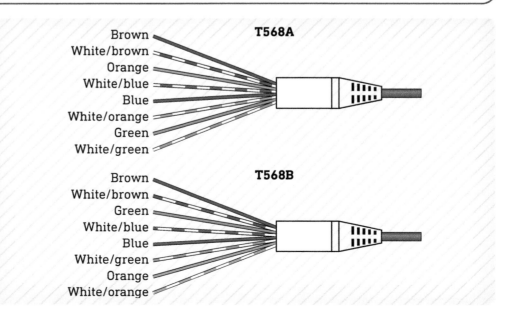

Figure 8.5: T568A or T568B wiring diagrams appear similar but have subtle differences

Practise

Think about the different networks you use every day.

1 Select the correct category for each network.

2 Identify the different types of devices connected to each network.

3 Write down the applications and services you use on each network.

A2 Explore network topologies, standards and protocols

Each point on a network is called a **NODE**. The shape formed when these nodes are connected and organised is called its **TOPOLOGY** (see Figure 8.6).

Topologies

A network topology can be either of the following.

- Logical: how devices appear to be connected to the network user.
- Physical: how devices are actually interconnected via wires and cables.

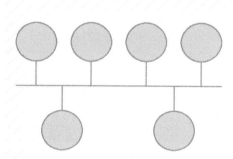

Bus: all nodes connected from a central 'bus' or spine.

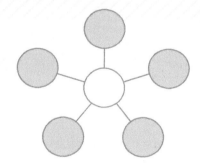

Star: all nodes connected via a central node. This represents a single point of failure, cutting off communication with the other nodes.

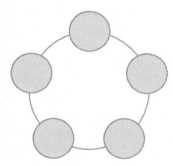

Ring: all nodes connected in a chain; **PACKETS** travel through each node on their journey from source to target, with each node taking it in turns to transmit.

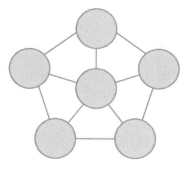

Mesh: all nodes connected via multiple routes. This topology is the most robust, coping well with many node failures and still transmitting successfully.

Figure 8.6: Network topologies provide a visual guide to basic connectivity

Link it up

Networking and Cybersecurity

For more on network layouts and topologies, go to Unit 11.

Protocols and standards

Many different protocols and standards are used in networking and the manufacturers of different network equipment follow them closely to ensure that their devices are INTEROPERABLE (that they work with each other). Below are some of the common protocols and standards.

- *802.x*: a group of network protocols and standards created by the IEEE (Institute of Electrical and Electronics Engineers) that cover various networking concepts, including:
  - *802.3 Ethernet:* the basis for the most common type of wired networks that now can operate at around 100 Gbits (gigabits per second)
  - *802.11 Wireless local area networks (WLAN):* popularly called Wi-Fi. Various revisions exist – for example, 802.11n where devices operate in the 2.4 Ghz (gigahertz) and 5 Ghz frequency bands. The 802.11 specifies both AD HOC and INFRASTRUCTURE MODES (where wireless devices are connected via a wireless access point (WAP).
- TRANSMISSION CONTROL PROTOCOL/INTERNET PROTOCOL (TCP/IP): the standard language used to communicate data on the internet. It is actually a suite consisting (originally) of two separate protocols, TCP and IP. In simple terms, IP is responsible for obtaining the target address where the data packet needs to go and TCP guarantees that it is actually delivered.
- IP addresses are important as they *uniquely* identify a client, server or device on a network. IP addresses for a client may be fixed (static) or change (dynamic). Problems occur when two network connections use the same IP address, causing an IP conflict.
- Each network device also has a permanent, hardware (or physical) address called the MEDIA ACCESS CONTROL (MAC) address that is assigned by the manufacturer.

  IP address   192.168.1.10
  MAC address   00-1A-4D-5D-B4-62

- *SMTP*: SIMPLE MAIL TRANSFER PROTOCOL is an internet standard for electronic mail (email) transfer usually between different email servers; email client applications often use IMAP (Internet Message Access Protocol) or POP3 (Post Office Protocol version 3) to retrieve email and SMTP only for sending to the server.
- BLUETOOTH®: a wireless standard for transferring data over short distances in the 2.4 Ghz frequency band. It is very commonly used in mobile devices to create PERSONAL AREA NETWORKS (PAN) that pair devices – for example, a mobile phone with a pair of stereo headphones, speakers or a portable keyboard.
- *3G and 4G*: third- and fourth-generation mobile technologies that are used to transfer internet data to and from devices such as mobile phones and tablets via telecommunication masts (or cells). Although local coverage is variable in rural areas, most cities and suburban areas enjoy widespread 3G and 4G connections, allowing high-speed internet connections while on the move for business and leisure applications.

Link it up

Networking and Cybersecurity

For more on network protocols, go to Unit 11.

Factors that affect network range and performance

A network's range and performance can be affected by a number of different factors. Some are specific to wired or wireless networks; others are general issues that affect both types.

- *Noise*: this is simply background electrical or electromagnetic energy that damages the signals carrying the network data. If the signal-to-noise ratio is high, data can be affected or corrupted, requiring it to be resent. Insulated and shielded types of cables are less susceptible to noise.
- *Distance*: the strength of a signal is lost when travelling over longer distances; this is called attenuation. It is often caused by reducing power as signals pass through various media components such as cables and connectors. Most media have maximum recommended lengths before the signal needs to be boosted. Wireless signals also degrade the further away a device is from the wireless access point or router. You may have noticed this at home, school or in public locations where Wi-Fi hotspots are available.
- *Cabling issues*: commonly include laying network cables too close to power lines (creating interference), badly crimped connectors, compressed or bent cables and loose wires.
- *Interference*: both wired and wireless networks can suffer from interference – stray signals that disrupt the network's intended signal. For wireless networks, these causes are often environmental in nature, for example signals being absorbed by thick walls or signals conflicting with devices operating on the same frequency (baby monitors or cordless phones).

A3 Understand network applications and software

Two key types of software are integral to a successful network.

1. Network operating systems (NOS).
2. Application services.

Network operating systems

Due to the advent and popularity of the World Wide Web and the internet, nearly all modern operating systems support networking as standard. Historically these were specifically referred to as network operating systems (NOS); however, this has quickly become a redundant term as the functionality has become commonplace. Common examples of NOS include:

- Microsoft Windows Server®
- Linux Server distributions, for example CentOS®, Ubuntu™, Debian™, Red Hat®
- Mac OS® Server.

Although Microsoft Windows Server is popular with modern businesses due to its easy integration with Microsoft Windows® 10 client desktop PCs, tablets and mobiles, it is different in other parts of the IT industry. In sectors such as web hosting, it is Linux-powered servers that claim the majority of the market, particularly due to their low cost, security and reliable 'up' times (periods between reboots). As such, you should be willing to learn about multiple OPERATING SYSTEMS as it is likely that you will encounter many NOS variations when completing your duties.

Common tasks performed by the NOS include:

- authentication, authorisation and accounting (known as AAA)
- sharing resources such as data, files and printers between multiple users
- communication, for example instant messaging or email
- collaborative working on documents, for example word processing, spreadsheets
- remote access to clients, particularly to allow teleworking
- centralised management of users, groups and security
- roaming user log-ins that provide access to personal files from different clients
- network application services.

Application services

Application services accessible on a network can run on either a peer-to-peer or client–server model using a compatible NOS. They aim to provide specific software for the user that takes advantage of the network environment, as shown in Figure 8.7.

Although some web services are commercial products, others are available for multiple NOS under the Open-Source Licence. This allows them to be freely used, modified and shared.

Figure 8.7: Application services are a core network resource

Web services	Relational databases	Anti-virus suites
• Provide **HTTP (HYPERTEXT TRANSFER PROTOCOL)** and **HTTPS (HYPERTEXT TRANSFER PROTOCOL SECURE)** protocols for the transfer and receipt of web content • Provide additional services that can be used to transfer data between different programming languages, applications and NOS – for example, combining SOAP (Simple Object Access Protocol) and XML (eXtensible Markup Language) • As well as providing access to the World Wide Web, it can also be used to host websites and corporate intranets • Apache®, Nginx® and Microsoft IIS (Internet Information Services) are popular web servers for various NOS	• Provide databases to store relational data, such as employees, customers, stock, orders, that a business might use • Have an interactive language (normally **STRUCTURED QUERY LANGUAGE (SQL)**) that is used to modify or interrogate the database to extract data and generate useful business information • Form part of a web stack for developers – for example, a LAMP is a combination of a Linus NOS, Apache Web Server, MySQL™ relational database and PHP scripting language • MySQL, MariaDB™ and Microsoft® MS SQL™ Server are popular relation database management systems	• These act as a central repository for anti-virus on a network • Downloads anti-virus update signatures from a remote server and then either 'pushes' or schedules updates for each network client so that it can remain protected • Anti-virus suites protect a network client from malicious software, adware and traditional viruses • **VIRUSES** such as **WORMS** use a network to spread and replicate themselves, making anti-virus protection essential in any network plan • Intel® Security, AVG®, Symantec™ Endpoint Protection and Kaspersky™ Endpoint Security Cloud are popular anti-virus suites suitable for small- to medium-sized businesses

Practise

Try to use different network services.

1 Install and configure an open-source web server.

2 Identify a suitable relational database and install it.

3 Access web pages and database tables from a different client on a network.

Skills and knowledge check

- ☐ What are the four different types of network?
- ☐ Can you describe the key features of network interconnection devices?
- ☐ What is the difference between Cat 5/6, coaxial and optical fibre cables and connectors?
- ☐ Can you list three types of network services and give examples of their everyday use?

- ○ I can identify a network topology.
- ○ I can describe different network protocols and standards.
- ○ I know what factors affect range and interference of a network signal.
- ○ I can use different network application services and operating systems.

B Develop a secure network

Secure networks are typically the result of thorough planning.

B1 Configure a network following a given plan

Network configuration depends greatly on the type of network being planned and the needs that have been identified.

Planning a network

Networks require planning for them to work effectively, be secure and meet the identified needs.

We can divide the building of a network into a sequence of different steps as shown in Figure 8.8.

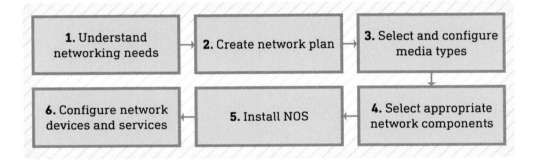

Figure 8.8: Following a defined plan helps to develop more secure networks

1. Understand networking needs

The first step is to understand the user requirements of the network. Typically, this involves answering the following checklist of questions.

- [ ] What will the network be used for?
- [ ] Who will be using the network?
- [ ] How many people will be using the network?
- [ ] How large is the network geographically, for example one room, one floor, multiple buildings or larger?
- [ ] Which network services are required?
- [ ] Will it be peer-to-peer or client–server?
- [ ] What type of media is required, for example wired, wireless or both?
- [ ] Is internet connectivity required?
- [ ] How secure does the network need to be?
- [ ] What permissions are required for different users and groups?

2. Creating a network plan

The following example uses a simple but realistic workplace scenario provided by a local business.

> We are a small local business that needs to network its computers. We currently have two main rooms. One contains four desktop admin computers and a networkable colour laser printer. The second room, which is the workshop, contains two desktop computers and a notebook. We would like to be able to print from any connected device and share files over the network. All devices also need internet access for web browsing and emails. The manager would also like to use his tablet and smartphone wirelessly. Our technician tells us that all devices currently have network capability.

Depending on the complexity of the user requirements gathered, you can usually sketch a simple network plan manually, or create it interactively using a **NETWORK VISUALISATION TOOL** (a software application that helps a network specialist to design and test a network in a virtual fashion).

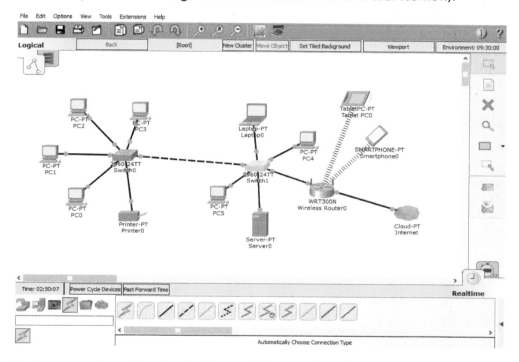

Figure 8.9: Cisco Packet Tracer can be used to create a working, virtual network

Software such as Cisco Packet Tracer® (free to download from www.netacad.com/about-networking-academy/packet-tracer) can be used to create and simulate a working network using a simple drag-and-drop approach as shown in Figure 8.9.

In Figure 8.9 we can see a network that solves the networking requirements of a small business. We can use this example to show the various decisions that have been made.

3. Select and configure media types

A small Ethernet LAN is suitable for this type of business requirement. This typically would mean a combination of wired (Cat 5 or Cat 6) cables and wireless devices.

Cat 5 or Cat 6 cables would be used to link the desktop computers, printer and notebook to the switches and connect each room's switch. Another cable would be used to connect the switch to the router.

The wireless features of the router would support connection for the manager's mobile devices (tablet and smartphone) and provide internet access via the business's ISP.

Link it up

Networking and Cybersecurity

Refer back to Unit 1 and also see Unit 11 to find more information about installing, configuring and testing software in computer systems and mobile devices to meet user requirements.

4. Select appropriate components

The three interconnection devices needed are:

- two network switches for each room (admin office and workshop) that can each support up to 16 devices (allowing for business growth)
- one wireless router that provides access to the internet for external services, such as email, and the world wide web, via the business's ISP, and supports wireless device connectivity.

In addition, a new server could be purchased to provide centralised data storage for shared files and improved security, although in theory a simple peer-to-peer solution may also be recommended depending on budget and whether the business wants to expand its network (client–server solutions are more scalable).

5. Install NOS

In general, the installation of a NOS is similar to the standard installation of a stand-alone operating system, although certain additional network services will be required.

6. Configure network devices and services

Various configuration tasks are required as follows.

Configure the IP address of each device. DHCP may be used by the server or the wireless router to provide dynamic IP addresses or these could be set statically.

Install an anti-virus suite to protect the server and network clients.

Create **USER ACCOUNTS** and permissions using directory services (an information store about network users, resources and services), for example using Microsoft Active Directory® to create suitable groups (Admin, Workshop) and identified user accounts for each employee.

Create shared folders for employees to access with appropriate permissions.

DNS may be installed on the server and/or remote DNS could be provided by the ISP, depending on the business preferences.

Practise

Use a network visualisation tool to design a simple home network.

1 What interconnection devices are needed?

2 Which media types are needed?

3 Which services need to be configured?

B2 Modify the network to specific requirements

Once you have developed a network, it is likely that further modifications will be required following client feedback. Sometimes this may be to improve security or simply change the way the network works.

Modifying a network to make it more secure

Common changes that are made to networks are listed in Table 8.1.

Table 8.1: Modifying the network

Configuring IP addresses	You can configure IP addresses manually (statically), that is, one client device at a time, or they can be assigned automatically using DHCP. The main advantage of using static IP addresses is that devices are tied to that address and its network traffic is easily identified and isolated for security purposes, for example for identifying suspect network traffic such as prohibited website visits. Static IP addresses are configured on the client device. Dynamic IP addresses are requested on the client device but a pool of available IP addresses must be set on the server (or router) and the DHCP service must be enabled. A typical IP pool of addresses could be: **192.168.1.1 to 192.168.1.250** This would provide unique addresses for 250 devices, including desktop PCs, network printers and mobile devices, for example: **192.168.1.1** **192.168.1.2** **192.168.1.3** ... **192.168.1.250** Even on a DHCP service it is possible for specific devices (particularly servers and printers) to have preferred addresses. DHCP IP addresses are leased for a specific time period, for example seven days. Once the lease has expired, a new IP must be requested. The renewed address may not be the same as the one leased previously.
Managing domains	A network domain is the name against which all user accounts, devices and permissions are registered on a network. Client–server networks have a primary domain to which all devices are connected. Peer-to-peer networks can often function without one, so moving from peer-to-peer to client–server will require the creation of a domain.
Adding user types and groups	Directory services on a network allow the administrator to create many different groups and user types. Different groups and user types may have access to different parts of the network and its services. Adding new groups or changing a user from one group to another is a common modification.
Installing and configuring an anti-virus suite	Installing and changing the configuration of an anti-virus suite is a common request, particularly in terms of its behaviour, for example when (and how often) it updates its virus signatures and its preferred action when it encounters an infected file, that is, whether it should delete it or **QUARANTINE** it.
Installing and configuring firewalls	Firewalls often need modification as new applications and network services are installed, as the firewall may attempt to block their access. This will require adding new rules to ensure that these applications and services are on the **WHITELIST**.

Always record any changes to the network that you have made and describe your reasons for doing so, linking them to the specific user requirements you have identified.

B3 Apply network security

You can use many standard techniques to secure a network and these often revolve around limiting the freedom of the network user. This is done because users frequently make inappropriate decisions when using the computer and/or network that can help others to crack the security.

Securing a network

Protection that is implemented in the network operating system software is collectively referred to as **LOGICAL SECURITY**, in contrast to the physical measures you will see later in this unit. As you will discover, there is no 'silver bullet' for network security, it requires a combination of many different techniques to provide the best possible protection.

Many organisations use recommended passwords' policies to reinforce network security. Many of these policies are actually built into the NOS as standard, such as Microsoft Windows Server to assist Network Administrators.

Passwords

Authentication occurs when a user attempts to gain access to a network, usually by entering a set of credentials, for example a unique **USERNAME** and a password, to prove their identity. Policies controlling password creation are often advisable, especially in a multi-user environment.

A good network password policy might require the following.

- Enforcing a minimum length of characters for the password, for example eight characters.
  Why? Longer passwords are harder to crack.
- Enforcing a password history, for example a new password cannot reuse any recently set password.
  Why? Users often alternate between previous passwords as it is easy to do (and therefore guess).
- Enforcing a minimum password age, for example how long users must keep a password before changing it.
  Why? Users often attempt to switch back to a preferred password as soon as possible.
- Enforcing a maximum password age, for example how long before users must change their password.
  Why? It forces users to change their password periodically, which helps keep it fresh and prevents it being guessed. Good values are 30, 60 or 90 days.
- Enforcing complexity requirements, for example passwords should not be real words or be the user's first or last name; they should be at least six characters long and use a mixture of lower case letters, upper case letters, numbers and symbols.
  Why? It makes passwords harder to guess and takes longer to crack.
- Enforcing password **ENCRYPTION**, that is, passwords are not stored in plain text on the server.
  Why? They cannot be read by unauthorised people.

Authorisation

After a user has been authenticated, the process of authorisation can begin. Authorisation occurs when the network system tries to determine which actions, services or resources a user can access, in essence, what they can and cannot do. For example, Figure 8.10 shows different levels of authorisation and access.

Link it up

Networking and Cybersecurity

Go to Unit 11, which looks at the tasks involved in ethical hacking, including password cracking, to give you another perspective on why network password policies should be enforced.

User 1	User 2	User 3
• Can change their password	• Cannot change their password	• Cannot change their password
• Can access the shared network printer	• Can access the shared network printer	• Cannot access the shared network printer
• Can access the internet	• Can access the internet	• Cannot access the internet

Figure 8.10: Selecting appropriate levels of authorisation for different users is crucial to securing a network

In this example, it should be obvious that User 1 has more authorisation than User 3, with more actions, services and resources available to them. The NOS will either not show the available option or refuse to permit access if the user does not have sufficient authorisation.

Permissions

Using directory services such as Microsoft Active Directory as a network administrator, you are able to create user accounts with various sets of permissions. These permissions can control:

- when the user can log in
- which settings they can access and change
- which network services they can use
- which applications can be run
- which folders can be traversed, read from or written to
- which files can be created, read, deleted or changed.

In Microsoft Active Directory, policies are used to control permissions and these can be assigned per user or by user group.

Access controls

NETWORK ACCESS CONTROL (NAC) is a more recent introduction that is designed to provide an assessment of the device that is trying to connect to the network and the identity of its user. This has become particularly important in businesses which encourage **BYOD**. Concepts such as BYOD have become a useful tool for businesses to keep their TCO (total cost of ownership) low by helping employees to use their own technology at work. However, it adds an extra layer of worry for cybersecurity professionals as they try to protect the business's network and resources.

A simple example of NAC would be to provide network 'guest' users with access to the internet and network printers without exposing sensitive network resources such as the server or shared folders. Employees may experience limited access to the business network depending on the security features available (and enabled) by their device.

Encryption

Encryption is the process of changing data into a code so that it cannot be read by anyone without the appropriate level of access or authorisation. For example, a website such as www.encrypt-easy.com uses the popular Blowfish algorithm to encrypt submitted text using a hidden password.

So the plain text '**Hello World!**' with a hidden password of '**SECRET**' would become the cipher text:

VmE8kllSqmoGZ+ZcytRn9A====

The *same* password would be required to decrypt the cipher text *back* to the original plain text. If this encrypted message was intercepted without the key, it would be difficult (and take time) to decrypt successfully.

HTTPS, SSL and TLS

Of course, it is common to encrypt data when it is 'at rest', that is, stored on a hard disk or **USB** flash drive. However, because it is possible to intercept data packets while they are transmitted across a network, it is common practice to encrypt data that is also 'in transit'.

In fact, you may have used many websites that use encrypted connections for tasks such as online banking, logging into a social media site or using an online shop. These are usually identifiable as the web browser shows a padlock in the address bar or the website's **URL (UNIFORM RESOURCE LOCATOR)** shows the page was transferred using HTTPS (Hypertext Transfer Protocol Secure) rather than the more commonplace HTTP.

An encrypted website connection is indicated by a padlock in Google Chrome

🔒 Secure | https://www.google.co.uk

Using HTTPS means that all traffic between the client device and the remote server is sent in an encrypted format using either the SSL (Secure Sockets Layer) or TLS (Transport Layer Security) technologies. For this reason, any data packets intercepted by a would-be hacker 'in transit' would be meaningless, including bank details, passwords and personal information.

Public key infrastructure

SSL and TLS rely on a technique called 'asymmetric' **PUBLIC KEY INFRASTRUCTURE (PKI)**. This happens when a server uses a private key (which only it knows) and a public key is issued to all the devices that want to securely talk to it. Any network data that is encrypted with the private key can only be decrypted by the associated public key and vice versa.

PKI works by installing an SSL 'digital' certificate on a server. When a device wants to talk to the server, the SSL certificate is sent to the device. This certificate contains the public key that the device needs in order to send and receive encrypted data from the server. Although a server can self-certificate, it is more typical for an organisation to purchase SSL certificates from a trusted third party known as a certification authority (CA).

Firewalls

Firewalls are used to physically inspect data traffic that is entering and leaving a computer network. A firewall can decide to block traffic based on a number of rules – for example, which network protocol or network ports are being used or which IP addresses the data is being sent from (source) or transmitted (destination) to.

Most firewalls permit standard network traffic, for example unencrypted World Wide Web HTTP traffic normally uses port 80, whereas HTTPS traffic uses port 443.

Network administrators can add rules to a network that will stop traffic they think may endanger the security of the network, for example downloading third-party applications (which may contain viruses) or congesting the network such as broadcasts of high-quality videos from entertainment websites that should not be accessed during business hours.

Legitimate web services need to be whitelisted in order to be sent and received correctly.

Anti-virus

ANTI-VIRUS SOFTWARE helps secure the network by protecting clients and the server from infected files that may be downloaded on to the network and executed by an unsuspecting user.

Some network viruses such as worms are specifically designed to travel round a network and cause maximum damage. If any node on a network becomes compromised, it is possible that the entire network could be accessed illegally by a hacker with potential data loss, data corruption or unauthorised distribution of sensitive data.

Physical security

In contrast to logical security measures such as passwords, authorisation, access control and permissions, tangible security devices can be used to secure networks.

Link it up

Networking and Cybersecurity

Refer back to Unit 3 for more on encryption as part of software- and hardware-based protection.

Biometrics

BIOMETRICS involves the statistical analysis or measurement of biological data. Computers are increasingly able to digitally scan and analyse human characteristics in order to provide additional levels of security. Common biometric techniques include:

- fingerprint
- handprint
- retina or iris scan
- voice print
- facial recognition
- handwriting recognition.

Previously only seen in popular science-fiction films, biometrics has now matured into a reliable technology and performs everyday jobs such as unlocking mobile telephones (by fingerprint) or confirming identities at passport control (using facial recognition).

In addition to data privacy worries, concerns exist about using biometric techniques as the only authentication measure; fingerprints are very easy to lift and duplicate, and voices can be recorded and replayed using a mobile telephone.

A common option is to use biometric techniques as a complement to traditional authentication, for example users requiring valid usernames, passwords and a biometric measure to form something called **MULTIFACTOR AUTHENTICATION**.

In this example, the usernames and passwords are **KNOWLEDGE FACTORS** (something you know) and biometric data is an **INHERENCE FACTOR** (something you are). A **POSSESSION FACTOR**, for example a swipe card with a magnetic strip or embedded chip, is something you have.

Locks

Traditional locks can be used to secure server rooms, client suites and desktop computers. Portable devices such as notebooks, tablets and smartphones use a Kensington security slot.

A Kensington security slot and lock system is a popular option for physically securing a device

---

Skills and knowledge check

- ☐ What is a DHCP lease?
- ☐ Can you describe the difference between network authentication and authorisation?
- ☐ What is PKI?
- ☐ What forms of biometrics can be used as security measures?

- ○ I know which steps are required to develop a secure network.
- ○ I know the difference between logical and physical security measures.
- ○ I can modify a network's configuration based on user feedback and changing needs.
- ○ I can use different techniques to secure a network.

C Review and troubleshoot a network solution

An important part of any network review is testing. As an IT professional, knowing the processes and tools available to you for this important stage is essential.

C1 Review a network solution

Most operating systems, for example, Microsoft Windows, Linux and Apple OS X®, have a range of networking tools that allow you to perform simple **BENCHMARKING** (evaluating something's performance against a standard or set criteria).

Testing a given network using available networking tools

Below are some common network tests that you will need to perform.

- *Checking configuration:* this should tell you the current state of the network card, for example IP address, MAC address, Gateway IP.
- *Checking connectivity:* this should tell you if you can transmit and receive data over the network connection quickly and reliably (without data loss).
- *Checking domain name resolution:* this should tell you if you are able to resolve an IP address from a domain name, for example if www.google.com can be resolved as 216.58.204.36.

This type of testing is performed from the command line interface (CLI). In Microsoft Windows this is called the 'command prompt'. In Linux and Mac OS X this is often called the 'terminal' or 'shell'.

These tests are summarised in Table 8.2 (overleaf).

Table 8.2: Common network tests

Checking configuration	The network interface card should always be checked to ensure it is working correctly. When it is working correctly it should have its own IP address and be capable of transmitting and receiving network data packets. At the Microsoft Windows command prompt use:

```
ipconfig /all
```

On Linux/Mac OS X terminal/shell use:

```
Ifconfig
```

To display the network interface card's current settings, including its IP address, Media Access Control (MAC) or physical address, its hardware description (make, model etc.) and whether it is using a DHCP-leased IP address (or a static one). If you cannot get information about the card from this command, it is probably not working properly and/or it is not properly configured – for example, missing drivers or there is simply a hardware fault.

In all operating systems, the ipconfig/ifconfig command will accept additional command arguments and switches that will provide additional information or allow network card settings to be changed – for example, in Microsoft Windows:

```
ipconfig /renew
```

will attempt to request a new IP address for the device from the DHCP network service.

Checking connectivity	It is always a good idea to first check your device's basic connectivity when fault-finding problems with a network; if basic connectivity is not present, no network service will be able to function and reviewing it will be extremely difficult.

In Microsoft Windows, Linux and Mac OS X it is possible to use the **PING COMMAND**, which transmits packets of test data to a target device and awaits a response. All that is required is a functioning network card (see ipconfig/ifconfig), a wired or wireless connection and the IP address of the target device.

The success of this process and the time taken to complete it can give you a good idea about the quality of connection your device has, irrespective of whether the connection is wired or wireless.

Checking domain name resolution	As previously discussed, the resolving of user-friendly domain names that are easy to remember into less-memorable IP addresses is achieved by the network's DNS. Sometimes this service will be run from a server on the network and sometimes it may actually be performed by remote servers that are accessed via the internet.

On Microsoft Windows or Linux, it is possible to discover the default server responsible for providing the DNS service by typing:

```
nslookup
```

In addition, it is possible to check the IP address mapping of a domain by adding the domain name to the command like so:

```
nslookup www.bbc.co.uk
Server: cache1.service.virginmedia.net
Address: 194.168.4.100
```

Non-authoritative answer:

```
Name: www.bbc.net.uk
Addresses: 212.58.246.91
 212.58.244.67
Aliases: www.bbc.co.uk
```

What if...?

You have received no response after performing a simple ping connectivity test from PC1 to PC2 and vice versa.

1 What is your next step?

2 What should you do if there is still no response between the PCs after performing this step?

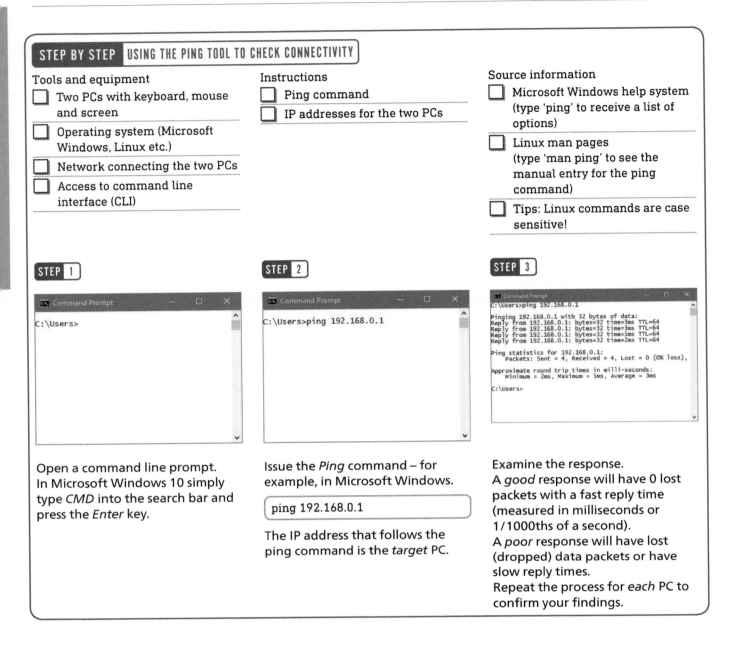

STEP BY STEP USING THE PING TOOL TO CHECK CONNECTIVITY

Tools and equipment
- [ ] Two PCs with keyboard, mouse and screen
- [ ] Operating system (Microsoft Windows, Linux etc.)
- [ ] Network connecting the two PCs
- [ ] Access to command line interface (CLI)

Instructions
- [ ] Ping command
- [ ] IP addresses for the two PCs

Source information
- [ ] Microsoft Windows help system (type 'ping' to receive a list of options)
- [ ] Linux man pages (type 'man ping' to see the manual entry for the ping command)
- [ ] Tips: Linux commands are case sensitive!

STEP 1

```
Command Prompt                    —  □  ✕

C:\Users>
```

Open a command line prompt. In Microsoft Windows 10 simply type *CMD* into the search bar and press the *Enter* key.

STEP 2

```
Command Prompt                    —  □  ✕

C:\Users>ping 192.168.0.1
```

Issue the *Ping* command – for example, in Microsoft Windows.

    ping 192.168.0.1

The IP address that follows the ping command is the *target* PC.

STEP 3

```
Command Prompt                    —  □  ✕
C:\Users>ping 192.168.0.1

Pinging 192.168.0.1 with 32 bytes of data:
Reply from 192.168.0.1: bytes=32 time=3ms TTL=64
Reply from 192.168.0.1: bytes=32 time=3ms TTL=64
Reply from 192.168.0.1: bytes=32 time=5ms TTL=64
Reply from 192.168.0.1: bytes=32 time=2ms TTL=64

Ping statistics for 192.168.0.1:
    Packets: Sent = 4, Received = 4, Lost = 0 (0% loss),

Approximate round trip times in milli-seconds:
    Minimum = 2ms, Maximum = 5ms, Average = 3ms

C:\Users>
```

Examine the response. A *good* response will have 0 lost packets with a fast reply time (measured in milliseconds or 1/1000ths of a second). A *poor* response will have lost (dropped) data packets or have slow reply times. Repeat the process for *each* PC to confirm your findings.

Benchmarking

To be able to review a network effectively, it is necessary to be able to generate network traffic and analyse its performance. This process is called benchmarking. Many different automated tools can be used to benchmark a network's performance with many being inbuilt into the NOS itself and others available from many third-party software developers.

Documenting network testing against benchmarks

Network testing should be documented in a professional manner for a range of user groups, including end-users and management. This essentially means recording test results accurately and using appropriate software (such as word processors, spreadsheets or databases) to store them in an accessible manner and present them. Spreadsheet applications are perhaps the most useful because their arithmetic functionality helps you to calculate minimum, maximum and average values from a large set of results very quickly with little fuss.

Identifying potential improvements

Potential improvement to the network can be identified by evaluating the following benchmarking factors.

- *Performance*: the basic everyday functioning of the network and its connected devices, including interconnection devices such as switches and routers, and servers and client devices.
- *Bandwidth or throughput*: data moved from source node to destination node in a given time frame. It is measured in bps (bits per second), mbps (megabits per second) or gbps (gigabits per second).
- LATENCY: time taken for data to move from source node to destination node and typically back again is called the ROUND TRIP TIME (RTT). It is measured in milliseconds (1000ths of a second).
- *Capacity*: the maximum amount of data that a particular network link can carry.
- *Accessibility*: how well the network can be accessed, its security and control measures.
- *Portability*: how well the network works with different types of devices and services, particularly different NOS, for example a Linux server with Microsoft Windows clients.
- *Reliability*: how often the network experiences 'downtime', for example power cuts which disrupt users, cost an organisation time and money and may inflict reputational damage.
- SCALABILITY: the ability for the network to continue to function well if it is reduced or (more typically) increased in size, for example supporting more nodes and users.
- *Manageability*: how easy it is to manage devices on the network, regulate it, change its configuration, add new nodes and so on.

Most network benchmarking tools will provide detailed information about bandwidth and latency. Factors such as reliability can be examined through specific tools such as Simple Network Management Protocol (SNMP).

Simple Network Management Protocol

On IP-based networks (for example, those using traditional Ethernet or Wi-Fi) a very common tool is the SNMP. This provides a rich collection of information about the operating status of the different devices connected to the network (for example, servers, clients, printers, switches).

This works by simply POLLING (checking at regular intervals) each device to discover its status. Over a period of time it is possible to create a useful picture of the network that includes many of the benchmark indicators listed above.

As a network protocol, it is supported by many different NOS and network devices and is relatively easy to configure.

C2 Troubleshoot a given network

Networks cannot meet user requirements when they develop faults, and although a network has no physical moving parts (like a car), technical faults often occur over the lifetime of a network for a variety of reasons.

Troubleshoot and repair routine issues

Table 8.3 shows some routine faults and ways to resolve them.

Table 8.3: Troubleshooting routine issues

Type of fault	How to identify	Possible causes	How to remedy it
IP address conflict	Usually the operating system will notify the user of this error with a pop-up notification – for example, in Microsoft Windows: Windows has detected an IP address conflict. Another computer on this network has the same IP address as this computer. Contact your network administrator for help resolving this issue. More details are available in the Windows System event log	One or more devices on the network having the same IP address. This is unlikely to occur on a network using DHCP as addresses are typically uniquely assigned from an available pool of addresses, so it is likely that two devices have the same fixed (static) IP address (see Figure 8.11).	✔ Identify the two devices with the same IP address. ✔ Change one of the two devices' IP addresses to an unused address or ensure both are switched to DHCP by obtaining their IP address automatically (see below).
Faulty cable	Usually this is identifiable when: ✘ a computer cannot connect to the network ✘ a computer cannot log in successfully (details cannot be verified on the server) ✘ shared drives become unavailable ✘ network services such as email or the World Wide Web are unexpectedly interrupted ✘ intermittent network connection is experienced ✘ NOS displays an error notification for network connectivity.	Ethernet network cables can become damaged over a period of time. Although flexible, wires can become stretched, broken or pulled from the RJ-45 plug. Laying network cables near power cables can also be problematic due to interference.	✔ Use a cable tester to check the cable's wiremap. ✔ Substitute a known (or new) cable and test connectivity using a ping again. ✔ If the cable has become disconnected from the RJ-45, it is possible to remove the jack and crimp a new one.

Table 8.3: *(continued)*

Type of fault	How to identify	Possible causes	How to remedy it
Faulty interface card	As above, but also the NOS might report issues with the NIC device – for example, missing or incorrect driver issues.	Although modern NICs are typically single chips onboard the device's **MOTHERBOARD**, traditional NICs can still be found that are inserted into expansion slots of the motherboard on servers and larger desktop PCs.	✔ Use the ifconfig (Linux) or ipconfig (Microsoft Windows) command to check the Ethernet card is recognised. ✔ In Microsoft Windows, check the device manager to see if the NIC is present and the driver is functioning properly. ✔ Try to update the existing NIC's drivers. ✔ If the NIC is inbuilt (on the motherboard), ensure the NIC is enabled in the BIOS (Basic Input Output System) or EFI (Extensible Firmware Interface) settings. ✔ Replace the NIC and install fresh drivers.
No wireless access	Usually this identifiable when a computer's NOS informs the user that it has no wireless connection. This is usually indicated through the use of a wireless icon on the NOS desktop or taskbar – for example: 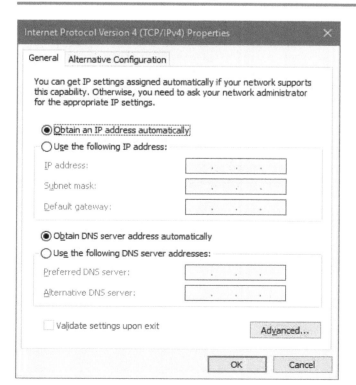	Wireless connections can fail for a number of reasons – for example: ✘ Wi-Fi password has been changed ✘ wireless router or wireless access point (WAP) has been switched off or its signal is weak or being blocked ✘ device's Wi-Fi has been disabled.	✔ Check the Wi-Fi password. ✔ Reboot the wireless router or wireless access point (WAP). ✔ Check for possible devices interfering with the Wi-Fi signal. ✔ Check that the device's Wi-Fi has not been disabled.

Link it up

Networking and Cybersecurity

Refer back to Unit 1 to find more information about internal computer hardware components such as replaceable network interface cards (NICs).

Figure 8.11: The Internet Protocol dialog can be used to select dynamic or static addressing for a device

What if...?

A computer has suddenly stopped downloading emails. It uses a wired connection to its home network. However, the user has been able to download emails via their mobile telephone.

1 What are the possible causes of this disruption?

2 How would you proceed to fix this problem?

Skills and knowledge check

- ☐ What kinds of network test can be performed?
- ☐ Can you describe the purpose of DNS?
- ☐ What is the difference between a MAC address and an IP address?
- ☐ Can you list three factors that could be investigated to improve network performance?

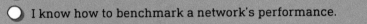

- ○ I can perform basic network diagnostics in different NOS.
- ○ I know how to benchmark a network's performance.
- ○ When troubleshooting a given network I can diagnose common faults and fix them.
- ○ I have solved simple networking issues and can describe their solutions.

Ready for assessment

- You will need to show that you can understand the protocols and applications used in networks.

- You should reflect on networking encountered during work placements, either as a user or when helping in technical support.

- You must be able to develop a secure network, review and troubleshoot it successfully.

- You need to develop a short report/presentation on the technologies used in networking and how they relate to topologies. It should include information on securing networks and how applications support efficient networking.

- You can gather evidence of your practical efforts in developing, securing and troubleshooting a network through the use of screen captures (for device and NOS configuration), photographs, video evidence and observation statements.

- Any review you produce for user groups on the network provided should include any observations made while troubleshooting the solution, including the issues diagnosed, the possible cause(s) and the solution found.

WORK FOCUS

HANDS ON

There are some important occupational skills and competencies that you will need to practise which relate to this unit. Developing these and practising them could help you to gain employment as a junior network engineer or in network support.

1 Thinking skills/adaptability

- Undertaking network installation, configuration and testing, for example using appropriate network configurations for different situations.

- Liaising with user groups, for example listening to feedback and making appropriate changes.

2 Problem solving

- Troubleshooting networks by identifying faults and their causes and selecting the most appropriate solution.

- Creating a network to meet client requirements by following a specific set of actions.

3 Self-management and development

- Developing the professional reports and documents used to review network solutions by understanding the correct formats in which to present the information and the most appropriate tools to create them.

Ready for work?

Networks can be used by a variety of different businesses for many different purposes. Part of your duties as a network engineer will be to understand the business's needs and translate this into workable plans for a secure network.

This requires using your thinking skills to investigate their needs, ask the right questions and start to formulate an appropriate networking solution. Be adaptable in your approach to ensure that you understand exactly what is required and be prepared to listen to users who will give you useful feedback that will help shape and refine your networking solution.

No network will work perfectly first time; there will be unexpected faults, slowdowns and features that annoy or do not fully support the business needs. Your problem-solving skills are important here as they will help you troubleshoot these issues and arrive at a better networking solution for your clients.

Having technical knowledge and being able to translate this into practical networking skills is important but it must be accompanied by a good standard of documentation. Employers appreciate fully rounded individuals who can also explain and document their solutions professionally.

9 Organisational Data Systems

Data is the lifeblood of organisations. Without it, organisations could not function. Every day organisations create and acquire a range of data and information items which they need to store so that they can be used in different ways.

In this unit, you will learn about how data is collected, cleaned and manipulated so that organisations can use it to make decisions and support their day-to-day activities. You will find out about the IT industry's newest phenomenon – big data – and learn how to use tools and techniques to visualise data.

You will analyse data and design a dashboard that displays visualised data. The final component of the unit will introduce you to the concept of data maintenance so that you will be able to apply tools and techniques to make sure that data is always of good quality.

How will I be assessed?

You will be internally assessed in this synoptic unit through a range of both written and practical work. You will be given an assignment to complete which comprises several tasks. The assignment itself will take the form of a vocational activity in which you will create a dashboard to allow users to access and manipulate data. In completing this activity, you will use the skills developed in other units to analyse and present data to different user groups in a meaningful way.

You will need to:

- manipulate data to produce reports for a range of audiences
- produce a dashboard solution to meet an organisational need
- produce an organisational data maintenance schedule.

You will need to produce evidence of your analysis, showing a range of queries that are also used to produce reports for different audience contexts. Evidence will be in the form of printouts and screenshots as appropriate. You will produce design documentation for a dashboard solution that allows for effective data visualisations. The assessment will culminate in a report detailing a range of data maintenance activities. You will also be expected to produce a portfolio that demonstrates a range of data maintenance activities, including data integrity checks and data cleaning activities.

Assessment criteria

Pass	Merit	Distinction
Learning aim A: Manipulate data to produce reports for a range of audiences		
A.P1 Perform data analysis techniques to produce results. **A.P2** Manipulate data, creating queries to produce reports.	**A.M1** Perform data analysis and manipulation techniques to produce reports, evaluating findings to provide informed statements about the data.	**A.D1** Perform data analysis and manipulation techniques to produce reports and demonstrate reasoned arguments, drawing conclusions about the data and making full use of specific examples.
A.P3 Use analytics software to present big data.	**A.M2** Use predictive analytics software to present big data in a range of formats, including numerical and graphical formats, and draw conclusions about the data.	
Learning aim B: Produce a dashboard solution to meet an organisational need		
B.P4 Create a user interface that provides data visualisations.	**B.M3** Create a user interface that provides high-quality data visualisations in a range of formats.	**B.D2** Create a user interface that provides industry-standard data visualisations in a range of formats.
Learning aim C: Produce an organisational data maintenance schedule		
C.P5 Create a data maintenance schedule for an organisational purpose.	**C.M4** Create a data maintenance schedule that supports effective data integrity checks and allows for effective, ongoing data management for an organisational purpose.	**C.D3** Create a data maintenance schedule that provides robust data integrity checks and provides guidance on effective industry-standard data management strategies, including future data migration techniques.

A Manipulate data to produce reports for a range of audiences

A1 Data analysis techniques to investigate, collect, cleanse and manipulate data

Organisations are generating or acquiring **DATA** all the time – even when they are closed, if they have an online shop or ordering system. Data is made up of facts and figures that relate to an organisation and its activities. It is collected and used to support activities, or analysed to help make decisions about future activities and direction.

Levels of data gathered, stored and used in organisations

> ### Practise
>
> Write down at least three things you do every day that generate data. For example, when you buy something, when you scan a bus pass, or when you use social media. Think carefully about your answers.
>
> Now write down at least three instances each day where you have to use or get data to be able to do something. For example, using a train timetable on an app, using Find My Friends® to locate members of your family, or using your course text to find information. Then consider the following.
>
> - How useful is it that you can access information this way?
>
> - If you didn't have internet access, how would you do it?

Link it up

Data Management

Refer back to Unit 2 for more information on the benefits of data systems to an organisation's efficiency, productivity and profit. Emerging technologies allow organisations to find new ways of innovating – making them more competitive and able to grow into new markets.

All data that is collected and generated by organisations has one thing in common – it reflects what the company does. Figure 9.1 shows how organisations use their data.

Figure 9.1: Data is used by organisations to provide three key levels of information

OPERATIONAL DATA: this is data that organisations generate and use every day. It includes customer information such as names, addresses, phone numbers, contact information, credit limits, and information about the product or service being sold (such as descriptions, stock levels, cost price of the item and the price the organisation will charge its customers for it). This data is used every day to process orders, generate invoices and despatch notes, and make sure that customers receive a satisfactory service.

People who work in operations do not often make decisions – they tend to follow set procedures which just repeat and so this information is vital.

TACTICAL DATA: this is data that helps managers to make decisions about what needs to happen in the medium term (usually the next few months or year). It includes stock level information and sales information, which are used together to make decisions about which products are selling well (enabling managers to decide whether to buy or make more to sell), or which are selling badly (enabling managers to decide whether to discontinue the product and sell off the remaining stock at a discount).

Tactical information helps managers make decisions that affect the next few months.

STRATEGIC DATA: this is data that is used to make decisions about the future direction of the organisation. It includes all the information discussed so far with additional information from outside the organisation. For example, this could be:

- a planned housing development (which might mean more customers)
- emerging technology (which might mean new opportunities)
- a large event such as hosting the Olympics (which might also mean more customers, although this will cause a spike (sudden increase) in sales which will not continue when visitors have gone home).

Strategic decisions are made to decide what the organisation wants to be doing in the future (the next few years). Data within the organisation can be analysed to help in this decision-making process.

Stages of data analysis

There is a process that should be followed by organisations in relation to their data needs and it begins with information requirements (see Figure 9.2).

Figure 9.2: Following each stage in the data analysis process enables organisations to convert data into meaningful information

Information requirements

Every organisation needs to understand:

- what data it needs to hold
- why it needs to hold it
- what it plans to do with it.

But when a problem arises that data can help solve, the organisation needs to establish:

- what data it holds that could be useful
- whether any other data is needed (that it may not already have)
- what it needs to do with the data to get the answers.

Data collection

An organisation will generate most of the information it needs through its activities, but sometimes additional information is needed, as shown in the examples below.

- An organisation wants to change the way particular processes happen to try to find ways to make things quicker. Observing and timing the different parts of the process will help the organisation understand the individual processes, how long they take and what they involve.
- An organisation is thinking about launching a new product but is not sure how its customers would feel about it. Interviewing some of the customers and showing them the product will help the organisation make decisions about whether the product is right and is ready for launch.

Data organisation

Data needs to be organised when it is stored, otherwise it can be difficult to find the information you need. This is particularly true if data is archived. When data is archived it is removed from the main **DATABASE**, but is stored somewhere else so that it can still be accessed. This makes the database run faster.

Also it is very important that organisations decide who should have access to their data. For example, it is not always necessary (or appropriate) for everyone in an organisation to see personal information about staff, such as information about salaries.

Data storage

Organisations can store their data in the **CLOUD** (a large and remote network of servers that work together to provide different types of service) rather than on their own physical machines. Even though the organisation has to pay for this, there are clear benefits to using the cloud.

- The service provider takes responsibility for making sure that the data is backed up and secure.
- The service provider will need to make sure that the technology stays up to date (this should mean that they replace hard drives before they fail).

One of the most common reasons for using the cloud is for storing data because it means that the data you are storing is not using any space on your organisation's hard drives.

The alternative to this type of external storage is to store the data on servers in-house. This means that all the activities described above will have to be carried out by in-house staff.

Data cleansing

DATA CLEANSING is a process that ensures that data is error free and complete. Part of this process is ensuring that there are good validation and checking routines when the data is generated or input. Checks should also be made for duplicate records (which should be deleted).

Data manipulation

There are many ways that data can be manipulated. It can be organised in different categories, such as in months, or quarters (periods of three months), or even in whole years. Data from different years can be compared to see if there is any obvious link between factors (for example, ice cream sales go up in the summer and at Christmas, or Wellington boots sell better between October and March).

Link it up

Data Management

Refer back to Unit 2 for more information on mobile technologies and the cloud.

Presentation of findings

Data that has been analysed should be presented in a way that visually highlights key points. It would be up to the analyst to draw attention to anything unusual about the data. For example, a nappy company is looking at why the number of nappies sold in September is different. All the other months have similar data across the same period in each year, but September stands out. Figure 9.3 shows how presenting the data visually helps draw out this key point.

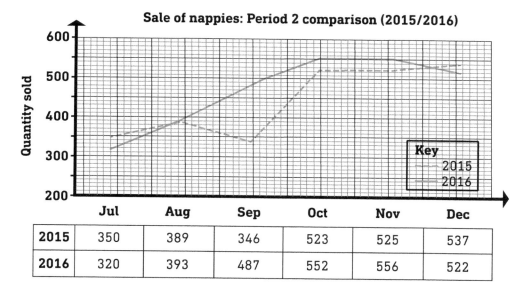

Sale of nappies: Period 2 comparison (2015/2016)

	Jul	Aug	Sep	Oct	Nov	Dec
2015	350	389	346	523	525	537
2016	320	393	487	552	556	522

Figure 9.3: Presenting findings visually helps highlight key points

What if...?

A manager has asked you to prepare data to be used to brief senior managers about product movement over a six-month period.

The table below provides the sales volumes for five key products.

Volumes	Jul	Aug	Sep	Oct	Nov	Dec
Shampoo	1,016	920	853	2,187	1,086	1,107
Conditioner	1,239	1,881	1,692	1,807	1,866	887
Toothpaste	1,395	2,326	367	1,354	1,437	1,751
Nappies	3,119	3,557	3,713	3,950	3,926	3,254
Aspirin	748	609	527	619	491	739

Although this shows the number of each item sold, the products vary in their profitability.

• Each bottle of shampoo contributes 117p to the **PROFIT** margin.

• Each bottle of conditioner contributes 123p.

• Each tube of toothpaste contributes 85p.

• Each pack of nappies contributes 15p.

• Each pack of aspirin contributes 37p.

Use a spreadsheet to produce two charts for the managers to compare. One should use the data as shown to communicate volumes. The other should communicate profitability.

If the organisation needs to stop selling one of the products, which would be the obvious product to select?

Link it up

Data Management

Refer back to Unit 6 for more information on design query techniques, queries and reports. In this unit, you can build on those skills by exploring new techniques that will help you to draw conclusions about data.

A2 Data manipulation

Organisations create large quantities of data every day. This data is stored, manipulated and used by managers to help them make decisions.

Design queries

To query the data in a database and to use the data to produce information, you will need to use a combination of **LOGICAL OPERATORS** (key words and symbols used in making decisions such as < (less than), > (greater than), AND, NOT and OR), **ARITHMETIC OPERATORS** (the +, -, / and * symbols used for the calculations) and **EXPRESSIONS** (these are calculations that occur when the database is used rather than being stored in the database – you will find out more later in the unit).

When you query a database, you must always begin by deciding what it is you want to know. What do you want the data to tell you? If you are managing a shop, you will always need information about stock so that you can order replacements (if stock is low), think about offering discounts on products (if stock is high) and understand the value of the whole stock for insurance.

STEP BY STEP | **CREATING A SIMPLE QUERY**

STEP 1

Look at the data below, which is part of a 48-record database for a music shop showing the stock table that identifies the instrument (description), its category, its price and the current stock level.

Musical Instruments

Product ID	Description	Category	Price	Stock	Add New Field
1	Violin (full size)	String	£123.00	6	
2	Violin (3/4 size)	String	£49.00	7	
3	Violin (1/2 size)	String	£47.00	9	
4	Violin (1/4 size)	String	£55.00	4	
5	Viola	String	£129.00	4	
6	Cello	String	£219.00	6	
7	Double Bass	String	£610.00	7	
8	Flute	Woodwind	£145.00	12	
9	Oboe	Woodwind	£246.00	14	
10	Clarinet	Woodwind	£95.00	17	
11	Saxophone (Tenor)	Woodwind	£475.00	2	

To extract data from a database you use logical operators such as > (greater than), < (less than) and = (equal to).

The use of the 'greater than' operator in this context might surprise you because you will be using it to check a letter of the alphabet (rather than a numeric value or date). You will already have seen the > and < operators used with dates (all entries after a particular date) and numbers (all items where there is more than a particular number in stock).

STEP BY STEP | CREATING A SIMPLE QUERY

STEP 2

Apply the **QUERY** as shown below. This is designed to display a list of musical instruments that start with the letter 'V' and go to the end of the alphabet.

Field:	Product ID	Description	Price
Table:	Musical Instruments	Musical Instruments	Musical Instruments
Sort:			
Show:	☑	☑	☑
Criteria:		> 'V'	
or:			

Here is the output.

Stock query

Product ID ▾	Description ▾	Price ▾
1	Violin (full size)	£123.00
2	Violin (3/4 size)	£49.00
3	Violin (1/2 size)	£47.00
4	Violin (1/4 size)	£55.00
5	Viola	£129.00
32	Xylophone	£13.00
43	Yamaha Keyboard	£84.00

This means that the logical operators work with more than just the numeric data types. But with a query you can go further. What about a query that calculates the value of the stock?

STEP 3

This value would not need to be stored in the database, because it must be calculated each time it is needed, as the stock values change. To demonstrate this, we will use the woodwind instruments only.

This is the query using Microsoft® Access query tools (which you will have seen before).

To calculate the stock value you use an expression that you write yourself.

To begin, you need to give the data a heading.

Total:

Field:	Product ID	Description	Category	Price	Stock	Total: [Price]*[Stock]
Table:	Musical Instruments	Musical Instruments	Musical Instruments	Musical Instruments	Musical Instruments	
Sort:						
Show:	☑	☑	☑	☑	☑	☑
Criteria:			"Woodwind"			
or:						

STEP BY STEP CREATING A SIMPLE QUERY

STEP 4

Then add the calculation, which is:

[Price] * [Stock]

Here is the value of the woodwind stock.

Product ID	Description	Category	Price	Stock	Total
8	Flute	Woodwind	£145.00	12	£1,740.00
9	Oboe	Woodwind	£246.00	14	£3,444.00
10	Clarinet	Woodwind	£95.00	17	£1,615.00
11	Saxophone (Tenor)	Woodwind	£475.00	2	£950.00
12	Saxophone (Soprano)	Woodwind	£230.00	0	£0.00
13	Saxophone (Alto)	Woodwind	£194.00	3	£582.00
14	Saxophone (Bass)	Woodwind	£300.00	1	£300.00
15	Bassoon	Woodwind	£694.00	1	£694.00
*	(New)		£0.00		

STEP 5

What you might not have seen before is the **STRUCTURED QUERY LANGUAGE (SQL)** (the language that is used to communicate with the database) that is actually running the query. It sits behind the query on a different tab, but can be viewed through Access by selecting the SQL view for the query. Use the menus as shown below to examine the SQL.

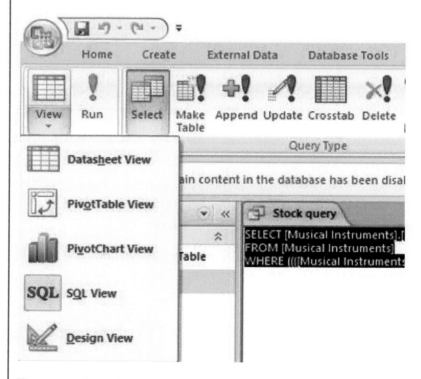

The query above looks like this when presented as an SQL query:

SELECT [Musical Instruments].[Product ID], [Musical Instruments].Description, [MusicalInstruments]. Category, [Musical Instruments].Price, [Musical Instruments].Stock, [Price]*[Stock] AS Total

FROM [Musical Instruments]

WHERE ((([Musical Instruments].Category)="Woodwind"));

Database queries

The simple query you created above contains a *Reading* query because it filters the database to look for specific records. But there are actually four key creation and editing functions or query formats that you can use in different contexts. To remember them, people in the industry refer to these formats with the acronym CRUD.

Creating

Reading

Updating

Deleting

Table 9.1 explains what each function of CRUD does.

Table 9.1: An explanation of the functions of database storage: CRUD

Function	Description
Creating data	This means adding data to the database. In Access, new records are always added to the bottom of a table. Using an SQL command, this would be an INSERT statement.
Reading data	This finds data against criteria to display. Using an SQL command, this would be a SELECT statement. SELECT [Musical Instruments].[Product ID], [Musical Instruments].Description, [Musical Instruments].Price FROM [Musical Instruments] WHERE ((([Musical Instruments].Description)>"V"));
Updating data	This is used to edit existing data. Using an SQL command, this would be something like: UPDATE Instruments SET Stock = 0 WHERE Product ID = 12
Deleting data	This function deletes a record or series of records. Using an SQL command, this would be a DELETE statement.

An example in context would be the following.

Creating tickets for a gig.

Reading the available tickets to find a suitable date and venue.

Updating the ticket database when a ticket is sold.

Deleting the ticket records after the gig has taken place.

Practise

Create queries in a database that filter the data for a particular purpose.

Add an expression that uses data in the database to produce new information.

Using queries to produce reports

As with queries, when you create reports (from queries or directly from tables) you must always begin by deciding what it is you want to report or display.

Although you can create reports using SQL commands in the same way as you can create queries, most users use the Report Wizard. The advantage of using the Wizard is that alignment of the data is automatic and Access makes the best use it can of the space provided.

Reports can be created from either a Query or a Table.

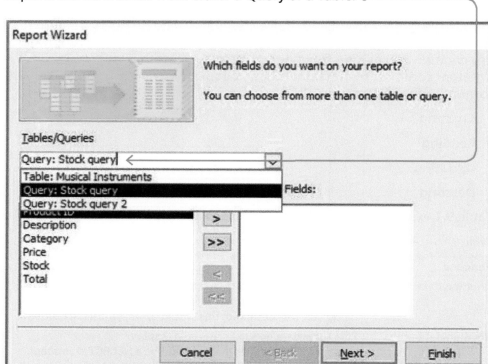

The process is simple.

1 Select the table or query that contains the data you want to report.
2 Select the columns you want to display.
3 You can choose to organise the data in ascending or descending order.
4 You have a choice of three layouts (Columns, Tabular and Justified and you can choose Portrait or Landscape orientation to display the report).
5 You can choose from a range of styles.
6 You can add a heading.

This is the query output.

Stock query

Product ID	Description	Category	Price	Stock	Total
8	Flute	Woodwind	£145.00	12	£1,740.00
9	Oboe	Woodwind	£246.00	14	£3,444.00
10	Clarinet	Woodwind	£95.00	17	£1,615.00
11	Saxophone (Tenor)	Woodwind	£475.00	2	£950.00
12	Saxophone (Soprano)	Woodwind	£230.00	0	£0.00
13	Saxophone (Alto)	Woodwind	£194.00	3	£582.00
14	Saxophone (Bass)	Woodwind	£300.00	1	£300.00
15	Bassoon	Woodwind	£694.00	1	£694.00

One of the biggest benefits of using reports is that you can add even more information to the report output based on the data in the report.

Using an expression, the total of the woodwind stock can be added to the report.

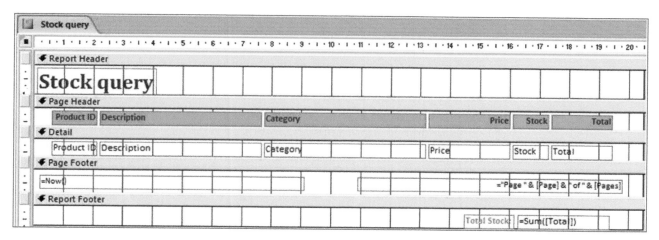

The expression is added to the footer of the report. You must make sure that you also format the output. The final result will look like this.

Stock query

Product ID	Description	Category	Price	Stock	Total
8	Flute	Woodwind	£145.00	12	£1,740.00
9	Oboe	Woodwind	£246.00	14	£3,444.00
10	Clarinet	Woodwind	£95.00	17	£1,615.00
11	Saxophone (Tenor)	Woodwind	£475.00	2	£950.00
12	Saxophone (Soprano)	Woodwind	£230.00	0	£0.00
13	Saxophone (Alto)	Woodwind	£194.00	3	£582.00
14	Saxophone (Bass)	Woodwind	£300.00	1	£300.00
15	Bassoon	Woodwind	£694.00	1	£694.00
			Total Stock:		£9,325.00

It is the job of the analyst to make sure that the reports are designed in an appropriate way for the intended audience.

This means only including the relevant data that is needed and using appropriate formats. This will be considered later in this unit.

Practise

Create reports using the queries (you may use the Report Wizard).

Add an expression that uses data in the report to produce new information.

A3 Use of big data

BIG DATA is a computing term used to describe very large sets of data, possibly from multiple sources, that can be acquired by organisations every day. The data can be analysed by the organisation to help it make better decisions and develop strategic plans.

Big data and how it is collected

As explained earlier, organisations generate data from their day-to-day activities. But there is far more data about them, about their customers and about the environment they operate in which can also be captured and used. This data can come from anywhere in the world.

Big data has three key characteristics.

- *Volume*: the amount of electronic data that organisations can collect is enormous compared with the data that would have been generated by organisations in a time before computers.
- *Velocity*: the data is streaming at a very fast speed from different sources and the organisation needs to have the technology to manage this.
- *Variety*: this describes the fact that the data will come in a range of different formats. It could be structured or unstructured, and it could contain text, images, numbers, sound, or video.

What is important to understand, however, is that this data needs to be gathered and stored and then analysed but most traditional data SOFTWARE does not have the capacity to work with it. For this reason, powerful software has been developed that can store data and has the technology to manage lots of different tasks at the same time. The most well-known software is called Hadoop®.

Practise

Use the internet to find out more about Hadoop or alternatives, such as Microsoft Azure®, Pega 7® Platform, SAS® Business Intelligence, Amazon Web Services®, IBM® Cognos® or QlikView®.

Sources of big data

Big data can come from many sources and can be used in a range of ways. Table 9.2 shows some examples.

Table 9.2: Sources and uses of big data

Source	Data and possible use by an organisation
Social media	Social media can be used to gather customer opinion about products – for example, using the number of likes or shares that a product post has achieved.
Online gaming	Gaming activity generates STREAMS of data about how players interact with the game: how long they play for and who they play with. The stream includes data about levels played and whether users leave games if they cannot complete a level, how many times they have tried the level and the time between attempts. In addition, there is data about how much players spend on online games (including in-game purchases).
Loyalty cards	When you sign up for a loyalty card you are asked to provide personal information, such as your gender, age, socio-economic status, location, marital status and the number of children you have. Every time you present the card with your purchases it builds up a profile of what someone like you buys. This is used to market products and services to you and to others like you.
Online commerce	All online stores will gather data about what you have purchased from them. They can also see the sort of products you have viewed. If you leave items in your basket, you might get a phone call from the catalogue inviting you to complete the purchase at a discount.
Questionnaires	Questionnaires are the most traditional way of gathering information and these now exist both on paper and online.

Table 9.2: *(continued)*

Source	Data and possible use by an organisation
Government records	The government gathers large amounts of data every year, including educational statistics (how many students passed qualifications and what these qualifications were), employment statistics (how many people there are working in different areas and how much they are paid), health statistics (to monitor illness trends in the population) and every ten years there is a census in which every person in the UK is registered and information about them is collected.
Subscriptions	**SUBSCRIPTIONS** and follows on Twitter® feeds, to Facebook® groups or to other websites, give organisations contact details for you that they can use to advertise goods and services.
Research	This could include asking customers directly about particular products or services, examining features and ranking them in order of importance.
Healthcare	Gathering and analysing information about the use of health services helps managers manage staff and other resources because they can establish when the services are most and least used.
Financial sector	Banks, loan and utilities companies share information about customer credit histories that are used by organisations such as ClearScore, which then provide services to help you understand your own credit status. Banks and loan companies can then use wider information to make decisions about lending you money.
Politics	Organisations use information about political policies to make decisions about their future strategy. In 2017 many organisations gathered data about how Brexit could affect them.
Weather	Weather patterns impact on sales of some goods and services – ice cream sells when it is hot, wet weather clothing when there is more rain than usual. Understanding what sells and when may provide additional opportunities.

If organisations gather enough data about individuals as users and consumers, they can make **GENERALISATIONS** (assumptions about groups or individuals) and target them for goods and services.

Users may not be aware of the data that is being gathered through their online activities, but the pages they visit and the content they click on will generate a trail of data that can be used commercially. It is possible to filter advertising, often by purchasing the application where the advertisement is being displayed.

Safety and security implications of big data

Regulations, such as the Data Protection Act 1998 and the Data Sharing Code of Practice, apply to big data in the same way as they apply to any other data stored and used by an organisation. This means that organisations have a duty to keep the data safe and secure. But what are the security risks and threats associated with big data?

Due to its sheer volume, big data can be distributed across multiple servers and networks and the locations of the different parts need to be mapped (so that they can be found later) – see Figure 9.4. **MAPPING TECHNOLOGIES** (software that acts as a reference guide to record the location of information so that the data can be found at a later date) can be attacked

Link it up

Data Management

Refer back to Unit 1 for more information on how data systems need to be secure to comply with legislation. All data needs to be backed up, protected from security threats such as **MALWARE** and protected from unauthorised access.

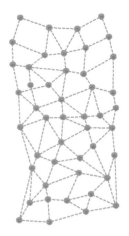

Figure 9.4: A distributed network can show how computers in a network are interconnected

by **HACKERS** who spy on transactions to find weaknesses in the system. This allows them to carry out **INJECTION ATTACKS** (where attack data is inserted into a data entry field through malware so that the attacker can steal the data in the database).

Data that has been compromised by hackers before being acquired by an organisation may further compromise the organisation's own data. Furthermore, if data is stored over multiple locations because of its volume, it means that there are potentially more people who could access that data, which has implications for privacy.

Ultimately, organisations have a responsibility to their customers to protect data that they have gathered about them. As a data analyst, this will be part of your role, and you will need to ensure that systems and policies are in place to protect the data. You will also have to review policy and processes regularly to ensure that the data protection is maintained.

A4 Big data analytics and analysis

In this section, you will find out about some of the software tools that are used to gather and analyse big data.

Link it up

Data Management

Refer back to Unit 3 for more information on how organisations protect their data systems from a range of threats, both internal and external, and how they can adapt to protect themselves against a range of vulnerabilities.

Use of software tools to gather and analyse big data

Here are some examples of software tools you might use to gather and analyse big data.

- *BI (Business Intelligence) systems*: these allow analysts to view data from multiple perspectives. Users can analyse data items to explore the reasons for anomalies and can **SLICE THE DATA** (reorganise the data and group it into different segments) so that comparisons can be made.
- *Data mining*: systems are used to process data and extract patterns, particularly in large data sets.
- *Predictive modelling systems*: these use the patterns in data to make predictions about future events.
- *Sentiment analysis*: this is often used in marketing to determine positive, negative and neutral responses to the features of products and services or to the product or service in its entirety.

Categories of data

There are many data categories that you can explore – but here are some examples of data that is regularly gathered for analysis.

- *Medical*: blood group information (for medical professionals who have to source blood for transfusions), medical conditions (for scientists to research cures).
- *Personal*: dates of birth, addresses, phone numbers combined with other information, which will be used for advertising.
- *Financial*: salary, credit rating, personal debt, mortgage payments and any fraud will determine your ability to borrow money.
- *Environmental*: temperatures, rainfall, sunlight hours, wind speeds and tides over longer periods. Measures of sea level, deforestation (cutting down trees without replacing them), air quality (pollution) and changes to glaciers and icebergs. This has enabled scientific claims about global warming that will impact on everyone in the future. Alternatively, this data could be used to warn people about developing natural disasters such as tsunamis, earthquakes and volcanoes.

- *Retail habits*: understanding consumers' preferred shops, spending habits and shopping patterns could cause stores to review their product ranges. This may result in them discontinuing certain products or starting to sell new ones.

Predictive analytics

PREDICTIVE ANALYTICS is used to make predictions about future events. It uses of a range of techniques such as data mining to find trends in data about past events, and **STATISTICAL ALGORITHMS** (these are the steps that are needed to calculate statistics) to work out the likelihood of the event or the severity of the event. It also uses simulations or data **MODELLING** tools such as **WHAT IF... ANALYSIS** to establish what might happen when a series of variables impact on a particular event. (What if…analysis is usually carried out using a spreadsheet and enables the user to change values in the spreadsheet to see what impact the changes will have.)

The main benefits of predictive analytics are shown in Figure 9.5.

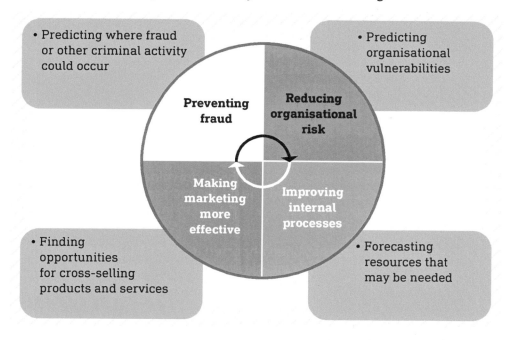

- Predicting where fraud or other criminal activity could occur
- Predicting organisational vulnerabilities
- Finding opportunities for cross-selling products and services
- Forecasting resources that may be needed

Preventing fraud

Reducing organisational risk

Making marketing more effective

Improving internal processes

Figure 9.5: Using predictive analysis helps organisations which are trying to make predictions about the future

The process of predictive analysis requires organisations to:

- define the data (this means the data they have and the information they want to produce)
- select the right algorithms to produce statistics
- choose the right data-modelling techniques to apply to the data
- understand how data could be mined and interrogated to provide the right data for an analysis.

Using analytics software

To demonstrate how you might use big data we will be using the UK's employment and labour market statistics published on 12th July 2017 by the Office for National Statistics (ONS). The data is published monthly and reflects national and local activity and changes in the workforce. The data can be manipulated to extract information at sector level, or the analyst can compare age groups, explore working trends in relation to gender, hours worked, earnings and much more.

The spreadsheet used in this example contains 1404 rows of data in 1302 columns, which is necessary to accommodate all of the classifications. This means that there are 1,828,008 cells containing headings or data items that need to be managed.

The data starts in 1891 with some limited entries, although more data is available from April 1992 onwards when the data was gathered monthly As an analyst, it would be almost impossible for you to filter and analyse that amount of data without the aid of software.

Preparation of big data for analysis

To begin, the data needs to be prepared.

- Under normal circumstances this would require data cleansing (removing data with errors, removing duplicated data), but in this example the data in the dataset downloaded has already been cleansed sufficiently to be used.
- Next you will code the data, which means defining the relationships between different pieces of data (such as linking tables in a database).
- Then you will extract and organise the data to make sure that the data you are using is valid for the purpose.
- Finally, you will check the data for integrity – this means checking that it is accurate and consistent.

Using software tools to process big data for a given business purpose

The data used in this demonstration has been downloaded fully prepared. This means that the data has already been cleaned and any errors eradicated. You can now go on to use software to interrogate the data to answer a series of questions.

For this example, the data has been imported into SAP® Lumira software. This software is easy to use, as it enables you to select the type of visualisation you want. The parameters you can use appear in a list that you simply choose from.

Data imported using SAP Lumira software. Clicking in any of the measures boxes will produce a list of data items that you can choose from

This example uses a bar chart (for more on this see B1 'Data visualisation methods') to compare the number of vacancies (per thousand) in the IT sector over a period of 15 years (using only December data in each year).

Converting the visualisation to a pie chart produces a different perspective and makes the differences between slices much more difficult to interpret, although you can use the mouse and hover over any slice of the pie to see its value.

For this reason, using either the bar chart, or the line chart is the most appropriate visualisation for this particular data.

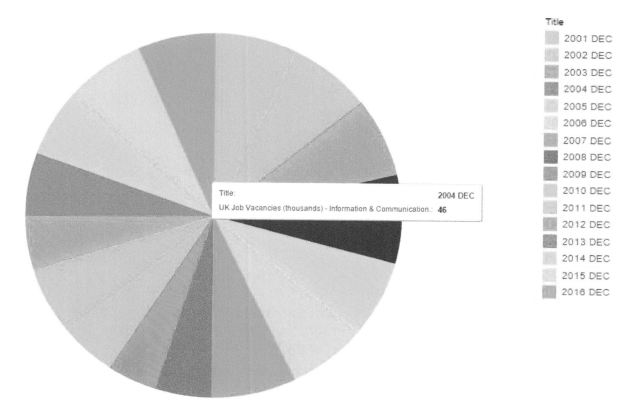

Title: 2004 DEC
UK Job Vacancies (thousands) - Information & Communication.: 46

Title
2001 DEC
2002 DEC
2003 DEC
2004 DEC
2005 DEC
2006 DEC
2007 DEC
2008 DEC
2009 DEC
2010 DEC
2011 DEC
2012 DEC
2013 DEC
2014 DEC
2015 DEC
2016 DEC

What are the advantages and disadvantages of displaying the data as a pie chart?

UK Job Vacancies (thousands) - Information & Communication.

What are the advantages and disadvantages of displaying this data as a line graph?

The data can also be visualised as a simple table.

What are the advantages and disadvantages of displaying the data in a table?

UK Job Vacancies (thousands) - Information & Communication.

	☐ Measures
Title	UK Job Vaca...
2001 DEC	41
2002 DEC	42
2003 DEC	41
2004 DEC	46
2005 DEC	40
2006 DEC	40
2007 DEC	43
2008 DEC	28
2009 DEC	25
2010 DEC	30
2011 DEC	34
2012 DEC	28
2013 DEC	33
2014 DEC	35
2015 DEC	40
2016 DEC	39

Evaluation of the results

It is not sufficient to simply produce results. These results need to be evaluated and checked to ensure that they are accurate and that they answer the questions that were the focus of the analysis.

Good practice for using analytics begins by defining what you want the data to tell you. You have to be specific.

- Data must be prepared:
  - cleansed
  - organised
  - assessed for validity and integrity.
- Data must be processed:
  - questioned
  - formulae applied
  - graphical information produced.
- Results must be evaluated:
  - were the questions answered
  - do the results meet the needs of the customer
  - what were the benefits of using big data analytics
  - what could be improved?

Skills and knowledge check

- ☐ Can you write a list of arithmetic and logical operators and explain each one?
- ☐ Can you create an expression to calculate output from a database?
- ☐ Can you explain big data and why it is different from data usually held by organisations?
- ☐ Can you explain why it is important to clean, organise and assess data for validity and integrity?
- ☐ Can you explain a range of tools that are used in data analytics?

- ○ I understand the difference between operational, tactical and strategic information.
- ○ I can explain the stages of the data analysis cycle.
- ○ I can demonstrate how data is collected, manipulated and stored.
- ○ I can create database queries and reports.
- ○ I can use basic analytics software.

B Produce a dashboard solution to meet an organisational need

B1 Visualisation tools and techniques

As a data analyst, there are many tools and techniques available for you to present data in the most effective way.

Data visualisation

Data visualisation is the process of exploring and viewing data graphically rather than in rows, columns, lists and tables. For example, the music shop owner wants to know how many instruments he has in stock in each category (woodwind, brass, strings, etc.). Here is part of the data.

Musical Instruments				
Product ID	Description	Category	Price	Stock
1	Violin (full size)	String	£123.00	6
2	Violin (3/4 size)	String	£49.00	7
3	Violin (1/2 size)	String	£47.00	9
4	Violin (1/4 size)	String	£55.00	4
5	Viola	String	£129.00	4
6	Cello	String	£219.00	6
7	Double Bass	String	£610.00	7
8	Flute	Woodwind	£145.00	12
9	Oboe	Woodwind	£246.00	14
10	Clarinet	Woodwind	£95.00	17
11	Saxophone (Tenor)	Woodwind	£475.00	2
12	Saxophone (Soprano)	Woodwind	£230.00	0
13	Saxophone (Alto)	Woodwind	£194.00	3
14	Saxophone (Bass)	Woodwind	£300.00	1
15	Bassoon	Woodwind	£694.00	1
16	Trumpet	Brass	£82.00	8
17	Trombone	Brass	£120.00	4

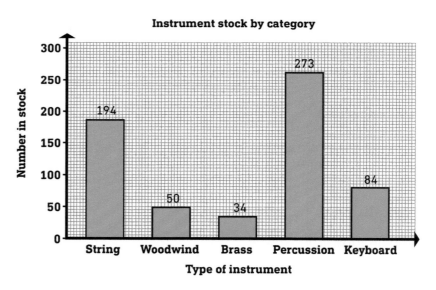

Figure 9.6: What conclusions can you draw from this graph?

From this, the music shop owner could do a visual count using the data and add up the columns manually. He could also use software that automatically adds up the categories and presents them as a bar chart.

This immediately tells the shop owner that most of his stock is percussion instruments and the category he stocks least is brass.

Having looked at the stock categories, he decides that he wants to know about the keyboard category, and, more specificially, which keyboards he stocks and how many. The pie chart in Figure 9.7 provides the answer.

Keyboard stock on 18 February

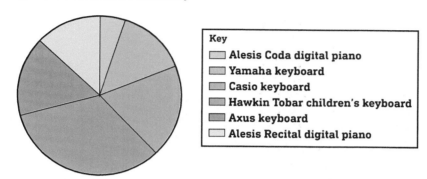

Key
- Alesis Coda digital piano
- Yamaha keyboard
- Casio keyboard
- Hawkin Tobar children's keyboard
- Axus keyboard
- Alesis Recital digital piano

Figure 9.7: Which keyboard does he stock the most of and which does he stock the least of?

As the data in the chart is linked to the actual stock levels in the database, if the shop owner revisits the chart two weeks later, the picture might be quite different.

Keyboard stock on 4 March

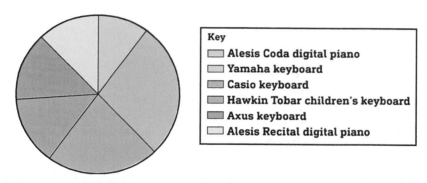

Key
- Alesis Coda digital piano
- Yamaha keyboard
- Casio keyboard
- Hawkin Tobar children's keyboard
- Axus keyboard
- Alesis Recital digital piano

Figure 9.8: Compare this pie chart with the one in Figure 9.7

For this reason, most organisations use dashboards with visualisations of their key data. You will find out more about dashboards in B2.

Data visualisation methods

There is an extensive range of charts and graphs that can be used in data visualisation. Each method looks different and is used in a different context. These are summarised in Table 9.3.

Practise

Once you have looked at Table 9.3, design and create a visualisation dashboard in Excel that uses a variety of techniques.

Table 9.3: Graphs and charts for data visualisation

Type	Example	Use
Arc diagram		Arc diagrams are used to visualise the repetition of patterns.
Area graph		Area graphs are used to display the changes in a data item over a period of time.
Bar chart		Bar charts are used to compare items.
Bubble chart		Bubble charts are different versions of scatter charts (see below). In some versions, the size of the bubble provides additional information.
Density plot		A density plot shows how data is distributed over a continuous period of time.
Donut chart		A donut chart demonstrates the relationships between data items as part of a whole.
Flow chart		**FLOW CHARTS** are used to display information about processes. They show what happens in what order, including events that are repeated and decisions where one thing or another happens depending on a particular value.

Table 9.3: *(continued)*

Histogram	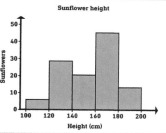	Similar to a bar chart, histograms display data in ranges. The first column shows the number of values between 100 and 120 – the second shows the number of values between 120 and 140 etc. There is no space between the columns.
Line graph	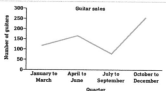	Line graphs demonstrate continuous data over a time period – so they are often used to show trends in information over equal periods of time such as monthly or annually.
Pictogram	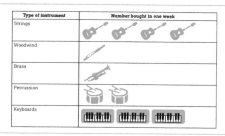	Pictograms display values using an image that is relevant. In this example, the number of musical instruments bought in one week is shown pictorially.
Pie chart	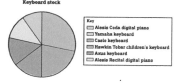	Pie charts, like donut charts, show values as a percentage or proportion of a whole value. The whole value here is the total number of items stocked in the keyboard category. Each slice of pie is the proportion of that total allocated to each individual keyboard stocked.
Scatterplot	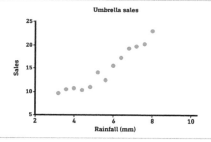	Also called an XY (Scatter) chart, scatterplots are used to show how much one value is affected by another value. A relatively straight line demonstrates correlation (in other words, shows that one value is affected by the other).
Tree diagram	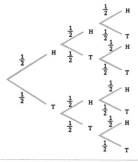	Tree diagrams are used to visualise probability. Each branch of the tree is a representation of a potential outcome. You have a coin – when you toss the coin it could be heads or tails. If it is heads, next time it could be heads or tails, and so on.
Venn diagram	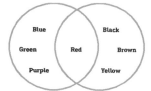	Venn diagrams are used to visualise when data overlaps. A group of boys and girls were asked about their favourite colours. The girls said blue, green and purple. The boys said black, brown and yellow. Both groups said red.
Word cloud		Word clouds display the data using the size of the words to represent the overall number. For example, most of the children in this class who had a pet had gerbils. The next highest value was dogs, then hamsters, cats, and so on. Guinea pigs were the least common pet.

B2 Interface design for data

Designing a **USER INTERFACE (UI)** for a visualisation is the same as creating an interface for a **DIGITAL APPLICATION** or a computer program. For this reason it follows the same rules.

User interface designing for a dashboard

It is common for organisations to create dashboards for key data that needs to be accessible. Figure 9.9 shows a dashboard presenting key stock information, and a price list for the percussion instruments.

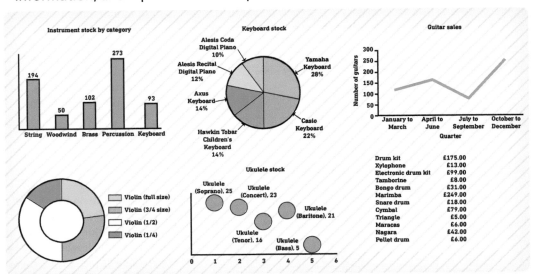

Figure 9.9: A dashboard is a useful way of presenting key data

Data visualisations

Your data visualisation interface could include some of the following components.

Input and output controls

LIST BOXES and **DROPDOWN BOXES** are a feature of database software and they work in a similar way. List boxes give users a full range of options from which they can choose one or more. With a dropdown box, users will again have a series of choices, but this time they can only choose one.

On a visualisation such as the dashboard shown in Figure 9.6, you might not have enough room to display everything you need to, so you might present the user with a list from which they will choose the visualisation they want to see.

Practise

Practise implementing both list boxes and dropdown boxes to enable users to input data without having to use the keyboard.

TOGGLES are **INPUT DEVICES** that are simply used to switch a feature on or off.

Navigational components

Your interface might make use of navigational components to help the user find the data or information that they want. SLIDERS are a good way of allowing users to choose a value between two limits that will filter data. For example, your slider could cover the year range 1900 to 2000. If the user wants to search for data from 1960, they can move the slider to this position and the data for the other years will be ignored.

SEARCH FIELDS are used to allow users to search for particular words or phrases in a set of data.

Information components

TOOLTIPS are pop-up messages that give the user advice about what to do. There are many different styles that you could use.

PROGRESS BARS show how far the machine has progressed while carrying out a lengthy task. They are very reassuring for users because it is obvious that the computer really is doing something and has not crashed.

MODAL WINDOWS are windows that prompt the user to make a decision. While this is happening the active window behind the pop-up is on hold. This means that the user is forced to make a decision before anything else can happen.

Link it up

Refer back to Unit 7 for more information on input and output controls, as well as navigational and informational components, in a user interface.

Design principles for creating interfaces

Figure 9.10 shows the key factors to consider in designing a user interface.

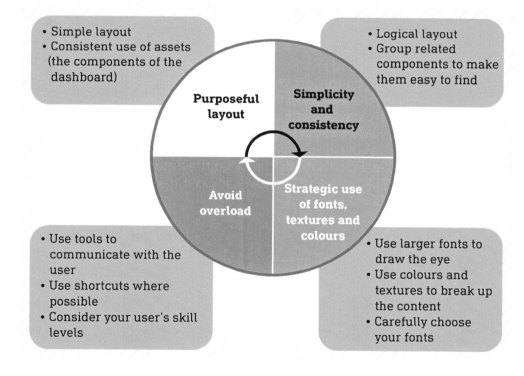

- Simple layout
- Consistent use of assets (the components of the dashboard)

- Logical layout
- Group related components to make them easy to find

Purposeful layout

Simplicity and consistency

Avoid overload

Strategic use of fonts, textures and colours

- Use tools to communicate with the user
- Use shortcuts where possible
- Consider your user's skill levels

- Use larger fonts to draw the eye
- Use colours and textures to break up the content
- Carefully choose your fonts

Figure 9.10: Key factors that make a user interface effective

Here are some other factors you should consider for your dashboard.

- The interface you create should be readable. Use text sizes, fonts and colours to draw attention to particular data.
- Be careful with backgrounds. Avoid coloured typefaces that are too similar to the background as this makes the text illegible. This is known as a colour clash.
- When you create a dashboard, there are many templates available that provide a range of functionality. Experiment with them for the environment you are using to see what is available – it might save time in the long run.

Data visualisation as part of interface design

Visualisations should always be **DYNAMICALLY LINKED** to the data that was used to create them. This means that the graphic represents the data *as it currently is,* not *as it was* when the visualisation was created. If any of the data that was used to create the visualisation changes, the graphs and charts on a dashboard should update.

You should always check that the visualisations you create are readable and usable. To make sure that this is the case you should thoroughly test your graphs and charts, and check how usable they are when values change. Not only can they become unreadable, but also in some circumstances the data can become distorted and even misleading.

For example, look at Figure 9.11.

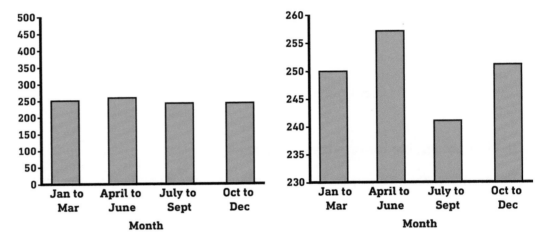

Figure 9.11: Where in the media might you have seen data become misleading because of the way it has been presented?

Both of them are displaying exactly the same data – but they look very different. In the image on the left, the differences between the values are harder to see than in the image on the right. This is because when you fix the range on an axis it stays exactly the same regardless of the data. For example, if the top value is set at 260 and the bottom value is set at 230, should the value fall above or below the range set, the numbers on the axis will not change to accommodate the fact that the data is not in the axis range. The column in Figure 9.12, however, looks different because you cannot see where the column ends.

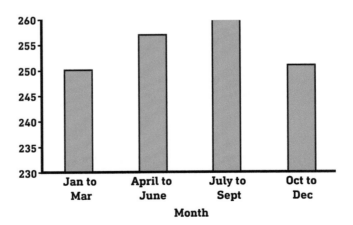

Figure 9.12: Always check your graphs to ensure you are presenting data accurately

When creating visualisations, you must therefore test your graphs and charts using a variety of images, including unusually high or low ones, and you should experiment with how the visualisation behaves with incorrect values (such as characters or symbols).

Data imports

Data can be imported from different sources into a visualisation. This includes:

- databases
- spreadsheets
- text.

These formats all contain data that could potentially change. The key is to make sure that the objects in your user interface (whether visualisations, text or spreadsheet content) link or embed the content rather than simply copy and paste it. For example, in a Word context, you would insert an Object (on the Insert tab). Notice that the link to file check box is ticked. This means that each time this Word file is opened, the file it is linked to will be checked to see if the data has changed. If it has, then the user will be given the option to update this file. If not, then no update will be needed.

Practise

Import data from a database into a spreadsheet.

Create a graph or chart.

Import the completed graph or chart into a Word document.

Skills and knowledge check

☐ Can you explain data visualisation?

☐ Can you demonstrate an understanding of the different input and output controls and navigational components used in a visualisation?

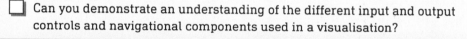

○ I can use a range of visualisation methods.

○ I can create an interface design for data.

○ I can import data from different sources.

C Produce an organisational data maintenance schedule

C1 Data management

If you drove your car around for years without having it serviced or maintained, parts would start to break down and, without some maintenance activity, this might not be noticed until there was a really serious problem and the car stopped running altogether. Most people service and maintain their cars on a regular basis – for example, every 12,000 miles, or every autumn and spring. In between, they check the levels of oil in the engine and water in the cooling system.

A similar maintenance approach is needed for database systems.

Investigate data maintenance activities

To make certain that the data is of the best quality it can be, it needs to be serviced and maintained in a planned way, just like a car.

What maintenance activities should be included?

1 Check the structure of the database regularly. If relationships, for example, have accidentally been deleted or the nature of the relationship has been changed in some way, the results that the system produces could have been compromised without anyone noticing immediately.

2 Make sample checks on the data to look for duplicate records, and if duplicate records exist, consider merging the records so that no data is lost (you might have some data linked to one record and more data linked to the other – so you should check before deleting anything).

3 Check that validation routines are still active.

4 Make regular backups of the data and store them offsite (in case of a fire or other disaster). How often backups are made will depend on how much activity affects the data each day. If only one or two records are created or edited each day, then a weekly back up would probably be acceptable. If, however, thousands of records get created or edited each day, it might even be necessary to back up more than once a day.

5 ENCRYPT the data and the backups.

6 WRITE-PROTECT the data (this means ensuring that it cannot be changed or removed by a user) and check that this protection is still in place.

7 Ensure that the data is PASSWORD PROTECTED (that users are required to enter a password to access the system), and that passwords are changed regularly (most organisations require staff to change their passwords on a monthly basis).

8 Check that the anti-virus protection is still up to date. It is not enough to simply install ANTI-VIRUS SOFTWARE – it has to be updated with information about new VIRUS SIGNATURES that the software should search for.

9 Create a training schedule for staff to make sure that they are working with the data in the right way.

Decisions made by the organisation in relation to these nine points will be written into a maintenance policy and plan that will itself be regularly reviewed to make sure it is still appropriate. Timings for activities will be set and if for any reason these are later found to be inappropriate, changes will be made to the plan.

Link it up

Data Management

Refer back to Unit 3 for more information on the legislation relating to storing and managing data.

Produce a detailed technical manual to accompany the database solution

All database solutions should have a **TECHNICAL MANUAL** that records all the key aspects of the database structure and operation. This is not the same as a user guide as it does not explain how to use the solution. This document is meant for technical staff who will be carrying out the maintenance activities discussed in the previous section.

A technical manual should include the following elements.

1   A table of contents that sets out exactly what the document includes.
2   The database structure diagram. In a multi-table database this means the relationships between the tables themselves. In Access you can view (and screen capture) this information on the Database Tools tab.

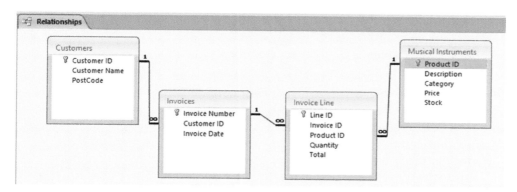

What then follows is a list of each of the tables, queries, forms, reports and the dashboard for the solution.

3   An explanation of the fields and their data types. Access has a Database Documenter, which can also be found on the Database Tools tab, but this can generate many pages of information, not all of which is helpful.

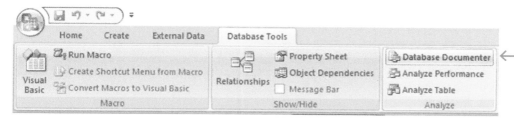

For example, the image on the following page shows a snapshot of the information for the musical instruments table in the music shop database. This image is just for part of the musical instruments table.

Practise

Use the Database Documenter to produce an electronic file in Access. Look at what the software produces, but do not print it. Save it to your user area.

```
C:\...\Music Shop.accdb                                          18 February 2017
Table: Musical Instruments                                             Page: 1


Properties
DateCreated:              16/02/2017 20:46:20       DefaultView:          2
DisplayViewsOnSharePointSit 1                       FilterOnLoad:         False
GUID:                     {guid {D25F5FAE-ACE5-41CA- HideNewField:        False
                          89ED-B96492A52755}}
LastUpdated:              18/02/2017 10:47:27       NameMap:              Long binary data
OrderByOn:                False                     OrderByOnLoad:        True
Orientation:              Left-to-Right             RecordCount:          48
TotalsRow:                False                     Updatable:            True


Columns
       Name                                         Type                  Size
       Product ID                                   Long Integer             4
               AggregateType:        -1
               AllowZeroLength:      False
               AppendOnly:           False
               Attributes:           Fixed Size, Auto-Increment
               CollatingOrder:       General
               ColumnHidden:         False
               ColumnOrder:          Default
               ColumnWidth:          1695
               DataUpdatable:        False
               GUID:                 {guid {36A32C4F-A0A9-4F2A-AE38-141D490E9ABA}}
               OrdinalPosition:      0
               Required:             False
               SourceField:          Product ID
               SourceTable:          Musical Instruments
               TextAlign:            General
```

Look at the information for the Product ID. Much of this information will never be used. The key point in this information is outlined. It is a field that **AUTO-INCREMENTS** (each record gets a new number automatically). The rest of the information might be needed if an administrator wanted to change the width or positions of columns – but otherwise it is unlikely it would be necessary. The detail for the Product ID would be replicated for every field in the table and for every table, and it would produce many pages of documentation.

Most of the necessary detail about the structure of the tables can be incorporated in a single page.

Field Name	Table	Key type	Data Type	Size (if applicable)	Description
Customer ID	Customers	Primary	AutoNumber		Customer unique identifier
Customer Name	Customers		Text	50	First and last name of customer
Postcode	Customers		Text	8	Contains an input mask: >LAAa\ 9LL (This will be explained later in the unit) >LAa&\ 9LL
Product ID	Musical Instruments	Primary	AutoNumber		Product unique identifier
Description	Musical Instruments		Text	50	Description of instrument
Category	Musical Instruments		Text	15	Contains lookup list of values: Brass, Keyboard, Percussion, String, Woodwind
Price	Musical Instruments		Currency	2 DP	Prices for each item
Stock	Musical Instruments		Number		How many are currently in stock
Invoice Number	Invoice	Primary	AutoNumber		Invoice number - unique identifier
Customer ID	Invoice	Foreign	Number		This is a number because in the Customer's table it is an AutoNumber
Invoice Date	Invoice		Date/Time		Contains input masking Date format: dd/mm/yyyy
Line ID	Invoice Line	Primary	AutoNumber		Identifies each line on an invoice
Invoice ID	Invoice Line	Foreign	Number		This is a number because in the Invoice table it is an AutoNumber
Product ID	Invoice Line	Foreign	Number		This is a number because in the Musical Instruments table it is an AutoNumber
Quantity	Invoice Line		Number		How many the customer is buying - contains validation: Must be greater than 0 and less than or equal to 20
Total	Invoice Line		Currency	2DP	Calculated field [Invoice Line].[Quantity] * [Instruments].[Price]

4 Each query should be recorded and explained.

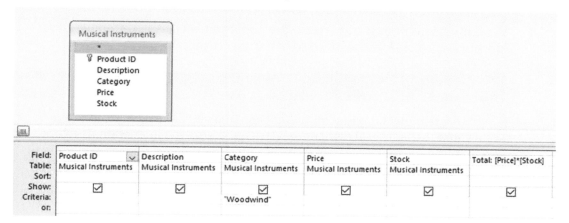

5 So should each form.

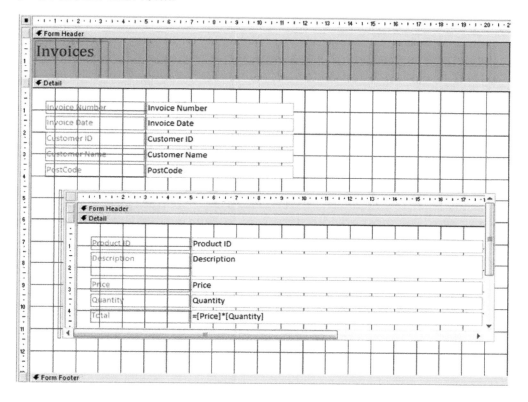

6 And each report.

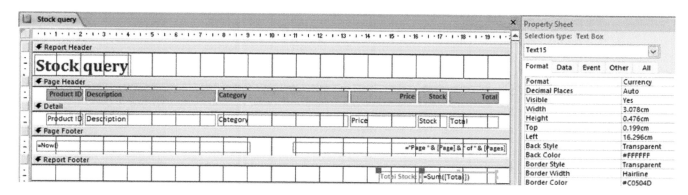

7 Finally, the dashboard should be explained in the same way, with a description of each object, what it is for and what it is linked to.

A technical manual should make the construction of the database and dashboard as clear as possible to other technical staff.

Practise

Create a technical manual for a database that you have developed. Make sure that the technical components are annotated to aid another developer who might need to understand the system.

C2 Data integrity and cleansing

To be useful, data must have integrity and be free of errors.

Validity and integrity checks of the data

DATA INTEGRITY (meaning the consistency and accuracy of data) and **DATA VALIDITY** (meaning that data has been checked to ensure that it is clean and correct) can be improved by using a range of techniques. These include limiting the values that can be input by the user, applying automatic formatting to inputs so they are all the same and using methods that allow the user to choose values from a list rather than requiring any direct input. In this section you will find out about some of these techniques.

Input masks

An **INPUT MASK** is a technique that requires users to input values in a specific way. The most obvious data item to demonstrate this technique with is the United Kingdom postcode.

Here are some example postcodes:

B90 8AH	Birmingham
GL3 1DB	Gloucester
OX13 7PP	Oxford
WC1V 7BH	London

Notice the different formats.

In order to make sure that the user does use one of these formats, you use an input mask, which forces numbers and characters to be input in a specific way.

>LAa&\ 9LL

This is how it works:

> Means character that follows will be capitalised (this does not mean that the user has to type a capital – the system will just make it one anyway)

L The user MUST enter a letter

A The user MUST enter a letter or a number

a The user CAN (but does not have to) enter a letter or a number

& The user MUST enter either a letter or a space

9 The user CAN enter a number

\ This outputs whatever the next character is (in the example it is a space).

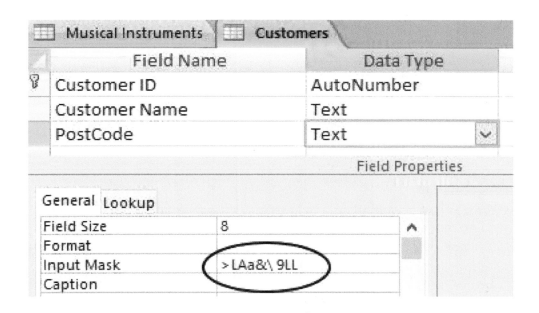

Example of an input mask

Practise

Create an input mask and a validation rule to improve the integrity of a database.

Default value

A **DEFAULT VALUE** is one that will appear unless the user types in something else.

This shows the default value is set to 0.

Field Name	Data Type	
Product ID	AutoNumber	
Description	Text	
Category	Text	
Price	Currency	⌄
Stock	Number	

General Lookup

Format	Currency
Decimal Places	2
Input Mask	
Caption	
Default Value	0 ←
Validation Rule	
Validation Text	
Required	No
Indexed	No
Smart Tags	
Text Align	General

This means that each new record has that value in the Price column before the user types anything in.

	Product ID	Description	Category	Price	Stock
⊞	46	Axus Keyboard	Keyboard	£104.00	13
⊞	47	Alesis Recital Digital Piano	Keyboard	£210.00	11
⊞	48	Alesis Coda Digital Piano	Keyboard	£364.00	4
✱	(New)			£0.00	

Validation rules

VALIDATION can be added on a field to make the user type in a value in a specified range.

For example, the music shop has decided that it will never sell more than 20 of anything at one time, and there would be no point in putting an item on an invoice if the number being sold was 0.

Here you can see how the database developer has added validation to make the user key in a number between 1 and 20.

Field Name	Data Type
🔑 Line ID	AutoNumber
Invoice ID	Number
Product ID	Number
Quantity	Number
Total	Currency

General Lookup

Field Size	Long Integer
Format	
Decimal Places	Auto
Input Mask	
Caption	
Default Value	
Validation Rule	>0 And <=20
Validation Text	Input must be between 1 and 20

If the user then attempts to key in an invalid number, an error message is displayed and the user will not be able to save the record until a valid number is present in the field.

Lists

Using a list means that users do not need to key in a value at all. They simply choose from a dropdown list. The Display is set as a list box and the Row Source Type becomes Value List. The values are then typed into the Row Source, separated by a semi-colon. This produces a list from which the user can choose.

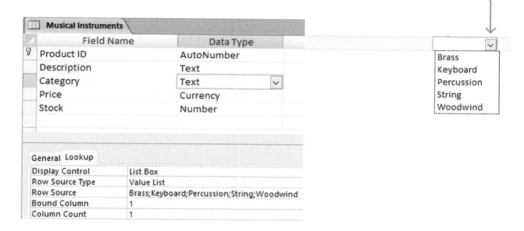

Exploring data management

To complete this unit, Table 9.4 summarises some of the other data management concepts that contribute towards good practice with data management.

Factor	Description
DATA MIGRATION and **DATA INTEGRATION**	Data migration means moving data from one system to another and data integration means combining data from two or more sources to create one set of data.
Data maintenance	In addition to the maintenance factors you have already considered, data should be checked against the master data definitions. This means checking that all the most critical data (the master data) is being correctly stored.
Data quality assurance and control	There are other techniques that can be used to improve the quality of data, but some of them are time consuming. For example: • asking users to input the same data on different machines. The computer then checks the two input files to ensure they are the same. This is sometimes done with extremely important data • making sure that users use consistent terminology • making sure data lines up properly (where values have decimal points, they should all line up properly (this is why you set the decimal places to 2) • making sure that data has not been contaminated with data that should not be there • using input masking, validation and lists to control incorrect or inaccurate data entry where possible.
Data archiving	Archive data that is no longer being used to reduce the chances of the data being compromised (particularly if it is not being used anyway). Users need to trust data, and data that has possible errors may no longer be trustworthy. Remember, data archiving is not the same as a data backup. A backup is made on data that is being used. A data archive is data that is being stored but that is not being used any more.

Table 9.4: Further data management concepts

Table 9.4: *(continued)*

Factor	Description
Risks to data integrity and quality controls (to minimise error and risk)	Ensure that you consider the full range of possible risks such as **VIRUSES**, hackers, users inputting incorrect, incomplete or wrong data.
How the quality of organisational data can be improved	• Cleanse the data. • Profile your data (check it for defects). • Take steps to prevent your data becoming defective.

Skills and knowledge check

☐ Can you identify the components of a technical manual?

☐ Can you explain the difference between data integrity and data validity?

○ I can explain data maintenance activities and carry out basic tasks.

○ I can write a basic technical manual.

○ I can create input masks.

○ I can create validation routines.

Ready for assessment

• Practise data analysis techniques by creating queries and reports on different databases you have created.

• Practise working with large data sets (big data) using the software recommended by your tutor.

• Before you start on your assessment, make sure you have practised a range of techniques that are important for data quality and integrity such as input masking, validation routines and reducing the potential risks to data by using lists to reduce data input requirements.

• When you create the interface, make sure you check the objects on your dashboard – remember to test by changing values (including some extreme values) to see what changes in data do to the visual objects. Do not forget to think about the users of your dashboard (their experience and skill).

• Create a data table for at least two other databases that you have created.

• Practise integrity checking and data cleansing to make sure you can use the techniques without creating issues with the data.

WORK FOCUS

HANDS ON

There are some important occupational skills and competencies that you will need to practise which relate to this unit. Developing these and practising them could help you to gain employment as a database developer or data analyst.

- Employers will expect you to be accurate and pay attention to detail.

- Always review your coursework and check it to make sure it is correct. Check your spelling and grammar, your layout and your headings.

- You will need to demonstrate that you can problem solve and that you can explain how you achieved your results.

- When you are working on this programme, you will be problem solving all the time. Practise writing an explanation about how you solved something.

- You will need to work under pressure and show that you can meet deadlines. You can practise this by always handing your work in on time.

- You will need to demonstrate that you are good at presenting and communicating.

- Practise your presentation skills as often as you can. The more you practise, the more confident you will become.

Ready for work?

A re you ready to work as a data analyst? Take this short quiz to test your knowledge.

1 Which of the following is not a key level of organisational information?
- [ ] A Operational
- [ ] B Strategic
- [ ] C Research
- [ ] D Tactical

2 What does data cleansing mean?
- [ ] A Making sure data is error free.
- [ ] B Organising the way data is stored.
- [ ] C Collecting data for analysis.
- [ ] D Presenting the results of analysis.

3 Which of the following is not a valid data visualisation method?
- [ ] A Bubble chart
- [ ] B Column of text
- [ ] C Pictogram
- [ ] D Scatter plot

4 Data can be dynamically linked. What does this mean?
- [ ] A The data can be used on any platform.
- [ ] B The data will automatically refresh if the source is changed.
- [ ] C The data can be used in any software.
- [ ] D The data will be automatically backed up.

5 What is >LAa&\ 9LL an example of?
- [ ] A An input error.
- [ ] B A value list.
- [ ] C A validation routine.
- [ ] D An input mask.

Answers: 1C, 2A, 3B, 4B, 5D

10 Organisational Uses for Digital Media Systems

Every day you make decisions about the organisations you choose to supply you with products and services. What digital technologies do you use to communicate with them and how do these technologies influence your decisions about who to do business with?

In this unit, you will learn how organisations design and build digital systems to interact with their customers to help achieve their business objectives. You will design and build an enhancement to an existing digital media system and gather feedback to help you assess its impact on the organisation.

How will I be assessed?

You will be assessed in this synoptic unit through a range of both written and practical work. You will be given an assignment to complete which consists of several tasks. The assignment will be based on an organisation that has an existing digital media system that needs to be improved.

You will need to:

- explore how organisations use digital media systems
- design and implement an improvement to an existing digital media system that will operate across a number of different channels
- test the functionality of your enhanced digital media system and use evidence you have gathered to assess its impact.

You will need to produce evidence of your research into existing digital media systems; this could be written reports or presentations. Evidence for the design and implementation of the enhanced system will include design documentation as well as the completed digital media system itself. Evidence of testing will include a completed test plan. Your assessment of the system's impact will include the evidence you have gathered as well as your analysis of it and the conclusions you have reached.

Assessment criteria

Pass	Merit	Distinction
Learning aim A: Explore current digital media systems		
A.P1 Present the purpose and business features of multichannel systems.	**A.M1** Investigate the impact of using a multichannel system to meet the goals of the organisation.	**A.D1** Investigate why organisations use multichannel systems and strategies and consider how the functions and features of their systems allow the achievement of their goals.
Learning aim B: Develop a multichannel digital media system enhancement for organisational use		
B.P2 Create a content plan for a multichannel system that enhances an organisation's objectives. **B.P3** Create well-structured prototypes for the development of a multichannel system to further enhance organisational objectives.	**B.M2** Develop a multichannel solution for an organisation, with consideration of the organisational goals and copyright issues.	**B.D2** Develop relevant enhancements for an existing digital media system that is suitable for multichannel platforms, considering the organisation's goals and purpose for the campaign with clear consideration of legal and ethical issues.
Learning aim C: Review the functionality and impact of a multichannel product		
C.P4 Test the full functionality and the features of the multichannel system, linking functionality to organisational goals.	**C.M3** Gather user feedback from a variety of audiences using different feedback methods for functionality and quality, and identify areas for development, with consideration of the key points suggested by feedback.	**C.D3** Evaluate changes to the multichannel system using analytics tools, organising data to an appropriate visual format to assess impact using key success criteria.

A Explore current digital media systems

You need to know how organisations use digital media systems. This will help you design improvements to an organisation's existing systems.

A1 Explore uses of digital media systems

You probably use digital media systems most of the time, but as a user you probably do not notice the platform that enables these systems to operate. As a starting point, consider all the different products that are available across many different platforms.

Exploring digital technology products available on multichannel platforms

A **COMPUTER PLATFORM** is where any piece of **SOFTWARE** is executed. For example, if you want to develop an app to be used on all mobile phones, you will have to develop different versions of the app to run on the main mobile platforms such as Android™, iOS® or Windows Phone®.

You probably use a range of digital products on different devices, across **MULTICHANNEL PLATFORMS** (different platforms). For example, you might start to watch a programme on your smart TV, then later on you might access a catch-up TV service on your laptop or video game console to finish watching it. The next day you might use your smartphone to watch part of the programme again when out with your friends.

As a user of digital products, you expect to be able to move between computer devices while enjoying using the same services. Organisations providing these services must:

- work out in advance which devices people prefer to use
- provide software that will operate on each of these devices, taking into account the different platforms that each system uses.

In other words, developers need to create **MULTICHANNEL PRODUCTS** (products that will work on different devices and platforms).

Practise

Make a list of the digital systems you have used in the past week.

- What different platforms did these systems use?

Compare your use with that of the other members of your family.

- What are the most common services and platforms used?
- Are there any services that do not work on all devices, that is, are there platform or channel restrictions?

Consumers demand that organisations provide multichannel solutions. These systems include both digital and non-digital platforms. For example, a department store might develop a system where:

- products can be bought online or in a physical store
- stores include kiosks connecting shoppers to the online store
- products can be bought online and collected from a store
- products bought online can be returned to a store for exchange or refund
- online services can be accessed from a website (PC and mobile versions) or app – each site or app will be optimised for different software platforms (for example, **OPERATING SYSTEMS** and **BROWSERS**)
- social media is used to communicate with potential customers and build brand loyalty, which is when customers identify with an organisation and its products and prefer to use them rather than competitor products.

Why do shops provide kiosks that link to their website in-store?

Exploring digital media systems

There are many different digital media products, some of which you have studied in Unit 7.

Some digital media systems enable organisations and their customers to create content and to share it with other users. Some of these systems are discussed below.

Blogs and vlogs

A **BLOG** is similar to a journal or diary written by an individual and made public for anyone to read using a platform such as WordPress®. Blogs are usually posted in reverse chronological order (newest post at the top of the page, older posts lower down). Many organisations use blogs to keep customers up to date on news and other developments, such as how the organisation is working on developing new products. Regular readers can be alerted to new blog entries by text, email or notifications from **AGGREGATOR APPS** (apps that display feed content from many different news sources that the reader can select). Examples include Google Play™ Newsstand and Feedly™.

A **VLOG** is a video-based blog. They are often posted on video-sharing platforms such as YouTube™ or Dailymotion®.

Link it up

Digital Applications

Refer back to Unit 7 for an exploration of a wide range of digital media products and how to create them, including media for printed visual products (for example, posters, packaging, point of sale promotions, magazine/brochures, leaflets, flyers) and media for digital products (for example, film, animation, **INTERACTIVE** media, augmented reality, web banners, digital adverts, CGI).

Podcasts

PODCASTS are audio versions of blogs and vlogs. They can be created using digital audio software and hosted on platforms such as iTunes® or SoundCloud®. Podcasts can be used to give news updates about products or services. Sometimes they can be used to provide additional information, for example to add value to an existing service by rewarding loyal customers with extra content.

Wikis

A **WIKI** is a website where the original creator of the site gives up all control over its future development – any visitor can edit or add new content directly from a web browser. In practice, many wikis are moderated – you have to be a registered user to edit the site so your contributions can be tracked and, if necessary, challenged or undone. A popular use of wikis is to develop 'fan sites' for popular TV programmes or movie series.

Forums

FORUMS are discussion sites where users can post messages and respond to other users' postings. Many organisations host forums about their products on their own websites. Also, third-party forums exist outside the control of the organisation.

What digital media features are used and not used by this video game site?

Video game websites

This is a good example of how digital media systems can be used together on a single site. On video game websites, users can read content created by the site, which will either be in text or video format (sometimes audio only). There will be several discussion forums, each focusing on a different game platform or genre. There may even be a wiki section where users can construct their own **DATABASE** of products and populate it with descriptions of content and playing strategies.

Practise

Visit examples of the digital content systems you studied in Unit 7 as well as those described above.

For each type of system, consider its purpose. Who are the systems aimed at? What are the strengths and weaknesses of each type of system for its users?

Identifying intended uses of digital media systems

Organisations use digital media systems for many different purposes, such as those listed below.

To advertise

Businesses will want to get existing and potential customers excited about new and upcoming products. Adverts can be posted on video-hosting sites and short messages sent using SMS-based services such as Twitter®. Businesses will encourage their customers to share posts and retweet messages to help spread the news to more followers.

To provide information

Potential customers want to find out about existing products. They may need to obtain detailed information or just an overview to help them decide which products to explore in more detail. The customers may have questions that need answering – so will look for a list of FREQUENTLY ASKED QUESTIONS (FAQS) and responses. They may be interested in reading the opinions of existing users on official and unofficial review sites.

To obtain feedback from customers

Businesses can find out the views of their customers by encouraging them to use feedback forms on websites or post replies to blogs and other social media updates. Sites such as SurveyMonkey® can be used to create short interactive questionnaires that can be used to gather customer feedback on a range of topics.

To communicate with employees and suppliers

Employees may work for an organisation remotely. They may need to access the digital media systems hosted on the organisation's own INTRANET (a collection of web pages that are only available to users on the LOCAL AREA NETWORK (LAN)). They may need to access existing content such as details of policies and procedures that must be followed or they may need to discuss an issue with a colleague or manager.

Organisations need to employ new workers when existing employees leave, or if the organisation expands and needs more staff. Having a strong digital presence can help to persuade more people that the organisation is worth working for. This will increase the pool of talent from which the organisation can select.

A supplier may need to connect with the remote systems of its client or customer, for example to check the specifications of the products it must deliver, or check delivery requirements such as time and place of delivery, as these may change at short notice.

Multichannel platforms are especially important to users who have access to more than one type of computer system. This might include people who have both home and work access or remote workers who need to work in both an office and while travelling.

A2 Evaluate the purpose and effectiveness of multichannel solutions

Some multichannel solutions are more effective than others. In this section, you will explore factors that will help explain why some solutions are better than others.

Considering the effectiveness of a multichannel solution

Organisations develop digital media systems for many different reasons, including to:

- communicate with existing customers
- reach new customers
- provide information about existing products and services
- promote new products and services
- enable users to share information and ideas about products.

How many of these brands do you recognise?

A digital media campaign is likely to be successful if some of the following goals are met.

- *Developing brand awareness*: how many different types of mobile phone can you name? Each one is a separate brand. You have brand awareness of the ones whose names you can remember. If you remember a brand and like it, you are more likely to ask for it when buying a product. Features of a strong brand identity include: a memorable name, a recognisable logo, strong colours and fonts that together make a visual style that makes you think of the brand each time you see it. Creating digital media is one way that the brand awareness can be developed.
- *Creating loyal customers*: products with strong brand awareness also tend to have loyal customers who return to the brand repeatedly and prefer using it to competitor products.
- *Being visible*: for consumers to be aware of the brand, it is necessary for it to be visible to them, for example some organisations sponsor sporting events so that their brand is visible to fans of that sport. Some organisations write blogs providing information about trends in their industry, so that people who find the information useful are reminded of the brand each time they read the blog.
- *Generating new customers*: new customers have either never bought the product before or are currently using a competitor. In either case, you will need to use strong reasons to persuade them to buy from you rather than a competitor. These reasons are usually to do with:
  - price – does your product offer better value for money than your rivals
  - product – does your product contain more, and better, features that people wish to use
  - promotion – can you persuade people that your product will benefit them more than rival products
  - place – can people buy the product conveniently for them?
- *Providing customer service and obtaining feedback*: it is important to help customers solve their problems and to obtain their feedback on your organisation and its products. This will help make customers happier – and therefore more loyal, as well as giving you feedback on how to make your products better.
- *Sharing views*: have you ever made a purchase because of a recommendation from a friend or a good online review? Then you will know why it is important to let customers share their opinions of products with each other.

- *Gathering data*: you can gather a lot of useful **DATA** about the people who visit your digital media products – both people who choose to use your products and those who do not. Feedback can be directly asked for by including feedback forms and review/rating opportunities. Feedback can also be indirect, such as how long users spend looking at particular parts of your website and which media they interact with.
- *Recruitment of staff*: most digital media activity is designed to attract customers, but recruiting new workers can also be thought of as a campaign to attract users. How and where the organisation advertises its vacancies is important as well as the messages it gives out on blogs about the type of organisation it is to work for.
- *Generating* **TRAFFIC**: if people do not see the digital media you have created, then there is less chance the other goals will be met. If fewer than one in fifty visitors to a mobile website make a purchase, then the more visitors there are, the more revenue you can earn per visitor.
- *The right channels*: as well as its wider goals, the organisation needs to know whether the channels it is using to reach users/customers are the right ones. If new media channels are developed, the organisation will need to know whether it should start using them.

Usually the organisation will have stated these goals in a digital systems content plan (see B1).

Evaluating the impact of an organisation's existing digital media systems in meeting its goals

You need to know whether your organisation's existing digital media systems are successful. If not, what can be done to improve them? Thinking about the following issues will help.

- *Does the system contribute to the organisation's goals?* You need to be clear what the goals are. Usually the organisation will have stated these goals in its digital systems content plan. (You will learn more about the digital systems content plan in B1.)
- *Feedback from clients*: what do users of the systems think of them? You may need to do research into the opinions and attitudes of users. However, a well-designed digital media system will include methods of obtaining feedback from clients embedded within it, such as example feedback forms and ratings opportunities (for example, rate service provided between 0 and 5 stars).
- *Limitations and restraints of the digital systems*: what does the system enable users to do? How do they interact with the organisation – just by interacting with the systems or are they able to use them to communicate directly with people such as customer service workers? Some systems have online chat facilities that start with the user chatting with a non-human **EXPERT SYSTEM** (a computer program designed to mimic the ability of a human to ask questions and then respond to answers with new questions or information). If the expert system cannot supply a solution, the user is redirected to a human operator.
- *Current and possible positive and negative impacts of the system*: for example, how much do the systems cost to operate? How does this compare with the original budget? Are the systems helping to make the organisation more or less **PROFITABLE**? (Profit is the money left when the cost of doing business is taken away from the money earned by the business.) Do the systems make the organisation's data vulnerable to loss or theft?
- *Recommendations for achieving long-term goals*: are the systems helping the organisation meet its long-term goals (such as expansion into new markets or increased profitability)? How could the organisation modify its systems to give it more chance of meeting these goals?

A3 Issues with media content management

Systems can have the potential to meet the organisation's goals, but there can still be reasons why the systems are not used well.

Link it up

Digital Applications

Refer back to Unit 3 to learn more about how disaster recovery policies can help organisations react when systems fail.

Link it up

Digital Applications

Refer back to Unit 3 for further details on a wide range of security threats and the actions that can be taken to protect computer systems against these threats.

Using digital systems in an organisational context

Think about the following questions organisations may face when assessing its use of digital systems.

- Are the staff employed to operate the systems clear about what they are expected to do? For example, who is supposed to deal with the system when it goes wrong?
- Are the staff managing the content under-posting or over-posting? Over-posting is a problem because users might start ignoring messages if they arrive too often. Under-posting is also a problem. If your social media profile has not been updated for several weeks, people might assume that you are no longer operating and so they may go to a competitor instead. It is important to decide how much time you are going to be able to devote to managing social media and writing blogs, then stick to the plan.
- Does the organisation respond to every post made on a review site, or just the positive ones? Does it write a unique response to each comment or does it paste the same comment on all postings? Does it respond positively to criticism or does it defend itself and attack the customer? How an organisation interacts with its customers on social media is very important in influencing its customer reputation. Organisations that respond badly to criticism can quickly develop negative customer-relations and a poor reputation.
- Are staff properly trained in how to manage digital media content? Do they know how to develop good customer relations and avoid over- or under-posting?
- Are systems vulnerable to **HACKERS** using **VIRUSES** and **MALWARE**? In early 2017, a popular blogging platform was subject to hacking attacks caused by some users not installing a security patch.
- Are systems able to meet the organisation's needs? If not, is it possible to modify them so that they do? For example, eBay® is mainly used by organisations to sell their products direct to customers, but it is possible to use the platform to sell your products via the stores of other eBay suppliers. A **BESPOKE SYSTEM** (one designed and created especially for you) is more likely to meet your specific needs than an **OFF-THE-SHELF SYSTEM** (one designed to be used by any organisation).
- How easy is it for the organisation to control the channel? For example, some channels, such as static html web pages, are under the direct control of the organisation. Others, such as social media pages, are in effect jointly edited by the organisation's followers.
- What restrictions do specific digital channels have in place? Can these limit the control the organisation has over its messages? For example, Twitter has a limit of 140 characters for each tweet.

Measuring outcomes

There are many ways that organisations can tell whether their systems are likely to be having a positive or a negative impact. Some positive outcomes include the following.

- *Viral content*: if each of three people share your blog posting with three others, then nine new people will see your blog. If each of these share your blog with three others, then 27 more new people will see your blog. If each of these shares with three others, then 81 more new people will see your blog. You can see how quickly a new posting can go viral with millions of people seeing the new content giving you many potential new users.
- *Press coverage*: if the digital media campaign is discussed favourably in the press, many more people will get to read about your messages and start to use your systems.
- *Brand awareness*: if customers are more aware of your organisation, you should be able to measure increase in:
  - sales of products
  - awareness of your products and your brand
  - the number of online conversations that mention your organisation favourably.

Some negative outcomes include the following.

- *Press*: the media may discuss your campaign in a negative way, for example a customer might complain about a social media posting.
- *Sales*: the campaign might result in reduced sales rather than increased sales.
- *Brand awareness:* customers may feel less positive about your brand image since the new digital media content was published.
- *Legal issues*: you may find your organisation faces the possibility of being taken to court, for example if you have used copyright content in your campaign and you have not been able to resolve the issue.
- *Viral*: your posting might go viral for the wrong reasons, for example people may criticise one of your recent postings.

Practise

Investigate a recent multichannel digital media campaign, for example a campaign to support the launch of a new product such as a car, mobile phone or video game.

- What were the aims of the campaign?
- What digital media products were involved? Why did the organisation choose to use these particular products?
- What channels and platforms were involved? Why were they chosen?
- Who were the intended audience for the campaign?
- What evidence is there that the campaign had a successful outcome?
- Is there any evidence of negative outcomes?
- Were there any issues within the organisation that had an impact on these positive or negative outcomes?
- In your opinion, was the campaign a success? What evidence is there to support your conclusion?

Skills and knowledge check

- ☐ Can you name four different digital platforms?
- ☐ Can you describe an example of a multichannel digital media system?
- ☐ Who are two intended users of the multichannel digital media system?
- ☐ Can you give four reasons why an organisation might develop a multichannel digital media system?
- ☐ Why is it important to evaluate the impact of a digital media campaign?
- ☐ Can you give four ways that the impact of a digital media campaign could be evaluated?

- ○ I can design a feedback form/rating system to gather user feedback on an item of digital media content.
- ○ I can recognise when an organisation is over-posting on a social media site.
- ○ I can recognise when an organisation is under-posting on a social media site.

B Develop a multichannel digital media system enhancement for organisational use

In this section, you will learn how to make improvements to an organisation's existing digital media systems. You will learn how to develop a plan that you will then use to create digital prototypes before moving on to create the final product. Finally, you will learn how to do this while thinking about factors that might influence what your improvements can and cannot contain.

B1 Plan for content

It is important to plan carefully the words, images, sounds and other content that will go into your digital campaign. As a minimum, this content needs to match the aims of your campaign.

Creating a digital systems content plan for a given scenario

A local cinema chain has asked you to help launch a new digital media campaign to attract more children and young families to its cinemas. You will need to produce a **DIGITAL SYSTEMS CONTENT PLAN** covering the digital technologies to be used as well as the digital media content to be communicated.

Your plan will help you to think about why and how the media systems will be developed. It will need to be approved by senior managers at the cinema because it could be expensive to put into practice. Table 10.1 shows the features of a digital systems content plan.

Table 10.1: Features of a digital systems content plan

Feature	Explanation
Aim(s)	What the digital system should achieve. For example, to increase attendance at films rated as U and PG.
Target audience	Who the digital system will be used by. This might be a list of the main groups of people within the population or a detailed description of one or two types if they are the main audience. For example, teenagers who visit the cinema without their parents/guardians, as well as parents with children aged between 8 and 16.
Financial implications	A breakdown of the likely costs. These will include developmental costs (the costs of developing the system) and running costs (the costs of operating and maintaining the systems). For example, the costs of developing and updating a new social media profile and smartphone apps.
Type of content	A description of the types of digital media content used in the systems. The plan should give reasons as to why this content is needed and how it will help the project achieve its aims. For example, the content of the mobile phone app might include links to upcoming films, booking screens as well as cinema-related games and quizzes.

Table 10.1: *(continued)*

Feature	Explanation
Themes	The main messages that the digital media content will contain. For example, the content for each new film might include links to trailers, reviews, forums where users can discuss the film and its actors.
Product links	How the content and themes link to the products that the organisation wants the systems to support. In other words, how the systems will support the aim of getting more people to visit the cinema.
Timescales and milestones	A description of the length of time needed to develop the systems (developmental phase) as well as how long the systems will be in use (implementation phase). For each phase, there will be **MILESTONES** (deadlines by which time important tasks must have been completed).
Channel(s)	How will users access the digital systems?
Legal/ethical constraints	What legal or ethical issues will limit what the systems can and cannot do? For example, how age restrictions on film audiences can affect who has access to what films (this could be achieved by requiring users to provide their date of birth when registering for the app).
General planning considerations	What issues have not been covered in the above sections? For example, who will be responsible for managing the project? What resources will be needed?

How to develop SMART targets

You will need to set targets for your project. A target is something that the project must achieve. There should be a target for each main stage of the project.

Your targets should be SMART (see Figure 10.1).

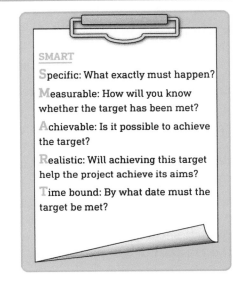

SMART

Specific: What exactly must happen?

Measurable: How will you know whether the target has been met?

Achievable: Is it possible to achieve the target?

Realistic: Will achieving this target help the project achieve its aims?

Time bound: By what date must the target be met?

Figure 10.1: What will happen if the targets are not achievable?

- You should start by identifying the main stages of the project – decide what needs to happen.
- Put each stage in order. Some stages must happen before others, for example you cannot test the final product before you have finished building it.
- Some stages can happen while others are still happening, for example you can be planning the launch-day activities while you are developing the systems themselves.
- Each stage should have a deadline – the date by which it must be completed.
- Some stages are time critical – if they are not completed on time, then the whole project will miss its final deadline.
- Work backwards from the planned launch date and forwards from the planned start date. Do you have enough time to complete the project?
- You can put all the above information into a **GANTT CHART** to get a visual overview of what the project will look like.

Link it up

Digital Applications

Refer back to Unit 7 where you can see how Gantt charts can help in planning a project.

Accessibility issues for the resources you need

Your plan should also consider the resources you need to implement the plan and their availability.

- What software do you need to create the content? Is this available or will it need to be purchased?
- What people will need to be employed to create the systems? How much time can they give to the project?
- How will you create the digital content (for example, obtain images and video)? What resources will you need (for example, cameras, microphones, locations)?

B2 Prepare prototypes

The next stage in the design process is to prepare **PROTOTYPES** of your products. A prototype is a simplified or test version of the final product. It is used to assess the look, feel and basic functionality of the product to help guide the creation of the final product.

Preparing prototypes

To develop the prototype, it is useful to plan an outline of what the product will look like. Depending on the type of digital media content being developed (for example, a digital mobile product or a web-based product), different types of visualisation designs are possible.

Planning

Consider the following tools and processes to help you with your planning.

Wireframe

A **WIREFRAME** is a diagram showing what an interactive multimedia object will look like (see Figure 10.2). Wireframes are typically used for websites, apps for mobile devices, kiosk displays (for example, museum information displays or station ticket machines). A wireframe will usually contain:

- a sketch of what the **USER INTERFACE (UI)** will look like
- where key elements will be placed, including:
  - navigation buttons
  - common elements on each page (logos, menu system)
- sketches for each screen
- an outline of the content of each screen
- location of text and video
- links between different parts of the system (for example, links to different screens)
- **HOUSE STYLE**, including choice of font types and colour schemes.

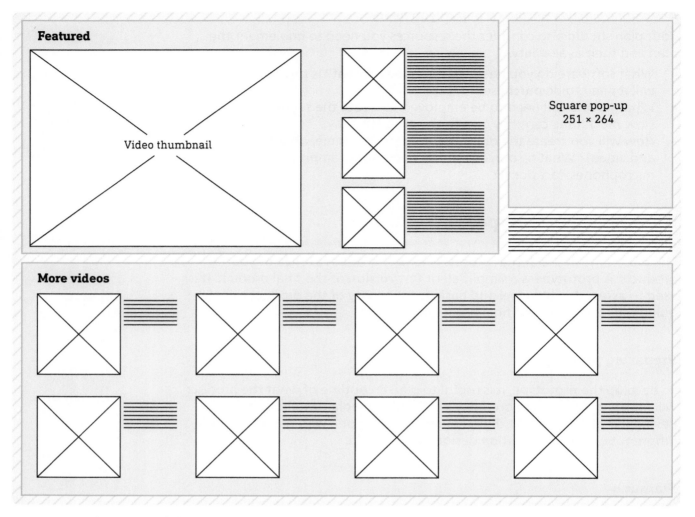

Figure 10.2: Why is it a good idea to produce a wireframe for an interactive digital media system?

Practise

A library wants to develop a mobile phone app. The app will need to enable users to:

- search for books using author/title/genre
- browse for books by author and genre
- request that a book be reserved for them to borrow when next in the library
- extend the loan period of an existing book.

The app must be in keeping with the library's existing visual style.

Design a wireframe for the new app.

Storyboard

A **STORYBOARD** such as that in Figure 10.3 is a visual technique for setting out the key parts in an unfolding story, for example the key moments in a 30-second video. The storyboard will include:

- a sketch for each key scene
- what the scene will look like
- how long the scene will last
- key events during the scene (with a sketch for each)
- audio (for example, dialogue, background music and sound effects)
- visual effects
- transitions between each scene (for example, fade-in/fade-out, dissolve).

Storyboard template 1

Production title:	Name:
Description of scene:	Scene:
Length of scene:	
Audio:	
Effects/Graphics:	Shot:
Transition:	

Figure 10.3: Why would it be hard to create an effective video without a storyboard?

Practise

A car manufacturer wishes to create a 30-second video to appear on its website. The video will support the launch of a new sports car. The manufacturer wants the video to give the following messages about the car.

- It is exciting to drive.
- It is stylish looking.
- Owning the car will make you feel good.

Create a storyboard for the video.

Mood boards

A **MOOD BOARD** is a collage: a collection of images, text and objects. The aim of the mood board is to evoke a specific mood or tone that the finished object might have. You might create a mood board to help explain to a client how you intend to evoke the mood of 'excitement' or 'fun' when creating digital media content. A mood board can be a physical object containing cuttings from newspapers, magazines or other found objects. It could be assembled using software to display digital objects.

Mind maps

A **MIND MAP** is a diagram that displays information and shows how ideas connect. A typical mind map starts with a single central idea that is placed in the middle of the diagram. Radiating out from this central idea are other, connected ideas with further connections coming from these. Different colours can be used to indicate different categories of ideas (see Figure 10.4). Mind maps can either be drawn by hand or can be produced using mind-mapping software.

How can a mood board make it easier to design a new product?

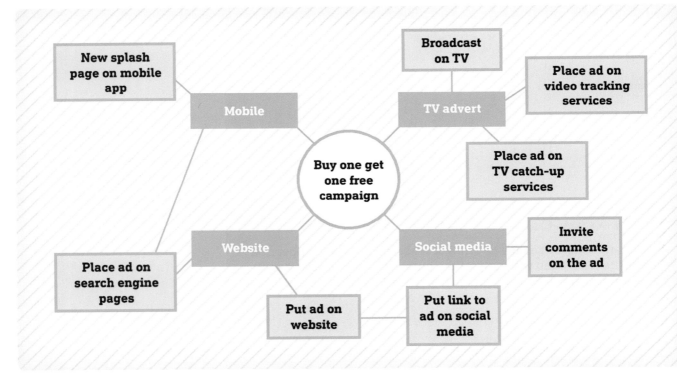

Figure 10.4: Why might it be easier to use mind-mapping software?

Practise

A local fitness centre wishes to create a digital media system to promote a new exercise class.

Create a mind map to help you plan its digital media system.

Sketching

Creating quick sketches will help others to understand what your finished product will look like. Sketches can complement a wireframe. A wireframe is more concerned with the specific design elements on each screen and where each object will be placed. A sketch can give a better idea of what the overall page will look like.

Audio-visual presentation

An audio-visual presentation will help others to understand how videos, animations and sound clips might play when they are finally created. There are two main types.

1. Create a draft of the finished product – concentrate on either the narrative (story) or the visual mood but make the product look and feel as close to the finished product as you can within the limitations of the design budget.
2. Create a SHOWREEL (a showreel uses clips from existing videos to give an idea of what the final product will be like). The creator of the showreel must be careful that when creating and sharing the showreel they do not break any COPYRIGHT restrictions placed on the clips.

Link it up

Digital Applications

Refer back to Unit 7 for details of a number of other useful design techniques, including user interface and screen layout.

Practise

A local bakery is planning to organise a competition for local adults to demonstrate their baking skills. The aim of the competition is to raise awareness of the bakery in the local community. The bakery has a website and a page on a social media website.

Produce a set of designs for a digital media campaign to support the competition and help the bakery achieve its aim.

Be prepared to amend your designs

There are two main reasons why you should produce designs for your digital media system.

1. To help fix what the final products will be like.
2. To enable you to test whether the design ideas will work, and if not, modify them.

One of the main reasons why systems do not succeed is that insufficient time is given to the design stage (see Figure 10.5). It is important that you spend time creating good designs, then showing them to intended users, then revising the designs and then testing them, and so on until you are sure that the designs will work. Only then should you move on to creating the content and the systems.

Figure 10.5: What kind of checklist would you need for each stage of this process?

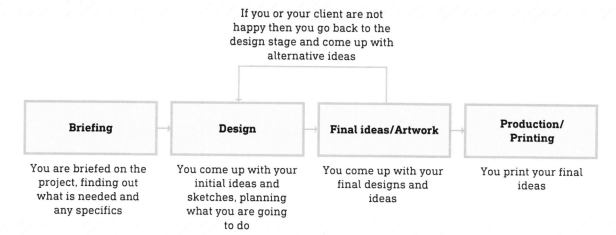

How to obtain verbal feedback on designs

At the design stage, it is important to obtain feedback that can help you to improve your designs. Ideally your feedback will come from intended users of the system but it could also come from whoever is available, for example your peers or work colleagues.

In C3, you will learn how products can be tested to obtain detailed written feedback that can be analysed. Consider the following forums for obtaining feedback.

- *Meetings*: a formal meeting will have a fixed start and finish time and will be dedicated to discussing the designs. Often the users will get a chance to review the designs before and come to the meeting ready to give their feedback.
- *Interviews*: an interview will be led by an interviewer who has a prepared list of questions that they will ask the members of the interview panel.
- *Discussions*: these will be with a small group of users. There might be a set of topics that the interviewer wishes to discuss, but otherwise the discussions will follow the points raised by users.
- *Focus groups*: these are discussion groups brought together to discuss specific aspects of the design, for example the music used in the designs.
- *Thought shower*: this is a problem-solving technique through which users give their immediate reactions to something without pausing to think whether the response is helpful (that comes later). For example, you might show your users a mood board and get them to give their immediate reactions – this will help test whether your mood board does convey the intended mood and whether your finished product will as well.

Practise

A local photography business is planning to organise a competition for adults to demonstrate their photography skills. One of the aims of the competition is to raise awareness of the photographer in the local community. The business has a website and a page on a social media website.

- Produce a set of designs for a digital media campaign to support the competition and help the photography business achieve its aim.

- Gather verbal feedback on the designs you have created, using at least two of the methods described above. Identify any improvements you need to make to the designs as a result of the verbal feedback.

B3 Develop a multichannel solution

You will need to show evidence of how you have developed your digital media content plan and how you used it.

Evidence showing the implementation of a digital media content plan

The evidence you show could include a production log (for example, a diary recording your progress each day), and screenshots of the product under development.

Your evidence must outline the ways in which your solution enhances the organisation's existing systems. You will need to demonstrate how this helps the organisation to meet its objectives. Below are two examples.

- The leisure centre has an objective of increasing membership of teenagers. It didn't have a mobile phone app, so I developed a new app which is designed for teenagers and young adults.
- The leisure centre has a Facebook® page but it was only updated once or twice a month. By updating it several times a week we have increased the number of active followers and so we expect to see an increase in attendance at classes and events among the under-35s.

Designing and creating content using a range of formats

To develop a multichannel solution, you will need to design and create content making use of a range of formats.

Link it up

Digital Applications

Refer back to Unit 7 where you studied how to create multimedia content in a range of formats, including interactive pages, sound, and still and moving images. Make sure you can remember the skills you used to create this digital content because you will need to apply them in this unit as well as in a future role as a digital content developer, or someone working in creative media support.

When you develop your multichannel solution you will need to make sure that you consider the following issues.

Creating images

As well as the issues covered in Unit 7, you should also consider the following.

- *Visualisation diagrams*: do you know what your finished images will look like?
- *Mood boards*: will your finished images convey the right mood?
- *Primary or secondary information*: will you be basing your final image on pre-existing images or will you need to create your own (for example, by taking photographs and then editing them)?
- *Copyright considerations*: if you are using secondary sources, then will any copyright restrictions prevent you from using your intended images? Are you able to comply with any copyright requirements?

Creating movies

- *Storyboards*: have you created a storyboard that meets the organisation's aims and user requirements?
- *Content*: will your movie contain still images, moving images and text? Do they fit well together?
- *Time limits*: do you know how long your movie needs to last? How long should each scene be?
- *File size*: do you know how large the final file size of the movie is? How will this affect download times and streaming performance? Could you reduce the file size by lowering the video quality and still produce a fit-for-purpose product?
- *File formats*: will the final movie be published in formats suitable for the intended channels and platforms?

Creating podcasts

- *Script*: does your podcast have a suitable script and does it convey all the required messages?
- *Narration*: do you know who will voice the script? Are their voices suitable and do they reinforce the messages?
- *Music*: is there appropriate background music? Does it support the main messages?
- *Time*: is the podcast the correct length?
- *File size*: do you know how large the file size is and how this will affect download times and streaming performance?
- *File format*: is the podcast available in a format that users can play on their preferred platforms?

Creating text

- *Character restrictions*: are there any text characters that cannot be used? For example, some foreign language characters, such as French and Spanish accents, may not display properly on all screens.
- *Tone and style*: are the words you are using giving the right message? If you are trying to be persuasive, is your tone convincing?
- *Font size*: do you know how large the text should be? Headings should be consistently sized and larger than the main text and all should be readable depending on the screen size of the user.
- *Accuracy*: is the information factually correct? Can you prove your claims are true? Are you legally allowed to say what you are saying?
- *Layout*: is your text laid out well on the page? Does it flow around images correctly? Does it all fit where it should?

Including a range of assets

Your product should contain a range of different ASSETS (types of content). These include:

- text
- still and moving images, graphics
- sound
- animation
- games
- interactive features and transitions – for example, menus/submenus, buttons, links, POP-UPS, video and sound clips.

Link it up

Digital Applications

For more on assets and how to create them, refer back to Unit 7.

B4 Consider legal and ethical constraints

How would you feel if you spent time and money creating a digital media product, only to find that somebody else had stolen your work and used it without asking you first?

Everyone who has their own digital property on the internet or has shared it with other organisations has the right to decide who can use it and how it is used.

Understanding the importance of digital property rights

Digital property includes:

- data, including **PERSONAL DATA**
- internet accounts
- intellectual property.

Following copyright requirements

Copyright laws aim to protect the creator or owner of **INTELLECTUAL PROPERTY** (an original piece of creative work such as text, images, sound or software code).

Below are some of the most common copyright restrictions placed on intellectual property.

- You must seek permission to use copyrighted work.
- You must acknowledge the owner or creator of the digital property when using their work.
- You must, if required, pay a fee to the owner of the copyright work to be able to use it.

In the UK, intellectual property is protected by the Copyright, Designs and Patents Act 1988.

If you fail to comply with copyright restrictions you could be:

- **SUED** (taken to court)
- required to compensate the digital property owner for your illegal use of their property
- required to stop using the digital property.

Avoiding plagiarism

PLAGIARISM happens when you use somebody else's ideas as if they were your own. Examples include:

- copying text from an online article and pasting it into your own document without acknowledging that it is a quotation from another source
- using somebody else's ideas to help write your own text without acknowledging that you are basing your work on somebody else's ideas.

Link it up

Digital Applications

Refer back to Unit 3 for an explanation of how personal data is protected by legislation.

Why should you check the copyright status of a digital asset before using it?

Monitoring usage and responding to comments

It is important that your digital media products meet legal requirements. But they should also meet ethical requirements. Ethical standards are about making sure you act in a way that is morally right, even if this is not enforced in laws.

Ethical organisations aim to go beyond simply meeting legal requirements and try to meet people's ethical concerns.

Below are some relevant ethical issues.

- Monitoring who uses your digital media products. For example, are your products used by your intended target groups? Is there an unintended imbalance in gender use or use by different ethnic or cultural groups? If so, does the product or company discriminate unintentionally in a way that puts some groups off?
- Responding to comments and feedback. Do you encourage your users to make comments and give feedback? If so, do you respond to the comments and do you act on the feedback received?

Potential of cyberbullying

If your channels include social media or blogs, you will need to take active steps to discourage and deal with the increasing risk of **CYBERBULLYING** (the online abuse and victimisation of other internet users).

Ways to manage cyberbullying on your social media site
- Produce a set of rules that users of the site agree to follow.
- Enable users to report acts of cyberbullying.
- Enable direct messaging (between the site owner and an individual user).
- Consider disabling direct messaging between individual users.
- Make it possible to block specific users from posting comments.
- Do not respond in public to comments made by possible cyberbullies.

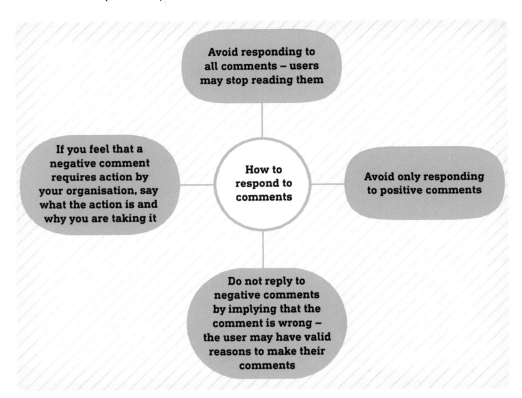

Figure 10.6: Knowing how to reply to comments requires tact and diplomacy

Copyright implications

It is vital that you understand the implications of using images and videos you find on the internet – and you should be able to justify your use of any media content you include. This includes seeking permission to use anything that is held in copyright by another party, and recording the evidence you have done so. Re-read this section if you are unclear on any of the relevant laws and the implications of plagiarism.

What if...?

You are helping to develop a new digital media system for a local independent cinema.

The cinema manager has identified some images that they would like you to include in the new system. The images were found using an internet search engine. The images include:

- film posters for well-known Hollywood films

- images of the covers of DVDs

- images of famous movie stars.

1 Explain the steps that would need to be taken to ensure that these images could be used in the cinema's new digital system.

2 Explain the possible consequences to the cinema if the images were used without these steps being taken.

Skills and knowledge check

☐ Can you list the features of a digital systems content plan?

☐ Can you describe three methods you can use to obtain verbal feedback on a digital systems content plan?

☐ What are digital property rights?

☐ What is intellectual property?

☐ Can you explain why it is important to meet copyright requirements when creating a digital media product?

○ I can create a digital systems content plan.

○ I can create a mood board.

○ I can create a storyboard.

○ I know how to prepare a prototype for a digital media product.

○ I know how to prepare a wireframe for a digital media product.

C Review the functionality and impact of a multichannel product

Now you have created your products in line within the legal requirements, you need to make sure that your digital media system works properly.

C1 Test functionality and features

One important part of this stage is to test that all the features and functions of your products work as intended.

Functions and features of the product

Link it up

Digital Applications

Refer back to Unit 7 for how to test digital applications, including creating and using test plans to test digital applications.

When testing your digital products, you need to make sure that all:

- features work as intended
- functions operate as expected and give expected results.

You should create a test plan which should include details of:

- what is to be tested
- how it is to be tested
- how you will know whether the item has passed or failed the test
- what action needs to be taken as a result (for example, to fix a problem and then a re-test to check the problem has been solved).

It is also a good idea to check that features work while you are building them. For example, if you plan that all pages have the same TRANSITION (a visual effect to smooth the move from one page to the next) on them, then you can check this as you build each page.

Test no.	Test type	Target file or screen	Purpose of test	Test data or situation	Expected result	Actual result	Outcome and actions required
1	Browser	Train_info.php	Rendering of departures timetable	Date set: 8 October 2016 Internet Explorer 11.0.0.0 Mozilla Firefox 49.0.1 Safari for Windows 5.1.7 Google Chrome 53.0.2785	Seven rows for departures, six coloured blue, one coloured yellow, displayed in ascending order by time. Column sequence: time, destination, platform, expected. Row 1 should contain an image (departures.jpg). Row 7 should contain an image in right-most cell (corner.jpg).	As expected As expected As expected As expected	All screens rendered as expected. No actions required.
2							
3							

Figure 10.7: Why is it a good idea to use a test plan?

Items that you should test will depend on the digital products that you will create as part of your system. These might include:

- text displays
- still and moving images
- graphics
- sound
- animations
- forms
- menus/submenus
- buttons

- pop-ups
- video and sound clips
- page transitions (see above)
- links, including INTERNAL HYPERLINKS to other pages of your product or EXTERNAL HYPERLINKS to other products or websites.

Gauging whether the system is fit for purpose

The aim of your system might be to persuade young adults to purchase more of your organisation's products. Your system will be fit for purpose if all parts of your system help to achieve this aim. There are two main ways that you can test whether your system is fit for purpose.

1. Monitor who uses your system, and how they use it (see C2).
2. Gather feedback from intended users (see B2 and C3).

C2 Analytics and impact

It is important to know whether your enhancements to the digital media system have had the intended positive impact on the organisation – helping it to meet its goals.

Measuring the impact of organisational digital systems usage

You should use indicators (data) to measure the impact of your campaign. Some of this data can be collected by asking your users questions. Other data can be collected using analytics services that monitor when and how users interact with your systems.

Common indicators

The following indicators can tell you how much your systems are being used. These USAGE INDICATORS are popular methods but you should be aware of their drawbacks.

- *Hits*: when you first visit a web page, your browser sends a request to the website host to send all the files the browser needs in order to download and display the full web page. These files might include the HTML PAGE (which contains the page's code and main text), files for each image and scripts needed to run interactive parts of the page such as search boxes or forms. Each request for a file that the website's server receives is a hit. The more hits received, the more popular the website. Hits can be counted to measure the popularity of the website. However, web pages that contain many files will register more hits than simple sites with fewer files. Also, some browsers will store a local copy of the files needed to view a page, preventing the need to re-download the pages in the future until the store is deleted. This can reduce the number of hits needed to view the page in future.

- *Visits:* when your browser requests files to view the web page, it gives your computer's IP ADDRESS. By logging the date and time that each IP address makes a hit you can measure how many times your website is visited.
- *Link clicks:* hits and visits record how many users visited your site. Link clicks can tell you how they got there. For example, are users coming to your website from your social media pages? Are users going to your online store only after browsing products or do they follow links in advertisements you have paid to have displayed on search engine results pages?
- *Length of visit:* how long are users staying on your website? Do they stay longer on some pages and not others?
- *Conversion rates:* how many visitors to your website buy your products? A conversion rate of 3 per cent is good – so for every 100 visitors you could expect one to buy something.

Useful benchmarks

It is good to know whether lots of people are using your systems. It is better to know whether your systems are having a positive impact – are they helping your organisation to achieve its objectives? You can use success criteria (also known as success indicators) to help you judge whether or not your campaign is successful.

Success criteria can be developed that are based on well-known BENCHMARKS (a level of performance that is generally accepted in a particular industry as being acceptable). For example, it is well known that only around 3 per cent of visitors to any online shopping website are likely to convert (buy a product). A business where the conversion rate is only 1 per cent will be performing below the benchmark standard and ought to try to improve its conversion rate to at least match the benchmark.

Key success indicators

SUCCESS INDICATORS are criteria that can be used to measure the impact of your digital system. The following is a list of some important success indicators.

- *Growth in client base:* are your systems helping you to increase the number of clients (users of your services or buyers of your products)?
- *Additional sales:* are you selling more products? Do you have more people paying more for your services? Is the income that you are earning going up? Are you earning more because you have more customers or are you earning more from each customer?
- *Increased profitability:* is the extra income you have earned from the digital media campaign greater than the costs of creating and running the campaign? In other words, is your extra income greater than the extra costs you paid out to earn the extra money? If yes, then your profitability has increased (profits are the difference between income and costs – they are the source of the money your organisation needs to pay the people who have invested money into it, including its owners).
- *Increased user interaction:* do you have more users using your products/ services for longer periods of time? This information can be used to sell advertising space on your digital products to other organisations.

- *Increased customer satisfaction*: are levels of customer satisfaction higher due to the campaign? Common ways to measure customer satisfaction include:
  - rating system averages (for example, if the average customer service rating increases from 3.5 to 3.7, then the campaign has increased customer satisfaction)
  - number of complaints/positive comments received
  - number of customers saying they are happy to use your services/ products again.

Practise

A doctors' surgery wishes to increase the number of registered patients by 10 per cent. It wants a new digital campaign to include:

- a redesigned website to include comments from patients

- an updated social media profile

- sponsored links on search engines – anyone who searches for health-related keywords from the town to see an advert directing them to the surgery website.

1 Describe the ethical issues the surgery should consider when running the digital campaign.

2 List key usage and success indicators that the surgery could use to judge whether the campaign is successful.

Tools to analyse the effectiveness of digital systems for organisations

Online organisations such as search engines and social media sites provide analytics services, for example Facebook has an analytics tool that helps organisations measure the impact of their Facebook pages.

Google Analytics™

Google Analytics monitors and records traffic to and around websites and other digital products such as mobile apps. Google Analytics works by using snippets of code using JavaScript as well as small data files called cookies placed on the user's computer or mobile device. These enable the service to track a user and collect data such as:

- how they arrived at the site (for example, by following links)
- browsing patterns (for example, which pages are seen, how long for, which digital assets are viewed?)
- number of page views (that is, the number of times a page is loaded).

Below are examples of information Google Analytics can provide.

- Do visitors to the site know what they want to find out before they get there? If not, how do they find the information they need?
- How many customers who visit a website attempt to make a purchase?
- How many customers start to make a purchase and then abandon the attempt? Why do they do this?

The owner of the site has to edit its properties to enable the analytics service to work, but this can be done to most digital products, not just ones that have, for example, been searched for using Google's search engine.

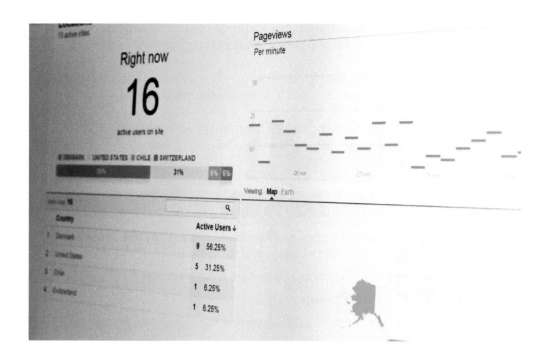

Why is it important to analyse how your digital products are used?

Facebook Insights®

This allows a Facebook site's admin user to track how their Facebook site is being used.

For example, the site's owner can check:

- how many users have visited the site (and how this number is changing over time)
- the total number of likes and dislikes (and how this is changing over time)
- how many friends your friends have (in other words how large your potential reach could be if you convert your friends' friends into new friends)
- which of your most recent posts were most popular (for example, by calculating their **VIRALITY** – how often they were reposted or linked to); this can help you build a positive image by producing new content that you know is going to be liked
- the profile of the people who 'like' you and your content, for example you see the age, gender and location profile so you can target people and places where you need to become more popular.

Hootsuite®

Hootsuite is a platform that enables a user to manage their social media sites. The service allows users to:

- view all their social media sites (including incoming messages) in a single location
- send messages to one or more social media outlets (for example, respond to a Facebook post and send the same message via Twitter).

This makes it easier for you to manage a digital media campaign because:

- individual messages are less likely to get lost
- you can respond to messages more quickly
- the same messages can be sent to different media sites so your users on each site get the same or similar messages.

Why is it important to keep your organisation's social media profile up to date?

Klout®

Klout is a tool that measures a user's social media profile on different social media channels (such as Facebook, LinkedIn® or Twitter) and gives them a score out of 100. The score is based on the number of social media followers and how they react to your messages.

As well as the Klout Score, the service also provides the following data.

- *True reach*: the proportion of your network who actively respond to your messages.
- *Amplification*: the likelihood that your social media activity will be met with a positive response from your network.
- *Network impact*: the extent to which your own social media network contains people who influence the behaviour of other social media users.

TweetReach®

TweetReach works with your Twitter account to measure:

- who reads your tweets
- who retweets your messages
- who reads your reposted messages
- the extent to which your messages become viral with multiple retweets.

You can use this data to make sure that your time spent posting messages on Twitter is put to good use. You can experiment with different types of message to see which ones are more popular with your followers.

Each of these systems presents data using a dashboard – a visual display of the data the user needs to analyse. For example, the dashboard could present summary data in tables and show trends in graphs.

C3 User feedback

As well as tracking the number of people who use your digital systems, you should obtain feedback from the users themselves. Ask your users questions about your products and how they use them. You can then analyse the responses to help you decide if your products are fit for purpose and are having the right impact.

Surveys or questionnaires

Give your users a set of written questions to which you want written answers. Good questionnaires are short and only ask relevant questions that do not take a long time to answer. Include a range of different response types, such as:

- yes/no buttons
- Likert scale (for example, rank your response to a statement as 1 (agree strongly) to 4 (disagree strongly))
- tick boxes
- free response questions.

Questionnaires can be put online, for example a pop-up could ask a user if they would like to complete a survey.

A drawback with questionnaires is that they can have a low response rate – unless users are given an incentive (such as a reward) to complete them.

Observations based on specific functionality

You can request feedback on a specific feature of your system by:

- asking a specific question about it (for example, using a pop-up)
- observing how users interact with it (for example, by inviting them to use the feature as part of a focus group meeting).

Focus groups

A **FOCUS GROUP** is a small group of users asked to spend time discussing your system. Focus groups usually have no pre-set questions but there might be a topic that you want to get feedback on – for example, their opinion of a new feature or ways to improve an existing one.

What are the drawbacks of using a focus group to obtain feedback from users?

One-to-one interviews

These are similar to a questionnaire but delivered face to face with an interviewer. The interviewer can either stick to a prepared set of questions or adapt them in light of the user's feedback. Good interviewers will prompt the user to give more detailed responses than they would give to a written questionnaire.

Written feedback

Invite users of a live product, or one under development, to give their written feedback on a specific feature.

Analysing data using spreadsheets/databases

Information collected from users can be analysed using spreadsheets or databases.

- Spreadsheet formulas could be used to calculate totals and averages, such as the average response to a Likert-scale question.
- A relational database could be used to analyse different types of respondent (held in one table) together with their opinions of different digital media products (each held in different tables).
- Charts can be used to display summary information that will be included in a presentation to senior managers.

Using data from analytics services or from user feedback is important. You need to know whether your digital media system is fit for purpose and is having a positive impact as well as helping your organisation achieve its goals. You also need to know whether your systems need to be improved and, if so, how. For all of this you need evidence, and your evidence will come from the data that you collect and how you analyse it.

Practise

You are developing a new multichannel digital system for a local charity. Your system includes a:

- mobile-friendly website

- new social media campaign where news about fundraising activities will be posted and feedback from fundraisers will be encouraged

- dedicated channel on video-hosting channels where new video content will be posted at least monthly.

1 Design a test plan to test the functionality of the mobile website.

2 Describe how you could use analytics services to both help manage your digital system and assess its impact.

3 List three potential problems that could limit the effectiveness of the digital media system and explain how you could overcome them.

Skills and knowledge check

☐ Can you list four usage indicators to measure the impact of a digital media system?

☐ Can you name three analytics services?

☐ Can you describe three methods to obtain user feedback?

○ I can create a test plan for a digital media product.

○ I can use a test plan to test the functionality of a digital media product.

○ I can produce success indicators for a digital media system.

○ I can use analytics services to monitor the impact of a digital media system.

○ I can create a questionnaire to gather user feedback.

○ I know how to gather user feedback using a range of different methods.

Ready for assessment

The practice tasks you have completed in this unit have been working towards your unit assignment. In the assignment, you will be asked to investigate existing digital media systems, then use this information to help you design, create, test and assess the impact of a multichannel digital media system for an existing organisation.

Understand existing digital media systems

You will need to:

- discuss the purpose of existing multichannel systems and the features they include

- investigate how the use of a multichannel system can help an organisation to meet its goals, for example by considering how the functions and features of the systems help the organisation to achieve its goals.

Design and create a multichannel digital media system enhancement for use by an organisation

Details of the organisation and its existing digital media systems will be given to you in the assignment. You will need to:

- produce a content plan for a multichannel system that will enable an organisation to meet its objectives

- prepare well-structured prototypes for the multichannel system. These should include storyboards, and wireframes where appropriate

- develop your multichannel solution, showing how it will:
    - meet the organisation's goals
    - respect copyright restrictions

- show how your enhancements will:
    - operate on different platforms
    - support the purposes of the organisation's digital campaign
    - meet legal and ethical issues.

Review the functionality of your multichannel product as well as its impact

You will need to:

- test the features of the multichannel system

- test the full functionality of the multichannel system, including whether the system helps the organisation to achieve its goals

- gather user feedback from different audiences using different methods

- consider the key points made in the feedback and use this to identify areas for development

- use analytics tools to analyse data on the impact of the system and organise this data into useful visual forms such as graphs, charts and tables

- use this information to assess the impact of the system by judging the impact against success criteria

- recommend suitable changes to the system.

WORK FOCUS

HANDS ON

Before developing your system, you may need to remind yourself of the skills needed to create a range of digital products, including:

- video
- animation
- web pages
- sound, including podcasts
- graphics and images.

When developing your ideas for the system you will need to consider the following.

- How will you decide which platforms you will use for your digital media system?
- Are your products compatible on different platforms?
- Do your products use file types that are compatible across different platforms?

- Have you tested your systems on all intended platforms?
- Do your systems work on all web browsers?
- How will your webpages look when displayed on mobile devices?
- Will you need to create separate websites for desktop and portable devices?

Your feasibility plans will need to include the following.

- What products will your system contain?
- What resources do you need to develop the system?
- How much will it cost to develop the system?
- How long will it take?
- Can you afford any delays to the development of your system?

Ready for work?

You have been asked by a local organisation to review how young people use social media networks and whether improvements can be made to the systems used.

Use appropriate methods to:

- gather information from users
- analyse the data you have obtained
- present your findings.

You should be able to:

- collect and use information from different sources
- determine the relevance and accuracy of information

- identify issues by being able to examine information
- ask questions to clarify information
- use IT to help solve problems
- organise information
- represent information in different ways using numbers.

Make sure that you:

- can ask questions that help you collect the information that you need
- can calculate totals and averages in a spreadsheet
- know when and when not to use line graphs, column and pie charts.

11 Installing and Maintaining Networks

What allows us to access our files over the internet? How can we log on to any machine in school or college and still access our work? How can we control our lights from the other side of the planet? What allows me to play my PlayStation® in a different room?

The answer to all these questions is networks! Networks require careful planning and development, as well as continual maintenance.

In this unit, you will learn about the different technologies that help build and support networks. You will also learn how to create and manage your own network using a range of tools and services.

How will I be assessed?

You will be assessed in this unit through a range of both written and practical work. You will learn about, and use, a variety of network management tools to test and document a network's performance.

Throughout the unit, you will learn all the necessary skills for both the creation and the maintenance of networks for a specific purpose. You will demonstrate and record skills such as configuring options for users, managing individual accounts, adjusting server settings and mapping drives for users. You will be making use of suitable documentation to evidence these activities as you progress through your assessment.

You will also produce evidence of using enabling network technologies, which will include a range of ethical hacking tools and developing networks to exist with new developing technologies, such as the Internet of Things (IoT).

Assessment criteria

Pass	Merit	Distinction
Learning aim A: Understand network management tools and systems		
A.P1 Use network management tools and activities to document a network.	**A.M1** Justify the effectiveness of documenting network management activities.	**A.D1** Evaluate network management tools.
Learning aim B: Implement network management procedures		
B.P2 Demonstrate how to manage a specific network, using tools.	**B.M2** Demonstrate that specific network management capabilities can be used to improve network speed and or capacity.	**B.D2** Manage a network, maximising its performance against user requirements.
Learning aim C: Use enabling network technologies		
C.P3 Use ethical hacking tools to demonstrate a network is secure. **C.P4** Develop a network that uses the IoT.	**C.M3** Justify how ethical hacking could be used to support networking professionals.	**C.D3** Demonstrate with confidence that you understand how ethical hacking can be used to improve the security of IT systems.
C.P5 Discuss how cloud systems operate and their differing types.	**C.M4** Justify key points for introducing a cloud solution.	**C.D4** Evaluate cloud solutions for a given network.

A Understand network management tools and systems

A1 Network management

Networks are an important part of many organisations. As well as setting up networks, it is important that you can effectively manage them to keep information up to date and make sure that the network is running at its best.

Network management functions

Figure 11.1 shows the wide array of tools and functions that can help you to make sure your networks are managed well.

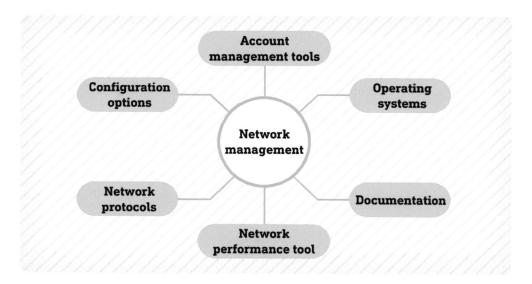

Figure 11.1: Network management tools allow for an efficient network

Configuration options (user groups)

User groups help you to manage what people can and cannot do on a network, as well as what people can access, by setting access by group type, for example employees, managers, customers. It makes things easier when you can group people together by what they are and are not allowed to do on a network, rather than on an individual basis.

Examples of the different types of user groups that could be used in your school or college are tutor and learner user groups. Tutors can be added to a group that has access to files containing important information (such as student contact details), and learners can be added to a group that has access to the specific **SOFTWARE** they need to complete their course.

Within organisations, the creation of user groups can help to manage large numbers of employees and what they can access on a network. For example, if a company needs to make use of software that has an expensive **LICENCE** (such as the Adobe® suite), it may only want its graphics or media department to have access to this software, and a specific group just for this makes sense.

Account management

ACCOUNT MANAGEMENT is used when you need to make changes to specific user accounts on a network, for example when a user needs to have their **PASSWORD** reset to log onto a machine.

As an IT support technician, you should be able to use account management tools to undertake tasks such as resetting passwords. However, users can often perform simple account management tasks such as this themselves, for example if a password is due to expire, a user can work though an automated helpdesk to change their password. In such cases, the user will usually have to carry out some form of validation to confirm they are the account holder.

Network performance

When you maintain a network, it is important that you monitor its performance to make sure it is operating at peak efficiency. There are many tools available to help you monitor network performance, some of which display network performance visually.

Some of these tools allow you to monitor specific elements, such as **TRAFFIC** on the network, and the **NETWORK RESPONSE TIMES** (the amount of time it takes for **DATA** to be transferred across a network). An example of this kind of software includes Wireshark™, which can provide visuals for network activity, generate reports and can even be set up to alert you of specific activities or events.

> ### Link it up
>
> #### Networking and Cybersecurity
>
> Refer back to Unit 3 to learn more about the types of account management policies organisations use and why they need them.

Using different operating systems software

An **OPERATING SYSTEM (OS)** is the core software we install on our devices that allows us to run our applications and control the **HARDWARE** we use. When it comes to setting up and maintaining networks, you need to remember the wide variety of operating systems that you could be using. As well as desktop operating systems, many networks now have to be configured to work with operating systems on mobile devices. Below are some of the networks you may encounter.

- *Microsoft Windows®*: the most common OS running on desktop computers. There is also a slimmed down version of the OS to run on mobile devices.
- *Linux®*: a free open-source OS. Although it is not widely used on PCs, it is a very common OS for servers.

With the increase in mobile technologies, you may also need to work with mobile operating systems. Below are some examples.

- *Android™*: this is an OS that runs on many mobile devices and tablets (apart from Apple® devices).
- *iOS®*: the mobile OS developed by Apple that runs on all its mobile devices, including iPhones®, iPads® and iPods®.

There are many operating systems you can encounter when configuring networks

Considering different protocols and layouts

When you set up networks, it is important to consider the different **NETWORK PROTOCOLS** available. (Network protocols are similar to a set of rules that tells parts of a network how to behave.) Below are some of the different types of network protocols.

Transmission Control Protocol/Internet Protocol (TCP/IP)

The **TRANSMISSION CONTROL PROTOCOL/INTERNET PROTOCOL (TCP/IP)** protocol is a set of rules for the transmission of data over networks. It makes sure that when data is sent, it is sent correctly and to the correct location. The protocol is made of four layers; these are the application, transport, internet and network access layers.

Application layer

The application layer is the section of the TCP/IP that directly links with the programs you use – for example, your web **BROWSER** when you access the web. This layer has its own protocols such as **HTTP** for accessing websites or the **FILE TRANSFER PROTOCOL (FTP)** for transferring files directly to a server over a network.

Transport layer

The transport layer splits the data being sent into **PACKETS** in order for the information to be delivered quickly and efficiently to the correct destination.

Internet layer

This layer attaches the **IP ADDRESSES** of the destination and sender. This makes sure that the packet knows where it is going as well as where it has come from before being passed on to the network layer.

Network layer

The network layer makes sure that the data is passed to the right physical machine on a network. This is important as in many cases there are lots of machines on any given network – so information needs to arrive at the specific machine for which it was intended.

Post Office Protocol (POP)

The **POP** is another example of a protocol on the application layer. This protocol allows users to access emails that have been sent to them. These emails exist on the email provider's servers, and this protocol allows users to retrieve, read and delete these emails (see Figure 11.2).

This is different to the **SIMPLE MAIL TRANSFER PROTOCOL (SMTP)**, which is responsible for handling the sending of emails.

Link it up

Networking and Cybersecurity

Refer back to Unit 8 to learn more about the different network topologies, standards and protocols.

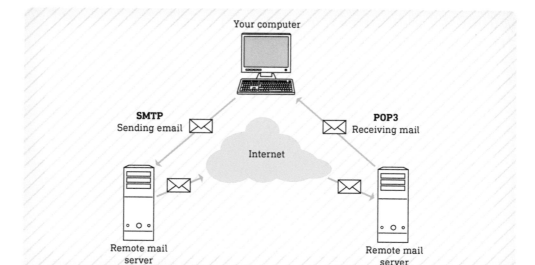

Figure 11.2: The process of sending and receiving emails uses POP and SMTP

Domain name system

The **DOMAIN NAME SYSTEM (DNS)** protocol is what allows you to navigate the web in a user-friendly way. Every site that exists on the World Wide Web has an IP address (like a phone number), for example 74.125.236.195. You can allocate domain names (for example, www.google.com) to these IP addresses. The DNS protocol then retrieves the correct site by matching the domain name to the correct IP address, which is much easier than having to remember all those numbers.

Network layouts

When you create your networks it is important that you consider the different options available for laying them out. The most common types of layout or **TOPOLOGY** are bus, ring, star, tree and mesh (see Table 11.1).

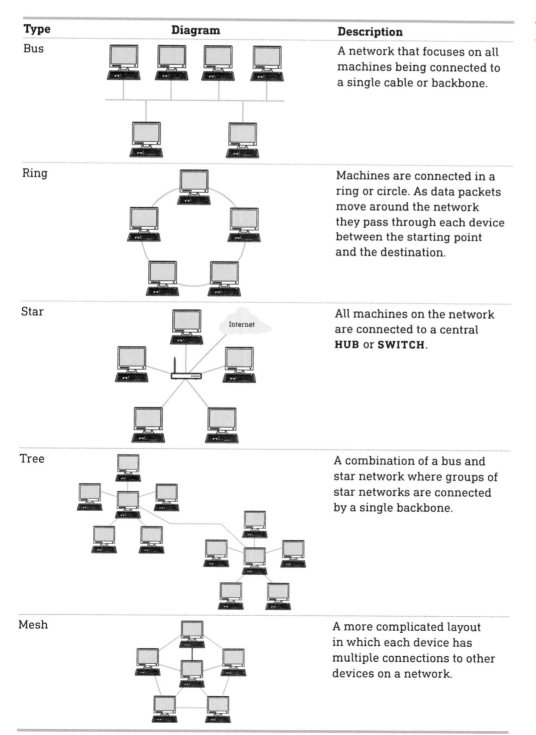

Type	Diagram	Description
Bus		A network that focuses on all machines being connected to a single cable or backbone.
Ring		Machines are connected in a ring or circle. As data packets move around the network they pass through each device between the starting point and the destination.
Star		All machines on the network are connected to a central **HUB** or **SWITCH**.
Tree		A combination of a bus and star network where groups of star networks are connected by a single backbone.
Mesh		A more complicated layout in which each device has multiple connections to other devices on a network.

Table 11.1: Common topologies

Networking tools

There are numerous tools you can use once your network is in place. The type of tools you will use will mostly depend on the type of activity you will be undertaking.

In most IT technician roles, you will want to be able to monitor and analyse the current condition of the network. In these cases, you will be looking at information based on how quickly data is being transferred over the network and current issues that are being detected.

In many cases, you can use software that generates a visual display of this information to help get an overall picture more quickly than by analysing the raw data. Examples of tools like this include Wireshark and HP® Intelligent Management Centre (see below).

Keeping a close eye on what happens on a network can help stop issues before they become a problem

A2 Network documentation

When you carry out the different tasks for network management, it is important that you keep accurate records of what you have done. Often different companies will have standardised documentation and systems to help keep track of this information. Examples of the types of systems that may be in place include standard formats for reporting and network testing or servicing, as well as systems such as electronic helpdesks for keeping track of reported network issues and their progress.

Documentation

The documentation in place within a company should record as much information about a network as possible. This is helpful for cases where you wish to make changes to a network or even if something goes wrong. The information documented can vary between organisations but tends to include, for example, details of current versions of software running on the network, hardware that currently exists and clear information on backups. If no documentation is used, it can be very difficult to keep track of what exists on a network, as well as making it harder to identify when and where an issue arose.

Testing reports

Clear testing reports are an important part of network documentation. As well as network performance, dates and times should be recorded clearly, just in case a report needs to be referred to at a later date. In most businesses, given how important a network is, you will be required to carry out and log the results of tests on a set time basis.

Service logs

Service logs will record when servicing (for example, updating and maintenance) has been carried out on both software and hardware on any network. In most organisations, these activities will take place at set intervals to make sure the network is running at peak efficiency. These logs are usually held and updated by the IT support team of a business.

In a technology support role in industry, you would normally be part of a team of employees who are responsible for maintaining and updating this type of documentation. It is important these are updated correctly to help others who may need to use them in future.

Practise

Make a list of the different elements you think should be recorded when carrying out network management activities, then use these to create a template for your own network documentation.

If possible, find a copy of the network documentation used in your school or college to see how they compare, and in order to refine and develop your own documentation further.

In class, try to review other people's documentation and discuss the elements each of you has included. Consider the following questions.

- What have you included that may not be necessary?

- What have you included that others have not? Could they have included this?

- Is there a definitive document that should be used? Or is it appropriate for different organisations to use different documentation?

Skills and knowledge check

- [ ] When would you set up a user group rather than modify a specific account?
- [ ] What is meant by a network protocol?
- [ ] What does DNS stand for and what does it do?
- [ ] What is meant by a protocol?

- ○ I can list three operating systems I am likely to encounter when setting up or maintaining networks.
- ○ I can list the different types of network layout.
- ○ I understand the role of TCP/IP.
- ○ I understand the importance of having relevant network documentation in place.

B Implement network management procedures

Once your networks are in place, there is a range of skills you need in order to configure and maintain them.

B1 Configuration options

In order to maintain a network effectively, there are multiple configuration options you need to consider. Ongoing configuration is part of the day-to-day role of any network technician and usually involves a wide range of activities.

Common configuration activities

User accounts

Once a network is in place you can set up **USER ACCOUNTS**. These accounts are often tailored to a user based on their requirements, for example learners need access to certain websites and resources in order to complete their work.

An example of how this could apply in a work environment may be where companies have limited access to social media for their employees. In a case like this, they may want to allow access to sites such as Facebook® and Twitter® for specific employee accounts (for example, this could be useful to the marketing team).

Roaming profiles

ROAMING PROFILES are what allow users to log on to any machine on a given network and still be able to access their files. This is possible as all the information and files for each user account is stored centrally on a server rather than on an individual's machine.

This setup is very common in organisations because of the flexibility it offers employees and employers in terms of where people carry out their work.

Server settings

Servers are the heart of any network, and require ongoing configuration and maintenance to make sure they run efficiently. Some networks may have a single server operating on them, but larger companies may have a number of servers to manage different aspects of the network, including, for example, **MAIL SERVERS** to store and send emails, **PROXY SERVERS** to monitor and block unwanted websites and **WEB SERVERS** for hosting websites.

Each of these servers has individual settings that will need to be configured in order to work effectively.

Link it up

Networking and Cybersecurity

Refer back to Unit 3 for more information on how to access wireless networks and how remote access works.

Local configurations

In some cases, you are required to set up a computer on a network on the specific PC you wish to connect. This process is called **LOCAL CONFIGURATION**. To do this, you access the network settings on each individual PC where you will need to enter all settings and specific IP information.

Fortunately, this type of configuration is far less common now as most PCs have automated network setups for the home, and network technicians are available in organisations.

Drive mapping

The drives that you store your files or applications on can be physical drives (such as the **HARD DISK DRIVES (HDD)** in your machine) or they can be **VIRTUAL DRIVES** (drives that do not physically exist, but can be used to store data).

Whenever you want to make use of these drives over a network, they need to be mapped correctly. Just like in the real world, the map allows the user account to find the drive by following directions, in this case a specific directory to look in. These drives can be mapped for one user for individual storage or for groups to help aid collaboration.

Virus scanning options

When your network is finally complete, you will need to make sure no **MALICIOUS SOFTWARE** is introduced that might cause issues.

To do this you should consider what virus-scanning options you have. When you set up virus-scanning software, you will need to think about the following.

- How often do you want to run anti-virus scans?
- What do you want to happen if a **VIRUS** is found on the network?
- How will you factor in people bringing in their own files/removable storage?
- How will people bringing in their own devices that are already infected have an impact?

As you can imagine, there is a lot to think about to make sure networks are kept safe.

Link it up

Networking and Cybersecurity

Refer back to Unit 3 for more information about the different threats to computers and networks and the methods we can use to protect ourselves from them.

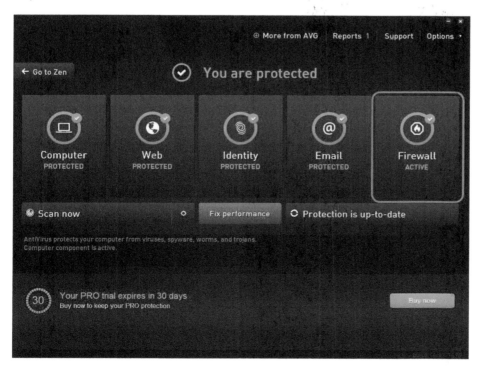

It is important that you configure your anti-virus software correctly, otherwise you risk opening your network to electronic infections

User interface configuration

Once you have set up your network, you can start to look at the configuration of **USER INTERFACES**. A business does this to make sure that the users have access to both the drives that they need and any specific software they require.

What if...?

A new school has decided to set up a new network to replace its old system. It requires the network to be able to perform several key functions, including the following.

- Students and staff should be able to log on to any machine and be able to access their work.

- Staff would like some drives set up so that they can collaborate on work that should be only accessible to staff.

- They would like another drive set up for students to submit work, which should be accessible to staff and students.

- They would like the network to be secured from viruses.

In pairs, devise a suitable plan for a network that meets the requirements for the school. As well as saying how you would configure the network, make sure you explain why you would choose that method.

B2 Maintenance activities

A significant part of making sure networks are set up and run efficiently is maintenance. Unlike the set-up process, maintenance is an ongoing process made up of different activities.

Regular maintenance activities

Once your network is set up, you must start the ongoing process of maintaining the network to make sure it works effectively. Figure 11.3 outlines the activities you need to consider when maintaining your network.

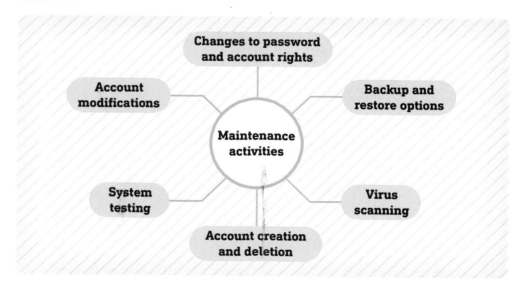

Figure 11.3: Regular maintenance activities are needed to ensure networks work efficiently

Backup and restore options

Imagine that you start your day and when you log on to your account, the assignment you have been working on seems to have disappeared. There may be numerous reasons why situations such as this happen, including human error, faults with software or hardware, or even the introduction of some malicious software such as a computer virus.

Fortunately, when using computer systems you have access to a range of backup and restore options. With these options, you can select parts of, or even an entire network to be backed up at regular intervals. If any issues occur, you can simply restore the network and its files back to its previous state. Sadly, performing this kind of restoration means any data generated since the last backup is lost, meaning you really have to think about how often you would like your network to be backed up.

Why is it important that you have a system in place for regular backups?

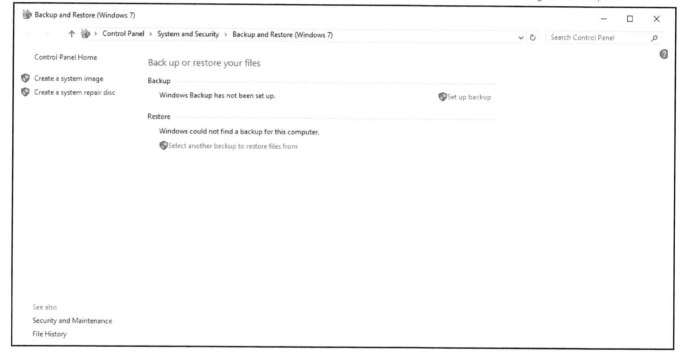

Account creation and deletion

The people who need access to networks change all the time. Think about your school or college: every year new learners start and older learners leave, meaning that the network needs to be updated.

The same applies in many organisations. Some organisations have a high turnover of staff, meaning that IT technicians need to create and delete accounts for employees regularly. In these situations, the network administrators need to make sure that new employees have accounts created and that anyone who leaves has their accounts deleted. Imagine how much storage would be taken up if no one ever deleted those old accounts.

Account modifications

Sometimes, instead of the creation or removal of a user account, you will need to make modifications to one instead. The kinds of modifications you can make include mapping a drive to an account that previously had no access, or increasing the amount of storage a user has on a network.

These modifications can quickly become complex to manage, for example in a large company that deals with protected information. As a network technician, it is your responsibility to make sure that only those who should have access to certain information do actually have access.

Password and account rights changes

One of the more common activities you will undertake while maintaining a network is changing passwords and accounts rights. If a user exceeds a set number of attempts, or has forgotten their password to log on to a network, often they will need to visit a network administrator to have their password reset or changed.

Changes to user rights are often required for activities such as giving specific users access to previously inaccessible areas like secure DATABASES or INTRANET pages.

System testing

As an ongoing process, the system should be tested and the results recorded at regular intervals. If problems develop in the future, these system tests can help you to identify when problems started to occur on your network.

System testing is a very important part of a network technician's role, as in many cases a network failure can often mean a loss of profit for a company.

Virus scans

Virus scans are set up to run at regular intervals on a network but you can also carry them out outside of these time frames. In order to make sure the scans are effective, it is important that the scanner's VIRUS DEFINITION FILE (a file that detects newer versions of electronic viruses) is as up to date as possible.

Depending on the size of the organisation, these scans could be run often, for example a web development company may have individuals working on projects at home, meaning external files are brought in and connected to the network all the time. In many cases, companies will also have ongoing email conversations with clients or customers with attached files – these could also be a source of electronic infection.

Virus scans and system testing is an important part of a technician's role, but also crucial for those who work in cybersecurity. If you are working in a cybersecurity role, you will need to be up to date with current threats to electronic systems to ensure that suitable protection methods are developed.

Link it up

Networking and Cybersecurity

Refer back to Unit 1 to learn more about the different security threats to computer systems.

Documentation updates

As the networks you create develop, so will the documentation you use. It is important that all of this documentation is updated regularly to reflect any changes or updates in your networks in order to be effective.

Work logs

WORK LOGS are important because they record any jobs carried out as well as any software that is installed. They can help you to clearly identify whether a specific activity or installation is at fault when problems arise.

Practise

Make a guide to help inform people of the different types of network available to them, as well as the importance of carrying out the various network maintenance activities that are needed.

If possible, interview your school or college's IT support team to get extra information on how these activities are carried out.

What if...?

Larry Jones has started his first day in a job working as a network administrator for a small company. When he arrives, there is already a major issue waiting for him: the network has malfunctioned due to an unknown error. Luckily Larry remembers his training.

- The first thing Larry checks is the most recent virus scans to make sure nothing was picked up on a routine scan. Fortunately, nothing was picked up so Larry moves on.

- Larry checks the latest networks tests to see if anything can be identified. Nothing is apparent there so Larry moves on to the next check.

- He checks the work logs and sees that on the previous day, the network team installed a new version of a piece of software on the server.

- Larry checks and sees that the team correctly set up a restore point before installing the software, so he restores the network from the backup and fixes the error.

In pairs, discuss the issues that could have arisen if the team had not properly documented the information above.

Skills and knowledge check

☐ What do you need to consider when configuring anti-virus software?
☐ What is meant by the term 'drive mapping'?

○ I know the difference between account creation and account modification.
○ I can explain why it is important that documentation is kept up to date.
○ I know the difference between backup and restoration.
○ I understand the difference between user accounts and roaming profiles.
○ I know why we need to keep accurate work logs.

C Use enabling network technologies

In order to ultimately secure a network, there is a range of network-enabling technologies you can use. These allow you to test the security of a network and in turn help secure it from threats.

C1 Ethical hacking in support of network management, penetration testing and firewalls

When you think of **HACKERS**, it is likely that an image of criminals will come to mind, but this is not always the case. Attempting to hack or test a network for vulnerabilities is actually a great way to find weaknesses and help us to secure them.

In order to do this, there are different tools available to you as a network technician to test a network for vulnerabilities and to protect it from any issues identified. Some companies (for example, Facebook) actually offer rewards to people who report any vulnerabilities that they find on their website.

Examining security features as tools for support

When considering making use of **ETHICAL HACKING** (using hacking techniques to gain access to a network of computers, to identify and secure weaknesses), there is a range of tools available for both testing a network for risks and then protecting it.

Firewall management

A **FIREWALL** is the first line of defence for any network. The best way to think of a firewall is as a barrier that sits between networks, for example this could be your home network and the internet.

The firewall interface usually requires a login to alter any of the settings. The firewall has a set of rules for **INBOUND AND OUTBOUND TRAFFIC** (data being received and sent out). If a connection follows these rules, then it will be allowed; if not then it will be blocked by the firewall.

Firewalls are essential to protect from a variety of threats, including viruses, hacking attempts and **DENIAL-OF-SERVICE (DOS) ATTACKS**. (A DoS attack is usually carried out by flooding a network with so much data that it becomes inaccessible to users.)

Access controls

Inside organisations you can use an **ACCESS CONTROL LIST**. This list tells the network what each user has access to, usually in terms of software and resources. The access control list can also manage who has permission to alter and view information. For example, as a learner you can see the grades that you have achieved in different subjects, but a tutor can view as well as update this information.

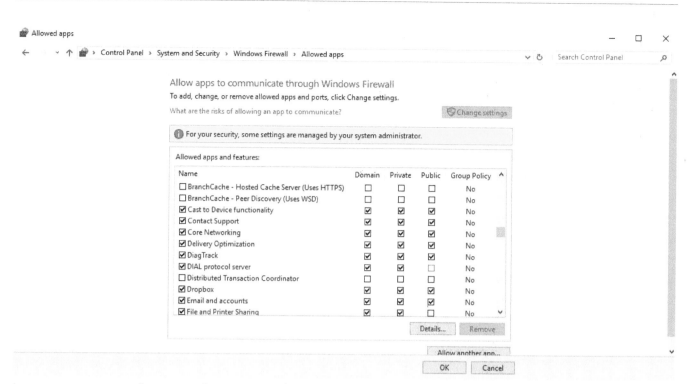

In some cases, we actually want to allow certain applications to pass data through our firewalls; to do this we configure the firewall settings to let this happen

User rights

The rights of a user are often specific to a profile. The rights defined here limit which areas of a network a user has access to. As you can imagine, getting these correct is very important in order to ensure that sensitive or confidential parts of the network remain private.

Virtual private network access

Sometimes an organisation will want to grant access to other people. To do this, you can use a **VIRTUAL PRIVATE NETWORK (VPN)**, which will allow you to create a secure connection for accessing and transferring data. Because data will be travelling between sites, it is important that it is **ENCRYPTED** and password protected to ensure its security. VPNs will allow you to create a secure connection for accessing and transferring data.

> ### Link it up
>
> **Networking and Cybersecurity**
>
> Refer back to Unit 1 to learn more about the different security practices for securing computer systems.

Applying penetration testing for network management

PENETRATION TESTING is a key method of checking a network's security. As part of this, you can make use of different software packages and techniques to help identify vulnerabilities in a network.

Port scanning

When you allow applications to pass information over a network, you do so by allowing it access through a **PORT** (think of it as opening a door for the data to pass through). Port scanners can be used to try to gain illegal access to a network by looking at which doors have been left open.

Network technicians or external security consultants can make use of the same techniques in order to find these vulnerabilities and safely secure them. This is classed as a form of ethical hacking as it is making use of techniques that would normally be employed by a criminal in order to help, rather than damage a network.

Password cracking

In many cases, access to your files on a network is secured using a password. You can use password-cracking software to test the security of your password. This type of software makes use of what are called **BRUTE FORCE ATTACKS** (a type of attack that keeps trying different possibilities in order to solve a problem). The software attempts a series of passwords from a database containing common sequences of numbers and letters until it gains access.

Using a brute force password-cracking word list will help to test the security of passwords

This is why when we create a password it often needs to contain special characters (for example, @$%#), capital letters, lower case letters and numbers to make our passwords harder to crack. Often a network will have a maximum number of attempts at a password before an account is locked and an administrator is required to unlock it. Some examples of these types of password can be seen in the Table 11.2.

Table 11.2: Strong and weak passwords

Password Type	Description	Examples
Weak	An obvious password using standard letters, often personal to the user (for example, home towns, pet names) so can be easy to guess	PASSWORD, 123456
Strong	Less obvious password, making use of special characters, numbers and upper/lower case letters, making it very difficult to guess	P@$$w0rd, H5avr48d

Vulnerability scanning

VULNERABILITY SCANS can check an entire network for anything that could be considered a security threat. These can show various methods that an intruder could use to gain access to the network as well as how authorised users may be able to access secure parts of a network through different exploits.

In a cybersecurity role, you would make use of a lot of these skills to test networks and to protect them from these vulnerabilities.

C2 The Internet of Things (IoT)

As technology has become more advanced, so too have the connections that link it. We now have appliances and mobile devices that are constantly connected to make the way we live our lives easier. The term for this new type of connectivity is the **INTERNET OF THINGS (IOT)**.

Technologies and services used in the IoT

Normally, when you think of networks and the internet, you tend to think of being able to access web pages on various devices. The IoT is a term that has been created to help define how new types of technology and services are being linked via the internet and networking services (Figure 11.4).

There are numerous examples that incorporate these, some of which are given below.

- Smartwatches and apps that help track health and diet information and update to a central store of information. This data can then be passed on to health professionals and in some cases has been known to save lives.
- Smart appliances, such as coffee machines that can switch themselves on when your morning alarm goes off or car satnavs that can update their routes in real time using live traffic information.
- Smart meters that connect to service providers for utilities, such as gas and electricity, to provide real-time updates on energy consumption and bills.
- Home services, such as network-controlled lighting, plugs and boilers.

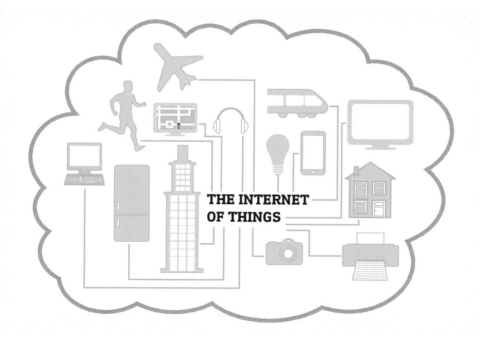

THE INTERNET OF THINGS

Figure 11.4: The Internet of Things creates connectivity to make our lifestyles easier

Security and ethical considerations

It may seem as if the IoT adds great convenience to the way we live our lives, but there are also multiple security considerations with these emerging technologies. One major consideration is that these devices (particularly in our homes) can help to provide security holes that can be exploited by hackers or to deploy denial of service attacks. Gaining access to these devices could give hackers access to controls such as the deactivation of home security systems or even unlocking front doors.

With the advent of any new type of computing technology, there are often people trying to find new ways to interfere with its function – the same can be true for the IoT. As the technology is developed, tailor-made IoT viruses have been developed. Some of these viruses take control of appliances and use them to conduct activities like flooding networks with traffic; or in some cases they can scan the network for the devices that are connected to it and report any vulnerabilities back to the person who sent the virus.

Other areas that need to be considered when we work with the IoT relate to people's rights with regard to the information they share. Are people really informed about the data they are sharing and how it can be used by different organisations? An example of this is the new Amazon Alexa®. Alexa works as a voice assistant that can be used to perform web queries as well as control different applications in the home. Although very helpful, there are some serious concerns. In order to carry out its job effectively, Alexa needs to be constantly listening to what is happening in a user's home in order to respond to queries. These recorded commands and sounds are stored on the Amazon server, meaning if the servers are hacked, then that information could be released into the public domain. In some cases, this information has been sought by the authorities in order to help with criminal investigations. For example, in Arkansas, USA, police requested access to recordings from a home linked to a possible murder investigation.

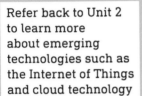

Link it up

Refer back to Unit 2 to learn more about emerging technologies such as the Internet of Things and cloud technology

C3 Bring your own device (BYOD) management

When employees take their own devices into work, they can often be connected to existing networks. Once connected, employees can use the different **PERIPHERAL DEVICES** within the organisation, as well as share connections (such as to the internet). The term for this type of network is **BRING YOUR OWN DEVICE (BYOD)**.

BYOD can be a major feature of a network. These types of networks allow individuals to bring in and connect their own hardware (usually mobile devices such as phones, laptops and tablets) to an existing network. For example, in your school or college you may be able to connect your phone to the network to make use of the internet connection.

Policies concerned with using own devices on a network

As you can imagine, allowing these external devices to connect can pose a serious risk to a network as well as having implications for the availability of resources. This is why when you set up a BYOD network, you often have to establish policies on usage as well as ensuring that hardware is maintained and configured correctly.

Viewing past histories

When you set up a network in an organisation, there is likely to be a policy in place relating to appropriate content such as access to social media or gambling, which the organisation may not allow.

In order to comply with these rules, there may be a policy in place allowing the organisation the right to review the browser history of anyone using the network. In some cases (such as educational establishments) this may even be a requirement of their service provider.

Sharing data

When you allow people to connect their own devices to a network you need to consider which elements of that network they can access. You need to think about whether or not you allow them access to the data that is stored on the network.

When you set up user accounts you can decide if that user has access to specific drives, as well as whether you allow them to read and write data to the drive. These security considerations are the same when you allow BYOD on your network – often an organisation will have a policy in place determining exactly what data people can and cannot see while using their own devices on a network.

BYOD maintenance support

Once set up, just like standard networks, BYOD networks need ongoing maintenance support to ensure they continue to work well.

Physical support

Physical support for a BYOD varies greatly depending on the requirements. A core part of a large-scale BYOD network is a **WIRELESS LAN CONTROLLER** (this works with wireless access points throughout an organisation to control the traffic and connections on a network).

Upgrading hardware and software

In order to put a BYOD network in place you should consider how this will relate to the organisation's hardware and software.

Hardware considerations

These can include looking at the likely areas where individuals will be trying to gain access to the network and putting wireless access provision (such as wireless access points) in these places. In some cases, this can prove to be very costly for big sites, so certain areas will need to be prioritised over others.

As technology develops, it may be necessary to upgrade these points to cope with the increase in connections or faster connection types. Servers may also need to be upgraded in order to cope with the increased amount of traffic on the network.

Software considerations

As part of ongoing maintenance of your BYOD network, **PROXY SERVER SETTINGS** (a kind of 'middle man' on a network that controls the connections between the network and devices) will need to be updated in order to allow people to connect devices. **WEB FILTERS** (pieces of software that can monitor traffic to and from the internet) will also need to be updated to ensure traffic from any extra devices is monitored while connected (administrators can use rules to make sure any content that is not allowed is blocked and not viewable by users on the network).

BYOD device configuration support

As a network technician, you will need to support BYOD users in a variety of ways.

User accounts

In many cases, user accounts for a BYOD network will be directly mapped to the standard account you use to log on to a machine. This means you can use your login details to access the network.

Link it up

Networking and Cybersecurity

Refer back to Unit 3 to learn more about the different types of networks.

In some cases, a new user account will be created to accommodate guests who wish to access a network wirelessly with external devices.

Access rights

In the same way that you configure **ACCESS RIGHTS** for individuals who access a network with set devices, you also need to configure the access rights that individuals have when they make use of their own devices. You will need to consider aspects such as whether:

- users can access any specialist software on the network
- databases with sensitive information are accessible through BYOD devices
- drives and data are accessible to BYOD users.

Often guest users will have very basic access (internet access, storage) when making use of their own devices.

Access to peripherals

People may wish to access peripheral devices (such as networked printers, scanners and photocopiers).

In many cases, server software (such as printer servers) must be configured to allow users to submit files for printing. Once the initial setup is complete, often these devices can be left on the network, but software configurations should be reviewed on a set-time basis.

Practise

Create a 'bring your own device' policy for your centre or college. If possible, find example policies on the internet to help you develop your own. When creating your policy, try to consider some of the following elements.

- What software or data will you allow people to access?
- Will this differ between individuals, or will there be a blanket (broad) approach?
- Will they have access to peripheral devices? If so, will this be limited?
- What content will BYOD devices be able to access online?

Link it up

Networking and Cybersecurity

Refer back to Unit 3 to learn more about BYOD networks.

C4 Business value of cloud technologies

As the capabilities of network technologies and connection speeds have improved, a new type of technology has developed – **CLOUD TECHNOLOGY** (this is a term used to describe internet-based storage and applications; see Figure 11.5).

Understanding cloud services from a business perspective

As cloud technology improves, businesses can make use of it to add value and become more effective in the ways they operate. Cloud technology has many uses, including:

- storing files that we can access anywhere with an internet connection
- being able to collaborate on files, working on them at the same time as others
- being able to access cloud applications that we can use anywhere, rather than just on our machine.

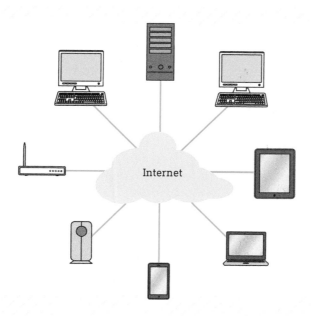

Figure 11.5: These devices can use cloud technology in a way that is extremely beneficial to businesses but there are many considerations that need to be taken into account from a business perspective

Scalability

One of the advantages of cloud computing is its **SCALABILITY**. A company making use of a cloud solution can cope with rapid increases in terms of storage and cloud application usage, by giving its employees an opportunity to make use of applications at home as well as storing files externally away from the organisation.

Security

Security is a serious consideration when deciding to implement a cloud strategy for an organisation. If an organisation plans to make data accessible through a cloud service, it needs to make sure that this data is secure. In some cases, this may even be a legal requirement in order to comply with the Data Protection Act 1998.

If a company decides to host its own cloud service, it needs to make sure it has taken the necessary steps to ensure this data is secure. In some cases, the company may opt to make use of an already established provider for its cloud storage or application, but even these can be hacked. In 2012, the well-established cloud storage service Dropbox™ was hacked with the login details of 68 million users being leaked on the internet.

Hardware independence

The term **HARDWARE INDEPENDENCE** refers to having applications and data stored separately from the hardware on which it will be used – a major advantage of using cloud computing. This means that the processing of these applications and software is carried out on the organisation's servers rather than the machines themselves.

Organisations can save money by making use of computers with much lower specifications (as they only need to manage the connection and the input to the server). These machines are referred to as thin clients.

Costs

Cost is a significant consideration when an organisation is looking at setting up a cloud solution. A benefit of making use of an external solution is that the set up and maintenance has already been carried out for you. Some services also offer tiered, pay-as-you-use options, so the cost implications can be affordable. The major trade-off for these services is the lack of control over how they work.

Internal cloud solutions, though costly to set up due to hardware, software and technical skill considerations, offer much more freedom in the way that they operate.

Either option will more than likely come down to the two following factors.

a. The size of the organisation: in many cases the amount a company can pay will be linked to its size.

b. The requirements: if a company wants to make use of a cloud solution for just sharing the odd file, it makes much more sense to outsource this to an external provider. If, however, the company needs a bespoke solution that meets specific requirements, it may find the flexibility of an internal cloud solution more appropriate.

Examining how cloud computing enhances organisations

There are numerous ways in which cloud computing services can increase the value and competitiveness of organisations that use it correctly. Cloud applications can offer employees the opportunity to make use of the software that they need even when they are not in the office. This in turn can help improve productivity as well as decrease cost implications for employees (as they will not need to pay for the applications themselves).

Another major benefit for a company is the ability to openly collaborate on files. Some services go beyond simple sharing and even allow multiple users to work on a single document at the same time.

Practise

This unit has looked at just some of the ways that cloud computing can help an organisation to gain an edge over competitors.

Look at your own study centre or college and consider how it could make use of cloud technologies to help improve the way it operates.

C5 Considering different cloud types

Before you implement a cloud solution you need to make sure you pick the appropriate solution based on your organisation's size and needs. To do this you will need to consider the different types of cloud and how you plan to use your cloud.

Cloud types

The type of cloud that a company will use often depends on several factors.

- What is the intended use of the cloud system?
- Will it be used for storage, running cloud applications or both?

Another consideration is the scale of use of these systems. Does the company think it could cope if the user base or amount of data drastically increased for any reason?

Cost and hardware/software requirements can also be a major factor. A company needs to assess whether it can afford a specific type of cloud system or whether it has the expertise to develop its own. The type of cloud it uses will fall into one of three categories:

- private
- public
- hybrid.

Private cloud

A **PRIVATE CLOUD** system is one that is developed in-house for a company to use. These tend not to be available for public use and are rarely for sale. Instead, this type of cloud is developed to service in-house needs such as cloud storage and cloud applications.

Although this type of cloud offers a company the greatest level of control, it can often be expensive to set up and requires specific technical knowledge that may not be accessible to some companies. This often means that a private cloud setup is more commonly found in larger, rather than smaller, companies.

Public cloud

PUBLIC CLOUD services are those offered by an external provider such as Dropbox, Google Drive™ or OneDrive™. These require little or no technical knowledge to use, which is a significant benefit. They are also an affordable solution, since the greater part of the setup cost and hardware is taken by the provider. It is for these reasons that public cloud services are often favoured by smaller companies.

Conversely, these services are limited in configuration options so they cannot be tailored towards a specific company requirement. In addition, a company has little control over the security of the information held on public cloud services, so any breach in a delivered service could mean a loss of data.

Hybrid cloud

In some cases, a company may decide to use what is called a **HYBRID CLOUD** solution, making use of both types of cloud. An example of this could be where an organisation uses its own private cloud and then expands into a public cloud if demand for application or storage increases during peak times.

Cloud deployment

Once an organisation has decided on a particular cloud type, the services will need to be deployed and accessed by individuals working there. In terms of a public cloud, this usually involves individuals using a set username and password to log in and access applications or storage. Once complete, any files are updated on the provider's server to be accessed again in future.

With a private cloud, deployment tends to be more complex. With this type of cloud service, the company will need to make sure servers and storage are in place to cope with the amount of traffic for accessing applications and any data that needs to be stored on the cloud system. The company will also be responsible for managing the security of the cloud system, so firewalls and **ANTI-VIRUS SOFTWARE** need to be set up and regularly maintained. These security considerations are essential, especially for organisations to comply with laws regarding the protection of data.

A hybrid system deployment requires consideration of both private and public deployment models, but also needs to be configured to ensure that even though two separate models are being used, they work together seamlessly to cope with increased workloads.

Link it up

Networking and Cybersecurity

Refer back to Unit 2 to learn more about the different cloud technologies.

Cloud storage

One of the main uses for cloud solutions is to store and manage data. These systems can exist internally or externally and often allow access from mobile devices as well as desktop machines. A major benefit of this type of storage is the flexibility in terms of collaboration as well as restorable backups.

Cloud storage solutions have become so easy to set up that there are even solutions for quick deployment of cloud storage for individuals at home.

Security

A major factor when setting up a cloud solution for running applications or storage is security. If a company outsources its cloud services, it should make sure that the company it uses has suitable security and **ENCRYPTION** methods.

If an internal solution is developed, then it is the organisation's responsibility to ensure these safeguards are in place. In these cases, the system should be tested to find any specific vulnerabilities, and firewall settings should be updated on a regular basis.

Other security methods for internal review could include making sure passwords adhere to **STRING CONVENTIONS** (combinations of letters, numbers and special characters) as well as reviewing the rights of individuals who have access to the data.

Skills and knowledge check

- ☐ Why is it important that we use strong passwords?
- ☐ Why is correctly setting user rights an important security feature?
- ☐ What are access controls?
- ☐ Why is security a major concern for the Internet of Things?
- ☐ What is meant by the term 'cloud technology'?
- ☐ What are the three different cloud types?

- ◯ I can list the security features used to protect a network.
- ◯ I can describe what penetration testing is.
- ◯ I know what is meant by the term the 'Internet of Things'.
- ◯ I can list three examples of the Internet of Things services and technologies.

Ready for assessment

As part of the assessment for this unit, you will make use of a wide range of network management tools on an existing network. This will be completed over the following tasks.

1 As part of this activity you will be required to keep accurate records of any management tools you use. To do this you can use either set documentation or documentation you have developed. This should include both testing reports and service logs.

   As well as learning about the theory behind these techniques, you will also gain an understanding of the technical aspects and how to perform both network configuration and maintenance.

   You will need to keep clear and accurate documentation on the activities you carry out and should be able to demonstrate an ability to use configuration options. For example:

- setting up user accounts and roaming profiles

- being able to configure server settings

- being able to set up mapping of drives and local configurations

- setting up virus scanning options.

2 Once the network is set up, your documentation will demonstrate you can carry out ongoing maintenance activities. For example:

- backing up and restoring

- account creation, deletion and modifying

- changing password and accounts rights

- performing systems tests and virus scans.

3 Now that you are familiar with the different types of enabling network technologies, you will need to apply this knowledge to develop a network that uses the Internet of Things.

4 Once set up, you will need to employ a range of ethical hacking techniques to help demonstrate that the network that has been developed is secure.

5 Finally, you will produce a report clearly outlining how the cloud systems operate, as well as justifying and evaluating cloud solutions for a given network.

WORK FOCUS

HANDS ON

There are some important occupational skills and competencies that you will need to practise which relate to this unit. Developing these and practising them could help you to gain employment in network maintenance.

1 Gain deeper understanding of managing complex systems

- Pick a small local business – imagine that business has asked you to develop and maintain a network for it. Provide valid suggestions for a networking solution.

- Consider the previous scenario – how do the suggestions you have provided differ from a scenario where this is a medium/large company?

2 Know how to produce formal documentation

- The same small company wants you to develop suitable documentation for it – would this differ from documentation that you would produce for a larger company? If not, why is this? Come up with an informative poster to outline the dos and don'ts for an organisation that is new to networking.

Ready for work?

Take this short quiz to find out whether you would be the person chosen for that dream job.

1 Which of these is not a network layout?
- ☐ A Bus
- ☐ B Star
- ☐ C Ring
- ☐ D Eye

2 What type of profile setup allows users to access data and applications on different machines?
- ☐ A Leaving
- ☐ B Roaming
- ☐ C Wandering
- ☐ D Walking

3 Which of these is a form of protection that sits between networks and limits connections?
- ☐ A Port
- ☐ B Anti-virus
- ☐ C Firewall
- ☐ D Router

4 What do we call the rules we put in place for people using our network?
- ☐ A Policy
- ☐ B Guide lines
- ☐ C Limits
- ☐ D Firewalls

5 What does BYOD mean?
- ☐ A Bring Your Own Dog
- ☐ B Bring Your Other Device
- ☐ C Begin Your Own Devices
- ☐ D Bring Your Own Device

Answers: 1D, 2B, 3C, 4A, 5D

Answers to Assessment practice questions

Shown below are some suggested answers to the questions in the Assessment practice features in Units 3 and 5.

Unit 3

Assessment practice, page 70

1 The organisation could put notices on all electrical sockets reminding computer users not to overload them, for example not to use extension sockets that can allow more than one plug to be connected to a single socket.

2 Computer users could avoid having any drinks on their desks.

3 The organisation could tell computer users not to use memory sticks to copy files to take home to work on outside the office.

4 Computer users should not visit websites unconnected with their work, for example social media sites.

5 Computer users should always save their work before shutting down their computer.

Assessment practice, page 71

1 Employees should never put confidential documents in the waste paper basket – they should use the shredder instead.

2 Employees should never install software themselves – it might contain a virus.

3 Employees should avoid working on confidential documents in public places, for example on trains or buses.

4 Employees should always ensure that they do not leave anything confidential lying on their desk or visible on their computer screen – it might be seen by visitors.

5 Employees should always lock their computer when leaving their desk so visitors cannot view any open documents.

Assessment practice, page 74

• You should keep your anti-virus software up to date because new viruses appear all the time. Your anti-virus software works by comparing the code in the computer programs and files you open with a library of code that is known to be used in viruses. If you don't keep your anti-virus software up to date, then it won't be able to detect that a new virus is in fact a virus, because it doesn't have the code of that particular virus in its library.

• You should set your anti-virus software to update automatically because otherwise you might forget to do it yourself. Most programs receive updates several times a day so it would be very time consuming to do it yourself – especially as you may not always be in the office and sometimes you might forget.

Assessment practice, page 77

1 Unauthorised users will find it harder to access the server. Any damage affecting the laptops is less likely to affect the server, for example water damage.

2 Someone needs to be responsible for the security of the room – for example, a keyholder. If the keyholder is absent it might not be possible to gain access to the server.

3 A laptop might contain a virus (for example, downloaded from an email) that can then spread to other parts of the LAN. Data transmitted wirelessly might be intercepted by a hacker, especially if the LAN is unencrypted.

4 An employee might forget to keep their anti-virus software up to date, resulting in a greater risk that viruses could be installed onto the LAN. An employee might disable their firewall – resulting in malware being uploaded to the laptop by a potential hacker.

Assessment practice, page 83

1 Advantages – no need to remember a password; every face is unique. Disadvantages – software is not 100 per cent accurate (could give access to an unauthorised user); a photo of the authorised user could be used to gain unauthorised access.

2 Advantages – more secure than just a password; an unauthorised user would have to gain physical access to the mobile phone. Disadvantages – if a mobile phone is lost then users are unable to gain access to the account; if there is no mobile phone signal then users are unable to access the account.

3 Advantages – hard for a robot (automated software) to complete the CAPTCHA request; ensures that only a human is able to interact with the system. Disadvantages – some CAPTCHA tests are hard to read; users who rely on screen readers may be unable to complete the CAPTCHA test.

Assessment practice, page 85

1 Read only

2 Read/write

3 Full access

4 No access

Assessment practice, page 89

- Website addresses using http are unencrypted. This means that any data sent using a form on this website will be sent in an unencrypted format, meaning it could be read by a third party.
- An out-of-date digital certificate could mean that someone other than the organisation that set the website up is in control of it. It could also mean that the website does not in fact belong to the organisation claiming to own it.

Assessment practice, page 98

1 Data protection policy

2 Disaster recovery policy

3 Backup policy

4 IT security policy

5 Internet use policy

Unit 5

Assessment practice, page 144

1 Benefits

- Staff are familiar with the system so there are reduced time and cost implications of training/re-training staff.
- Compatibility with current systems – the system is well established and should be compatible with all current systems as all bugs/incompatibility problems will have been discovered.
- Keeps costs low – upgrading the operating system on all computers in a large organisation will cost a lot of money, both for purchasing the licence of the upgraded operating system and the cost of the staff time required to carry out the upgrade.

  Drawbacks

- May not support newer software – as other systems are upgraded, such as application software or new computers purchased, the chances of compatibility issues are increased.
- Older operating systems will not make effective use of newer hardware. For example, the OS cannot support/make use of a computer's maximum amount for RAM, which will affect the performance of a system.
- Publishers/developers, for example Microsoft®, stop providing support or security updates for older systems, leaving them vulnerable. (Learners may wish to investigate the 2017 'WannaCry' ransomware attack.)

2 Alternatives

- Upgrade current version of the operating system to the next version using the publisher/developer's upgrade software – some publishers allow an 'upgrade' to be run which updates the base operating system without touching any of the user's data, allowing the upgrade to be run in place without the need to uninstall and reinstall all other software and files.
- Remove all software (including operating system) and install the newest version on an empty computer.
- Change to a different operating system, for example move from Windows XP to Linux/GNU.
- Use virtual machines/thin clients allowing the current computers to be used as stations while running all software from the server.

3 Implications of keeping current operation system

- Security risks – no updates mean the latest viruses and vulnerabilities are not addressed, which could affect user data and impact on the organisation's operations and stakeholder confidence in the organisation.
- Maintenance – may require constant maintenance and 'work arounds' to get new systems and software working with the older OS.
- Staff familiarity/training – as new staff join they may not have experience with the outdated system, meaning they will require some re-training/support.

  Implications of upgrading to a newer operating system

- Cost – licences for a new OS can be expensive. If low cost/free (open source) alternatives are used there may be additional costs in terms of training staff and/or support packages from developers.
- Compatibility – if companies are using old operating systems then it is likely that the computers they run on are also quite old. Many new operating systems do not support some older hardware (for example, 32-bit computers are not supported by many OSs).

- Down time – upgrading will require systems to be taken offline. This could affect when systems are available, which may impact on staff and customers.

Assessment practice, page 147

Delivering services

- Ensure there is a website and phone line for customers to use to communicate with the company and to book delivery/collection.
- Ensure drivers have data relating to destination, customer name, delivery time, etc. This may need to be live and tracked to identify the closest drivers and estimate delivery times.
- Ensure robust security for maximum uptime of the website.

Customer relations

- Ensure 24/7 access to the website and booking to allow customers to be flexible as to when they conduct their business.
- Ensure there are enough phone lines and staff to deal with phone calls.
- Train staff on how to deal with customers, including tone and methods of communication.
- Ensure company policy is clear and shared with staff and, where appropriate, the customer to ensure all customers are dealt with equally.

Contracting supplies

- Source equipment such as a server for data/websites and handheld devices for the drivers (for example, smartphones) to allow them to communicate with the office, receive updates on deliveries and collections, use GPS, and so on.

IT support

- Install and maintain the supporting infrastructure, for example set up the website/server and select appropriate devices for drivers and workers.
- Write IT use policies and ensure security of systems.

Marketing and sales

- Web and social media presence – ensure staff are trained appropriately on how to communicate (for example, tone and choice of medium such as private/public messages).
- Use analytical data to target people on the web/social media to maximise potential sales.
- Use a range of different marketing and advertising medium.

Financial

- Process payments from customers – consider a range of payment options, for example credit card, bank transfer, PayPal®.
- Internal finance, for example buying supplies, payroll processing.

Assessment practice, page 161

NB: You should investigate an actual organisation. This is an example to show scope only.

Aims	Tasks to be performed
Provide local 'high street' store	<ul><li>Track current stock</li><li>Manage sales figures</li><li>Manage store finances</li></ul>
Provide online store	<ul><li>Provide 24/7 access for customers to purchase goods</li><li>Track stock – stock 'in store' and online should match</li><li>Deploy the web store and associated website</li><li>Select third-party hosting or self-hosting</li></ul>

Aims	Tasks to be performed
Customer experience	• Provide similar experience in terms of availability of stock online as well as in store, e.g. if a customer purchases an item online showing as 'in stock', a purchase in store should not then affect the ability to deliver that product • Choose a suitable platform for the site that balances security and usability • Protect user data to keep customers happy and ensure the system is reliable, providing as much uptime as possible • Create a usable interface that provides an appropriate experience, e.g. adaptable design (desktop and mobile version of the site). The interface must support all users so needs to include accessibility features • Customer support provisions – decide how these provisions can be made – website with online chat, social media presence, phone lines?
Staff needs and working styles	• Shop staff – interact with customers, scan products at the till, check prices for customers, stock shelves • Warehouse/web order processing staff – prioritise orders, pack products for collection/posting, locate products in the warehouse • Staff training – staff will need training specific to their role, e.g. the systems used by warehouse staff may be slightly different to those used by staff in the shop or those providing customer support
Location	• Are the warehouse and shop in the same location? • Ensure balance between what is in stock in the shop and what is kept in the warehouse, allowing for a suitable balance between web sales and in shop sales • Are some staff able to work remotely, e.g. can customer service staff work from a different location to the shop/warehouse?

Assessment practice, page 170–171

As well as the specific information in the case study, you should think about similar organisations you may have studied to explore different ways of solving common, and specific, organisational tasks.

1 Office, sales and management staff

- Internal communication.
- Management tasks, for example managers delegating work to different staff, monitoring progress and quality of work.
- Advertising – generating new business and communicating special offers, new products, and so on, to new and existing customers.
- Supply management:
  - source raw materials for use in the manufacturing process, ensure enough materials are ordered and 'on-time' delivery will ensure there are no breaks in the production process
  - ensure material is bought at the correct price. Balance quantity bought at any one time against storage capacity and possible fluctuations in price. Consider when to buy if any materials have an effective 'shelf-life'.

Warehouse and manufacturing

- Communication between the warehouse and supply management staff to ensure appropriate quantities of the correct materials are bought and delivered at the right time.
- Locate batches of product that have been produced when they have been placed in storage so orders can be fulfilled and dispatched to customers.

- Communication between office staff and manufacturing:
  - order details – quantity, due date and so on, to ensure orders are fulfilled on time
  - custom orders – some customers may want customised versions of a product. The manufacturing staff will need to receive the specifications of this order.

2   There is no set response here and alternatives change as new technologies are released. You should look critically at the systems listed and consider how else they might be achieved. You could think about other solutions you have seen.

3   Example diagram for remote/home working staff.

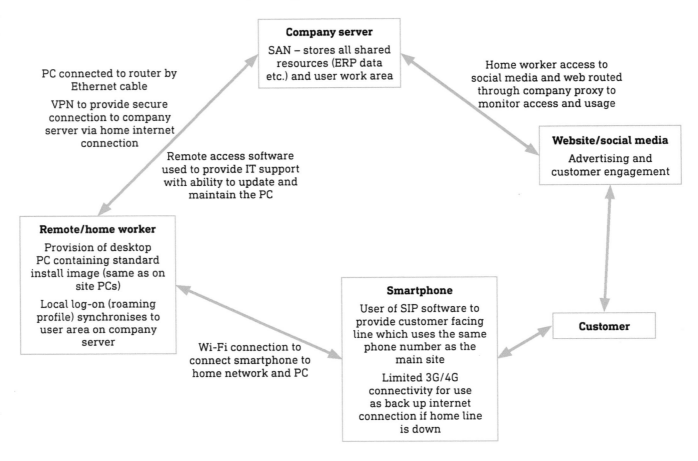

Learners should develop similar diagrams for other areas of the organisation.

4   You should think about the benefits and drawbacks of a proposed IT solution and what you need to consider when thinking about the potential impact of a proposed solution.

Glossary of key terms

ACCEPTABLE USE POLICY (AUP): a policy that states what users of a computer network can and cannot do

ACCESS CONTROL LIST: a list that tells the network what each user has access to, usually in terms of software and resources

ACCESS RIGHTS: the different permissions that are given to different users or groups of users on a computer network

ACCESSIBILITY DEVICES: sometimes referred to as 'assistive technology', these are peripherals designed to enable users, who would otherwise have difficulty, to use an IT system

ACCOUNT MANAGEMENT: used to make changes to specific user accounts on a network, for example when a user needs to have their password reset to log onto a machine

AD-HOC MODE: where two wireless devices are connected directly to each other

AD-HOC NETWORK: a network created by the temporary use of existing networks, such as connecting to public Wi-Fi

ADWARE: software designed to impose unwanted adverts on the user

AGGREGATOR APPS: apps that display feed content from many different news sources that the reader can select

ALPHA TESTING: in-house testing of a product to detect any design flaws

ANTI-VIRUS SOFTWARE: software that protects a device from malicious software that may be designed to damage or steal data

APPLICATION SOFTWARE: software that can be used to carry out a task or to produce products such as documents and presentations

ARITHMETIC OPERATORS: the +, -, / and * symbols used for the calculations

ARTIFICIAL INTELLIGENCE (AI) SYSTEMS: systems that are different from most computer solutions because they can make decisions and also be programmed to learn

ASCENDING ORDER: going up in order from lowest value to highest

ASSET: a component of a digital application

ATTENUATION: where the data signal loses strength over distance

AUDIO/SOUND CARDS: perpipheral devices that are added when more demanding or specific processing is required

AUGMENTED REALITY (AR): a technology used to overlay an image that has been generated by a computer onto what the user can see in the real world, providing a merged view

AUTO-INCREMENT: add a new number automatically

BACKDOORS: bypasses the security methods used to protect computers from unauthorised remote access (such as firewalls and encryption systems)

BANDWIDTH: the maximum amount of data a connection can transfer at any one time

BENCHMARK: a level of performance that is generally accepted in a particular industry as being acceptable

BENCHMARKING: evaluating something's performance against a standard or set criteria

BESPOKE SYSTEM: a system designed and created especially for an individual, organisation or specific group

BETA TESTING: testing where intended users of the application begin to try it out

BIASED: providing one particular opinion or influencing people's views in a certain direction

BIG DATA: very large sets of data, possibly from multiple sources, that can be acquired by organisations every day

BIOMETRICS: the statistical analysis or measurement of biological data

BITMAPS: files made up of a grid of tiny dots called pixels – each pixel is a different colour and these pixels can be changed individually

BLACK BOX TESTING: testing a database to ensure it works as expected. The database or program is the 'box', which is 'black', as the tester does not see anything inside it

BLOG: (short for weblog) similar to a journal or diary entry, written by an individual and made public for anyone to read

BLUETOOTH: short-range wireless connection used in mobile phones and other devices such as tablets

BOTNET: a robot network that can be used to send spam emails and attack other computers

BREACH: a breaking of a law or agreement

BREADCRUMBS: controls that show users where they are in an application

BRING YOUR OWN DEVICE (BYOD): employees are encouraged to use their own devices (such as notebooks and tablets) to perform their duties rather than relying on business-provided desktop PCs

BROWSER: a piece of software designed to allow users to view web content

BRUTE FORCE ATTACKS: a type of cyberattack that keeps trying different possibilities in order to solve a problem

CACHE: a small, high-speed memory location

CAPTCHA: Completely Automated Public Turing Test to Tell Computers and Humans Apart. This is used to ensure that the user is human and not an automated system

CENTRAL PROCESSING UNIT (CPU): the internal component responsible for controlling the computer, handling instructions and performing calculations

CHECK BOXES: input controls that make it possible for users to easily select items from a list

CLOUD: a large and remote network of servers that work together to provide different types of service

CLOUD STORAGE SYSTEM: a remote storage device where data is read-to and written-from via an internet connection

CLOUD TECHNOLOGY: remote technologies that use internet-based resources to store and process data

COLLABORATION SOFTWARE: software typically implemented through the use of cloud technologies

COMPLIANCE: working within legal requirements

COMPRESS: modify the content of a file to make it smaller

COMPUTER NETWORK: a set of computers connected together to share resources

COMPUTER PERIPHERAL: any external device or component that is not part of the core computer system

COMPUTER PLATFORM: the location where any piece of software is executed

CONNECTOR: the part of the wire that attaches to the device

CONTENT MANAGEMENT SYSTEMS: software that allows users to create and modify a range of digital assets

CONTROL PANEL: the set of functions that allow you to change settings on a computer

CONVERGENCE TECHNOLOGY: the combining of multiple technologies into one device such as providing a camera, GPS and internet capabilities in a smartphone

COPYRIGHT: a legal term that means that the person who created the material – music, images, writing and so on – needs to give permission for it to be used

CORE: part of the central processing unit of a computer that processes the instructions

CORRUPTED: damaged beyond use

CRIMP: to compress something into small ridges

CYBERBULLYING: the online abuse and victimisation of other internet users

DATA: single or collected quantities, characters or values on which the computer performs operations

DATABASE: an organised collection of data used to store, manage and extract large amounts of information for a user

DATABASE REPORT: presents information from a database simply and efficiently in different formats and layouts

DATA-BUSES: internal computer connections that carry data and instructions between internal components

DATA CLEANSING: the process of changing or removing data in a database that is incorrect, incomplete, improperly formatted, or duplicated

DATA DICTIONARY: a set of information that describes the content, format and structure of a database and the relationship between its elements

DATA ENTRY FORM: a form designed to make it easier to enter information into a database

DATA FLOW DIAGRAMS: diagrams showing how data and information flow through an IT system, including data required or generated, and the stakeholders involved

DATA INTEGRATION: combining data from two or more sources to create one set of data

DATA INTEGRITY: the consistency and accuracy of data

DATA MIGRATION: moving data from one system to another

DATA MINING: the process of analysing data to discover meaningful information that can be used to predict future outcomes, discover new opportunities and improve performance

DATA VALIDITY: whether or not data has been checked to ensure that it is clean and correct

DATE FIELDS: fields that enable users to input dates in a consistent format

DEBUGGERS: programs used to test and debug other programs

DECRYPTION KEY: used with encryption software to restore the encrypted data back into useable data

DEFAULT VALUES: the value placed within a numeric data field before a user inputs information. Typically, the value tends to be zero, although this can be changed from the field properties

DELIMITER: a character used to separate fields when data is stored as plain text

DENIAL-OF-SERVICE (DOS) ATTACK: a cyberattack usually carried out by flooding the network with so much data that it becomes inaccessible to users

DESCENDING ORDER: going down in order from highest value to lowest

DIAGNOSTIC SHEETS: these contain a list of initial questions/tests that can be answered or carried out to see what a fault may be

DIGITAL APPLICATIONS: software used on computers or electronic devices

DIGITAL SIGNATURE: a code embedded within a document which confirms that the sender is genuine and the document has not been edited after being sent

DIGITAL SYSTEMS CONTENT PLAN: a plan covering the digital technologies to be used as well as the digital media content to be communicated

DIGITAL VISUAL INTERFACE (DVI): a digital output at a higher resolution than VGA which is gradually replacing VGA usage in modern computers

DIRECTORY SERVICES: an information store about network users, resources and services

DISASTER RECOVERY POLICY: a policy designed to help an organisation recover quickly from fire, explosion, earthquake or other disaster

DOMAIN NAME SYSTEM (DNS): allows you to navigate the web in a user-friendly way, by matching domain names to correct IP addresses

DRONE: an unmanned aerial vehicle

DROPDOWN BOXES: input controls that show users a range of options from which they can only choose one

DUMPSTER DIVING: the searching of rubbish bins in order to find confidential information

DYNAMICALLY LINKED: when a visualisation is dynamically linked to the data used to create it, the graphic represents the data as it currently is, not as it was when the visualisation was created

ELECTROSTATIC DISCHARGE: a sudden release of low-level electricity caused by friction from anything from clothing to human skin

ENCRYPTION: a process for converting data into a scrambled code that only someone with a translation key can unscramble

ENCRYPTION KEY: used with encryption software to turn data into scrambled code

END-USER: the person who is using the hardware or software on a computer

ENTERPRISE DEPLOYMENTS: basic versions of software that have added functionality

ERGONOMICS: the study of people and their working environment and how this affects their efficiency

ERROR CODE: a code produced after a fault, which you can use to see what the problem is

ESATA: a data port which uses the same connection type that is typically used to connect internal hard drives (SATA)

ETHICAL HACKING: using hacking techniques to gain access to a network of computers system, in order to identify and secure weaknesses

EXPANSION CARDS: components that plug in to the computer's motherboard to provide additional or enhanced functionality

EXPERT SYSTEM: a computer program designed to mimic the ability of a human to ask questions then respond to answers with new questions or information

EXPRESSIONS: calculations that occur when the database is used rather than being stored in the database

EXTERNAL HYPERLINKS: links to other products or websites

FANS: used in a computer to keep air flowing around the inside of the case in order to cool the central processing unit

FAQS (FREQUENTLY ASKED QUESTIONS): a predicted list of common questions that users are likely to ask

FAULT-DIAGNOSTIC PROCESS: the staged process that is used to find out the fault with hardware or software so a solution can be found

FETCH-EXECUTE CYCLE: the basic instruction cycle of a computer involving retrieving program instructions from memory, determining the action to be taken, then carrying out that action

FIELD: a single piece of data, such as name, date of birth or telephone number

FIELD FORMATS: options within a database application to change how the data is displayed

FIELD SIZES: determine how much memory space should be set aside for a particular field

FILE-NAMING CONVENTIONS: a method of allocating file names in a consistent way. It is usually agreed by technical staff in an organisation and is applied to all files

FILE TRANSFER PROTOCOL (FTP): the system for transferring files directly to a server over a network

FILE TYPE: generated when a piece of software saves or creates a file

FIREWALL: monitors connections to a device and ensures that no connections are being made to the device by a malicious or unauthorised source

FLASH MEMORY: electronically written memory

FLOW CHARTS: diagrams created to communicate the steps of a process in a visual way

FOCUS GROUP: a small group of users asked to spend time discussing a system

FOREIGN KEY: a field in one table that refers to the primary key in another table, in order to link tables together

FORUMS: discussion sites where users can post messages and respond to other users' postings

FUNCTIONAL TESTING: testing to compare the solution provided by the application to the business requirements – does it have the expected functionality (and does it all work)?

GAMIFICATION: using game concepts and techniques outside a gaming environment

GANTT CHART: a technique used when different tasks need to be planned out over time – it is easy to see which tasks can run side by side or which have to be completed before the next task can begin

GENERALISATIONS: assumptions about groups or individuals

GRAPHICAL USER INTERFACE (GUI): an intuitive system for users to interact with and control a computer through a series of windows, icons, menus and pointers

GRAPHICS PROCESSING UNIT (GPU): a processing chip optimised for computer graphical operations

GROSS MARGIN: the difference between the price a customer paid and the cost of the actual resources (raw materials) used to create the product

HACKERS: unauthorised people who use network functionality to gain access to systems with the intention of stealing or destroying data or disrupting the operation of the system

HAPTICS: the use of feedback through the sense of touch, such as vibration features when interacting with a smartphone's touch screen

HARD DISK DRIVE (HDD): a mechanical secondary storage device that uses spinning disks and magnetic read/write heads

HARDWARE: the different physical parts, or components, that make up a computer

HARDWARE INDEPENDENCE: where applications and data are stored separately from the hardware on which it will be used

HDMI (HIGH-DEFINITION MULTIMEDIA INTERFACE): this provides high-quality video and audio data transmission. This connection is typically used to connect monitors and other similar output devices

HEAT-SINK: a component attached to the central processing unit using a heat conductive gel, designed to draw heat away from the chip

HOSTED/CLOUD COMPUTING: a method of deploying or providing access to application software

HOUSE STYLE: the way that an organisation's printed documents or digital screens look: the font type, size and styles and the colour combinations that are used

HTML PAGE: a page that contains a web page's code and main text

HUB: a simple networking component that allows computers to communicate

HYBRID CLOUD: a storage solution, making use of both types of cloud, both private and public

HYPER TEXT TRANSFER PROTOCOL (HTTP): text that is sent as plain, unencrypted text

HYPER TEXT TRANSFER PROTOCOL SECURE (HTTPS): a more secure version of HTTP that uses data encryption to send data to and from the website

INBOUND AND OUTBOUND TRAFFIC: data being received and sent out

INFRASTRUCTURE MODE: where wireless devices are connected via a wireless access point

INHERENCE FACTOR: user authentication credentials that are unique to the individual, in the form of biometric data such as fingerprints and voice patterns

INJECTION ATTACKS: situations where attack data is inserted into a data entry field through malware so that the attacker can steal the data in the database

INPUT DEVICES: devices that enable the user to interact with, or control, a computer system

INPUT MASK: a technique that is used to control what users are allowed to enter as input in a text box

INTEGERS: whole numbers

INTELLECTUAL PROPERTY: an original piece of creative work such as text, images, sound or software code

INTERACTIVE: where software or a product responds to a user's actions or inputs

INTERCONNECTION DEVICES: devices used to connect clients and servers together

INTERNAL HYPERLINKS: links to other pages of a product

INTERNET BACKBONE: the main data routes that connect internet service providers across the world

INTERNET OF THINGS (IOT): a term which groups together all technologies that have internet connectivity

INTERNET SERVICE PROVIDER: a company that provides the internet to organisations and individuals

INTEROPERABLE: able to work with each other

INTRANET: a collection of web pages that are only available to users on the local area network

IP (INTERNET PROTOCOL) ADDRESS: a unique identifier/address for a device connected to a network

IT SERVICE CATALOGUE: a document where all IT services for an organisation are identified and their requirements described

IT SERVICE LIFE CYCLE: a way of identifying, defining, planning and evaluating a solution to meet the IT service needs of an organisation

KNOWLEDGE FACTOR: user authentication credentials in the form of information the person knows, such as a PIN number or password

LATENCY: the delay between when a signal is sent and when it is received

LEGACY IT: where, historically, organisations were responsible for their entire IT systems and all the functionality that was needed by the organisation

LICENCE: a permit issued when you buy a piece of software, specifing exactly how you can use the software

LINKS: the parts of the network that join (or link) the nodes

LIQUID COOLING: a process designed to reduce the overall temperature inside a computer system by pumping a cooled liquid through pipes distributed inside the computer

LIST BOXES: input controls that show users a range of options from which they can choose one or more

LOCAL AREA NETWORK (LAN): a network based on geographical location such as an office or a school

LOCAL CONFIGURATION: setting up a computer on a network on the specific PC you wish to connect

LOGICAL OPERATORS: key words and symbols used in making decisions such as < (less than), > (greater than), AND, NOT and OR

LOGICAL SECURITY: protection that is implemented in the network operating system software

LOSS OF SERVICE: when a service that is run on the network is either not performing as it should or not performing at all

MAIL SERVERS: software systems for storing and sending emails

MALICIOUS SOFTWARE: harmful programs that are intended to cause damage to computer systems

MALWARE: software designed to cause damage to a computer system or to steal its data

MANUAL: the guide that comes with the equipment when it is first bought

MAPPING TECHNOLOGIES: software that acts as a reference guide to record the location of information so that it can be found at a later date

MEDIA ACCESS CONTROL (MAC): a unique identifier that is assigned during the manufacturing process and cannot be changed

MILESTONES: deadlines by which time important tasks have to be completed

MIND MAP: a diagram that displays information and shows how ideas connect

MOBILE APPLICATIONS: software that is optimised for use on mobile devices such as tablets and smartphones

MOBILE/CELLULAR NETWORK: a network that uses a data connection provided by a mobile phone

MODAL WINDOWS: pop-up windows that temporarily suspend the active window and force the user to interact with the process

MODELLING: processing data to identify trends and patterns to ask 'what if…?' questions

MOOD BOARD: a collage or collection of images, text and objects

MOTHERBOARD: sometimes referred to as the mainboard, this is a printed circuit board that holds the central processing unit and its supporting components

MULTICHANNEL PLATFORMS: different platforms that support software

MULTICHANNEL PRODUCTS: products that will work on different devices and platforms

MULTIFACTOR AUTHENTICATION: a way of controlling access to a computer using a combination of valid usernames, passwords and biometric data

MULTIFUNCTIONAL: able to perform more than one specific task

NET MARGIN: the difference between the price a customer paid and the cost of the actual resources (raw materials) used to create the product added to a proportion of the overheads

NETWORK ACCESS CONTROL (NAC): designed to provide an assessment of a device that is trying to connect to a network and the identity of its user

NETWORK INTERFACE CARD (NIC): an electronic device that allows a computer to connect to a computer network

NETWORK PROTOCOLS: a set of rules that tells parts of a network how to behave

NETWORK RESPONSE TIMES: the amount of time it takes for data to be transferred across a network

NETWORK SERVICES: provide services to clients connected to the network

NETWORK/SYSTEM DIAGRAMS: these show how all the component parts of a solution will work together as a complete solution

NETWORK VISUALISATION TOOL: a software application that helps a network specialist to design and test a network in a virtual fashion

NODE: any connected computing device (such as a server or desktop) or network device (such as a router)

NON-FUNCTIONAL TESTING: testing focused on how the application behaves – how it performs on the system it is loaded on, or how it manages lots of users using it at the same time

NON-VOLATILE: storage that holds data in the long term, even when the power is turned off

OCULUS RIFT® TECHNOLOGY: technology that takes the user into a virtual world

OFF-THE-SHELF SYSTEM: a system designed to be used by any organisation

ON-BOARD DIAGNOSTIC SOFTWARE: software that tests each individual component and then generates a report about the working status of each one

ONLINE FORUMS: internet sites where information and ideas and advice can be exchanged

OPEN NETWORKS: networks that are unencrypted, which means anyone can access the data sent and received

OPEN-SOURCE SOFTWARE: software that is free and in the public domain

OPERATING SYSTEM (OS): the most important piece of software on a computer as it controls all the computer's major operations and ensures that it functions

OPERATIONAL DATA: data that organisations generate and use every day

OPTICAL DRIVE: a drive that uses disk lasers to write to disk media – for example, CD, DVD and Blu-ray

OPTIMISATION TECHNIQUES: when using media assets in a digital application, optimisation techniques make the assets as efficient as possible in terms of size, quality and so on

OUTPUT DEVICES: devices that provide a user with feedback from a computer system and send data to users or other systems

OVERHEADS: the salaries and building costs that an organisation has to pay all the time, whether it sells products and services or not

PACKETS: sets of data for sending over the internet or a network

PASSWORDS: words, phrases and numbers used to confirm that the person entering the user name is genuine

PASSWORD PROTECTED: a system that requires users to enter a password before allowing them access

PATCHES: a small section of code designed to replace a vulnerable part of an existing program

PATCH PANEL: a rack-mounted wiring panel used to connect cables directly to a network

PEER-TO-PEER FILE-SHARING SERVICE: files are shared directly between computer users and not downloaded from a legitimate business

PENETRATION TESTING: a key method of checking a network's security. This uses different software packages and techniques to help identify vulnerabilities in a network

PERIPHERAL DEVICE: any device that connects to, and works with, a computer to provide some form of additional functionality

PERSONAL AREA NETWORK (PAN): made up of a single user's devices such as their laptop, smartphone and wearable technologies (for example, a fitness tracker)

PERSONAL DATA: information about people, such as name, date of birth, National Insurance number, that can be used to identify an individual or to carry out identity theft

PHARMING: using malware to direct the user to a fake website that requests information

PHISHING: sending many users the same spam messages in the hope that at least some people will be tricked into replying with desired information

PING COMMAND: transmits packets of test data to a target device and awaits a response

PIRATE: illegally reproduced copy of copyrighted material

PLAGIARISM: using somebody else's ideas as if they were your own

PLUGIN: a prewritten module that has a particular function that you can choose to add to your software

PODCASTS: audio versions of blogs and vlogs

POLLING: checking each device at regular intervals

POP-UPS: new windows that open when the user clicks on a link

PORT: the place on the computer which the connector attaches to, or plugs into

POSSESSION FACTOR: user authentication credentials based on items the person has with them, such as a smartphone

POST OFFICE PROTOCOL (POP): a protocol on the application layer that allows users to access emails that have been sent to them

PREDICTIVE ANALYTICS: used to make predictions about future events. It uses of a range of techniques such as data mining to find trends in data about past events

PREVIOUS FAULT LOG: a list of faults that users of a computer network have reported in the past

PRIMARY INFORMATION: new data that has not been collected before

PRIMARY KEY: a single field or combination of fields that uniquely identifies every record

PRIVATE CLOUD: a storage system that is developed in-house for a company to use

PRODUCTIVITY SOFTWARE: software associated with tasks required in an office or similar environment, such as word processing, spreadsheets, databases and email

PROFIT: the difference between the amount of money you receive for a product or service and what it costs to provide that product or service

PROFITABLE: when an organisation or individual makes money after the cost of doing business is taken away from the money earned by them

PROGRESS BAR: this helps users to see how much more time is needed before the component is loaded and shows progress that has been made

PROPRIETARY SOFTWARE: software that is usually paid for and, for which intellectual property rights have been claimed

PROTOTYPES: simplified or test versions of the final product

PROXY SERVERS: software systems that monitor and block unwanted websites

PROXY SERVER SETTINGS: a kind of 'middle man' on a network that controls connections between the network and devices

PUBLIC CLOUD: a system of storage such as that offered by an external provider, for example Dropbox, Google Drive™ or OneDrive™

PUBLIC KEY INFRASTRUCTURE (PKI): a technique to ensure that when a server uses a private key (which only it knows) and a public key is issued to all the devices that want to securely talk to it, any network data that is encrypted with the private key can only be decrypted by the associated public key and vice versa

QUALITATIVE DATA: data that can only be written in words (not numbers – for example, 'What were your thoughts on the usability of the database?'

QUANTITATIVE DATA: data that can be written in numbers – for example, 'What is your age?'

QUARANTINE: place in a safe location on the hard disk

QUERY: allows users to see different views of the information in a database in order to analyse it quickly and efficiently

RADIO BOXES: input controls that force the user to choose only one of the options as only one of the buttons can be selected at a time

RANDOM-ACCESS MEMORY (RAM): the computer's volatile short-term memory, used as a temporary store for program data and instructions

RANSOMWARE: a type of malicious software that, once downloaded, encrypts the user's data then demands the user pays money in order for the data to be decrypted back into useable information

RASTER: a grid of co-ordinates that maps a display space

READ/WRITE HEADS: a mechanical part of the hard drive that transfers data to and from the storage part of the hard drive

RECORDS: a complete set of fields, for example a student's school record

REFERENTIAL INTEGRITY: the description used for data that is consistent where it is not possible to add a record to the second table that does not exist as a primary key in the first table

REMOTE DESKTOP SOFTWARE: software that allows you to control a computer and fix a fault without having to visit the location where the fault exists

REMOTE DIAGNOSIS TOOLS: tools that allow you to monitor a computer system without being where the hardware or software is actually located

RESOLUTION: the amount of detail that can be seen in an image

RJ-11: a slightly smaller data connection than an RJ-45, used almost exclusively in telephone connections

RJ-45 (REGISTERED JACK-45): a data connector commonly used in computer networks. RJ-45 refers to the connector type at each end of an Ethernet cable, not the cable as a whole

ROAMING PROFILES: these allow users to log on to any machine on a given network and still be able to access their files

ROOT CAUSE: the basic cause

ROOTKITS: software that reaches protected parts of an operating system

ROUND TRIP TIME (RTT): the time it takes for data to move from source node to destination node and back again

ROUTER: a device used to connect computer networks by sending data packets from one router to the next

SANDBOX TESTING: the testing of software or software updates before they are installed on a computer

SCALABILITY: the ability for software to support more users as necessary

SCAMS: subtle methods for targeting individuals to obtain confidential information

SCHEMATICS: technical circuits

SEARCH FIELDS: allow users to input words or phrases so that they can quickly find what they are looking for within the application

SECONDARY INFORMATION: existing data that has already been produced

SELECTION AND ITERATION TECHNIQUES: 'if' statements and loops in a program

SERVER–CLIENT MODEL: a network model in which a central computer (server) controls access to files and data on the network

SERVICE-LEVEL AGREEMENT (SLA): an agreement that has been made between two groups, usually those accessing a service and those providing the service

SERVICE SET IDENTIFIER (SSID): the name assigned to the access point that allows the user, and the connected devices, to tell what network they are connecting to

SHOULDER SURFING: someone watching you at work and seeing you using or entering confidential information

SHOWREEL: uses clips from existing videos to give an idea of what the final product will be like

SIDE-LOADING: unofficially installing applications onto a mobile phone

SIMPLE MAIL TRANSFER PROTOCOL (SMTP): an internet standard for electronic mail (email) transfer usually between different email servers

SITE LICENCE: a licence that tells you how many computers across the entire building can use the software

SLICE THE DATA: to reorganise the data and group it into different segments

SLIDERS: input controls that are used to limit a range – for example, if you want to limit the results of a search to all items between £20 and £50, the slider can set the upper and lower values

SOCIAL ENGINEERING: attempts by third parties to get users to reveal secure information such as passwords

SOFTWARE: programs and other operating information used by a computer

SOLID-STATE DRIVES (SSD): a secondary storage device that uses electronically written memory rather than mechanical parts

SPYWARE: software that collects information about the user (for example, web-browsing history, keystrokes made on a keyboard) then shares this information with other people

STAKEHOLDERS: individuals or organisations who have an interest or a stake in something – this is particularly true of investors

STATISTICAL ALGORITHMS: the steps that are needed to calculate statistics

STORAGE DEVICE: any device or component that provides non-volatile, long-term storage for data, programs and files

STORAGE MEDIA: devices that can be used to store data

STORAGE SERVER: the space available centrally that will be used to store all data that is used by everyone on a network

STORAGE SPACE: the space each user has to store their files

STORYBOARD: a visual technique for setting out the key parts in an unfolding story, for example the key moments in a 30-second video

STRATEGIC DATA: data that is used to make decisions about the future direction of an organisation

STRUCTURED QUERY LANGUAGE (SQL): language that is used to communicate with the database

STREAMING: listening to music or watching videos on a device without downloading them

STRING CONVENTIONS: combinations of letters, numbers and special characters

SUBSCRIPTION: paying regularly in advance for a purchase

SUCCESS INDICATORS: criteria that can be used to measure the impact of a digital system

SUED: taken to court

SWITCH: a network component that directs internal network traffic

SYNCHRONISATION: allows users to use the same files and data across multiple devices by ensuring the most recent copy of the data or file is available on any of the connected devices

SYSTEM SOFTWARE: software specifically designed to provide access to, or control of, a function of a computer or device, such as its operating systems and utilities

TABLES: used to store raw data for a particular category

TACTICAL DATA: data that helps managers to make decisions about what needs to happen in the medium term (usually the next few months or year)

TECHNICAL MANUAL: a document that records the key aspects of the database structure and operation

TECHNICAL SPECIFICATION: this outlines the components and processes required to solve a problem using a digital application

TECHNOLOGY SYSTEMS: complete computing systems – this is often what people think about when they say the word 'computer'

TELECOMS SERVICES: services that provide popular facilities such as email, web access, remote access and remote desktop

THREAD: the number of instructions each core can process at the same time

THUNDERBOLT™: a combination port that provides data, video and DC power output

TICKETING SYSTEM: a piece of software that can help record and monitor the progress of fixing problems

TOGGLES: input devices used to switch a function on or off

TOOLTIPS: messages that can be added to components to give the user hints about how to use the feature

TOPOLOGY: the shape formed when all the nodes in a network are connected and organised

TRAFFIC: incoming and outgoing data

TRANSITION: a visual effect to smooth the move from one page to the next

TRANSMISSION CONTROL PROTOCOL/INTERNET PROTOCOL (TCP/IP): the standard language used to communicate data on the internet

TROJAN HORSE: any malicious software that pretends to be something harmless

TYPOGRAPHY: the techniques you use to arrange text and make it readable and appealing when displaying it in printed or digital media – the style and approach that you take

UEFI/BIOS (UNIFIED EXTENSIBLE FIRMWARE INTERFACE/BASIC INPUT OUTPUT SYSTEM): a set of permanently stored data that specifies the order in which connected devices should be checked for an OS

URL (UNIFORM RESOURCE LOCATOR): a website address

USABILITY: whether something is fit for the purpose for which it was intended

USAGE INDICATORS: ways of telling you how much your systems are being used

USB (UNIVERSAL SERIAL BUS): a data connection port used to connect a range of peripherals such as printers and external storage media

USER ACCEPTANCE TESTING: where users carry out a final test to confirm that the application is working as it should

USER ACCOUNTS: specific accounts given to individuals in an organisation so that they can log on to a network

USER INTERFACE (UI): the screen that the user works with

USERNAMES: an identification used to help a system match a user with a specific account

USP (UNIQUE SELLING POINT): something that makes people want to use/buy/own a product

UTILITY SOFTWARE: a set of tools that allows a user to maintain and optimise the performance of a computer

VALIDATION: the process of checking that data entered into a database (or system) is reasonable and in the correct format

VECTORS: graphics which are made up of objects. Each object can be changed. You can change the colour of an object, its size, its shape and its position on the display

VIDEO CARD: a device containing additional processors dedicated to graphical possessors

VIDEO GRAPHICS ARRAY (VGA): an analogue output that provides relatively low (by modern standards) resolution output

VIRALITY: how often a post is reposted or linked to

VIRTUAL DRIVES: drives that do not physically exist, but can be used to store data

VIRTUALISED SERVERS: a server where storage has been split into different parts and each one behaves like a server in its own right

VIRTUAL PRIVATE NETWORK (VPN): operates like a local area network but uses the internet to connect its users together

VIRTUAL REALITY: a computer-generated simulation that people can interact with in a physical way

VIRUS(ES): once installed on a computer, a virus attaches itself to an existing program then copies itself

VIRUS DEFINITION FILE: a file that detects newer versions of electronic viruses

VIRUS SIGNATURE: a short extract of code from a virus program

VLOGGER: a person who owns, runs or contributes to a vlog

VLOGS: weblogs that are largely made up of videos

VOLATILE: describes memory that holds data only when powered

VULNERABILITY SCANS: scans that can check an entire network for anything that could be considered a security threat

WARRANTY: an agreement whereby if there are any faults with the equipment, the manufacturer will fix the faulty equipment and cover the costs

WATTS: a standard unit for measuring electricity consumption

WEB FILTERS: pieces of software that can monitor traffic to and from the internet

WEB SERVERS: software systems for hosting websites

WHAT IF... ANALYSIS: analysis that is usually carried out using a spreadsheet and enables the user to change values in the spreadsheet to see what impact the changes will have

WHITELIST: a list of trustworthy sites

WIDE AREA NETWORK (WAN): a network across a wider geographical area – for example, connecting two buildings on opposite sides of a city

WI-FI PROTECTED ACCESS (WPA2): the most up-to-date and secure method of encrypting a WLAN

WIKI: a website where the original creator of the site gives up all control over its future development – any visitor can edit or add new content directly from a web browser

WIRED EQUIVALENT PRIVACY (WEP): the oldest and least secure method of encrypting a wireless network

WIREFRAME: a diagram showing what an interactive multimedia object will look like

WIRELESS ACCESS POINTS (WAP): devices that plug into a wired network and provide additional wireless access

WIRELESS LAN CONTROLLER: a device that works with wireless access points throughout an organisation to control the traffic and connections on a network

WIRELESS LOCAL AREA NETWORK (WLAN): a local area network that is wireless

WORK LOG: a function to record any jobs carried out as well as any software that is installed

WORM: a form of malicious software that operates as a standalone program and can infect other connected computers

WRITE PROTECT: ensure that data cannot be changed or removed by a user

ZERO-DAY ATTACKS: viruses or hacking attempts that exploit software weaknesses that have not yet been patched by the software company

Index